Home Games

Home Games

Essays on Baseball Fiction

JOHN A. LAURICELLA

McFarland & Company, Inc., Publishers
Jefferson, North Carolina, and London

Library of Congress Cataloguing-in-Publication Data

Lauricella, John A., 1961–
    Home games : essays on baseball fiction / John A. Lauricella.
       p.   cm.
    Includes index.
    ISBN 0-7864-0625-9 (library binding : 50# alkaline paper)
    1. Baseball stories, American — History and criticism.
    2. American fiction — History and criticism.   3. Baseball
in literature. I. Title.
   PS374.B37L38   1999
   813.009'355 — DC21   99-10933
                                       CIP

British Library Cataloguing-in-Publication data are available

Manufactured in the United States of America

McFarland & Company, Inc., Publishers
  Box 611, Jefferson, North Carolina 28640
  www.mcfarlandpub.com

For my wife
Risa M. Mish
She believes

In memory of my father
John August Lauricella
July 19, 1934 — February 16, 1999
Godspeed

Acknowledgments

Several friends and former colleagues deserve thanks for their interest in this book. Jim Green persuaded me that baseball fiction was worth a book and that my knowledge of the game would enable me to write uniquely about the subject. I hope that *Home Games* resembles his conception of what it could be. The encouragement of Paul Cody has been a source of renewal; I might have given up this book any number of times without his pep talks. Jack Sherman, having undertaken several research trips with me to the Baseball Hall of Fame in Cooperstown, has shown bemused curiosity about what a book like *Home Games* might have to say. Perhaps some part of it will justify his interest. Cornell Professor Lamar Herrin monitored the chapter-by-chapter development of *Home Games* as it evolved, some years ago, into my doctoral dissertation. His insightful comments have helped me write a better book. Professors Pete Wetherbee and Dan McCall, also of Cornell, read the earlier manuscript and contributed useful ideas for its revision. At a time when the prevailing academic chic dismisses interpretative approaches that do not serve the agendas of ethnic or gender politics, these professors regarded my ideas with respect. For such considerate treatment, I am grateful.

Others lent support at crucial times. To Liz Holmes, Diane Sherman, Jim LeBlanc, Ernie Roberts, Sarah Ross, Ed Hardy, Beth Lordan, Deidre Jackson, Sondra Morris, Tim Young, Tamar Katz, Hugh Jenkins, Bill Carleton, Fiona Cheong, Anne Whitaker, Cathy Tufariello, and Professors Daniel R. Schwarz and Edgar Rosenberg, my sincere thanks.

My parents, John and Lucille Lauricella, have been supportive observers of a process whose purposes must have seemed obscure. If I have accomplished anything worthwhile in these essays, it begins with the special self-confidence they instilled in me as a child and the lessons in independent thinking they have imparted since.

My brothers, Jim Lauricella and Ken Lauricella, encouraged me to complete this book when the reasons for doing so had disappeared. I take their faith as a sign of brotherly love.

My greatest thanks belong to my wife, Risa Mish. She has suffered the composition of these pages firsthand and shown exceptional patience with my slow, sometimes desultory writing habits. How she tolerates my ways I do not know, but she endures and I am grateful. Her faith in this quixotic project has allowed me to complete *Home Games* in its present form. Its publication is the least of all I owe her.

Table of Contents

Acknowledgments   vii

Preface. A Remarkable Question   1

Introduction. Baseball by the Books   9

Part I

◆ ONE ◆ "I See Great Things in Baseball"
The Game and Its Contexts   23

◆ TWO ◆ The Black Sox Signature
Baseball in The Great Gatsby   37

◆ THREE ◆ A Picture's Worth a Thousand
Baseball Subtext in The Sound and the Fury   51

◆ FOUR ◆ "A Nation of Frustrated Baseball Players"
Realism and Impressionism   61

◆ FIVE ◆ "How to Live in It"
Synecdochic Naming and Hemingway's Baseball Games   85

Part II

◆ PROEM ◆ The Baseball Novel
Writing a Good Game   115

◆ SIX ◆ A Portrait of the Ballplayer as a Young Man
Busher Keefe's Dramatic Monologues   121

♦ SEVEN ♦ "Only Connect"
The Tragicomic Romance of Roy Hobbs   143

♦ EIGHT ♦ The Game's the Thing
Adventures of Henry Wiggen   161

♦ NINE ♦ Writing Baseball
J. Henry Waugh's Game-Within   187

Conclusion. Coming Home: Baseball in American Fiction   215
Appendix. Views from the Press Box: The Critical
Literature   221
Index   235

Books are the best of things, well used; abused, among the worst. What is the right use? What is the one end, which all means go to effect? They are for nothing but to inspire.

One must be an inventor to read well. As the proverb says, "He that would bring home the wealth of the Indies, must carry out the wealth of the Indies." There is then creative reading as well as creative writing. When the mind is braced by labor and invention, the page of whatever book we read becomes luminous with manifold allusion. Every sentence is doubly significant, and the sense of our author is as broad as the world.

Emerson, "The American Scholar"

◆ *Preface* ◆
A Remarkable Question

"Who is Babe Ruth?"
— a Cornell graduate student

This book began with a single question. "Who is Babe Ruth?" is simple enough, but the candor with which it was asked is still astonishing. Of the questions I have heard literature provoke, it remains the most remarkable — not only for the particular ignorance it implied but for the answer it invited.

Context is all. The forum was a graduate seminar on American literary modernism, which concerned itself with prose and poetry by William Carlos Williams, Wallace Stevens, Gertrude Stein, Marianne Moore, William Faulkner, F. Scott Fitzgerald, and Ernest Hemingway. The questioner was a young woman, serious and smart, devoted to the study of American literature. The text to which her question referred was the third chapter of *The Sound and the Fury*, Jason Compson's virtual monologue of comedic horror. In the process of unpacking the metaphors that describe the obsessions of the last sane Compson, the seminar collectively addressed the dialogue in which Jason tells Mac that he would never "bet on any team that fellow Ruth played on." "That fellow Ruth" is, of course, Babe Ruth, although Jason and Mac refer to him simply as "Ruth" in their half page of baseball talk.

Some confusion is understandable. We are more than seventy years removed from April 6, 1928 (the date of Jason's narration), and the details of that baseball season — and the one before it — are unlikely to be uppermost in the mind of a contemporary reader. Moreover, "Ruth" looks as much like a first name as a surname; when the student asked, "Who's Ruth?" other students may well have been secretly assisted by the professor's clarification, "Babe Ruth." Yet no explanation save ignorance (or episodic amnesia) can account for the follow-up — delivered without a blink or pause or second thought (or so it seemed to me, seated next to her) — "Who is Babe Ruth?" Silence fell in answer, an interval of stop-time; everyone, I assumed, was watching for a sign that she was feigning, that her question was a pretense designed to exhibit an innovative critical maneuver, a sophisticated reading. But no. Her countenance,

1

unsmiling and expectant, showed that the name "Babe Ruth" meant nothing to her. The professor's nonplussed expression indicated his surprise, which he quickly covered by supplying some standard background. A few students, I noticed, took notes, their postures saying that it was minor but useful. The identity of Babe Ruth, however, did constitute information; the silence had been unknowing, contrary to what one might have expected. Seated between professor and student, I was caught in the interstice of their exchange. I wanted to turn to her and say, "You're kidding, right?" but to have called attention to the surprising gap in her knowledge would, in that forum, have been considered unseemly, if not insulting. So I held my tongue, and for the balance of the session, the explanations and anecdotes that had been part of my own knowledge since boyhood spilled back into my conscious mind from wherever they had been sequestered. Later, the trivial confusion I had witnessed seemed fortuitous, for it suggested a series of similar questions that, to me, required an extended response.

Given Babe Ruth's status in the semiotics of American culture, to be unaware of his identity—or to go blank at the appearance of his name in an American novel—is to beg the question of what baseball means in American literature. In researching the topic of baseball fiction and in writing *Home Games,* I have assumed that "Who is Babe Ruth?" is a specific instance of a general question: How does serious, or what is conventionally called "literary," American fiction represent baseball and its significance in American culture? The larger question has many specific answers, and these are as complex as the texts to which they refer. Baseball appears in *The Great Gatsby* (1925) and *A World I Never Made* (1936), two novels that could hardly be more different; it figures prominently in *The Old Man and the Sea* (1952), a story whose meaning greatly depends on the reader's recognition of baseball names less famous than that of Babe Ruth; it embodies major themes of *A Farewell to Arms* (1929) and *Of Time and the River* (1935), although it expresses different ideas in each novel. Various as they are, these examples do not begin to exhaust baseball fiction's rhetorical permutations.

In contemporary fiction the matter is even more complicated. The genre that has come to be called, rather too simplistically, the "baseball novel" encompasses both Bernard Malamud's *The Natural* (1952) and Mark Harris's *The Southpaw* (1953), as well as *The Universal Baseball Association, Inc., J. Henry Waugh, Prop.* (1968), by Robert Coover.[1] Although these books have baseball in common, they are, in terms of voice, structure, and narrative method, quite unlike one another. The discerning reader notices the differences and understands

---

[1] *I classify the "baseball novel" as a genre merely for the sake of argument and taxonomic convenience. What Christian K. Messenger claims for sports fiction generally—that it is "not a genre, unique in itself, as much as sport in fiction is a structure, a symbolic universe, a referential activity in society, a competitive paradigm, a heroic conferral, a shaping against mortality"—also describes the baseball novel. See Christian K. Messenger,* Sport and the Spirit of Play in Contemporary American Fiction *(New York: Columbia University Press, 1990), 425.*

that these books are not "about" baseball so much as they are expressions of American values, preoccupations, and concerns. Baseball is, of course, crucial to these novels — it is their guiding metaphor and their subject matter — and the reader must know baseball, particularly its history and the definitive form of the game, to read them perceptively. For instance, to appreciate the emotional drama of *You Know Me Al* (1916), the reader must be aware of the severe hazing to which rookie ballplayers were subjected by their established teammates. This experience underlies Jack Keefe's apparent loneliness and emotional isolation, yet remains partially obscured by the linguistic vagaries and superficial hilarity of the busher's letters home. Similarly, readers of *The Great Gatsby* who do not know the story of the Black Sox Scandal, like the reader of *The Old Man and the Sea* who knows nothing of Joe DiMaggio — and the reader of *The Sound and the Fury* who does not recognize the apostrophe, "that fellow Ruth" — will misconstrue allusions to these figures. To discover the metaphoric sense of baseball fiction, one must read it with a sensitivity to its contexts, both literary and cultural. Strong contextual readings yield a richer understanding of baseball's place in the American literary imagination.

The interpretative exercise begins with the stories that loom behind the baseball material. Thus, to appreciate Jason's allusion to "that fellow Ruth," one must know the stories, true and fictitious, associated with Babe Ruth. The simplest account is the one supplied by the professor in answer to the student's remarkable question. Something along the lines of "Babe Ruth is the most famous baseball player ever and hit more home runs than anyone before him and helped the New York Yankees win many championships" is adequate. However, to do justice to the manifold significations of "Babe Ruth" — and to interpret the version of American culture inscribed in baseball fiction — one must tell a fuller story. The story must locate the athlete within a context, for context is indispensable to the construction of meaning; without context, no gesture, whether physical or linguistic, has significance beyond its transitory presence. The critic's task is to (re)construct context from the available material: baseball history and legend, literary theory, the volatile practices of writing and reading, literary texts and the rhetorical cues they supply to help us read them.

Because writing a critical essay is akin to assembling a puzzle, one should begin with the easy pieces: Babe Ruth, a major league baseball player from before the First World War until the middle of the Great Depression, is generally believed to have been the greatest all-around player in the history of the game and is, among Americans, known by this reputation. He is celebrated in the written histories of baseball and in the less-structured, usually oral, accounts of ex-players, sportswriters, and fans. These discourses, typically anecdotal in form, facilitate the dissemination of Babe Ruth's life-stories even among non-fans and make "Babe Ruth" a distinctive element of the American lexicon. Indeed, the name possesses as much rhetorical currency as "home run" or "baseball" itself. The processes of word-of-mouth, if not of literature, have enabled

"Babe Ruth" to transcend the circumscribed parameters of baseball subculture and to enter our popular culture, the domain of public knowledge and public use. As a figure of mythic tales and legendary deeds woven into the greater tapestry of what may be called American mythology, the signifying potential of "Babe Ruth" in the semiotics of American culture is comparable to that of "George Washington." Americans, even when they are indifferent students of history, recognize this name because "George Washington" has become, for rhetorical purposes, a sign; the expression, "He is as honest as Washington," troping on the tale of young George admitting that he has chopped down the cherry tree, is an intelligible simile without recourse to quantifying the integrity of the historical Washington or the accuracy of the cherry-tree tale. Similarly, if one could justly say of a politician, "He is the Babe Ruth of American politics," one would be understood by an American audience (although perhaps not in every seminar room at Cornell). As vehicles of metaphoric expression, "George Washington" and "Babe Ruth" equally retain the potential to signify. Reasonable expectations lead one to assume that the soldier and statesman will cut a more significant figure than the ballplayer in the collective memory: hero of our Revolution, our first president, the Father of our Country, Washington's graven image is never far from our minds — nor from our fingers, appearing as it has for decades on quarters and dollar bills. Babe Ruth's moon face is not reproduced on United States currency, but a bat-wielding rendition of the Babe does adorn a 20¢ U.S. postage stamp, thereby becoming, if only temporarily, almost as common as the Washington quarter and itself a form of legal tender. Such commemorative stamps suggest that the novelists, poets, musicians, scientists, and baseball players (Ruth is not the only one honored by a stamp[2]) whose images we affix to our envelopes merit almost the kind of remembrance we have, however fleeting, of generals and presidents.

The story of Babe Ruth is worth remembering. Part history, part legend, it is a recurrent trope of many baseball novels and informs many of the baseball allusions in canonical works. Its appearance in American fiction is inevitable, for in contour and detail it resembles, like Jay Gatsby's fictive biography, a

[2]*The first baseball stamp appeared in 1939 to mark the centenary of the game's reputed invention, was worth three cents, and depicted boys playing ball. The second baseball stamp (6¢) was issued in 1969 to commemorate one hundred years of professional baseball. It pictures a red-capped batter set in a yellow background; the figure, cropped at midchest and composed from an irregular black-and-white geometry, was a generic representation. The first stamp to depict an individualized baseball player was the 20¢ Jackie Robinson stamp of 1982, issued 35 years after Robinson broke the color barrier and became the first Negro to play in the modern major leagues. A Babe Ruth stamp was issued in 1984, some 36 years after the Babe's death, and featured the high follow-through of his home run swing. Another 20¢ stamp, also issued in 1984, memorialized Pittsburgh Pirate great Roberto Clemente 12 years after his untimely death while on a mission of mercy to earthquake-shattered Nicaragua. A 1989 stamp commemorated Lou Gehrig 50 years after the end of his streak of 2,130 consecutive games played. Gehrig, fatally ill in 1939 with amyotrophic lateral sclerosis, died in 1941. In 1992, a series honoring Olympic sport included a 29¢ stamp that showed a generic ballplayer sliding into a generic catcher, who held the ball in his mitt. A second Babe Ruth stamp (32¢), issued in May 1998 as part of a series commemorating the 1920s, placed the Babe in Yankee Stadium, its stands draped with tricolor bunting, again having just completed his home run swing.*

permutation of the American Dream. The child, not an orphan but held as such in the popular imagination, proves too troublesome to be cared for by his father, a peripatetic saloon-keeper, and his mother, a saloon-keeper's wife in ruined health, and at eight years old is signed over to a Baltimore reformatory and orphanage.[3] The reason is noted succinctly on the commitment papers: "Incorrigible" (Creamer 29, 31). The boy is high-spirited, periodically violent, invariably repentant. He is taken in charge by a stern but gentle man under whose tutelage he learns necessary lessons of discipline, respect, and the importance of playing the game by its rules. The boy tries to emulate the man, experiences success and failure, and grows up a baseball player, having learned the game from his mentor.[4] As a young man, he develops into not just another professional paid good wages to play a boy's game but the most spectacular (his exploits especially please the eye), most exciting (endowed with athletic ability in felicitous disproportion, he often performs a feat others seldom attempt) player of his era, perhaps of any era. Nicknamed "Babe" when, inimitably boyish, he joins his first professional team, he is renamed frequently thereafter: the Bambino, the Big Guy, the Behemoth of Bust, the Colossus of Clout, the Maharajah of Mash, the Rajah of Rap, the Wazir of Wham, the Sultan of Swat.[5] The proliferation of names documents the excesses of sportswriters, yet the people's recognition that one personality fits all the names delineates the size of Ruth's presence in popular culture, takes the measure of his influence on the national mind. Star pitcher and hitter both, possessor of an athletic genius capable of transforming the 50-year-old (by 1920) strategic conventions of "inside baseball" into the modern (1920 until today) preoccupation with the home run, Babe Ruth wrought a revolution in the style and psychology of baseball and embodied, in his play on the field and his play off it, the zeitgeist of America's Roaring Twenties: the flamboyant individual who could produce great changes with seeming effortlessness — in a "single stroke" — and precipitate desired results in an instant of concentrated action.[6] Consider the name "Babe Ruth"

---

[3]*Robert W. Creamer's* Babe: The Legend Comes to Life *(New York: Simon and Schuster, 1974), the definitive biography, provides a full account of Ruth's early life and experiences at St. Mary's (24–40). Other versions include Marshall Smelser's* The Life That Ruth Built *(New York: Quadrangle, 1975) and* The Babe: A Life in Pictures, *by Lawrence S. Ritter and Mark Rucker (New York: Ticknor and Fields, 1988). According to Creamer, young George Herman Ruth entered St. Mary's on June 13, 1902, when he was eight years old (or seven; there is some uncertainty about the Babe's birth date). See Creamer 26–27). He stayed one month. In November he spent another month inside St. Mary's. "The real incarceration," as Creamer describes it, began in 1904 and lasted four years (Creamer 29–31).*

[4]*Brother Matthias, a powerful, physically imposing man, was the prefect of discipline at St. Mary's and the pre-eminently influential figure of Ruth's formative years (Creamer 35–38, 44).*

[5]*Lawrence S. Ritter and Mark Rucker,* The Babe: A Life in Pictures, *101.*

[6]*Baseball fans applauded the Babe's home run hitting, but many "experts" (or purists), including Ring Lardner and John McGraw, denigrated the new style of play. Such traditionalists continued to prefer Ty Cobb's method of place-hitting (for a higher batting average), judicious bunting, and slash-and-burn baserunning because (they argued) Cobb's tactics were more effective in winning games. For a discussion of the controversy as it was played out in the sporting press, see Leverett T. Smith,* The American Dream and the National Game *(Bowling Green, OH: Bowling Green University Popular Press, 1975), 189–207.*

a synecdoche of this *Zeitgeist,* and the home run, which Ruth did not invent but brilliantly perfected, reveals itself as a sports-obsessed culture's expression of Wall Street's "get rich quick" credo and that ardently wished-for phenomenon of Broadway, the "big hit."[7] In his journey from St. Mary's Industrial School for Boys to Yankee Stadium (named for him: "The House That Ruth Built"), George Herman Ruth exchanges days of drift and spin for a life of celebrity and fame, material riches, and popular adulation. When he dies of cancer in 1948 at the age of 53, Babe Ruth is America's foremost cultural icon (sharing this status, perhaps, with the Hollywood cowboy).

The legends embroidered on a famous life ultimately become more significant to us, particularly to our endeavor of retelling exemplary tales of a career and of fashioning new fictions out of old material, than the simple cloth of fact. Many stories, some of them apocryphal, are told of the Babe: how he promised to hit a home run for a dying boy, and did; how he ate so many hot dogs that the resulting bellyache disabled him for half a season; how he "called his shot" in a 1932 World Series game against the Chicago Cubs by pointing at the center field bleachers and blasting Charlie Root's next pitch into the spot; how he saved baseball from the ignominious demise threatened by the Black Sox Scandal by clouting an unprecedented 54 home runs in 1920, exploding his own record of 29 (chalked up the summer before) and providing a season of incredulous expectation and joyous fulfillment for fans betrayed by the fixed World Series of 1919.[8] This last tale is a telling representation of how Babe Ruth single-handedly delivered baseball into the modern era, a dramatic way of reporting an event of baseball (and American) history, and an exciting story in its own right. Evaluating its truth, like taking the measure of Washington's honesty, seems beside the point. If the story is a lie, that is, a fiction, then like other fictions it enriches its audience by constructing an internally consistent and plausible smallworld: the self-sustaining ontology of a text.

The name itself engenders texts, inspires stories so expressive of the capacities of the American imagination — for faith and skepticism, for the adulation of heroes and their destruction, for idealism and pragmatism — that these stories have been retold in American fiction practically since Ruth's death half a century ago. "Babe Ruth" evokes familiar images, mostly the one of a barrel-chested, spindly-legged slugger whose long, looping swing imparts to a baseball something of its own powerful elegance, delivering the bright sphere into

---

[7]See Robert J. Higgs, Laurel & Thorn: The Athlete in American Literature *(Lexington: University Press of Kentucky, 1981),* 7: "*[Literature] invariably reflects the Zeitgeist of a society in much the same manner as sports and games and the heroes emerging from those events.*"

[8]Eight Men Out *(1963; reprinted, New York: Henry Holt, 1987), by Eliot Asinof, is a meticulous recreation of the scandal, hard news of which began to break in late summer 1920 after months of rumors. Asinof says little about Ruth's 1920 season but notes that his "fiftieth and fifty-first home runs [propelled] fans into a wild hysteria" (Asinof 157). In the introduction to Asinof's book, Stephen Jay Gould advances a cogent explanation of how Ruth's home run hitting was made possible by the very scandal it appeared, to some extent, to redeem (xvii–xviii). See also Bill James,* The Bill James Historical Baseball Abstract *(New York: Villard Books, 1988), 124–125.*

a high parabola that reaches even in its descent toward some distant place, like the evaporating arc of a rainbow. The impulse to overreach, to vouchsafe to a crowd of spectators a glimpse of transcendence, the peculiar beauty of performing a feat wholly inaccessible to an ordinary person, finds its expression in the home run and its incarnation in fictions tailored to the Babe's pattern. In Bernard Malamud's *The Natural,* Roy Hobbs's prowess as pitcher and hitter, like his gargantuan appetites for food, sex, and money, cast him in the Ruthian mold. Indeed, Roy's feats (as well as his errors) during his single season in the game exceed even the Babe's exploits, marking Roy as an exaggerated, fatally flawed hero who might succeed splendidly were he not doomed to awful failure. In Mark Harris's *Bang the Drum Slowly* (1956), New York Mammoth slugger Sid Goldman chases the Babe's single-season home run record (60, set in 1927) through the long summer and into September only to fall short by a handful, as home run hitters from Hack Wilson (56 in 1930) to Ralph Kiner (51 in 1947, 54 in 1949), from Jimmie Foxx (58 in 1932, 50 in 1938) to Willie Mays (51 in 1954, 52 in 1965), from Hank Greenberg (58 in 1938) to Mickey Mantle (52 in 1956, 54 in 1961) have done. Here is failure made more splendid by its very proximity to success. Until the record-shattering season of Mark McGwire and Sammy Sosa, only Roger Maris had bettered Ruth's mark. That Maris's "61 in '61" occurred five years after the publication of Harris's novel helps to insure what is all but fated: that Sid Goldman will fail. In a realistic baseball fiction, no player can manage to eclipse a legend.

Idol-toppling, however, is characteristic of hyperbolic forms like satire, fantasy, comedy, and farce, which Philip Roth synthesizes in *The Great American Novel* (1973). In subjecting two traditional artifacts of American culture, baseball and the novel, to an iconoclastic revisioning, Roth's story depicts Luke Gofannon, consummate hitter of the homeless Ruppert Mundys, as having broken the home run record the year after Ruth established it; Smitty claims that Luke hit 63 home runs during the repressed and now forgotten Patriot League season of 1928. Elsewhere, *The Great American Novel* portrays Ruth in savvy caricature as a means of demythologizing the legend. This process, instigated in Smitty's narration by Angela Whittling Trust, abets Roth's intention, evident throughout the novel and stated as such in another context, of reducing the mythic status of several historical ballplayers (Ty Cobb and Walter Johnson are two of the most obvious) and of deconstructing the literary standing of certain writers (Hawthorne, Melville, Twain and, most graphically, Hemingway) enshrined in the American literary canon.[9] Similar manic designs drive other baseball novels, including *Babe Ruth Caught in a Snowstorm* (1973) by John Alexander Graham, *The Seventh Babe* (1979) by Jerome Charyn, and *Sam's Legacy* (1974) by Jay Neugeboren, toward distortions of the historical and mythic Babe Ruth. These idiosyncratic representations, sometimes shockingly original,

---

[9]*Roth explains his purposes in a self-interview, "On* The Great American Novel," *reprinted in* Reading Myself and Others *(1975; expanded edition, New York: Penguin Books, 1985), 75–92.*

at times outlandish, attempt to create a repleteness of allusion and symbol. Their literary merit is negligible, however, because of the uncertainty of their language and the periodic incoherence of their form.[10] The prose, pedestrian at its best, is typically loose and often awkward. Scenes with a potential to achieve genuine pathos, and others retaining a discernible but repressed intellectual energy (the repression of which often seems anxious or guilty, almost hysterical, as if the text — or its author — were fearful of appearing to take its subject or itself seriously), are either abandoned prematurely or diminished by some bit of trifling slapstick or nonsense. The narrative lapses, details become gratuitous, and entire chapters strike the reader as superfluous to the progress of plot and the articulation of character. The result is a compromised, badly written novel. Because so many baseball novels suffer from these infirmities, much more accomplished works — for example, *The Río Loja Ringmaster* (1977) by Lamar Herrin, *Almost Famous* (1982) by David Small, *Blue Ruin* (1991) by Brendan Boyd — tend to be undervalued. Serious readers innocent of baseball knowledge aggravate the problem: *The Natural* is deprived of much of its rhetorical power by readers for whom Babe Ruth is a sound without resonance — especially because the *name* does not appear in the text.

The possibilities of what baseball can mean in American fiction are rich and various, surprising and inevitable. Discovering them is less a task of strangeness or complexity than a matter of faith: the faith that literary baseball is not an empty sign. Each of the following chapters is an essay in defense of this faith. Each essay attempts to read the baseball content of American fiction with the commitment and aesthetic discernment that scholars have brought for decades to their studies of canonical texts. This attitude shapes the interpretations of both baseball allusions (in Part I) and baseball novels (in Part II). Each essay associates the baseball text with ideas related to literary studies; in some cases I link the baseball text to works that stand more firmly within the tradition of Anglo-American literature. The intention of this strategy is to place baseball fiction within this literary tradition. When baseball fiction proves itself in this context — when it can be understood as belonging to the ongoing, evolving legacy of literary art — its claims on the attention of readers will be justified. At that point, the student's remarkable question will generate greater interest and its answers become occasions of genuine excitement.

---

[10]*This view of some allegedly first-rate baseball novels takes issue with the roster of "Baseball's Dozen Outstanding Contemporary (post–1973) Adult Novels" compiled by Peter C. Bjarkman in "Baseball Novels from Gil Gamesh to Babe Ragland to Sidd Finch" in* Cooperstown Symposium on Baseball and the American Culture *(1989), edited by Alvin L. Hall (Westport, CT: Meckler, 1991), 32–59.*

◆ *Introduction* ◆
Baseball by the Books

"The game has four bases, a ball, a bat, and lots of outfield. Fences and dugouts. We call the area within the four bases the diamond, the hill at its center the mound. He who runs the bases begins and ends at home. The shape is significant. It's not up and down, end to end, as in football, basketball, tennis, or soccer. It's an enclosure, it's the circle squared. The object is to strike something as white as your own good name and as hard as your ego into the outer-reaches of the park and then get back to where you began before that insulted ego and battered name gets to you. That wins you a point. A point— certainly mysterious scoring, to lie panting and torn where moments earlier you stood as photogenic as a lord. But an even wilder mystery— the fans prefer you in your disarray! ... No, this is no common game...."
— Lamar Herrin, *The Río Loja Ringmaster* (1977)

Home Games: Essays on Baseball Fiction is a series of interpretative essays about the baseball content of selected American prose fictions. Part I explicates allusions to baseball in canonical works, including *The Great Gatsby* (1925), *The Sound and the Fury* (1929), *A World I Never Made* (1936), *You Can't Go Home Again* (1940), and *The Old Man and the Sea* (1952), and illustrates how baseball allusions engage signature themes of American literature: versions of the American Dream, ethnic prejudice, city work and pastoral play, cultural identity, and the relationship of father and son, among others. Whatever their thematic import, baseball allusions retain a concern with "home," in various senses of that word. Notions of home, always underlying or metaphoric in baseball allusions, provide the unifying theme of Part I, just as the prospect of home or "coming home" shapes the readings that constitute Part II. The four novels discussed in Part II —*You Know Me Al* (1916), *The Natural* (1952), *The Southpaw* (1953), and *The Universal Baseball Association, Inc., J. Henry Waugh, Prop.* (1968)— inaugurated the baseball fiction genre and staked its claims to artistic legitimacy. In narrative strategy and mimesis,[1] one or more of these books is the precursor of every baseball novel written since; having established the tonal

---

[1]*"Mimesis" follows Eric Auerbach's definition of the term in* Mimesis *(1946; translated by Willard R. Trask, Princeton, NJ: Princeton University Press, 1968): "the literary representation of reality" (Auerbach 23).*

and representational parameters of literary baseball fiction, these books continue to inspire authors to approach the genre with seriousness of purpose. Although distinct from one another in story and verisimilitude, these books share at least one important element: the quest for home.

The major conceptual argument that, to a greater or lesser degree, underlies each of these essays is the structural analogy that exists between baseball fiction and the basic movement of baseball itself. Just as a player undertakes a solitary transit of the bases in order to return "home," so does the protagonist of a baseball novel endure physical, psychic, or emotional separation as a result of his devotion to the game. Like the player, the protagonist begins "at home," a state of confidence and relative contentment; unlike the player, who tries to reach base by any means, the protagonist suffers a traumatic wounding that casts him into exile.[2] The protagonist's task is to return to his original condition or something like it, to find a way to play the game that will allow him also to live a satisfying home life, apart from baseball. Such a plot, especially in a formulation stripped of embellishment, might easily evolve into a story-too-simple; in itself, the trope[3] of exile and homecoming is a template for drama, a mechanical gadget that threatens, in inexpert hands, to produce silhouettes and routines rather than to create compelling characters and events. As is true of other prefabricated narrative forms (allegory, murder mystery, romance novel), the main interest of the journey and return lies in the details of the player's experience. It is not where he is going or if he arrives but how he gets there or why he fails that creates aesthetic tension. In this sense, the playing of the game is more significant than its outcome; the progress of the season holds greater meaning than the final result.

The baseball fan, if he is observant and thoughtful, understands that the basic action, indeed, the manifest purpose, of baseball might aptly be described as a movement of journey and return. Habitual readers, if they also watch baseball, apprehend that a baseball game is like a story, that the baseball season is a kind of book. The reader who is less well-versed in baseball, like the fan whose love of literature is limited to the sports page, might perceive the analogy of game to book more clearly if he thinks of baseball and the novel as cultural artifacts. At this level of abstraction, the artifice available to the author or player of one pastime suggests that the other is, in many ways, its counterpart.

As cultural artifacts, both novel and game are self-contained, largely self-referential systems of signification that create a limited alternative reality,

---

[2]*Christian K. Messenger discusses similar ideas (within a specific theoretical framework) in relation to baseball fiction in* Sport and the Spirit of Play in Contemporary American Fiction *(New York: Columbia University Press, 1990). See 10–20, 24, 316–318, 322, 344–345. Cited as CAF.*

[3]*I use "trope" flexibly throughout* Home Games *to refer to figurative or metaphoric rhetorical constructions on various levels, from similes to metaphoric narrative structures, from strong verbs and figures of speech to emblematic or symbolic actions. The specific use of "trope" and its referent ought to sort themselves out in context.*

ontology, or "other world." Each artifact is conventionally understood to be internally coherent and sustaining. Each devises its own significant form based on its implementation of the rules that govern it.[4] The conventional novel is a prose text of some 90,000 words that is divided into chapters that are, theoretically, infinitely variable in length and substance yet tend, practically, to be of a piece in subject matter and duration. The reader is expected (by the author; by himself) — indeed, is implicitly obliged by their sequential deployment between bound covers — to read these words in a predetermined order. The reader pays special attention to beginnings and endings and is especially alert to words and actions ascribed to major characters. Similarly, a baseball game is an athletic performance conventionally consisting of nine innings (each divided into halves that are themselves divided into three outs each) of roughly equal duration that may nonetheless differ infinitely in length and interest. For the spectator, the game unfolds in an inevitable sequence that is both simple and various: the excitement of the first pitch and the anticipatory thrill of the early innings; the more leisurely tempo of the middle-game; the urgent, "now-or-never" quality of the late innings; and the decisive significance of the endgame. The spectator regards all players' actions as meaningful, or at least consequential, yet attributes particular importance to the exploits of pitchers, hitters who bat at the cruxes, the middle infielders, and catcher of each team. Baseball and the novel are simplified here according to their conventional forms; both artifacts are protean in their respective possibilities of inspiring hope and delivering, or denying, fulfillment. The generic versions only begin to illustrate the rules by which each generates its own significant form and its own meaning.

The rules, really a code of (il)legitimate actions, are adjusted according to experience: The efficacious are retained, the affectless changed or abandoned. Rules are essential to the maintenance of novel and game, for only through the rules are the participants, whether they be players or fans, novelists or readers, able to recognize the gestures (of narrative or character development, of home run or double play) that create meaning, that are meaningful in themselves. By defining these gestures, rules distinguish important from incidental effects. At the same time, the rules disallow actions that may be said to cancel meaning by contradicting the artifact's internal logic. Thus, the significance or value of certain acts, like the illicitness of others, is conventional — and ultimately arbitrary. It is not too extreme to say that a novel's meaningful effects, like the important

---

[4]*The idea that a game is a self-defining artifact is a common one. A. Bartlett Giamatti, trained as a Renaissance scholar and once president of Yale University — and a former National League president and commissioner of baseball — describes the conventional nature of the game (without explicitly differentiating "game" from "sport") in* Take Time for Paradise: Americans and Their Games *(New York: Summit Books, 1989): "The conventional quality of contests or sports ... lies in the fact that games are rule bound. Rules — complete and completely arbitrary — are what set these activities off from work, and make them doorways to leisure. Or, in the terms of this essay, make them artifacts, that is, entirely created by human will and imagination, social agreements for organizing energy that make no sense except in their own terms. ¶ Sports are conventional, and are self-contained systems of convention"* (Giamatti 55).

actions of a baseball game, are possible only because the participants agree on what "counts" and conform their behavior and expectations to these standards. In this sense, the meaning of a novel or a baseball game is a fiction — an agreed-upon fiction, but a fiction still — and a fiction on a prior level than the manifest fictiveness that insists on the divisibility of both novel and game from real life.[5]

For either fiction or baseball to have meaning, writer and player (as well as the reader/fan) must know the rules; without these conventions, language (action) becomes a babble and reading (watching) dissolves in chaos. Within the rules the novelist enjoys greater freedom, and therefore retains more responsibility, than the baseball player in redefining the form of his game. As the author(ity) of his novel, the writer's prerogatives are multitudinous and include bending or breaking what have been hitherto regarded as the formal constraints of prose fiction. Indeed, the Novel really has only one immutable "rule": Be interesting. Any of its formal elements may, in theory, be modified or discarded (although it is difficult and, in practical terms, probably not worthwhile to conceive of a novel without characters), and such a change is judged not by the degree to which it diverges from any preexisting rule but by its effect. A successful performance is its own justification: What works, works. By the same token, if the novelist botches an innovation of narrative form, for example, or of character development or mimesis, the reader resists this "rule breaking" and loses faith in the author's expertise. Similarly, if a player hits away despite the manager's bunt sign, an observer might doubt his professionalism; and yet, this prerogative, illicit under the protocol of organized baseball, might be authorized *ex post facto* if the player delivers a base hit. Both in baseball and in writing, performance is the justification sufficient unto the day.

The novelist's freedom to redefine his genre exceeds the player's ability to reshape his game in two ways. First, the Rules Committee, not an individual athlete, establishes the rules of Organized Baseball, whereas each writer is responsible for the significant form of his fiction — for his own soul, as it was once thought. Second, the writer is not restricted by the contingencies of strict chronology, whereas the player cannot, unilaterally or in concert with his teammates, choose to play the eighth inning first, then flash back to the third inning, and so forth. To counter the first distinction, one might argue that the Novel has come to be defined by a complex set of conventions that have, over many generations, accumulated from the aggregate writings of practicing novelists and working critics, who together constitute an informal and unbinding,

---

[5]*Conversely, many theorists conceive of real life and life's games (or play) as continuous or identical. Neil Berman argues that "It no longer seems appropriate to say that play and sport are like 'life'; play and sport are life — or should be, if sport were always play" (Berman 15). Berman cites Jacques Erhmann's view that "the distinguishing characteristic of reality is that it is played. Play, reality, culture are synonymous and interchangeable" (quoted by Berman 7). See* Playful Fictions and Fictional Players: Game, Sport, and Survival in Contemporary American Fiction *(Port Washington, NY: Kennikat Press, 1981). See also CAF 3–10.*

yet still "rule" defining, "rules committee" of the Organized Novel. A particular novel, then, is analogous to a single baseball game, of which each player is an author, within which each player (and manager, coach, and umpire) is a character.[6] To this extent, a baseball game is a story written by its characters, its plot unfolding quite apart from any single author's intention or control. To address the second distinction, temporal constraint, one is virtually obliged to note that the baseball player does play against simple chronology in two ways. First, a baseball game is not limited by clock time; it is calibrated in innings that are measured in "outs." Set free within the context of its rules from ordinary time, a baseball game is theoretically timeless, the temporal field of its play set in what Frank Kermode calls *kairos,* or "a significant season": "God's time."[7] Second, in his progress around the diamond, the baseball player moves counterclockwise, thereby undoing clock time in metaphor if not in fact. In this way, the achronological option of the novelist is symbolically preserved for the player in the signifying structure of baseball.

It is this structure, the definitive shape of a baseball game and the essential scheme of its play, that suggests the most fruitful analogy to literary art. Conventionally described as a diamond because the arc of the infield bends elegantly between two divergent rays that originate at a single point, baseball's interior field is, geometrically, a square. The pivotal point is home plate, which is distinguished from the three bases (also squares) by its shape: a five-sided polygon that resembles a diamond with elongated sides and a flattened crown. Regarded from its front end — from fair territory — home plate resembles a child's drawing of a house: a silhouette or modernist archetype of home. The small diamond of home plate (formerly called home base, now referred to simply as home) is the irreducible emblem of baseball's gesture toward an immutable "nodal point"[8] or origin: the player's counterclockwise movement around the square that ends, ideally, where it began; a journey that reaches its point of arrival in returning to its point of departure; an exile redeemed by a homecoming. For all of the lines and angles that demarcate the diamond, baseball's defining movement is circular. The player leaves the security of home to travel the bases, enduring separation from his teammates and a conspiracy (on the part of his opponents) to "put him out," to have him "die" on base. A player who completes the 360-degree, 360-foot circumnavigation is a comrade

[6]*One might refine the analogy and liken discrete baseball games to a novel's chapters. A team's full complement of games might then be said to compose the book of its season. To press the point further, one might match a baseball game to a novella. For the audience this analogy might be the most exact, for the time required to read a novella approximates the time consumed in watching a typical baseball game (a little shy of three hours). At this point, however, hairs are being split to little purpose. The important element is not duration, which almost always varies, but structure, sequential development, and variable pacing. See CAF 316.*

[7]Frank Kermode, The Sense of an Ending: Studies in the Theory of Fiction (New York: Oxford University Press, 1967), 46–49.

[8]*Home plate is a profane version of "the World Navel," as Joseph Campbell defines it in* The Hero with a Thousand Faces *(1949; second edition, Princeton, NJ: Princeton University Press, 1968), 40–46.*

returned from an embattled exile, a brother or son reclaimed by kith and kin, a hero met by a handshake of congratulation, of welcome, of gratitude for having accepted the challenge.[9]

From Bunyan's *Pilgrim's Progress* to Vonnegut's Billy Pilgrim unstuck in time, from Chaucer's pilgrims bound for Canterbury's restorative shrine to Leopold Bloom navigating the reefs and shoals of Dublin in search of an emotional pathway back to 7 Eccles Street, where Molly lies in waking dreams, the greater part of Anglo-American prose fiction describes an outward journey and eventual homecoming. The trope is as old as the *Odyssey*, Homer's epic of exile and cunning, and defines, Giamatti reminds us, "the literary mode called Romance" (Giamatti 90), which reunites exiled children and erring parents, and realigns a social order temporarily set awry. In the romances of Shakespeare, the dramatic action culminates in marriage, demonstrating that a fully achieved homecoming restores coherence to a disordered world.

In baseball novels, the action of exile and homecoming lends structural coherence to a compelling narrative. The protagonist suffers a psychic, physical, and/or emotional wounding, by his own hand or by another's, that causes an estrangement from his friends and family — from "home." The plot depicts the protagonist's journey through a hostile land and, possibly, back to his origins. He travels, sometimes in time and space, always in a dimension of psychic and emotional flux, toward reunion with his estranged, lost, or absent loved ones. The success of the final homecoming varies. Sometimes, the protagonist's return to an originating scene — which might be his hometown — fails to consummate the long-sought process of reconciliation. In other narratives the protagonist never returns to his "nodal point," pursuing instead an extended exile in a dismal landscape. In some renditions the player comes home, physically or symbolically, to a reconciliation with family and friends that is made possible by the acts of expiation and penitence he continues to perform. In such novels, of which *The Southpaw* and *Almost Famous* (1982) are outstanding examples, the means of homecoming is, in part, baseball, a shared experience of the game that seems to recapture a time before wounding and separation. Baseball proffers a neutral ground, sometimes literally a grass-covered field, on which wounded heroes enact ceremonies of atonement.

This scenario becomes more complicated when baseball itself is the cause of the debilitating wound. Many baseball novels generate creative tension in representing the hero's devotion to the game as the source of his transgression against what Hawthorne calls (in "Ethan Brand") "the human heart" and what one may, in the present context, define as the protagonist's responsibilities to his teammates, friends, and family. In these novels the resolution of exile in homecoming entails another kind of resolution: an explanation of the paradox

---

[9]*See A. Bartlett Giamatti's foreword to* The Armchair Book of Baseball II, *edited by John Thorn (New York: Scribner's, 1987), xi–xii; and Michael Novak,* The Joy of Sports *(New York: Basic Books, 1976), 57–58.*

that casts the means of reunion equally as the agency of estrangement. "How to live?" is the implicit question such narratives pose. The answer, not surprisingly, is that baseball itself is neither holy nor evil, good nor bad. Baseball is a game, not a moral philosophy. It is the player who is a moral agent, and his actions within the narrative scheme reveal the errors and abuses, as well as the correct choices, that define his involvement with his game. The only acceptable ethical position for these characters is one that balances the demands of the game against life's many obligations. Right and proper conduct, an ethics of holding the middle ground between conflicting extremes, as Aristotle conceives it, suggests a continuum that in its linearity cuts across the baseball diamond's encircled square. In what may feasibly be called antibaseball fictions, the linear model supplies a clarifying image for the protagonist's stepping off the field of play, of removing himself from the diamond-inscribed world and retreating from his obsession, in order to attain a proper perspective on the anguish of his times and his own reintegration. Such narratives posit a game so insistently nonreferential, so artificial in form and meaning, so divorced from the concerns of real life as it is encountered by men and women in real worlds, that the protagonist must abandon the game (in the more docile antibaseball fictions) or escape from it (in the more nightmarish) if he is ever to become a whole person wholly re-engaged with human intimacies of thought and emotion. And yet, if the protagonist is able to balance his devotion to baseball against a conscientious engagement with life's demands, game and life can become mutually enriching. The investigation of this paradox and its possible resolution animates novels as different from one another as *You Know Me Al* and *The Natural*, *The Río Loja Ringmaster* and *The Universal Baseball Association, Inc., J. Henry Waugh, Prop.*

To clarify the basic assumption of *Home Games*, one might simply quote the epigraph of a baseball novel:

> He wiped his face with the towel again. "Old man, a book can have Chicago in it, and not be about Chicago. It can have a tennis player in it without being about a tennis player."
> I didn't get it. I probably looked it, for he went on, "Take this book here, old man — " and held up one of the books he had swiped from some library. Along with the numbers I could see Hemingway's name on the spine. "There's a prizefighter in it, old man, but it's not about a prizefighter."
> "Is it about the sun rising?" I said. I knew that was part of the title.
> "Goddamn if I know what it's about," he said....

These lines serve as the epigraph of Mark Harris's *Bang the Drum Slowly* (1956). Harris lifts the passage from Wright Morris's *The Huge Season* (1954) and in the process makes a basic point: A novel with baseball in it is neither necessarily nor exclusively about baseball — just as *The Sun Also Rises* (1926) is not about bullfighting (to shift the epigraph) and *The Old Man and the Sea* is about neither baseball nor fishing.[10] Although critics assiduously tell us what these novels might be about, the baseball content of American fiction has received relatively modest analysis. Some critics explicate the baseball references in well-known fictions, like Hemingway's "The Three-Day Blow," yet often only to date the fictive events. As useful as this enterprise is, it does not exhaust the possibilities. Others offer interpretations of individual baseball novels, yet this attention usually occurs as part of an investigation of sports fiction as a whole. *Home Games* limits its inquiry to baseball's place in American fiction by focusing on selected baseball allusions and baseball novels.[11]

One virtue of concentrating on a small sample is the opportunity to tease out implications that must be ignored in studies of wider focus. As the following essays attest, the import of baseball fiction is often subtle, sometimes complex, and always more important than it seems at first glance. In both symbolic and realistic forms, baseball provides the subject matter of successful modern novels and serves as the vehicle of metaphor and allusion in canonical texts. Writers as stylistically diverse as William Faulkner and Ernest Hemingway fashion effective allusions from baseball history (which in their own temporal context is often baseball contemporaneity) despite evincing scant interest in baseball itself and no self-conscious awareness of the novel-as-game. Far from being disposable outbreaks of local color or arcane topical references, baseball allusions are rhetorical artifices as cunning as any metaphor, zeugma, or synecdoche in foregrounding meaning.[12] Read within their respective literary and historical contexts, baseball allusions reveal new perspectives on classic American novels, enriching an initiated reader's understanding of familiar texts and showcasing the agility of their authors' subtle genius.

Part I establishes the rhetorical contexts of baseball in canonical American fiction and explicates allusions to the game, particularly allusions to certain

[10]*Cordelia Candelaria makes this point in* Seeking the Perfect Game: Baseball in American Fiction *(New York: Greenwood Press, 1989), 92. Mark Harris explores the idea more fruitfully in* "Horatio at the Bat, or Why Such a Lengthy Embryonic Period for the Serious Baseball Novel?" *reprinted in* Aethlon *5:2 (Spring 1988): 1–11. Harris believes that the genre has compromised itself because he, Malamud, Roth, and others have felt obliged to cast their baseball fictions as being about something more serious than a game for fear of being thought idle, mentally deficient, or "not serious."*

[11]*Cordelia Candelaria employs a similar strategy in* Seeking the Perfect Game, *which limits its inquiry to baseball literature and addresses many of the primary texts that the present work attempts to explicate. The nature of the critical approach, however, and its individual readings, differ significantly from those presented here. A number of other studies explore baseball fiction within the context of American sport literature and that genre's reflection of or influence on American culture. To facilitate further reading, I have appended a brief summary-review of those works (including* Seeking the Perfect Game) *that have been most helpful in the composition of* Home Games. *Readers who are new to sport literature and its criticism might wish to consult the Appendix now. For scholars, the footnotes will be sufficient to indicate how* Home Games *incorporates the work of prior critics.*

[12]*Synecdoches are common in baseball; a proficient hitter is called a "good bat" or "good stick," a pitcher an "arm," and so forth. Zeugmas are less typical, although Ring Lardner contrives a pithy example in* You Know Me Al; *having married the busher's ex-girlfriend and having just struck him out with the bases loaded, an opposing pitcher tells Jack Keefe, "'I don't want nothing more of yourn. I allready [sic] got your girl and your goat.'"*

players and events that are famous or legendary in baseball history. The subtextual presence or metaphoric trace of "home" inscribed in these allusions links the canonical texts to the baseball novels addressed in Part II. In the interest of thematic unity, the contextual readings of baseball allusions attempt, in part, to locate or identify these traces of "home." This project begins, in "'I See Great Things in Baseball,'" with a brief recapitulation of the development of baseball in the nineteenth century and the attention the "New York Game" received from literary notables Walt Whitman and Mark Twain. The invention of American baseball was to some extent a literary endeavor, for the story of its origins and the codification of its rules both required a purposive effort of creative writing. As chapter one recounts, Whitman and Twain witnessed this process and celebrated what they separately understood as the identifiably American qualities of America's home game. Chapters two through five investigate the rhetoric and imagery of baseball allusions in selected canonical American prose fictions. Jay Gatsby's apostrophe of Meyer Wolfshiem as "the man who fixed the World's Series back in 1919" is the occasion of "The Black Sox Signature" in much the same way as that oft-quoted dialogue with Nick Carraway is the signature scene of *The Great Gatsby*. Fitzgerald uses the ambiguous circumstances of the Black Sox fix to illustrate Gatsby's cynical dishonesty and Nick's feckless ethics, as well as to objectify the concern of some observers that certain home truths are susceptible to subversion by pernicious foreign influences. In "A Picture's Worth a Thousand," the subject is the partially obscured identity of "that fellow Ruth" and the question of why Jason Compson so detests Babe Ruth in *The Sound and the Fury*. Faulkner's allusion to the triumphs of Ruth and the New York Yankees reveals the obstinacy of Jason's grudges, as well as the frightening reach of his prejudice. Jason, too, is preoccupied with defending his home turf from what he perceives as the threat of distant enemies, real and imagined. The focus widens in "'A Nation of Frustrated Baseball Players'" to encompass some of the most evocative baseball allusions, variously realistic and impressionistic, in the respective novels of Thomas Wolfe and James T. Farrell. Both authors represent baseball's subtleties and fine points at such length, with such peculiar "accuracy," that other allusions read, by comparison, like secondhand information. Farrell juxtaposes baseball-playing and spectatorship to Danny O'Neill's erratic home life and youthful insecurities, while Wolfe embodies the notion of finding one's way back home in the figure of his fictive baseball hero, Nebraska Crane. Part I concludes with "How to Live in It," an extended appraisal of the deft allusiveness and metaphoric potency of Ernest Hemingway's baseball games. The allusion to Babe Ruth in *A Farewell to Arms* (1929) is so minor that it seems like an example of name-dropping, yet it indicates Frederic Henry's sense of isolation in a foreign land and suggests his repressed longing to return home. Similarly, Nick and Bill's baseball conversation in "The Three-Day Blow" (1925) ostensibly reveals the boys' interest in the pennant race and their latent disdain for baseball, yet also offers an elaborate subtextual commentary on Nick's mistaken assumptions and confused emotions in his relationship with Marjorie, with whom he might establish a truer, more satisfying home than any he and Bill can counterfeit. The baseball allusion attains its perfect pitch in *The Old Man and the Sea*, in which Hemingway invokes the name of Joe DiMaggio and his reputation as the professional's professional to deepen the reader's response to Santiago and his plight as a wounded warrior who must summon up the courage and faith to see the fight to its end. As readers of this immaculate short novel will recall, Santiago ventures far from home and nearly perishes on "the true Gulf" yet lives to return to Manolin, his surrogate son. The old man's relationship with the boy is a complex, emotionally compelling reiteration of his love of baseball and his imaginative kinship with the famous baseball player. Hemingway's inscription of "the great DiMaggio" as a powerful talismanic presence in this story sets the artistic standard of the baseball allusion. Whether or not subsequent authors realize it, they are responding to or recapitulating some aspect of Hemingway's method in their own literary ball games.[13]

Part II concerns itself with baseball novels, beginning with the first work in the genre,[14] Ring Lardner's *You Know Me Al*. Like Part I, the contents of Part II are highly selective: Far too many baseball novels have been written since the publication of *You Know Me Al* in 1916 — indeed, since *The Natural* appeared in 1952 — for each one to receive detailed attention here. I have limited the selection to four novels that represent the origin of the genre and have established its mimetic parameters. These four works — *You Know Me Al, The Natural, The Southpaw,* and *The Universal Baseball Association, Inc., J. Henry Waugh, Prop.* — are the first notable "literary" fictions to take their subject matter from baseball. Each of these books shapes its narrative to some variation of the exile

---

[13]*The foregoing works have been selected for two reasons: Their literary quality is established, and they are standard texts for students of American fiction. To understand the essays of Part I, the reader must have a competent knowledge of these works and their major themes. Other examples, such as the baseball content of novels like* Ironweed *(1982),* Never Come Morning *(1942),* The Catcher in the Rye *(1951),* The Field of Vision *(1956),* Portnoy's Complaint *(1969),* Ragtime *(1975),* Rabbit at Rest *(1990),* Mao II *(1991),* Underworld *(1997), and so on, might have been cited. These novels use baseball to illuminate a character or scene, as a guiding or encompassing metaphor, or evoke in passages of lyric intensity its sights, smells, and sounds, the atmosphere of its performance.*

[14]*You Know Me Al* is first if one agrees to set apart novels like Our Baseball Club and How It Won the Championship *(1884), by Noah Brooks,* Baseball Joe on the School Nine *(1912), by Lester Chadwick, as well as collections like Zane Grey's* The Red-Headed Outfield and Other Baseball Stories *(1915), which were written for boys. Juvenile baseball fiction also includes serial publications like the Frank Merriwell tales of Gilbert Patten, which first appeared in Tip Top Weekly under the author's "Burt L. Standish" pseudonym. This subgenre, formerly called "boys' books," is generally held to have introduced baseball subject matter to American fiction writers, who subsequently devised their own variations of its formulaic plots and stock characters. See Christian K. Messenger,* Sport and the Spirit of Play in American Fiction *(New York: Columbia University Press, 1981), 155–179, for a comprehensive appraisal of what he calls "The Boys' School Sports Story." See Michael Oriard,* Dreaming of Heroes *(Chicago: Nelson-Hall, 1982), 27–52, for a detailed account of baseball in juvenile fiction and 333–334, note 28, for a sampling of its titles. Also, see both Leverett T. Smith's "John R. Tunis's American Epic; or, Bridging the Gap between Juvenile and Adult Sports Fiction," 46–61, and Wiley Lee Umphlett's "Formulaic Sources of the American Sports-Fiction Tradition: The Code of Quality Performance in Juvenile Sports Fiction," 25–45, both in* The Achievement of American Sport Literature: A Critical Appraisal, *edited by Wiley Lee Umphlett (Madison, NJ: Fairleigh Dickinson University Press, 1991).*

and homecoming trope, and each protagonist attempts to live and play the game in such a way that participation will lead him home. The protagonist's concern with home is sometimes explicit and manifest in the plot; at other times this concern is repressed or marginalized in symbolic action or rhetorical configurations. And yet, the reader eventually perceives that all narrative energy moves homeward.

You Know Me Al is the story, told in his "letters home," of Jack Keefe, a rookie pitcher trying to succeed in the major leagues in spite of his own ignorance and recklessness (of which he is infrequently aware). The vicissitudes of Jack's baseball career are complicated and, to a great extent, precipitated by his unruly personal life, which revolves around the complementary desires of getting married and establishing a home. The harried, nearly desperate nature of Jack's "romantic" relationships, like his reflexive references to the "little yellow house," indicate that his matrimonial intentions and domestic dreams are sincere — and possibly obsessive — if only marginally coherent. Jack's manner of wooing, like his strategy of securing a home of his own, dramatizes his myopic optimism and general imprudence, as well as his lack of self-knowledge. In combination with his assorted stupidities, these traits create an atmosphere of hilarity that masks the pain and isolation, the real sense of displacement, that he suffers as a small-town boy "on the road" in the major leagues. Jack's efforts to marry one girl or another read like farce, and his attempts to come home to Bedford are thwarted by circumstances that are variously humorous and vexing. Finally, circumstance itself matches Jack's own wish, belatedly acknowledged, to postpone his long-deferred homecoming indefinitely. Lardner's mimetic mode is one of comic hyperbole; the language is plain and often ungrammatical, the situations superficially absurd and implicitly pathetic. By permitting Jack Keefe to narrate his trials and tribulations in the form of the letters he writes to "Friend Al," Lardner demonstrates that the epistolary form of prose fiction can be as unselfconsciously revelatory of the fictive writer as the dramatic monologues of Robert Browning are of the poetic speaker.

In *The Natural*, Bernard Malamud requisitions familiar myths of sacred quest and vegetative regeneration to lend structure and substance to the story of Roy Hobbs, an unreformed natural caught up in a tragicomic romance.[15] Delivered into his profession some fifteen years too late, Roy strives to outhit, outrun, outplay chronological time by cramming a career's worth of success into a single summer. His gestures harken back to his boyhood idyl in a primeval western forest, the only home he seems to remember with unambiguous contentment and the immediacy of "felt life." Unlike the forbidding "bone-white farmhouse," the forest is the place where, safe from care and anxiety, Roy has known an easy solitude uncomplicated by great expectations and all-consuming goals. Ghosts from this time haunt Roy's consciousness, but the past remains inaccessible. Roy cannot go home again, nor recapture the time he has lost.

---

[15]Roy is a "natural" in the Shakespearean sense of an uneducated, naïve character.

Similarly, a future home exists for Roy only as fantasy or delusion, for the version of it he prospectively constructs around Memo Paris is impossible within the narrative's symbolic universe and its archetypal demands. The mixed genre of *The Natural* tends to lead readers into confusion: Written in a language that often echoes the vernacular of sports journalism, the book inscribes ancient paradigms in a baseball context, then adds signs of magic — a silver bullet, a disintegrating baseball — to alert the reader to the symbolic implications of the baseball events. Like Roy, the reader risks missing the metaphorical import of events if he insists on reading them in terms of the story's nominal realism. The narrative is, in mimetic terms, a modern American romance of the type Nathaniel Hawthorne might have written had he been born a century later.

The Southpaw presents another first-person narrator, Henry Wiggen, who is also a baseball player and, like Lardner's busher, the author of his own story. Posing as the book's editor, true author Mark Harris helps his surrogate to improve sufficiently upon Jack Keefe's ungrammatical language and abbreviated self-awareness to produce a quintessentially American *Bildungsroman* in the manner of *Adventures of Huckleberry Finn*.[16] The "inside" story of Henry Wiggen's early life and coming-of-age, including the left-hander's first season in the major leagues, recounts his formative adventures from a perspective of greater knowledge. In its narrative strategy *The Southpaw* truly does contain its end in its beginning. Only after traveling the arc of experience — from home, into a kind of professional's exile, and back home again — does "author" Wiggen begin to write his story. The process of composition, directed by Holly Webster and critiqued by Aaron and Pop, completes his reunion with the values that have shaped his character until the inception of his professional career. It also yields a book. Henry Wiggen's autobiography of initiation is the first baseball novel that adopts the genre's formal realism to achieve self-consciously literary goals. Events and characters are credible, the language maintains its colloquial register without becoming a grotesquery of American English, and the baseball is recognizable as the game played on fields of grass and dirt. By allowing the game to be itself and resisting the impulse to overburden it with symbolic claims, *The Southpaw* distills life-wisdom from a written text of baseball. In some respects the mimetic realism, or verisimilitude, of its baseball scenes has yet to be bettered.

Distinguishing between fictiveness and reality in a baseball game and in a life (or what passes for one) is the object of the many games that Robert Coover plays in *The Universal Baseball Association, Inc., J. Henry Waugh, Prop.* Originality of form and rhetorical ingenuity give Coover's novel a literary stature that few subsequent baseball fictions have approached; for sheer inventiveness, the story of J. Henry Waugh and his tabletop baseball game has not been

---

[16]A Bildungsroman, *or novel of initiation, features a young protagonist whose trials, successes, and defeats chart his evolving consciousness of himself and his relation to the greater world.*

matched. The playing of this game on the sun-bright fields of Henry's imagination dominates the narrative process, which, in turn, describes the evolution of the UBA from game to ritual. The result is a metafictional narrative that dramatizes the mental processes that invest language, thought, and action with meaning. For Henry, every UBA contest is a home game played in the familiar solitude of his kitchen. The invented players inhabit his consciousness with the felt presence of family members and easily seem more "real" than Henry's few friends and associates. Gradually, inexorably, Henry retreats from his life of accounting firm and delicatessen, allowing his imagination to take up residence permanently within the space of his game. Dissatisfied with his life and its deprivations and banalities, Henry resorts to the UBA for moral coherence. He discovers, however, that the game is amoral. Its outcomes are decided by chance; any pattern of meaning it seems to describe is a confluence of serendipity and coincidence. Frustrated by the game's failure to reflect the meaning that he projects upon it, Henry attempts to remediate the vagaries of play with the intentionality of art. This self-conscious meddling leads to a severe psychic wounding that seems to approach mental illness. During the dark night of his soul, Henry drifts in virtual exile from both his real life and the life of the Association. The resolution implicates player and game in a sinister homecoming that is also a greater exile, and the ceremony and foreboding of the final chapter illustrate that the game, like life and all art, is contained within parameters of its own devising. The novel's interpenetrating fictions and multiple crossovers among life, art, and game propose that these endeavors are often complementary and equally (un)real. Their outward forms might differ, but each artifact always threatens to escape its player/author's intention and control.

Throughout *Home Games,* I am interested in the aesthetic qualities of literary texts. I believe that it is as art, as a form of entertainment and an expression of moral value (rather than as an expression of political ideology or agenda), that prose fiction makes its claims on our attention. I focus, therefore, on the genre's major aesthetic components — language and structure, metaphor and imagery, contingencies of plot, articulations of character — and how these components create meaning. Some of this meaning begins in baseball itself. Because baseball fiction often refers to baseball in the real world, the anterior reality of players, games, and seasons exerts a decisive influence on literary representations of the game. The baseball material that appears in *Home Games* (in the form of historical background, brief player biographies, and game accounts) should enrich the reader's understanding of the text to which it pertains. Baseball is part of the relevant context, and the effort of interpretation must take it into account. To some, the game is and always will be extraliterary; indeed, watching it played, one can hardly escape the physical evidence of its having nothing to do with *belles-lettres.* However, in relation to the fictions discussed in *Home Games,* baseball knowledge constitutes an indispensable element of the critical method. Thus, the essays that follow attempt to interweave two discourses: a historical account of baseball that is relevant to the literature under review and a critical interpretation of literary texts in which baseball has a demonstrable effect on meaning. If this attempt is successful, the reader will recognize not only the importance of baseball in American fiction but also the power of creative literature to inspire baseball — as it is remembered and written down — with an embellished literary life. The reader may observe this effect in an allusion, such as the one that informs Thomas Wolfe's description of "a man named Speaker, quick as a deer to run, sharp as a hawk to see, swift as a cat to strike," as well as in the game-within that Robert Coover's dark diceman plays at his kitchen table, on the interior diamond of his mind. In baseball fiction it is the game itself — its gestures and language, the spectacle of its performance, the achievements of its players, the progress of its seasons — that enjoys a heightened existence and enchanted afterlife.

PART I

♦ *One* ♦

"I See Great Things in Baseball"

The Game and Its Contexts

Some baseball is the fate of us all.
— Robert Frost

Walt Whitman knew baseball. As a boy he played the game with his brother, Thomas Jefferson Whitman, and was described by another brother, George Washington Whitman, as an "old-fashioned ballplayer." Hale, athletic, Whitman in his prime stood six feet tall, weighed two hundred pounds, and played an underhand-slow-pitch soft-ball game in the years before written rules, in New York City and its environs. Coming of age in the place and time of American baseball's (re)invention from English rounders, America's great inimitable poet evolved toward a mature aesthetic during the same years that the National Pastime underwent the refinements that would transform it from a schoolboy's diversion into a man's contest of strength and skill.[1]

Credit for these refinements, and for codifying the *de facto* rules of "base ball" (its antebellum orthography), belongs to Alexander Joy Cartwright, volunteer fireman, professional bank teller, and amateur ballplayer. Cartwright was the chief founding member of the Knickerbocker Base Ball Club of New York, formed from a group of merchants, clerks, brokers, and other white-collar men who had been gathering for several years in Manhattan (at 27th Street and 4th Avenue) to play "base ball."[2] Although they did not invent the game, the Knickerbockers did invent themselves by drawing up a constitution in 1845.

[1]*Ed Folsom's "The Manly and Healthy Game: Walt Whitman and the Development of American Baseball," in* Arete *2:1 (Fall 1984): 43–62, is the definitive investigation of Whitman's involvement with baseball and is the main source of the details about Whitman and baseball presented here.*

[2]*Harold Seymour,* Baseball: The Early Years *(1960; reprinted, New York: Oxford University Press, 1989), 15–16.*

Crowded out of the city's busy streets, the Knickerbockers crossed from Manhattan Island via ferry to the Elysian Fields of Hoboken, New Jersey, where they rented a playing field and dressing rooms.[3] By no one's fancy (including their own) a professional team, the Knickerbockers devoted equal attention to social activities ("balls, suppers, hops, promenades, skating parties" [Goldstein 19–20]) as they did to ball-playing and relished the customary postgame banquet as much as the day's game (Seymour 15, 20–21). They are significant in baseball history neither for their athletic performances nor for the lavishly laden tables they proffered to "guest" clubs but for the rules they, principally in the person of Cartwright, committed to paper. The distance between pitcher and batter (45 feet), the distance between bases (90 feet), the number of players to a side (nine), the number of outs to an inning ("three hands out, all out"[4]), as defined in the Knickerbocker Rules, became the standards of the game, circa 1845.

Baseball's first set of codified rules rewrote some of the game's nineteenth-century practices — conventions that heretofore had remained unwritten. Most significant are the specifications for a harder ball and a caveat governing its use.[5] By restructuring established practice, this rule obliged the players to develop a new technique: To put a base runner out, the fielder must touch him with the ball or, in possession of the ball, touch the base to which the runner is forced ahead of the runner's arrival. Before the Knickerbockers took the matter in hand, fielder put out runner by hitting him with the ball. "Soaking," or "plugging," as the contemporary lexicon named it, was prohibited by Knickerbocker rules, and the base runner touched ("tagged" today) with the ball was put out with more decorum and a diminished risk of injury. Later (1858), the Knickerbockers tried to change the rule that allowed balls caught on one bounce to be counted as outs; outs, they averred, should have to be caught "on the fly," a feat demanding more skillful fielders. Other clubs demurred, but the "fly rule" prevailed and the "New York game" (so-called in contradistinction from the "Massachusetts game") became the model of American baseball.[6]

Several features made the New York game preferable, but its dissemination and acceptance depended on writing: The Knickerbockers wrote everything down, and through the simple yet definitive act of writing endowed their rules with a semblance of authority. Their written words proved sufficiently impressive to make the Knickerbocker code of behavior normative as well:

[3]*Warren Goldstein*, Playing for Keeps: A History of Early Baseball *(Ithaca, NY: Cornell University Press, 1989), 12.*

[4]*"Three hands out, all out" was a common phrase in nineteenth-century baseball. See* The Old Ball Game *(Alexandria, VA: Redefinition, 1990), by Mark Alvarez, 17.*

[5]*The new ball consisted of a leather cover sewn over yarn wound around an india rubber core. It was 6–6¼ ounces and 10–10¼ inches in circumference (Seymour 18). The specifications for the modern baseball were fixed in 1872 and remain in effect today: 5–5¼ ounces, 9–9¼ inches in circumference (Seymour 182).*

[6]*For the operative differences between the New York and Massachusetts games, see Seymour 26–29 and Alvarez 22–23; for "plugging" see Alvarez 50–51.*

Other amateur base ball clubs, as if bidding for legitimacy, adopted the Knickerbocker bylaws of personal deportment, thereby enjoining their members to refrain from arguing with umpires, using profanity, and turning out for club meetings and games in a state of drunkenness. Some clubs emulated the Knickerbocker custom of wearing stylish uniforms (Seymour 17, 20).[7] The upshot of this process was a practical (re)invention of base ball in the image that the Knickerbockers conceived for it. Thus, an aggregation of pen-strokes revised the folk games of "Base," "One-Old-Cat," "Stool Ball," and "Town Ball," each relying for decades on the oral tradition to communicate its particular conventions, into a literate (in its written rules and records) precursor of modern baseball.[8] Of which precursor, Whitman, precursor of poets, knew.

About which game, Walt, newspaperman, wrote.[9] As a young newspaper editor in 1846, Whitman observed the unfolding of the American game and extolled the practice of "several parties of youngsters playing 'base,' a certain game of ball" in an editorial written for the *Brooklyn Daily Eagle* and printed one month after the Knickerbockers played the first game under their new rules at the Elysian Fields (Folsom 46). "Let us go forth awhile," Whitman writes in this piece, "and get better air in our lungs. Let us leave our close rooms.... The game of ball is glorious."[10] Twelve years later, Whitman is editing the *Brooklyn Daily Times* and becomes one of the first baseball writers (Folsom 48) when he reports on matches played between amateur clubs: "The game played yesterday afternoon between the Atlantic and Putnam Clubs, on the grounds of the latter club, was one of the finest and most exciting games we ever witnessed. The Atlantics beat their opponents by four runs, but the general opinion was that the defeat was as much the result of accident as of superior playing" ("On Baseball" 417). Judging the game's quality, Whitman writes as an experienced observer; evaluating its outcome, he distinguishes misfortune from ability by identifying true causes: Several Putnam players suffered injuries (hence, "accident") that put their team at a disadvantage, but the performance of the Atlantics did merit their reputation as "the *Champion Club*" (Whitman's italics). His citation of "the general opinion" might proceed from postgame conversations with lingering fans, but an anonymous vox populi serves the reporter's purpose, corroborating his interpretation of the game as if by popular vote. Similarly,

---

[7] *Among nineteenth-century enthusiasts, uniforms were considered mandatory for any self-respecting club nine. See Goldstein 108–111 for a commentary on early baseball uniforms.*

[8] *For a distinction between folk versions of baseball and Organized Baseball's literary quality, see Tristram Coffin, The Old Ball Game: Baseball in Folklore and Fiction (New York: Herder and Herder, 1971), 3–5.*

[9] *Folsom notes that two pieces of Whitman's baseball reportage remain extant, both from 1858 and chronicling Putnams' games (Folsom 48). The ensuing quotation is the first paragraph of the latter article, reprinted (with a rudimentary box score) as "On Baseball, 1858" in* The Armchair Book of Baseball II, *edited by John Thorn (New York: Scribner's, 1987), 417–418; cited as "On Baseball."*

[10] *Quoted by John Bowman and Joel Zoss in* Diamonds in the Rough: The Untold History of Baseball *(New York: Macmillan, 1989), 258; cited as* Diamonds.

the collective "we," a rhetorical gesture, underscores the communal nature of spectatorship and suggests that the reporter is one of the people and free of professional bias. Whitman's recourse to popular opinion aptly characterizes the "reader-response" quality of the people's game and offers a prosaic example of Whitman's poetic interest in the people's voices. The reporter ends his column with a conventional naming of key players: "Messrs. M. O'Brien, P. O'Brien, Boerum, Pierce, and Oliver of [the Atlantics] cannot easily be surpassed in their respective positions. Messrs. Master, Gesner, and McKinstry, of the Putnam Club, also deserve special commendation" ("On Baseball" 418).

Here is a hint of why baseball pleases Whitman so well: The victory of the club is primary, but the efforts of individual players may, even in a losing cause, be applauded. Congratulation of honest effort is a sign of civility that accords with the spirit of the game. Indeed, in its manicured field, its unencumbering uniforms, in the orderliness of its play, baseball is among the more genteel of our major sports. The game inhabits an open space, a garden within the steel city, a village green where people gather. Its field provides a great stage, its difficult feats offering ample occasion for the exhibition of individual prowess, as well as the tasking of solitary frailty. The progress of baseball is highly visible, its gestures discrete. At bat the player is poised, expectant, yet relaxed; in the field he is nonchalantly alert, ready to sprint, reach, dive, or pivot to "field" his position. Always in the midst of play, the ballplayer is exposed to the scrutiny of spectators, his only privacy depending on the extent to which he is able to dissemble his vulnerabilities behind the mantle of his skills. And even then, the consequence of each least action is available to the eye and, afterward, to the mind in reflection. Like the poet and the man who walks the high wire, the baseball player constantly risks absurdity.

In a related analogy, baseball's foregrounding of individual performance within a context of team play suggests a metaphor for the part played by a productive citizen within the institutions of democratic capitalism.[11] Whitman, democratic man, "neither for nor against institutions,"[12] chronicler of Americans in their labor and their indolence, does not waste his poetic power on the getting and spending of specie, does remark the manifest freedoms and salubrious fringe benefits of playing ball as an activity apart from the day's toil.[13] Speaker of "long dumb voices," speaker of "forbidden voices" ("Song of Myself" 211), singer of the body electric, singer of himself, Whitman celebrates America's possibilities for all persons created unabridgably free, inalienably equal;

---

[11]See Christian K. Messenger, Sport and the Spirit of Play in Contemporary American Fiction (New York: Columbia University Press, 1990), 17. Cited as CAF. See also Michael Oriard, Dreaming of Heroes: American Sports Fiction, 1868–1980 (Chicago: Nelson-Hall, 1982), 59–60.

[12]Walt Whitman, "I Hear It Was Charged Against Me," in Complete Poetry and Collected Prose, edited by Justin Kaplan (New York: Literary Classics of the United States, 1982), 281. All quotations of the poetry follow this edition and are cited by titles and page numbers.

[13]See Folsom 46 for Whitman's association of baseball with health. In "Song of Myself" (221) Whitman associates "base-ball" with "the race-course, or enjoying picnics or jigs."

claims an ineffable intimacy with nature, an interchangeability of his vital substance with the air and earth of his native land[14]—

> My tongue, every atom of my blood, form'd from this soil, this air,
> Born here of parents born here from parents the same, and their parents the same,
>
> ******
>
> I bequeath myself to the dirt to grow from the grass I love,
> If you want me again look for me under your boot-soles.

—recognizes in baseball a manifestation of America's fitful energy, a synecdoche of the nation's politics—

> "That's beautiful: the hurrah game! Well—it's our game; that's the chief fact in connection with it: America's game; has the snap, go, fling, of the American atmosphere; it belongs as much to our institutions, fits into them as significantly, as our constitution's laws: is just as important in the sum total of our historic life" [*Diamonds* 258].

—and in a free-verse cataloguing of activities that define the spirit and temper of the American people and the contours of the landscape through which he walks, recommends "a good game of base-ball" as something to be enjoyed as recreation, as if part of a holiday ("Song of Myself" 221). Something about the game, the ever-expanding playing field, the coordinated deployment of young men, long-limbed and lithe, within the precise geometry of the diamond, the antagonistic intimacy of pitcher and batter, charms the poet's imagination. Yet Whitman's remarks suggest that his attraction to baseball is inspired less by its nice aesthetics, many of which concern static qualities and often are reflected by a language of stasis, than by its action: the players' vigorous motions, the darting flight of the ball, the kinetic energy that every play sets free. It is better, Whitman intimates, to act, to stretch and bend and enliven oneself with physical exertions describing the accomplishment of a material challenge. Man attains wholeness not only through contemplation but equally in articulations of force; exercise strengthens weak limbs, the mind becomes more alert by focusing it periodically on the demands of the body. To heal the wounds that debilitate us, Whitman prescribes play. In the aftermath of the Civil War and its four years of catastrophic slaughter, Whitman spoke of baseball as a tonic for all America: "I see great things in baseball; it's our game—the American game. It will take our people out of doors, fill them with oxygen, give them a larger physical stoicism. Tend to relieve us from being a nervous, dyspeptic set, repair these losses, and be a blessing to us" (quoted by Folsom, 50). Therapeutic, rejuvenating, compensatory, a benediction for body and soul: "I am the poet of the Body and I am the poet of the Soul" ("Song of Myself" 207).

Whitman's alignment of physical and metaphysical well-being with baseball

---

[14]*The following lines are from "Song of Myself," pages 188 and 247, respectively.*

is characteristic of the theory, propounded from the earliest days of ball playing and proclaimed at times with propagandistic fervor, that baseball fosters
moral rectitude.[15] Baseball history testifies to the contrary, but the myth endures,
and as a sustaining fiction this myth is valuable. Valuable, too, is Whitman's
reaction to the curveball, a recent (in 1889) device, for his disapproval registers what is commonly called the purist baseball mentality. The purist mind
recoils before every change in the rules, style, and field of play and discerns in
any alacrity to accept such change (and in the new ways themselves) a sign of
unequivocal corruption. The subtext of this attitude is that baseball was, once
upon a Golden Age, perfect. Whitman did not often speak in a conservative
voice and in his poetry evinces an appreciation of the impure as well as the
pure, but in baseball matters the poet tends to display a conservative, purist
temperament. To Whitman, the curveball is a devious stratagem practiced in
bad faith by pitchers upon batters. The intention, obscured by the immediacy
of play, is ultimately transparent: to induce, through trickery (in how the ball
is thrown) and deceit (in hiding this trickery), the batter to miss the pitch, to
swing where the ball is not, to counterfeit plenitude in the midst of absence.
The end, predictable for being commonplace, is the professional's credo: to
win. Whitman, an "old-fashioned ballplayer," condemned the curveball, judging it a symptom of degraded morals; its practioners, prizing victory more than
honesty and readily resorting to deception in the pursuit of one-upmanship,
were, to Whitman, guilty of an ignoble competitiveness unworthy of human
beings. Accordingly, the poet places them within a traditional bestiary: "The
wolf, the snake, the cur, the sneak all seem entered into the modern sportsman —
though I ought not to say that, for a snake is snake because he is born so, and
man the snake for other reasons, it may be said" (quoted by Folsom 55). To
Whitman, curveball pitchers are morally culpable because they fail to conform
their behavior to the standard of personal integrity that each person ought to
maintain; they are cheating. In Whitman's eyes, a pitcher who throws the curveball exploits not only superior physical ability but, what is more to the point,

---

[15]*Albert Goodwill Spalding, one of baseball's progenitors, championed this theory, which happened to
serve his interests. As cofounder of the National League, owner of the Chicago White Stockings, and
prime mover in the establishment of the sporting goods company still named for him, Spalding became
a rich man. See Peter Levine's* A. G. Spalding and the Rise of Baseball: The Promise of American
Sport *(New York: Oxford University Press, 1985). Spalding is also the central mythifier of the Doubleday Creation Myth, which identifies Civil War general Abner Doubleday as baseball's immaculate con-
ceiver. See Seymour 8–12 for how and why Spalding and his cohorts perpetrated this fiction; see Seymour
4–8 for baseball's evolutionary development from various stick-and-ball games, primarily English
rounders. Spalding's intentions in falsifying the origins of baseball are recounted by Levine 112–115.
Stephen Jay Gould interprets the success of Spalding's creation myth as indicative of our yearning to
discover a definite time, place, and agency of origin — an "originating scene"— for the phenomena that
matter to us. In "The Creation Myths of Cooperstown," reprinted in* The Best American Essays, 1990,
*edited by Justin Kaplan (New York: Ticknor and Fields, 1990), 99–111, Gould analogizes the fiction of
baseball's instant creation to the Cardiff Giant fraud. In a coincidence almost too aesthetically satisfying to be believed, the great gypsum relic has found its resting place in "a shed behind a barn at the
Farmer's Museum in Cooperstown, New York" (Gould 99), home to the National Baseball Hall of Fame
and the supposed site of baseball's rural birth.*

excessive intelligence, a variety of efficacious but low cunning that is, from old-fashioned baseball's viewpoint of fair play, indistinguishable from treachery.[16] The poet rebukes, in effect, a guilty mind, his verdict charged with moral censure: Of the curveball, Whitman concludes, "I should call it everything that is damnable" (quoted by Folsom 55).

Perhaps damnable, surely regrettable, is Whitman's failure (assuming he tried) or reluctance (if he did not) to compose a poem about baseball as he knew it. One might, from his spoken comments, imagine the verses he might have written, but Whitman did not find in baseball either subject matter or metaphor congenial to his poetic enterprise. American novelists who wrote primarily before the Civil War share this implicit neglect of baseball. Nathaniel Hawthorne, for instance, typically drew his subject matter from an earlier landscape, mostly Puritan and preindustrial, that was haunted by crueller hardships than the pagan rites that baseball re-enacts on a sunlit field. The Passion of Hester Prynne occurs in seventeenth-century Boston, where the prevailing Puritan ethos relegates game-playing to the margins of social interaction; it is inconceivable that Hawthorne's moral romance of secret sin and public expiation could be leavened by the shouts of boys playing rounders. Ball games of different kinds did exist in Puritan New England, but sport generally was a subject of opprobrium.[17]

Of the great American novels one commonly reads in college, none takes its subject matter from the great American game. Baseball was a cipher to virtually all nineteenth-century authors, becoming a national pastime only (and somewhat ironically) during the Civil War and arguably a national preoccupation in 1869.[18] Like Hawthorne, America's great early novelists — James Fenimore Cooper, Charles Brockden Brown, Herman Melville — did not imaginatively possess baseball as a feature of American life that they could use in their respective fictions. A general deficiency of cultural resources, valued by Henry James as the very stuff of fiction, presented these innovators with a considerable challenge as they initiated what has become the hodgepodge tradition of

---

[16]*When Whitman played the amateur game, the batter requested a high or low pitch and the pitcher obligingly tossed the ball to that spot. Seymour points out this accommodating feature of early baseball (Seymour 19) and notes that the pitcher was known as the "feeder" (Seymour 5).*

[17]*Christian K. Messenger,* Sport and the Spirit of Play in American Fiction: Hawthorne to Faulkner *(New York: Columbia University Press, 1981), 29–30.*

[18]*In that year, the Cincinnati Red Stockings formed the first all-professional team and traveled across the continent by train, playing whistlestop baseball from Brooklyn to San Francisco. The Red Stockings compiled a record of 56 wins, 0 losses, and one tie, but the 17-17 game against the Troy Haymakers is reputed to have been corrupt. On the pretext of a sham protest over a caught (or muffed) foul tip, the Troy nine walked off the field in the sixth inning so that the New York gamblers who had wagered heavily on them would not have to pay off their bets (Seymour 56–57). Other accounts note that the umpire declared a forfeit and awarded the contest to the Cincinnati club, and that the Haymakers came to accept this decision and even apologized to the Red Stockings the following winter. This version credits the Red Stockings with a perfect season of 57 and 0. If one counts the six "picked nine" games (in which their opponents were essentially all-star teams of a given town or city) in addition to the 57 club matches, the Red Stockings of 1869 won 63 games without a loss. See Alvarez 89, 92–94.*

the American novel. James himself artfully catalogues the "stuff" that Hawthorne so acutely lacked[19]:

> The negative side of the spectacle on which Hawthorne looked out, in his con-
> templative saunterings and reveries, might, indeed, with a little ingenuity, be made
> almost ludicrous; one might enumerate the items of high civilization, as it exists
> in other countries, which are absent from the texture of American life, until it
> should become a wonder to know what was left. No State, in the European sense
> of the word, and indeed barely a specific national name. No sovereign, no court,
> no personal loyalty, no aristocracy, no church, no clergy, no army, no diplomatic
> service, no country gentlemen, no palaces, no castles, nor manors, nor old coun-
> try-houses, nor parsonages, nor thatched cottages nor ivied ruins; no cathedrals,
> nor abbeys, nor little Norman churches; no great Universities nor public schools —
> no Oxford, nor Eton, nor Harrow; no literature, no novels, no museums, no pic-
> tures, no political society, no sporting class — no Epsom nor Ascot! Some such list
> as that might be drawn up of the absent things in American life ... [*Hawthorne*
> 351–352].

James himself registers the place of sport among the institutions of "high civilization," reserving an incredulous exclamation mark for "no sporting class —
no Epsom nor Ascot!" More suggestively, The Master's interest in edifices seems
to refer to the activities that occur within: to social context, and the opportunities that context provides for bringing fictive characters into revealing
relationships. In this spirit, one might add, "no baseball parks, nor sandlots nor
diamonds; no box seats nor Superstation coverage." Baseball today, its sub-
sidiary industries and peripheral employments as well as the game itself, figures
in our shared lives — and in many individual imaginations — as an elastic context that encompasses distinctive elements of American culture: labor unions,
labor relations, corporate identity; fast foods, "pop" fashions, physical fitness;
modern architecture, revival architecture, gentrification; newspapers, radio,
television; spectatorship, exhibitionism, the excesses of celebrity. To this vast
context an audience brings prejudices and fantasies, a readiness to applaud
cooperative achievement and individual success. The ballpark, with more
demonstrable efficacy than the theater, the museum, the novel one reads in solitude, serves the democracy as a locus of communal witnessing, a forum in which
the citizens look upon the rough beauty of athletic competition, which, because
it is evanescent, can become even more beautiful in the imagination's reflective
eye.

    In the one hundred and seventy years that have passed since Hawthorne's
predicament of, in James's phrase, "terrible denudation,"[20] America's cultural
contexts have changed many times over, giving modern American writers a

---

[19]*In* Hawthorne, *reprinted in* Henry James: Literary Criticism; Essays on Literature; American Writers; English Writers, *edited by* Leon Edel (*New York: Literary Classics of the United States, 1984*),
315–457.

[20]*Writing in 1879, Henry James refers to Hawthorne's predicament in terms of "the conditions of intellectual life, of taste ... in a small New England town fifty years ago" (Hawthorne 340–341).*

more colorful and expansive, and at the same time more inclusive, social scene to transpose into narrative art. Delivered into the national consciousness late in the nineteenth century, baseball matured as a professional sport during the first three decades of the twentieth. While the American novel was passing through the successive transmutative phases of Realism, Modernism, and Naturalism, baseball was invigorated by Ty Cobb's perfection of hustle-as-artform, the surgical batting and fleet, fierce baserunning that dominated the game before 1920, then was reinvented by Babe Ruth through the sudden power of his prodigious bat. With the formation of the American League in 1901 and the playing of the first World Series in 1903, American novelists after the turn of the century could not fail to notice baseball. Even writers who knew little and cared less about the game were virtually obliged by the representational nature of their medium to consider its hold on the popular imagination, for some of the people who frequented the ballpark on summer afternoons might also read their books.[21]

Of the period's canonical authors, only Ring Lardner, a first-rate writer who has remained marginal, wrote what is often dismissed as "baseball fiction." His short stories, and particularly the epistolary baseball novel *You Know Me Al* (1916), stand with the genre's most accomplished works.[22] Other authors — whose books, unlike Lardner's, one usually reads in college — use baseball only as incident and allusion in novels designed to represent a reality nominally more complex than that of the game. Allusive baseball proves to be a potent metaphor; taken as the game played on the diamond or in rhetorical terms as a symbol of American culture, baseball allusions serve as emblems of American values, tropes of American beliefs, the signature of our national myths.

Like Whitman, Mark Twain knew baseball. The author of *Adventures of Huckleberry Finn* (1884) recognized in baseball's competitive vigor a manifestation of nineteenth-century America's distinctive vitality. In 1899, Twain defined baseball as "the very symbol, the outward and visible expression of the drive and push and rush and struggle of the raging, tearing, booming nineteenth century."[23] This encapsulation seems similar to Whitman's comments, yet the vigorous (violent?) verbs evoke a different image of baseball than the one woolgathered by the good gray poet in his rocking chair in Camden. The nouns

---

[21]*Among the exceptions, Henry James and Edith Wharton come readily to mind. By age and temperament attuned to the nineteenth century, both authors belonged to a social class that looked on professional baseball players much as the "better sort" of Elizabethan Englishmen regarded actors. Ty Cobb's father held a similar attitude when his nineteen-year-old son told him that he would rather play professional baseball than study law or medicine; see Charles C. Alexander,* Ty Cobb *(New York: Oxford University Press, 1984), 13–16. Rube Marquard's father was of the opinion (in 1906) that "'Ballplayers are no good ... and they never will be any good,'" as Lawrence S. Ritter reports in* The Glory of Their Times *(1966; reprinted, New York: Vintage Books, 1985), 2.*

[22]*Like "My Roomy" (1914), "Sick 'Em" (1914), "Horseshoes" (1914), and "Alibi Ike" (1915).*

[23]*Twain's description is oft-quoted in histories of baseball. See Diamonds 67, 396 and Seymour 345.*

"drive and push and rush and struggle" strike the reader simultaneously as active verbs and seem to allude not only to Gilded Age acquisitiveness but also to an energetic, possibly belligerent, male sexuality. So, too, do these words reflect the heedless industrialism of late nineteenth-century laissez-faire capitalism, suggesting on all counts an impulse to dominate, an assertion of power, ambition, and desire. Twain's associating these qualities with baseball is appropriate, even predictable, for the game has practically always been both a business enterprise and a sport played and watched predominantly by men. Twain's characterization of the "raging, tearing, booming nineteenth century" also seems identifiably male, for it echoes qualities stereotypically attributed to men. Joining the two series—"drive and push and rush and struggle" and "raging, tearing, booming"—yields an unpleasant sense that something (perhaps Nature, in the form of the North American continent) is being raped in the tumult of capitalist expansion, however alien such an implication might be to the author's intended meaning.

In fictive incarnations as well, baseball serves Twain as a portmanteau metaphor for values, proclivities, and traits that he takes to be uniquely American. In *A Connecticut Yankee in King Arthur's Court* (1889), Twain uses baseball to mark the American modernness of his hero, Hank Morgan, who visits a long-past and demonstrably foreign world.[24] Knocked unconscious in a fight (he suffers a crowbar blow to the head), Morgan awakens in a bucolic landscape. All is not well, however, for he finds himself imperiled by an armored knight, mounted on horseback and charging with leveled lance. Having no alternative but to surrender, Morgan soon realizes that he has slipped the bonds of chronological time and the time-bound context of history and has been transported from nineteenth-century Connecticut to King Arthur's medieval court. Modern scientific knowledge and his native Yankee shrewdness enable Morgan more or less to take charge of sixth-century Britain, to which he introduces innovations like sewing machines, telephones, electricity, steamboats — and baseball. Baseball, Morgan decides, will replace jousting as the knights' main recreational diversion. The game is competitive, does not jeopardize life or limb, and allows for individual confrontations within a context of team play. In keeping with the New England tradition of applied common sense, Hank Morgan fills his rosters with monarchs and designates a person of unimpeachable authority to act as umpire:

> This experiment was base-ball. In order to give the thing vogue from the start, and place it out of the reach of criticism, I chose my nines by rank, not capacity. There wasn't a knight in either team who wasn't a sceptred sovereign.... Of course I couldn't get these people to leave off their armor; they wouldn't do that when they bathed. They consented to differentiate the armor, so that a body could tell one

[24]*Mark Twain,* A Connecticut Yankee in King Arthur's Court *(1889), reprinted in* Mark Twain: Historical Romances *(New York: Literary Classics of the United States, 1994), 213–539. References and quotations follow this edition.*

team from the other, but that was the most they would do. So, one of the teams wore chain-mail ulsters, and the other wore plate armor made of my new Bessemer steel. Their practice in the field was the most fantastic thing I ever saw. Being ball-proof, they never skipped out of the way, but stood still and took the result; when a Bessemer was at the bat and a ball hit him, it would bound a hundred and fifty yards, sometimes. And when a man was running, and threw himself on his stomach to slide to his base, it was like an iron-clad coming into port. At first I appointed men of no rank to act as umpires, but I had to discontinue that. These people were no easier to please than other nines. The umpire's first decision was usually his last; they broke him in two with a bat, and his friends toted him home on a shutter. When it was noticed that no umpire ever survived a game, umpiring got to be unpopular. So I was obliged to appoint somebody whose rank and lofty position under the government would protect him.

Here are the names of the nines:

BESSEMERS.	ULSTERS.
King Arthur	Emperor Lucius
King Lot of Lothian	King Logris
King of Northgalis	King Marhalt of Ireland
King Marsil	King Morganore
King of Little Britain	King Mark of Cornwall
King Labor	King Nentres of Garlot
King Pellam of Listengese	King Meliodas of Liones
King Bagdemagus	King of the Lake
King Tolleme La Feintes	The Sowdan of Syria

UMPIRE—Clarence.

The first public game would certainly draw fifty thousand people; and for solid fun would be worth going around the world to see. Everything would be favorable; it was balmy and beautiful spring weather, now, and Nature was all tailored out in her new clothes [Twain 507–508].

This humorous digression is the last pleasant moment Hank Morgan enjoys in the Middle Ages. His mind is taken from baseball by the illness of his baby daughter, for the sake of whose health he and his retinue have been sojourning on the French coast. When the little girl is on the mend, Morgan realizes that the ship he has sent to England for supplies has been gone for more than two weeks without a word. Fearing that an armed invasion or an outbreak of plague has occurred, Morgan returns to England to find that civil war has broken out and the Pope has placed an Interdict on the nation, to remain in effect as long as Morgan remains alive. Now *persona non grata,* "The Boss" retreats with Clarence and a band of English boys to fortifications at Merlin's cave. Twelve concentric electrified fences, with a raised battery of thirteen Gatling guns at their heart, enable Morgan to annihilate a host of some 30,000 knights arrayed against him, but the resultant slaughter effectively collapses civilization back into medieval times. Merlin's magic delivers up the Connecticut Yankee to thirteen centuries of stony sleep, and the novel ends.

The baseball allusion is a fanciful, comic invention that Twain introduces because the game is an obvious feature that distinguishes his native land from other countries, and specifically from England, where the people favor cricket, rounders, and their most popular game, football (American soccer). Twain is having some fun here in making the assorted kings of Arthur's English court play America's National Game, for cricket and rounders are two of the ball-and-stick games generally recognized as baseball's precursors (Seymour 4–7). The English believe cricket to be superior to baseball, but in the second half of the nineteenth century baseball supplanted cricket forever in the United States. Further, baseball is the game that sets the nineteenth century apart: It is certifiably modern, like electricity and the telephone, and a reference to it would have been recognized by Twain's contemporary readers as being quite up to date. On the other hand, by the time *A Connecticut Yankee* was published, baseball was no longer a novelty.[25] Indeed, the historical context is evident in the allusion: Morgan's claim that "The first public game would ... be worth going around the world to see" alludes to the around-the-world baseball tour of Albert Spalding, his team, the Chicago White Stockings, and a team of National League All-Stars. Spalding organized the tour, which lasted from October 1888 to April 1889, as a business venture: He hoped to disseminate baseball as widely as possible, then reap great profits from selling bats, balls and gloves to new players all over the world.[26] When Spalding and the touring players returned to New York City on April 6, 1889, they were welcomed with public adulation and a banquet at Delmonico's. Some three hundred guests attended the festivities, including Teddy Roosevelt, baseball officials, members of the New York Stock Exchange — and Mark Twain. Amid the hoopla and hyperbolic falderal that often attend a roomful of affable fellows who have surrendered themselves to food and drink, Abraham G. Mills, the National League president, staked the claim of "No rounders!" to the noisy approval of his audience, thereby setting in motion the effort to establish a purely American origin for baseball (Seymour 8–9). Twain's own claim that baseball is "the very symbol ... of the ... nineteenth century" was part of his address at this banquet. Its contemporaneity with the baseball allusion in *A Connecticut Yankee,* published in America on December 10, 1889,[27] suggests that Hank Morgan's introduction of baseball to medieval Britain is Mark Twain's contribution to the project of reversing the order of precedence between American baseball and English rounders.

The other remarks that one might make about Hank Morgan's account of baseball in the Middle Ages are, perhaps, a bit more esoteric. The prospect of 50,000 Englishmen coming out to watch a baseball game, for instance, is a

---

[25]See *"The American National Game"* in Seymour's Baseball: The Early Years, *for a thorough account of baseball's expansion after the Civil War.*

[26]*These details are highlights of Spalding's tour. The two teams played exhibition games against each other not only in England, Ireland, and Scotland but in such far-flung places as Sidney and Melbourne, Florence, Rome, Paris, Ceylon, and Cairo, where a game took place at the Pyramids. To the consternation of the Egyptians, some ballplayers climbed the Sphinx to pose for pictures. For various reasons, baseball's foreign reception was lukewarm, and Spalding lost $5,000 on the adventure. For a complete account see Levine 99–109.*

[27]Allison R. Ensor, preface to the Norton Critical Edition of A Connecticut Yankee in King Arthur's Court, *edited by Allison R. Ensor (New York: Norton, 1982), xi.*

terrific bit of optimism on Morgan's part, a rare attitude for him at the best of times and especially unlikely in the latter stages of the novel. Even in America the average attendance at National League games in 1889 was less than 10,000.[28] Doubtlessly, Morgan is counting on the novelty of baseball to attract curious natives. Manning his nines by rank — every player is a "sceptred sovereign" — rather than by athletic ability indicates his opinion that the English remain illogically impressed by social and political status and ignore the talents, however impressive these might be, of ordinary men. The problem of umpires' being assaulted plays off of class prejudice, for only Clarence, Hank Morgan's right-hand man, possesses enough authority to restrain the ball-playing kings. Their abusive treatment of umpires without rank also registers the traditional antipathy of American baseball fans. The cry "Kill the umpire!" is seldom heard today because it sounds corny, but it was in Twain's day a favorite epithet of the baseball "fanatic," or "krank" (Seymour 329–330, 337–344). The monarchs, with little regard for the lives or well-being of commoners, do not hesitate to enact what was otherwise an empty threat that only occasionally led to physical violence (Seymour 340). The balance of the allusion, which depicts players wearing full-body armor and baseballs ricocheting 150 feet, seems farcical to anyone who knows baseball. Chain-mail ulsters and plate armor are remote, indeed, from the wool flannel uniforms of the nineteenth century. Images of chain-mail and steel are difficult to incorporate into any vision of baseball, for the game is invariably figured as a pastoral diversion despite its major inventions having taken place in urban centers. Morgan's noting the onset of spring reinforces the element of pastoralism and clashes more discordantly with the metallic uniforms than any errant pitch. Each additional detail distorts the allusion further, suggesting baseball's dependence on its American context; to impress observers and be favorably received, the game must be played at home. Twain's incorporation of baseball at so late a stage of the novel's composition is quirky, even undisciplined, although it does afford an interlude of comic relief.

To state the case plainly, for Mark Twain and Walt Whitman, "base ball" is a happy occasion. As one might expect, both authors allude to the game in general terms: A certain amount of history had to happen before the stories that surround baseball became usable material for creative writers. In the nineteenth century, baseball was still new enough to count as a topical allusion, yet was also sufficiently familiar to be recognized by most readers. The comments that Whitman and Twain make about the game are almost invariably affirmative — Whitman's condemnation of curveball pitchers is an anomaly addressed to a circumstance that is, to Whitman, a startling break with the young game's amateur tradition — and the contexts of these allusions are usually celebratory. The latter quality reflects the historical context as much as it expresses the affinity of Whitman and Twain for baseball. Like the whole of American society, the

---

[28]Bill James, The Bill James Historical Baseball Abstract *(New York: Villard Books, 1988), 26. By 1889 the largest crowds to watch a professional baseball game numbered upwards of 30,000.*

National Pastime became more complicated as it entered the twentieth century, and allusions to the game in novels written after the First World War reflect the changing nature of both baseball and American culture. The optimism reflected in Twain's and Whitman's respective remarks, so generalized and pervasive that it seems atmospheric, shifts gradually toward cynicism, melancholy, and dread in the works of F. Scott Fitzgerald, William Faulkner, Thomas Wolfe, James T. Farrell, and Ernest Hemingway. At the same time, the national dissemination of baseball enabled these authors (and others of the early twentieth century) to draw on specific events, like the World Series, and on famous players, like Babe Ruth and Joe DiMaggio, for potent allusions that define theme and reveal character. Whether to convey optimistic or pessimistic sentiments, these authors have made baseball signify by having incorporated it into their creative work. If baseball means more in American fiction than what it is as a recreational diversion, the credit goes first to the writers who have written about it, or have written it into prominent fictions, in ways that invest it with meaning.

◆ *Two* ◆
The Black Sox
Signature
Baseball in
The Great Gatsby

Since sports are so much of boyhood, boys who turn away from sports
frequently seem crippled in humanity, poisoned against their peers,
driven to competitiveness in intellect or lost in the acquisition
of power and wealth, never graced by the liberty of play.
— Michael Novak, *The Joy of Sports*

During the first half of the twentieth century, baseball was the nation's single major professional sport and incontestably the favorite athletic diversion of the eastern section of the country. Despite its popularity, however, baseball did not impress F. Scott Fitzgerald (a midwesterner) as being anything more than a boy's game. For mature men, and for a serious writer, Fitzgerald considered baseball a waste of time. In the case of his friend and Long Island neighbor, Ring Lardner, Fitzgerald believed that too great an involvement with baseball had proven debilitating. His attitudes and imagination having been formed by the game and the personalities associated with it, Lardner was never able, in Fitzgerald's estimation, to transcend the limits of its milieu. Thus, on the occasion of Lardner's death, Fitzgerald writes that "one is haunted not only by a sense of personal loss but by a conviction that Ring got less percentage of himself on paper than any other American of the first flight."[1] It was not a matter of Lardner's having trifled away his days watching ball games but one of his having to interpret "the horribly complicated mess of living" ("Ring" 37) largely on the basis of ideas, values, insights, and assumptions he had learned from his experiences at the ballpark. The effect on his fiction was, according to Fitzgerald, devastating:

[1]F. Scott Fitzgerald, "Ring" (1933, The New Republic), reprinted in The Crack Up, edited by Edmund Wilson (New York: New Directions, 1956), 34–40; cited as "Ring."

37

> During those years, when most men of promise achieve an adult education, if only in the school of war, Ring moved in the company of a few dozen illiterates playing a boy's game. A boy's game, with no more possibilities in it than a boy could master, a game bounded by walls which kept out novelty or danger, change or adventure. This material, the observation of it under such circumstances, was the text of Ring's schooling during the most formative period of the mind. A writer can spin on about his adventures after thirty, after forty, after fifty, but the criteria by which these adventures are weighed and valued are irrevocably settled at the age of twenty-five. However deeply Ring might cut into it, his cake had exactly the diameter of Frank Chance's diamond.
>
> Here was his artistic problem, and it promised future trouble. So long as he wrote within that enclosure the result was magnificent: within it he heard and recorded the voice of a continent. But when, inevitably, he outgrew his interest in it, what was Ring left with? ["Ring" 36].

Fitzgerald's argument typifies the intellectual prejudice that posits an absolute hierarchy between the proper sources of literary fiction and the physical, contestatory nature of baseball.[2] Despite the concession that Lardner's treatment of baseball material is successful — You Know Me Al is, by Fitzgerald's reckoning, one of the best things Lardner ever wrote ("Ring" 38) — Fitzgerald maintains that baseball itself is insufficiently instructive or "real" to serve the embryo-author as a usable core experience; despite the passion of its fans, not enough is at stake. Two assumptions underlie Fitzgerald's theory: (1) Baseball is "only a game," and the people who play and watch it have neither thought nor existence, to say nothing of inner lives, apart from it; and (2) Lardner mistook the playing (and watching) of the game for the living of a life — he either did not perceive the emotional and psychological truths that underlay the superficial aspects of the physical contest, or failed to translate the qualities of human character displayed on the diamond into more general, non-sporting contexts. The first assumption surely is incorrect; if it were true, the present book could not have been written, must less conceived. The second assumption might be correct, for there is little evidence to refute Fitzgerald's contention that, without baseball, Lardner was a writer without resources. In this sense the example of Lardner's fiction-writing career serves Fitzgerald well, if his purpose is to discredit baseball's aesthetic currency. And yet, as Fitzgerald himself reminds us, Lardner was often cynical about the value of his work and given to insincere dismissals of his abilities as a writer ("Ring" 36, 37).[3] If an author regards his own writing with insufficient faith in its quality, it is unlikely that he will write either very well or for long. Lardner's limitations, therefore, might have been exactly that: inherent and attributable to his own disposition rather

[2]See Michael Oriard, Dreaming of Heroes: American Sports Fiction, 1868–1980 (Chicago: Nelson-Hall, 1982), 93–94: "The weaknesses Fitzgerald cites are, in fact, Lardner's strengths, as they are the strengths of the sports fiction genre."

[3]See Lardner's preface to You Know Me Al in the paperback edition (New York: Vintage Books, 1984), 17–18. See also Christian K. Messenger's assessment in Sport and the Spirit of Play in American Fiction: Hawthorne to Faulkner (New York: Columbia University Press, 1981), 108, 110.

than a result of his having come intellectually of age at the ballpark. Indeed, the successful use of baseball in literary fiction suggests that a writer's attention to the game need not culminate in failed or compromised work. Fitzgerald's own fiction might be cited as a case in point, for the baseball allusion in his single truly classic novel, *The Great Gatsby* (1925), can be read as a sign of the author's recognition that, in the cultural consciousness of America, baseball retains a great deal more significance than "a boy's game, with no more possibilities in it than a boy could master."

To be sure, Fitzgerald does not afford the game pride of place in *The Great Gatsby;* he is at least as interested in other sports and their players as he is in anything having to do with baseball. In Tom Buchanan, Fitzgerald depicts an ex-college football player grappling with civilian life, with brutal results, and plays on the popular associations of golf with affluence, leisure, and privilege to heighten the aloofness of Jordan Baker. Like Tom, Jordan's fanatical devotion to her sport is the touchstone of her solipsistic personality; both characters express in physical appearance and posture the *quidditas* of their respective games.[4] Observing Tom, Nick notices "a great pack of muscle shifting when his shoulder moved under his thin coat,"[5] as Buchanan's physique mimes even in ordinary movement the exertions of football's line of scrimmage. It is entirely appropriate that Tom shatters Myrtle Wilson's nose with "a short deft movement" (*Gatsby* 31). As if in counterpoint, Jordan Baker first appears "extended full length at her end of the divan, completely motionless and with her chin raised a little as if she were balancing something on it which was quite likely to fall" (*Gatsby* 10). Jordan's posture of relaxed equilibrium embodies the professional golfer's physical grace, as well as suggesting the particular endeavor of lining up a putt on a tricky green.[6]

Curiously, Gatsby himself eschews conventional games, preferring the serious play of his ostentatious parties, his hydroplane, his baroque automobile, his beautiful shirts — all of which contribute to the antic self-portrait he fashions to woo the former Miss Daisy Fay of Louisville. Gatsby is associated with sports on only two occasions[7]: In a photograph taken at Oxford, he holds a cricket bat (*Gatsby* 53); after his death, his dog-eared copy of *Hopalong Cassidy* reveals a detailed SCHEDULE, penciled onto the back fly-leaf, that reserves the half hour between 4:30 and 5:00 P.M. for "Baseball and sports" (*Gatsby* 134–135). Because of the shuffled chronology, the photo of Gatsby as an insouciant Oxford cricketer appears before his earlier incarnation as a boy baseball

---

[4]*James Joyce*, A Portrait of the Artist as a Young Man, *edited by C. G. Anderson (New York: Viking Penguin, 1968), 213: "'quidditas, the whatness of a thing.'"*

[5]*F. Scott Fitzgerald*, The Great Gatsby, *edited by Matthew J. Bruccoli (New York: Cambridge University Press, 1991), 9. Quotations and references follow this edition and are noted as* Gatsby.

[6]*In these readings of Tom and Jordan, I am developing an idea proposed by Richard Lessa in "'Our Nervous, Sporadic Games': Sports in* The Great Gatsby," *Arete 1:2 (Spring 1984): 69–79.*

[7]*"Old sport," Gatsby's signature phrase, is a pretense that indicates only its speaker's presumption that other men play at life as he does.*

player. Knowing the bad end of Gatsby's reinvented life, the reader cannot fail to appreciate the pathos of the second image. Its poignance is especially affecting because it is Gatsby's father who disingenuously directs Nick's attention to his son's SCHEDULE of September 12, 1906[8]: "'It just shows you, don't it? ... Jimmy was bound to get ahead'" (*Gatsby* 135). Fitzgerald avoids what might have become a maudlin moment by having Mr. Gatz produce only the sparsely notated list of his son's activities rather than, say, a sepia photograph of young Jimmy holding a baseball and fielder's glove. Mr. Gatz's silence on the baseball detail accords with Fitzgerald's unsentimental characterization of him and underlines the author's resistance to the cliché that figures baseball as a metaphor of the combative love that binds sons to fathers and fathers to sons.

The meager evidence that Jimmy Gatz played baseball might seem inconsequential, yet it links the boy to the man Gatsby has become by the time of the novel's major baseball allusion. In light of the fact that Fitzgerald does not use baseball elsewhere in his fiction, its presence in *The Great Gatsby* is especially provoking.[9]

---

[8]*As Bruccoli points out, the 1906 date of Jimmy's* SCHEDULE *is an anachronism, for* Hopalong Cassidy *was published in 1910. See Bruccoli's "Explanatory Notes" to the Cambridge edition of* The Great Gatsby, *204.*

[9]*In speculating on Lardner's influence on Fitzgerald during the composition of* The Great Gatsby, *Christian K. Messenger asserts, "At no other time did [Fitzgerald] evince an interest in professional baseball" (Messenger 203). Although Fitzgerald does not use baseball elsewhere to comparable effect, in* This Side of Paradise *(1920; reprinted, New York: Charles Scribner's Sons, 1970) Amory Blaine wonders "whether Three-fingered [sic] Brown was really a better pitcher than Christie [sic] Mathewson" (16). This preoccupation, like his interest in "chameleon ties" and "how babies were born," seems designed to mark Amory as a callow adolescent, the "Young Egotist" of his formative years (15). And yet, the rivalry between Christy Mathewson and Three-Finger Brown represented to partisans more than just a rooting interest, for the different backgrounds of the two men seemed to express the era's class consciousness. Mathewson, the son of a gentleman farmer and a mother of independent means (both born in England), grew up in an affluent home in Pennsylvania. He attended Keystone Academy and Bucknell University, where he starred in three sports, was a member of the Glee Club and literary society, and served as class president. A devout Methodist, Mathewson seldom drank liquor or swore, and chose not to pitch on Sundays — a preference to which his manager, John McGraw, deferred. Tall, lean yet strong, fair-haired and handsome, Christy Mathewson embodied the polite, polished, middle-class qualities that Organized Baseball wanted to call its own. It is fitting, as the context implies, that Amory favors Mathewson. Mordecai Peter Centennial Brown was born in Indiana; the middle name "Centennial" commemorates his 1876 birth date. He grew up on the family farm, yet teammates and friends called him Miner because he was a miner before becoming a ballplayer. A husky, friendly midwesterner, Brown pitched primarily for the Chicago Cubs and was a great favorite in the City of the Broad Shoulders. He was nicknamed "Three Finger" Brown by sportswriters because his pitching hand was deformed. When he was seven years old, Brown lost his right index finger below the second joint and broke his middle finger when his hand was caught in a feed cutter. Before the wounds had healed, he fell while chasing a hog, breaking the other two fingers and jamming the mangled middle finger up into his hand. Brown referred to this hand as his "paw." It enabled him to throw a curveball with a rapid downward break — "the most devastating pitch I ever faced," Ty Cobb called it (quoted by Kerrane 48). Three Finger Brown defeated Christy Mathewson nine times consecutively from July 12, 1905, to October 8, 1908, the final victory clinching the pennant for the Cubs. Brown was elected to the Hall of Fame in 1949, but Christy Mathewson is still known as "the master of them all" for combining strength, speed, and finesse. In 1936, Mathewson became one of five charter members of the Hall of Fame. See Noel Hynd,* The Giants of the Polo Grounds *(New York: Doubleday, 1988), 115–117, 193–197; Gene Karst and Martin J. Jones,* Who's Who in Professional Baseball *(New Rochelle, New York: Arlington House, 1973), 110–111, 647–649; Kevin Kerrane,* The Hurlers *(Alexandria, VA: Redefinition, 1989), 48, 122–125.*

Considering Fitzgerald's aspirations — he wanted *The Great Gatsby* to have "the very best I'm capable of in it or even as I feel sometimes, something better than I'm capable of" and thought of the novel as "a consciously artistic acheiment" [*sic*][10] — one wonders why he permitted an allusion to the 1919 World Series to intrude upon Nick's account of Gatsby's doomed love. The inclusion of baseball in so self-conscious an artifact of literary art suggests that Fitzgerald's instincts as a working novelist were keener than his principles as a critic.[11] The baseball allusion in *The Great Gatsby* is often quoted, for it bears directly on Fitzgerald's representation of his narrator and on Nick's portrayal — which becomes, finally, his judgment — of Gatsby. Indeed, the moment is so well known and so thoroughly characteristic of both Nick and Gatsby that it may be read as the novel's signature scene:

> "Who is he anyhow — an actor?"
>
> "No."
>
> "A dentist?"
>
> "Meyer Wolfshiem? No, he's a gambler." Gatsby hesitated, then added coolly: "He's the man who fixed the World's Series back in 1919."
>
> "Fixed the World's Series?" I repeated.
>
> The idea staggered me. I remembered of course that the World's Series had been

[10]*Fitzgerald states these intentions in a letter to Max Perkins of early April 1924, when Fitzgerald was still writing the novel (quoted by Bruccoli in his introduction to* The Great Gatsby, *pp. xi–xii).*

[11]*Fitzgerald deleted a second baseball allusion from* The Great Gatsby, *possibly because of its effect on his prose style. In a subsequently rewritten version of the "confrontation scene," in which Tom and Gatsby each claim Daisy's love (Gatsby 88–114), the impromptu mint julip party at the Plaza Hotel does not exist. Instead, there is an excursion to the Polo Grounds to watch the New York Giants play the Chicago Cubs, then a public scene enacted by Gatsby, Tom, and Daisy — with Nick and Jordan as semi-willing spectators — in "a little café set amid the hot sparse shrubbery of Central Park" (Gatsby, Appendix 6, 218–219). The deleted scene contains lines ultimately published in the novel's extant Chapter VII, as well as the following account of Nick's day at the ballpark: "I enjoyed that afternoon. It was so hot that my underwear climbed like a damp snake around my legs, so hot that when I took off my coat beads of sweat raced cold across my back — but the smell of peanuts and hot butter and cigarettes mingled agreeably in the air and someone was thrown violently from the bleachers for being drunk or sober or wrong, and a pitcher with an exquisitely eccentric delivery warmed up near us on the grass. The Chicago Cubs were the visiting team and Tom applauded with perfunctory patriotism whenever they hit safely or pulled off a good play. But when he urged Daisy to do likewise she answered that she and Gatsby were for New York — after that he took no interest in the game. ¶ Somebody won and we swept out with the crowd into the late afternoon" (Gatsby 218–219). Nick's description of the Cubs-Giants game is brief and impatient, its language all-purpose. The teams on the field are nondescript. Faceless players hit and field an invisible ball, as if glimpsed through shadow, and even the pitcher with the "exquisitely eccentric delivery" performs anonymously. Believing the action of the game too familiar — or too dull — to merit a detailed account, Fitzgerald describes the spirit of play by resorting to the unlikely spectacle of "someone [being] thrown violently from the bleachers," which sounds like one of the sophomoric hi-jinks that mark college football games. Tom's Midwestern partisanship's being rendered as "patriotism" harkens back to antebellum America's regional fractiousness and underlines Tom's manic prejudices of race and class (later, Tom raves, "You begin by sneering at family life and family institutions and the next thing you'll throw everything overboard and have intermarriage between black and white!" [Appendix 6, 219; see Gatsby 101]). Nick's lack of interest in the game seems to mirror Fitzgerald's own disengagement from the material. A comparison of the deleted confrontation scene to the published Chapter VII reveals the latter's neater, more succinct creation of its effects and the former's uncoordinated energy and relative sprawl. It is unclear if the baseball scene itself led Fitzgerald's prose awry, but he did choose to rewrite the chapter without it.*

fixed in 1919 but if I had thought of it at all I would have thought of it as a thing that merely *happened*, the end of some inevitable chain. It never occurred to me that one man could start to play with the faith of fifty million people — with the single-mindedness of a burglar blowing a safe.

"How did he happen to do that?" I asked after a minute.

"He just saw the opportunity."

"Why isn't he in jail?"

"They can't get him, old sport. He's a smart man" [*Gatsby* 58].

The so-called Black Sox Scandal of 1919 is the most infamous event of baseball history, and its story has been retold by many commentators. Eliot Asinof's *Eight Men Out* (1963) remains the single most comprehensive and readable account of the fix, which for baseball aficionados requires little explication.[12] Arnold Rothstein, the millionaire New York gambler who is the model for Fitzgerald's Wolfshiem,[13] was generally identified as the brains and bankroll behind the fix. No incriminating evidence was presented, however, and his own testimony (in September 1920) persuaded the Cook County Grand Jury that his name had been bandied about by scurrilous small-time gamblers; incapable of funding such a project themselves, they had (the argument went) used his phantom involvement to convince the players that they

[12]*Readers not familiar with the story should read* Eight Men Out: The Black Sox and the 1919 World Series *(1963; reprinted, New York: Henry Holt and Company, 1987). In lieu of Asinof's book, the facts are these: In 1919, the lavishly-talented Chicago White Sox were heavy favorites to defeat the Cincinnati Reds in the World Series, but gamblers and eight — actually seven, for third baseman Buck Weaver knew of the fix but refused to participate — players on the White Sox conspired to lose the Series. The gamblers intended to make the most of betting long odds on the underdog Reds, and the players coveted the offered bribes ($10,000 apiece) as compensation for the substandard salaries paid by Charles Comiskey, the notoriously tightfisted owner of the White Sox. The players, led by first baseman Chick Gandil and including star pitcher Eddie Cicotte and baseball's original "natural," Shoeless Joe Jackson, agreed to lose the Series, while the gamblers, chiefly Sport Sullivan and Abe Attell, promised to deliver the entire $80,000 (Gandil did not mention that Weaver would play it straight) before the first game. The gamblers, who were even more unscrupulous than the players — and eager to bet every dollar on a Reds victory — did not honor the agreement. Cicotte, the starting pitcher, was paid in full, however, and he and the others engineered a White Sox loss in the first game. The gamblers made a killing despite having depressed the odds by betting so much money on the Reds. In combination with rumors that Arnold Rothstein, "the Jew from New York," had instigated a fix, the gamblers' heavy betting on a Reds victory trimmed the profits before the Series even began. The eventual payoff, although substantial, was nothing like the one anticipated by the principals. Considering how the gamblers strung along the disgruntled players, appeasing them with token payoffs sporadically during the Series but always withholding the full $80,000, it is remarkable that the fix did not unravel (in a sense, it did unravel — or would have, if the gamblers had not threatened violence to hold it together; see Asinof 112–119). Late in the 1920 season, Cicotte and Jackson confessed to having thrown the 1919 Series. The White Sox were contending to win another pennant, but Comiskey suspended the conspirators. At trial, the eight "Black Sox," as the newspapers called them, were acquitted of conspiracy to defraud (the confessions having opportunely disappeared). They were, however, banned from Organized Baseball for life by Kenesaw Mountain Landis, baseball's new plenipotentiary commissioner. None of the eight, including Buck Weaver, ever played in the major leagues again.*

[13]*The spelling "Wolfshiem" follows the Cambridge Edition, which emends the long-standard "Wolfsheim." Bruccoli's explanation — that the manuscript spelling is "Wolfshiem" and that such a spelling is "uncommon but possible" (Gatsby 148)— appears in "Substantive Emendations and Textual Notes" (Gatsby 143–154).*

would be paid off. Handled by the court like a defamed gentleman, treated as a friendly witness by State's Attorney Maclay Hoyne, Rothstein was exonerated. Popular opinion, however, as well as chronicles of the Black Sox Scandal have ever after linked Arnold Rothstein to the fixed World Series of 1919, from which he is reputed to have garnered $350,000.[14]

Both Nick and Gatsby are impressed by Meyer Wolfshiem's having finagled the fix, yet only Nick displays shock or incredulity. Gatsby's "coolly" describing Wolfshiem as "'the man who fixed the World's Series'" and Nick's "staggered" reaction have been read by critics as an index of their respective moral positions (Messenger 203). Nick is so nonplussed that his reply — "'Fixed the World's Series?'" — is mere reiteration, words uttered to occupy what would otherwise be silence while his mind gropes for a handle to Gatsby's astonishing revelation. Readers generally accept Nick's subsequent words at face value, chalking them up as an example of the moral rectitude, admittedly vague at times, that marks his reaction to untoward social situations and entangling alliances. Nick's scrupulous honesty does not operate alone, however; here and consistently throughout the novel, Nick betrays an elusiveness that does not quite mark him as a hypocrite so much as it buffers him from unpleasant realities, the contemplation of which might tax what one assumes is his genuine midwestern naïveté.[15] Indeed, the story of Gatsby's romantic lost cause and the excesses of morbid emotion that occur in its wake seem designed to offend callow Nick Carraway with special persistence.

When he learns that Meyer Wolfshiem is "'the man who fixed the World's Series,'" Nick's outraged innocence would be almost endearing if it were not too jejune to be taken seriously. He claims to remember the incident but seems to have paid little attention to its aftermath. It is, to Nick, something that has happened in a world apart from his own; obviously not implicated, he can afford to remain unconcerned. Curiously, Nick's presumption of indifference seems to entail a freedom from responsibility not just for himself but for the "fixers" as well; this particular dishonesty seems to have "merely *happened,*" to constitute "the end of some inevitable chain." Nick assumes an absence of agency, a

---

[14]See Asinof 26–31, 216–221, 286. See also Leo Katcher, "The Man Who Fixed the Series" reprinted in The Great Gatsby: A Study, edited by Frederick J. Hoffman (New York: Charles Scribner's Sons, 1962), 148–159. Katcher contends that Rothstein had inside knowledge of the fix and was partially responsible for bringing it about, yet refused to pay the bribes or bet to the limit on a Cincinnati victory. Katcher pegs Rothstein's take at $350,000 but cites no source for the figure. Asinof notes that Rothstein's personal fortune in 1920 approached $4 million and that an FBI search of the gambler's files (after Rothstein was shot and killed during a poker game) uncovered a record of $53,000 paid for four affidavits testifying to his part in the fix — including his payment of $80,000 to the Black Sox. These affidavits, however, were given by two of the gamblers accused of organizing the fix, so their veracity is questionable.

[15]Critics generally attribute the incredulity with which Nick reacts to not-quite-proper situations to his innocence, which they align, in turn, with his Midwestern origin. See also Messenger 184; and Robert Ornstein, "Scott Fitzgerald's Fable of East and West," 58, reprinted in Twentieth Century Interpretations of The Great Gatsby, edited by Ernest Lockridge (Englewood Cliffs, NJ: Prentice-Hall, 1968), 54–68.

void where there should be a clever mind calculating the ways and means, and seemingly attributes the fix to the working out of nature's evolutionary processes, as if it were a by-product of natural selection. This attitude is strange and leads finally into illogic: All business ventures, legal and otherwise, begin in an individual imagination. Nick seems to believe that such deals can enter the world spontaneously from no particular source merely because they are possible. This notion is characteristic of Nick's reactive personality and is incongruous with his job as a bond salesman. It is no surprise that Nick decides to leave the East after the fuss and tumult have subsided, for he has doubtless sold precious few bond issues while exhausting the year of financial support to which his father has staked him. This retreat and his assumption of a no-fault fix reveal Nick as either too credulous or too sentimental to adapt himself to the stratagems and dissimulations of East Coast life. One begins to think that Nick is too much of a neophyte even to have formulated a plausible interpretation of the irregular relationships he observes in West Egg.

It is worthwhile, moreover, to consider what Nick might mean when he analogizes debasing the World Series to "play[ing] with the faith of fifty million people." It might be that he is merely alluding to the fact that the World Series is advertised as an unrehearsed sporting event and that the people who watch it have implicitly committed themselves to believing that the games are just what they purport to be, neither more nor less. Nick's use of the word "faith," however, is charged with a moral judgment of Wolfshiem's duplicity. By using this figure of speech, Nick indicates his awareness that the World Series has attained the status of a cultural event; for those who pay attention to baseball, the Fall Classic achieves a relative importance that is, within its secular context, virtually religious.[16] Clearly, Nick regards baseball as something more than an inconsequential diversion and the World Series as more than a string of boys' games. Assuming that Fitzgerald does not wish to discredit his narrator (by making Nick seem to overvalue baseball), one must either attribute Nick's judgment of Wolfshiem's role in the Black Sox Scandal to the author or conclude that Fitzgerald, himself indifferent to or disdainful of baseball, recognized its importance to his readers and calculated the scene's rhetorical effect with the dispassion of Stephen Dedalus's dramatic artificer.[17] In either case, the relationship

---

[16]Michael Novak likens sport to religion in The Joy of Sports (New York: Basic Books, 1976), 24, 30–31, and passim.

[17]In A Portrait of the Artist as a Young Man, Stephen Dedalus theorizes that the literary artist allows his art to subsume his personality as his formal expression evolves from the lyric to the dramatic: "The personality of the artist, at first a cry or a cadence or a mood [lyric form] and then a fluid and lambent narrative [epic form], finally refines itself out of existence, impersonalises itself, so to speak. The esthetic image in the dramatic form is life purified in and reprojected from the human imagination. The mystery of esthetic like that of material creation is accomplished. The artist, like the God of the creation, remains within or behind or beyond or above his handiwork, invisible, refined out of existence, indifferent, paring his fingernails" (Joyce 215). My point is, provisionally, that Fitzgerald may have attained the Joycean ideal of the disinterested artist in his use of baseball in The Great Gatsby yet not in the novel as a whole.

between sport and religion doubles back ironically on itself: By "play[ing] with the faith of fifty million people," Wolfshiem has treated their "religion" as if it were a game — which, in the case of baseball's acolytes, it already is.

Thus, Wolfshiem is the chief culprit in Nick's estimation, and the reader who respects the integrity of any game must concur. Some commentators discern in the depiction of Wolfshiem the author's shrewd and, presumably, cynical representation of a twentieth-century American folk hero; bootlegging and racketeering in the urban jungle have supplanted the nineteenth-century attributes of trailblazing, physical prowess, and self-sufficient living in the heart of the country (Ornstein 58). Styling Meyer Wolfshiem a citified, post–World War I version of Gatsby's earlier mentor, the rough-and-tumble, self-made Dan Cody, tends to romanticize the figure of the gangster and to propose, somewhat incongruously, that a man likened to "a burglar blowing a safe" is an archetypal confrère of Daniel Boone. One may extend the analogy to the baseball heroes whom Wolfshiem's shenanigans have betrayed, for the ballplayer has traditionally been represented (in "boys' books") as an icon of folk virtue and ingenious self-reliance. Many commentators identify the baseball player as the heir of rustic knowledge, a modern-day "natural" who lives in respectful cooperation with a bucolic landscape, judging the effects of wind and sun on a batted ball with the same expertise the frontier farmer relied on to gauge the viability of his crop in relation to the conditions of soil and weather.[18] For millions of baseball fans, however — and for at least one writer, Ring Lardner — the Black Sox Scandal discredited this association of the baseball player with American folk heroes (see Asinof 197–199). Banned for life from Organized Baseball, the Black Sox came to be defined in the popular mind as a coterie of rogues given over to dishonesty and greed. By implicitly linking the banished players to Meyer Wolfshiem and analogizing Wolfshiem to Dan Cody, Fitzgerald devises a complex metaphor of a fulfilled American Dream (Cody) and its faithless adulteration by grasping white-collar charlatans and cynical unlettered crooks (Wolfshiem and the Black Sox). As a sporting institution, baseball extols the self-made man ethos represented by Dan Cody, yet the Black Sox Scandal falsifies baseball's traditional claims of honesty and mutually supportive teamwork. The latter qualities might have been most completely possessed by players during baseball's amateur era, when men played the game for the simple satisfactions and salutary effects of athletic competition, or during the period of fledgling professionalism prior to the game's evolution into "big business." When money becomes the measure of success, what was a game becomes an "opportunity"— Gatsby's word (*Gatsby* 58)— or a "transaction"— Nick's word (*Gatsby* 133). Similarly, the

---

[18]Michael Oriard reads the baseball player as "the self-sufficient but social man whose imaginative origin as the rugged individualist of the American frontier makes him in many ways the most distinctly American of sports heroes" and as "the descendent of American frontier heroes who lived close to the land ... also a 'natural'" (Oriard 59–60). Oriard notes that the baseball player is "dependent on nature— on climate, on wind direction and velocity, on even the smallest pebble that can turn a routine grounder into a base hit" (Oriard 60–61).

American Dream becomes a grubby nightmare when a baseball player plays purposively to lose, prostituting rare physical abilities to "get ahead," to "score big," while the democratic game, in which every man succeeds according to his ability, goes begging.

The interplay between Wolfshiem and Gatsby underscores the careerism and social fawning that characterize their world of a booming stock market, silk shirts, and bootleg liquor. The point, besides warning the reader that Gatsby's impeccable bearing is compromised by moral corruption (he lauds Wolfshiem's crime), is to allow the reader to register (through Nick's incredulity) an unambivalent disapproval of something in Gatsby's world that shows itself to be sullied beneath the surface glitter. In this scene (*Gatsby* 55–58), Wolfshiem acts as a corrosive that tarnishes Gatsby's shining image. Fitzgerald deftly exploits Wolfshiem's minor role, yet achieves a convincing caricature by trafficking in the so-called polite anti–Semitism that taints many early twentieth-century American novels.[19] Fitzgerald, presumably intending that Wolfshiem impress the reader as faintly humorous but essentially unsavory, foregrounds the details that he believes will suspend the reader's sympathy and reduce the gambler to an exotic figure, slightly grotesque and slightly bizarre. Speaking Yiddish-inflected English, affecting a humble persona, Wolfshiem plays the "colorful" ethnic Jew whom both narrator and reader quickly recognize as a "foreign element"—inevitably a locus of culpability[20]—who corrupts the American institution of baseball for his own enrichment. When Nick accuses Wolfshiem, in a narrative aside, of "play[ing] with the faith of fifty million people," he successfully evokes the whole of America's spiritual heritage, from the first Puritans to the present day, while tacitly reminding the reader that this particular faith does not also reside in Wolfshiem's soul. To Nick, and to most of Fitzgerald's contemporary readers, the Jew is implicitly unknown, alien, "other"—the kind of presence they would prefer to exclude from their careful lives, their sheltering homes, their native land. Similarly, the trope of "a burglar blowing a safe" likens Wolfshiem's sacrilegious confidence game to an invasive yet ordinary theft, a petty wrong almost beneath the notice of morally

---

[19]The "polite" or "fashionable" anti–Semitism to which I refer appears in novels as unlike one another as The Sun Also Rises (1926)— in Jake's grinding resentment of Robert Cohn— and The House of Mirth (1905), in the narrator's particular bias against Lily Bart's would-be suitor, Simon Rosedale.

[20]Fitzgerald's depiction of Meyer Wolfshiem might owe something to the sporting press, which was ready to blame the most pernicious gambling influences on one subset of gamblers. As Leverett T. Smith documents in The American Dream and the National Game (Bowling Green, OH: Bowling Green University Popular Press, 1975), The Sporting News of October 9, 1919, was insistent in making an overt— and implicitly anti–Semitic— distinction between "sportsmen" who wagered unprofessionally and "the crop of lean-faced and long-nosed gamblers," the "hook nosed gentry," who "organize betting syndicates and make a 'business' of anything there is a chance to filch a dollar out of, however sacred it may be— to Americans" (quoted by Smith, 131). By presenting Wolfshiem as the brains behind the fix, and by evoking the notion of faith in Nick's response, Fitzgerald seems to be responding to the cues provided by The Sporting News ("hook nosed gentry"; "sacred"). In any case, Wolfshiem's portrayal and his alleged role in the 1919 World Series suggest the subtextual presence of anti–Semitism and religious bias.

upright Americans — if not outside the purview of the criminal justice system. In this rendition, Gatsby, guilty by association, figures as hypocrite and sycophant, a traitor to his American birthright.

Although he strives to pass himself off as an American aristocrat, Gatsby strikes the reader as persistently, almost compulsively, suspect. His flippant remarks to Nick about Wolfshiem seem designed to make one pause, if only to notice how Gatsby, suddenly coy, seems to tease Nick with a revelation of "inside" knowledge. Reluctant at first, Gatsby "add[s] coolly," as if he were uttering a throwaway line, that Wolfshiem is "'the man who fixed the World's Series.'" Gatsby's diffidence then shifts toward an ambivalent (un)ease that sends a mixed signal. He is not certain that he wants to trust Nick with information of so flagrant and infamous an illegality yet does not want to forestall Nick's allegiance to his greater scheme by withholding the story of what he, Gatsby, considers a peripheral affair. Thus, Gatsby speaks imprudently and with a kind of hidden desperation, hoping to impress Nick with a piece of choice gossip. What probably troubles Gatsby most is his inkling that Nick is too straight an arrow to understand the revelation about Wolfshiem with the necessary moral aloofness. Perhaps Gatsby, a clever judge of character except in the instance of Miss Daisy Fay, already senses that in every morally challenging situation Nick's instinct is to "telephone immediately for the police" (*Gatsby* 16). At the moment, Gatsby is less concerned about what Nick could say to the police than with the report Nick might choose to make to his cousin Daisy about Gatsby's business associates. When Nick turns in short order to asking (of Wolfshiem), "'Why isn't he in jail?'" the question comes to Gatsby almost as a relief; it is predictable, thus unthreatening. Gatsby's answer — "'They can't get him, old sport'" — is spoken with an obvious calm that implies Gatsby's sense of his own insulation from discovery and punishment. The general import of his comments incriminates him as an opportunistic confidence trickster motivated purely by cash. His approval of Wolfshiem's crime — "'He just saw the opportunity'" — indicates that Gatsby regards the fix as just one more business deal, while his praise of dishonesty as intelligence — "'He's a smart man'" — reveals Gatsby as an amoral financial operator with his eye turned shrewdly on the main chance. In baseball terms, really in the terms of any game, Gatsby is the worst kind of cheater. He allows others to take the risk, reaps profits for himself, and tasks his own conscience not at all. His disposition toward Wolfshiem suggests not only that the rules have been made to be broken but that breaking the rules and, further, manipulating the odds are precisely what the savvy sportsman does. In this sense, Gatsby himself is a fictional representation of Arnold Rothstein, the big-shot gambler who allowed small-timers to organize the Black Sox fix while he sat by in New York and quietly bet on the Series with smart money (see Asinof 1–38, 61, 64–65).

Gatsby applies his sporting credo, which is also his business ethos, to sportswomen as well: Of Jordan Baker, lady golf professional, who was accused of changing a bad lie in her first important tournament, Gatsby opines, "'Miss

Baker's a great sportswoman, you know, and she'd never do anything that wasn't all right'" (*Gatsby* 57). It is certainly possible, perhaps even likely, that Gatsby is ignorant of Miss Baker's contretemps (Nick reports that "The thing approached the proportions of a scandal—then died away" [*Gatsby* 47]), yet one is tempted, given Gatsby's consorting with Meyer Wolfshiem, to propose that, to Gatsby, any form of cheating is "'all right'" if it makes the player (or gambler) a winner. At this point, one wonders why Nick, who is at some pains to establish his own ethical credentials (even going so far as to state with a directness matched only by its unabashedness, "I am one of the few honest people that I have ever known" [*Gatsby* 48]), has anything more to do with Gatsby, much less why he agrees to abet Gatsby's secretive, manifestly illicit courtship by staging a private meeting with Daisy. The rhetorical brilliance of the prose persuades most readers that Nick's admiration for Gatsby—despite his representing "everything for which [Nick has] an unaffected scorn" (*Gatsby* 6), despite Nick's having "disapproved of him from beginning to end" (*Gatsby* 120)—is uncompromised by ulterior motives, that his attraction to Gatsby is sincere, pure in the way of a higher calling that does not provoke Nick's customary "provincial squeamishness" (*Gatsby* 140), finally that Nick's fascination is a kind of aesthetic response to a charismatic personality that is always executing another "unbroken series of successful gestures" (*Gatsby* 6). Ultimately, one concludes that Nick is not as honest as he claims or that he sacrifices honesty to Gatsby's notion of romantic idealism. In either case, the dialogue that reveals Wolfshiem's duplicity also pegs Nick as Gatsby's co-conspirator after the fact, a role he accepts fully when he plays Pandarus to Gatsby's Troilus and lures Daisy to his safe house between the opposed hosts. Gatsby haunts the rooms of his splendid mansion, keeps night vigil on his dock and sighs his soul toward Grecian tents greenly lit, and Nick delivers the girl into his arms.

Reappraised at novel's end, young Jimmy Gatz's half-hour of "Baseball and sports" buzzes with an ironic undertone of which Fitzgerald is perhaps unaware. Mr. Gatz, certainly, does not notice any contradiction, and Nick, whose consciousness Fitzgerald uses to record the palpable incongruity between Gatsby's dream and the actual conditions of Daisy's life, does not register either surprise or even amused disappointment at the shadow that falls between James Gatz's recreational ball playing and what one infers to have been Jay Gatsby's crass baseball transactions (in connection with either the 1919 World Series or game-fixing thereafter, or both). Like the hollow men of T. S. Eliot's poem, who sense a shadow falling between idea and reality, emotion and response, Gatsby experiences in his life's penultimate moments the disorder and belated sorrow that come with watching the shadow fall between his idealized scenario of love recaptured and that scenario's degradation in the world. And yet, it is easy to overstate the purity of Gatsby's dream. Like his scheduled ball playing, Daisy Regained is part of a plan, a necessary ingredient in the concoction of a certain kind of lifestyle that implies the fabrication of a certain kind of self. The James Gatz who pencils in—with perhaps a little too much self-conscious circumspection — a half-hour of "Baseball and sports" becomes a credible antecedent of the calculating Jay Gatsby who presumably traffics in the nefarious business of betting on fixed baseball games. Ideal rapidly devolves to deal, and Gatsby becomes the "(i)dealist" of his own imagining, a social climber who covets Daisy Fay as the final accoutrement of his shining mansion — most unlike his persona of a devoted swain seeking reunion with the golden girl whose absence makes his accumulated riches seem like pasteboard and glass.

Thus, boy and man each strive to attain a goal that is ulterior to participation in or spectatorship of a game, whether it is baseball or love. Like the athlete who plays only for money, each is a kind of perversion. The crucial difference is that, in the iconography of American culture, a boy playing baseball participates in an honest, wholesome means of self-improvement, whereas the man who bends the game to force-fit capitalism's profit motive destroys its integrity and makes himself a thief. One might recuperate the innocence of James Gatz's boyhood baseball play by reading the SCHEDULE as a document designed by Fitzgerald to remind the reader of Benjamin Franklin's detailed list of daytime duties, "The Precept of *Order*," in *The Autobiography*.[21] Mimicking the officious yet superlatively practical, resourceful, and efficacious Franklin, young James Gatz may be taken at his word as having in mind for himself a fulfillment of the American Dream quite different from the destiny he begins chasing on board the yacht *Tuolomee* at the feet of Dan Cody. And yet, it remains uncertain whether Jimmy Gatz turns to baseball joyfully, in a spirit of play, or if he dutifully allocates himself a too-brief half-hour of recreation merely because he thinks that he should — as if he were trying to guarantee himself worldly success by drawing up a schedule calculated to cultivate it. In either case, James Gatz's approximate reproduction of a Poor Richard–like plan for achieving a Good & Productive life retrospectively suggests that these better sensibilities — the spirit of play and conscientious discipline — must have atrophied for him to have arrived at Jay Gatsby's amoral romanticism. Thus, Gatsby's "gonnegtion" with Meyer Wolfshiem, criminal meddler in America's National Game, is an index of the corrupt means that this decadent romantic (i)dealist exploits to serve his unattainable end.

---

[21]*Benjamin Franklin*, Writings, *edited by J. A. Leo Lemay (New York: Literary Classics of the United States, 1987), 1389. Franklin, too, sets aside time (from six until nine in the evening) for "Musick, or Diversion, or Conversation." He does not, however, seem to participate in athletics: According to his "Scheme of Employment for the Twenty-Four Hours of a natural Day," Franklin occupies himself during the daylight hours entirely with "Work."*

Three

A Picture's Worth
a Thousand
Baseball Subtext in
The Sound and the Fury

The idea of a ballplayer making more than the President was almost incomprehensible. An apocryphal story, often told, says that someone asked Ruth if he thought it was right for him to be paid more than President Hoover and that Ruth replied, "Why not? I had a better year than he did."
— Robert Creamer, *Babe*

In William Faulkner's Yoknapatawpha County, baseball is an event of little moment. Temple Drake visualizes the Starkville ballfield that she and Gowan Stevens will never reach, but the "scene" does not possess enough narrative weight to posit baseball as the sanctuary, or home, that Temple so desperately needs to find[1]:

> She said nothing, thinking of the pennant-draped train already in Starkville; of the colorful stands; the band, the yawning glitter of the bass horn; the green diamond dotted with players, crouching, uttering short, yelping cries like marsh-fowl disturbed by an alligator, not certain of where the danger is, motionless, poised, encouraging one another with short meaningless cries, plaintive, wary and forlorn [*Sanctuary* 204].

One might argue that the violence awaiting Temple (in the corn-crib inside Lee Goodwin's barn; in Miss Reba's whorehouse in Memphis) is foreshadowed by the image of marsh-fowl imperiled by a prowling alligator, except that the narrator does not, either in the quoted passage or elsewhere in *Sanctuary*, liken the abused coed to the poised, "yelping" players. When one considers Temple's

---

[1]In Sanctuary *(1931). Quotations follow the text reprinted in* William Faulkner: Novels 1930–1935 (As I Lay Dying, Sanctuary, Light in August, Pylon*), edited by Joseph Blotner and Noel Polk (New York: Literary Classics of the United States, 1985) and are cited as* Sanctuary.

ordeal, the sexual abuse and virtual slavery to which she is subjected by the rep-
tilian Popeye, such an analogy seems false, if not perverse. Temple, certainly, does
not think of herself or her situation in terms of baseball; even going home, in
the prosaic sense, does not seem particularly interesting to her. She merely envisions a ballpark spectacle that impending misadventure will prevent her from
seeing. The most that one can claim for this baseball allusion is that it expresses
a sense of foreboding so vague that the anxiety is practically disassociated from
the consciousness of the character who conceives it. It is also less descriptive of
a baseball game than it is indicative of its author's studious circumlocutions.

In his many fictions, William Faulkner has little to say about baseball players and seldom turns to the game itself for allusion or metaphor. Faulkner does,
however, complicate his portrayal of certain characters by making them players of games that have nothing to do with athletics. Flem Snopes and Thomas
Sutpen are two figures who come to mind; Jason Compson is another. In *The
Sound and the Fury* (1929) Jason plays on Caddy's affection for her daughter and
on his mother's trust, both of which he exploits for selfish ends; he plays with
language, launching aggressive metaphors and perverse hyperboles at other
characters;[2] and he plays the ultimate ironic joke on himself when he chases his
niece so persistently that at last she runs away for good, having stolen Jason's
own hoard of cash together with the money that he has been, over many years,
filching with painstaking stealth from her. Every "game" he plays draws Jason's
character in bold strokes; each example of his driven "play" adds detail to the
figure. The final portrait reveals a character whose obsessions are as startling
and definitive — and as long-established — as his narrow-minded certainties. The
game that most concerns Jason, however, does not focus on his macabre family or its legacies of promiscuity, alcoholism, and madness. It centers on money.

As any reader of *The Sound and the Fury* can hardly forget, Jason is partly
occupied on Friday, April 6, 1928, with playing the cotton market. He does not,
one must hasten to add, regard this activity as a game; rather, he considers it
deadly serious business. Jason believes that he can outsmart the Commodities
Market and its investors just as he has outsmarted his mother, sister, and niece.
He ritually burns his own worthless forgeries in place of the checks that Caddy
sends to Quentin, thereby appeasing his mother's sense of honor and answer-
ing his own cry for justice. By stealing his sister's money (and thereby robbing
his niece), Jason believes that he is taking nothing more than what is rightfully
his: compensation for the job lost to him through Caddy's sexual indiscretions.
Similarly, Jason thinks of his cotton investments as a business strategy that he
must pursue to restore his patrimony, which he believes has been squandered
in financing the foibles of his siblings. And yet, Jason's buying and selling of
cotton via Western Union Telegraph seems like long-distance gambling,

---

[2]*For interpretations of the humor of Jason's language, see James M. Cox, "Humor as Vision in Faulkner,"
and William N. Claxon, Jr., "Jason Compson: A Demoralized Wit," both reprinted in* Faulkner &
Humor, *edited by Fowler and Abadie (Jackson: University Press of Mississippi, 1986), 1–20 and 21–33,
respectively.*

sanctioned by the financial institutions that facilitate it, fueled by chimeras of profit and promptings of greed. Given Jason's mean-spirited parsimony, any sense of him as a gambler is bound to seem ironic; as the market drops and Jason continues to lose money, the ironic is compounded by the comic. This impression deepens when one remembers the vagaries of the stock and commodities markets, particularly the reckless speculation that occurred during the years preceding the Crash of 1929. It might be accurate to distinguish Las Vegas from Wall Street primarily by the outward forms of the games and the disposition of the odds, although the investor must contend with the additional anxiety of not always knowing against whom he competes. Jason, an unsophisticated player many miles and a world away from Manhattan, flounders in the cotton market as a neophyte might at the roulette table, repeatedly playing the same number — or laying his chips on a different number for every spin. All stratagems bear small fruit in a game of chance, for luck and the odds seem always unfavorable.

Perhaps Jason's losses in cotton temper his response to betting in general. After he learns that cotton has closed down 40 points, Jason refuses to wager even on the 1928 New York Yankees, as sure a bet to win the pennant as any gambler could hope to find:

> "Well," Mac says, "I reckon you've got your money on the Yankees this year."
> "What for?" I says.
> "The Pennant," he says. "Not anything in the League can beat them."
> "Like hell there's not," I says. "They're shot," I says. "You think a team can be that lucky forever?"
> "I dont call it luck," Mac says.
> "I wouldn't bet on any team that fellow Ruth played on," I says. "Even if I knew it was going to win."
> "Yes?" Mac says.
> "I can name you a dozen men in either League who're more valuable than he is," I says.
> "What have you got against Ruth?" Mac says.
> "Nothing," I says. "I haven't got any thing against him. I dont even like to look at his picture." I went on out. The lights were coming on, and people going along the streets toward home[3] [*Fury* 314].

This conversation allows Jason to ignore, albeit for only a moment, the preoccupations that have goaded him all day. Quentin's sexual shenanigans and the roller-coastering price of cotton fade from his attention while he throws in his two-cents' worth of analysis of the impending pennant race. And yet, the frustration that Jason has felt since breakfast — and possibly, one is invited to imagine, all of his adult life — is evident in his tense, joyless rejoinders to Mac's baseball small talk. Believing that he has been duped by the cotton brokers, whom he suspects are in cahoots with Western Union Telegraph for the purpose

---

[3]William Faulkner, The Sound and the Fury (*1929; reprinted, New York: Modern Library, 1956*). All quotations and references follow this edition and are cited as Fury.

of defrauding "a few more country suckers" *(Fury* 282, 305), Jason will not risk being misled again by experts (in this case, sportswriters and bookmakers), whose highly touted favorites usually fail in ways that cost him money. As a result, he will not play the gambler when the game is baseball.

Oddly, Jason seems to recognize, despite his vehement denials, that the New York Yankees are baseball's best team in 1928 and will probably win the American League pennant. His insistence that he will not bet on the Yankee team "'even if [he] knew it was going to win'" inspires some readers to declare Jason decidedly *not* "The first sane Compson since before Culloden" *(Fury* 420) but rather a character whose mind does not work according to the principles of logic — or even to the exploitative, "main chance" standards of smart business. Indeed, Jason's refusal to put his money on the Yankees suggests to some readers that he is given to quixotic gestures bearing "the mark of a curious idealism"[4] — as if Jason were rooting for some other, underdog team. Others interpret this attitude as a demonstration of independence that sacrifices Jason's single true talent, his business savvy.[5] This view depends in part on Jason's opinion that the universe, far from possessing any systematic and morally coherent teleology, is driven wholly by luck and the vicissitudes of chance working through random events. His riposte to Mac — "'You think a team can be that lucky forever?'" — captures the essence of Jason's complaint about the cosmos and his sense of himself as its plaything. Although these readings are essentially valid, they underemphasize two key elements: Jason will not bet on the Yankees because the team represents, to his xenophobic Southern mind, New York; and because its star player is "that fellow Ruth."

Jason's antipathy for Babe Ruth and the New York Yankees is his reflexive response to a matrix of unspoken resentments and subtextual circumstances. He can hardly be expected to like the team's name, which must sound, on some level of his consciousness, a note of Northern gloating over the South's defeat in the Civil War. For Jason, reminders of Yankee dominance are unwelcome and unnecessary. He has fought ceaselessly — and with only partial success — to free himself of his mother's archaic notions of Southern gentility, to distance himself from the sad fascination with the Old South's hallowed Lost Cause — which may be said to have killed both his father and his brother Quentin — and yet he seems still to live in the war's desolate shadow, a twilight of diminished expectations and stillborn dreams. To be sure, a baseball team is not an invading

---

[4]Donald M. Kartiganer, "[The Meaning of Form in] The Sound and the Fury," *in* The Sound and the Fury, *edited by David Minter (New York: Norton, 1987), 372; reprinted from Kartiganer's The Fragile Thread: The Meaning of Form in Faulkner's Novels (Amherst: University of Massachusetts Press, 1979), 3–22.*

[5]Duncan Aswell, "The Recollection and the Blood: Jason's Role in The Sound and the Fury," *Mississippi Quarterly 21 (Summer 1968): 211–218. In discussing Jason's subservience to the imperatives of family and memory, Aswell notes that Jason, in scorning the 1928 Yankees, compromises his "business sense" and relies on "personal whims and prejudices for the sake of demonstrating his independence." The manifest supremacy of that Yankee team is no obstacle: "Even in the face of logic and sense, [Jason] insists on reducing all experience to temporary status, as if he were his father" (Aswell 212–213).*

army, but a man confident of the deterministic formula "Once a bitch always a bitch" *(Fury* 223) will find much in a name. Further, New York is home to one of Jason's chief nemeses — "'those damn eastern sharks'" *(Fury* 270), "'those rich New York jews'" *(Fury* 240), "people to take the money away from us country suckers" *(Fury* 291–292)—who, Jason is convinced (at the outer edge of his paranoia), have "guaranteed inside dope" *(Fury* 292) that allows them to anticipate the fluctuations of the financial markets, thereby preventing him and "'the sucker gamblers'" *(Fury* 238) from making a profit. Given Jason's paranoid distrust of New York's monied professionals, it is reasonable to conclude that he regards them as a present-day version of the Union army. This time, the Yankee legions will not have to march *en masse* through Dixie burning cities, for the physical destruction has already been accomplished. Now the despoilers of his life and livelihood need only to hoodwink him about his investments, which they are able to do simply by manipulating the financial markets, instruments of their own invention. The calculated deceptions of "that New York crowd" *(Fury* 283) cause Jason and "these small town gamblers" *(Fury* 292) to lose money, which means that Jason Compson — and all of the New South — will remain forever cash-poor and powerless in relation to the economic and political hegemony of affluent, privileged New York.

By placing Jason's vituperations against the New York Yankees within the context of his doomed New York investments, Faulkner reminds the reader of the extreme regionalism that precipitated the South's secession from the Union on the principle of states' rights. Despite the Civil War's having ended more than 60 years ago (in the time of the novel), Jason holds to notions of states' rights just as he clings to a simple wish for his own independence — from the losing game he plays against Wall Street ("I just want to hit them one time and get my money back" [*Fury* 292]) and from "a kitchen full of niggers," whom he works "ten hours a day to support ... in the style they're accustomed to..." *(Fury* 298). As Jason judges the situation, he is a decent, hardworking man beset on every side by confidence tricksters, freeloading servants, and degenerate relatives. He feels besieged within his (mother's) own house and dogged at work by Earl, his presumptuous partner and virtual overseer in the hardware trade. Forced to live under such conditions, Jason believes that he must act vigorously to defend hearth and home — both of these finally reducible to himself, although including, perhaps, his mother — from outside forces, whether they be "'a bunch of damn eastern jews'" *(Fury* 237) or the commercial drummers (traveling salesmen) who pursue Quentin, having learned "where to pick up a hot one when they [make] Jefferson" *(Fury* 286). Jason's sense of himself as put-upon, as a good man whose kindness and tolerance are abused, first strikes the note of humor soon picked up by this thwarted cotton trading. However, Jason's racism — or ethnicism — particularly against Jews and Negroes, makes the laughter he provokes discomfiting at best and often insulting. Even at their funniest, Jason's words are unkind and frequently sadistic. His blatant anti–Semitism makes Nick's presumption of this attitude, in his conversation with Gatsby about Meyer Wolfshiem, seem trivial by comparison, although the difference is mostly a function of the anti–Semite's own sense of being threatened.[6]

Indeed, ethnic prejudice is an important subtext of the baseball talk, for it explains Jason's apparently incomprehensible, almost manic dislike of Babe Ruth. To claim in 1928, as Jason does, "'I can name you a dozen men in either League who're more valuable than [Ruth] is,'" is brazenly to represent as a statement of fact what an examination of the record book and a consultation of contemporary accounts reveal as fustian hyperbole. True, Babe Ruth did not win the Most Valuable Player Award for the prior season (1927), when his teammate Lou Gehrig was selected the league's MVP, but "that fellow Ruth" had already won the honor in 1923.[7] Even more apposite is the reader's recognition that the bestowal of a specific trophy for one season's performance is beside the point when one attempts to measure the degree of Babe Ruth's sustained excellence and its impact on baseball. The Babe's cumulative batting records from 1920, his first year with the Yankees and the first season in which he played every day instead of pitching, through 1927, the summer of his famous 60 home runs and the season immediately preceding Jason's comments, mark him as baseball's best offensive player and preeminent home run hitter.[8] Indeed, Ruth's performance on the diamond throughout the 1920s was such that he often seemed a man playing among boys — or a demigod striving against mortal men.[9] Journalists' accounts attest to Ruth's dominance. Sportswriters

[6]See page 46 supra for Nick's anti–Semitism, and page 42 supra, note 13, for "Wolfshiem."

[7]From 1911 through 1914 the Chalmers Motor Company presented a car to the Most Valuable Player in each league, as judged by a committee of newspapermen (one from each major league city). From 1915 to 1921, no award was given. From 1922 to 1929, the Most Valuable Player was selected by a special committee of each major league. This practice fell silently into disuse in 1930. Beginning in 1931, the Baseball Writers Association of America began selecting the MVP of each league based on the vote of its members, an office it still exercises. See Harold Seymour, Baseball: The Golden Age (1971; reprinted New York: Oxford University Press, 1989), 285–286, and The Baseball Encyclopedia, 7th ed., edited by Joseph L. Reichler (New York: Macmillan, 1988), 31, 35.

[8]During the war-shortened 1918 season, Ruth split his play among the outfield, first base, and the pitching mound, managed to bat .300 and hit 11 home runs, and took the Boston Red Sox into the most recent World Series they have won, in which he pitched two winning games. His 11 home runs during the regular season tied him for the league title. In 1919, his final year with the Red Sox, Ruth appeared primarily as a full-time player and hit 29 home runs, unprecedented at the time. His batting statistics from 1919 through 1932 testify that Babe Ruth was the single most potent and dominating offensive player in both major leagues. See Robert Creamer, Babe: The Legend Comes to Life (New York: Simon & Schuster, 1974), 158–170, 197–198, 200–204; Baseball Encyclopedia 1419, 2116; and Bill James, The Bill James Historical Baseball Abstract (New York: Villard Books, 1988), 422–423, 603.

[9]The exceptions are 1922, when Ruth was suspended for the season's first five weeks by baseball commissioner Kenesaw Mountain Landis for disregarding the prohibition of barnstorming tours for players on pennant-winning teams, and 1925, when the Babe collapsed on the trip north from spring training and subsequently underwent surgery on April 17 for an intestinal abscess. He returned to the Yankee lineup on June 1 (too soon: he had lost thirty pounds), played in only 98 games, and was suspended on August 29 by Yankee manager Miller Huggins for general insubordination and rule breaking. Ruth hit 35 home runs in 1922 and 25 in 1925, the only years from 1918 through 1931 that he did not lead the league. See Creamer 244–256, 289–301 and James 603. For the confrontation with Commissioner Landis, see Leverett T. Smith, The American Dream and the National Game (Bowling Green, OH: Bowling Green University Popular Press, 1975), 180–189.

Heywood Broun (author of *The Sun Field* [1923], a baseball novel whose hero is a Ruthian figure), John Kieran *(New York Times)*, Jimmy Cannon *(New York Post)*, Red Smith *(New York Times)*, and Fred Lieb[10] (who dubbed Yankee Stadium "The House That Ruth Built") laud Babe Ruth's ball playing and celebrate the persona he created: the boisterous baseball hero, uncouth, undisciplined, and unlettered, whose athletic prowess makes him the crowd's favorite. The Babe's antics, his dramatic performances and self-indulgent pleasures, kept typewriters clattering in the newspaper rooms of every big-league city. Contemporary accounts of Babe Ruth sound like tall tales, legends of an unlikely anthropomorphic god whose large-mannered motions describe a presence too great to be circumscribed by ordinary language. This persona seems, to a contemporary reader, a product of exaggeration and embellishment.[11] And yet, almost everyone who knew the Babe or saw him play responds with awe and delight[12]:

> [Babe Ruth] was sublimely aware that he transcended records and his place in the American scene was no mere matter of statistics. It wasn't just that he hit more home runs than anybody else, he hit them better, higher, farther, and with more theatrical timing and a more flamboyant flourish. Nobody could strike out like Babe Ruth. Nobody circled the bases with the same pigeon-toed majesty [Red Smith 151].

******

> Ruth did everything big. His appetite for food was enormous. I've seen him eat ten hot dog sandwiches, washing them down with beer, and then ask for more. He could drink the same way, since he had an abnormal capacity for handling beer and liquor. ... In addition to being the greatest home run hitter, he also was the game's foremost showman. He sizzled with charisma. He was worshipped by the multitudes, and boys followed him in droves wherever he went. He may have been dumb in some things, but he knew he was good as an athlete and as the center of attraction. He glorified in it and he acted accordingly [Lieb 150].

Although Jefferson's local newspaper probably does not sing Ruth's praise as loudly as New York's sports press, Jason can hardly be unaware of or indifferent to the Babe's popularity and success. His gaudy $70,000 salary (in 1927–1929; Creamer 346),[13] in particular, probably irks Jason more than the New York Yankees' dominance of the American League.[14] Jason sees himself as a man who must struggle grievously for every advantage, a man who must,

---

[10]*Fred Lieb's baseball books include* Baseball As I Have Known It *(New York: Grosset and Dunlap, 1977)* and The Story of the World Series *(New York: G. P. Putnam's Sons, 1965).*

[11]*See the preface to the present work.*

[12]*These excerpts are quoted in* The Baseball Hall of Fame 50th Anniversary Book *(New York: Prentice-Hall, 1988), by Gerald Astor. See 143, 145, and 136 for remarks by Brown, Kieran, and Cannon, respectively.*

[13]*Babe Ruth's annual salary peaked in 1930 and 1931 at $80,000, although he believed he was worth $100,000. The Yankees' second-highest salary was $17,500 (Creamer 348–351). The Bill James Historical Baseball Abstract reports that Ruth's $80,000 would be worth about $520,000 in 1988 (James 133).*

[14]*From 1920 to 1928, inclusive, the Yankees won six American League pennants.*

if he is ever to know affluence or merely redress the financial injury done to him, scrape together and hoard "in niggard and agonised dimes and quarters and halfdollars" *(Fury* 421), "at the price of sacrifice and denial, almost a nickel and a dime at a time, over a period of almost twenty years" *(Fury* 425), a private cache of $2,840.50 of his own money and another $4,000 he has stolen from his niece. The disparity that Jason doubtlessly perceives between the degree of his misfortunes, the extremity of his efforts to remediate them, the modest level of his gains, and the riches that accrue to Babe Ruth merely from playing baseball are more than sufficient to elicit his resentment. And yet, something beyond either resentment or simple envy of a wealthy sportsman lurks within Jason's acerbic "'I dont even like to look at his picture.'"

Babe Ruth's picture or, more accurately, his photograph, appeared often in newspapers during the baseball season, and Jason would doubtlessly have come across it — perhaps while scanning the financial listings for price quotes and "inside dope" on cotton. Provided that Jason does not rely wholly on Western Union for his information, he is likely to have encountered Babe Ruth's moon face every week even if he is indifferent to the baseball news, simply because many American newspapers typically print sports columns, especially baseball box scores, in the pages immediately before or after the price quotes from the stock and commodities exchanges.[15] Perhaps the Babe's photograph reminds Jason of falling cotton prices, his face grinning from a sunny ball field, a too-provocative sign that his easy good fortune occurs in a distant world, cleaner, fairer, more brightly lit than the one that plays witness to Jason's dark frustrations.

More significant is the face itself: a broad, flattened nose, a heavy brow and full lips, together with the dark tan that Ruth's complexion took on in spring training and retained all summer. These attributes of contour and hue led many of the Babe's contemporaries to remark that he had some admixture of "nigger blood," as they called it.[16] Comments to this effect were made so often that Babe Ruth's mixed ethnicity became the assumption of many players and fans, including the players of the Negro League. Barred from the major leagues despite their abilities by an unwritten "gentleman's" agreement among the owners, Negro League players reportedly thought of Ruth as "a secret brother" and rooted for his continuing dominance of "white baseball" (Creamer 185). Throughout his playing career, Ruth was the object of bench-jockeying that usually reverted to baiting him with the word "nigger" and the imputation that his family's bloodlines were not "pure." To Ruth, born of German-American parents and reared on the South's threshold in Baltimore, this rumor was "an insufferable calumny" (Creamer 185), which accounts for the opposition's

---

[15]*The week-day editions of the* New York Times, *the* New York Daily News, *and the* New York Post *follow this format. Jason is unlikely to see a New York tabloid in Jefferson, but small-town presses generally mimic metropolitan newspapers.*

[16]*The rumor began at St. Mary's, where Ruth's boyhood nickname was "Niggerlips" (Creamer 38).*

resorting to it. Although the rumor is not credible — its possible truth is, in any case, beyond recovery — one ought to emphasize that the "evidence" rests wholly in the beholder's eye.[17] Photographs of Babe Ruth show a large, round face favored with the strong features generally taken to indicate Northern European ancestry. If one were not told to seek the shadow of a more exotic visage, one would hardly imagine its presence.

Some observers, however, believed they saw in Ruth's face the secret of a black man passing for white — another chimera that continues to interest some imaginations.[18] When he looks at Ruth's photograph, Jason Compson notices the same illusory signs that bigots and vulgarians before him have exploited for their own purposes and (sub)consciously aligns Babe Ruth with Uncle Job and the "kitchen full of niggers" who, he supposes, eat the food that would otherwise feed him. This conflation, together with the figurative sense of the New York ballplayer's being a modern Yankee encroacher, explains why Babe Ruth's fame and fortune raise Jason's anger to the level of outrage. His disgust even in "'look[ing] at [Ruth's] picture'" is a symptom of Jason's rabid racism, just as the subtextual allusion to the myth of Babe Ruth's African-Caucasian ethnicity indicates the extent of Jason's paranoia about threats, real or imagined, based on racial difference: "And then a Yankee will talk your head off about niggers getting ahead. Get them ahead, what I say. Get them so far ahead you cant find one south of Louisville with a blood hound" *(Fury* 288). These sentiments, which constitute Jason's unspoken response to Uncle Job's enthusiasm about the traveling show playing in Jefferson over Easter weekend, display the misanthropic spirit of a man debased by his myriad prejudices. They also express Jason's derision toward all things "Yankee" — the Yankee financial gamesmanship he distrusts, the Yankee notions of social justice he holds in contempt, the Yankee baseball team he wishes would lose, and the Yankee ballplayer whose personal downfall he would, for reasons derived from nothing more than dollar-envy and a racist misprision, relish more than any other.

Thus, while his animosity toward Babe Ruth seems superficially to suggest Jason's uninterest in baseball, its subtextual content analogizes the last "sane" Compson's racist assumptions to a variety of paranoid delusion. Similarly, its

---

[17]*Pictures are worth one thousand words. See* The Babe: A Life in Pictures *(New York: Ticknor and Fields, 1988), by Lawrence S. Ritter and Mark Rucker, especially 40, 53, 57, 189, 195, 203, the frontispiece, and, most poignantly, 144, which shows Ruth with Negro baseball fans segregated to unchoice bleacher seats.*

[18]*In* Sam's Legacy *(New York: Holt, Rinehart and Winston, 1974), author Jay Neugeboren plays an inventive reversal on the myth of Babe Ruth's passing for white by creating Mason Tidewater, a fair-complected black man and aged Negro League veteran of unsurpassed baseball talent who could have easily passed but chose to affirm his ethnic identity. Mason becomes a fictive secret-sharer with an equally fictive "black" Babe Ruth, whom Neugeboren writes into the novel primarily so that Mason can vanquish him on the baseball field and, in an expansion of history that would be comic were it not absurd, become Babe Ruth's homosexual lover. Although the novel's thematic premise is the revelation of hidden or denied identities and marginalized truths, this part of the plot is unconvincing to anyone familiar with the unexpurgated version of Babe Ruth's biography.*

juxtaposition to his losses in the cotton market foregrounds the economic grudges that Jason bears against his family and his willfulness in extracting a petty but not penurious economic revenge. Looming behind Jason's reserve of bitterness, resentment, and disappointment is the defeat of the Confederacy and the destruction of the Old South, both of which were accomplished by blue-uniformed Yankees fighting, as Jason sees it, for the cause of Negro Emancipation — an event that, in Jason's skewed understanding of men and things, makes a phenomenon like Babe Ruth possible. The legacy of the antebellum world, and of the Compson family's lost status, weighs on Jason almost as heavily as it has burdened his brother. Quentin surrenders to its palpable sense of suffocation, drowning himself rather than continuing to compromise the ideals of a vanished society with the relentless ticking of America's clocks and pocket-watches. Jason, trying mightily to tame the vital spirit of Caddy's legacy, scours town and countryside practically blinded by pain, having forgotten in his haste the camphor-soaked handkerchief that would help him breathe. Quentin (the niece) escapes with the money and Jason goes back to work, renouncing the Compsons' own lost cause but not giving up a fevered image of recompense, "of catching her without warning, springing on her out of the dark, before she had spent all the money, and murder[ing] her before she had time to open her mouth" (*Fury* 426).

Rather than being a throwaway allusion, the short passage of baseball talk signals the narrator's preoccupations without the narrator's acquiescence or knowledge. Herein lies the rhetorical genius of the passage and of the larger chapter: Jason's unwitting revelations of himself to his implied audience. Like Robert Browning's monologuists, who speak always in the reader's presence whether or not they share the poetic space with a silent auditor, Jason speaks more words than he merely says. Rhetorically as well as practically, he "'fools a man whut so smart he cant even keep up wid hisself,'" as Uncle Job tells it: "'Dat's Mr Jason Compson'" (*Fury* 312). The disjunction between the manifest intentions of Jason's narration — to depict himself as the honest, smart, hard-working victim of his family's improvidence, cunning, and madness — and the rhetorical effects of his comments is discernible only to the extent that the reader understands how context shapes the possible meanings of utterance.

◆ *Four* ◆
"A Nation of Frustrated Baseball Players"
Realism and Impressionism

Wolfe sought to make monuments, to "set down America as far as it can belong to the experience of one man." He was not "celebrating" America, as Whitman had done; he was trying to record it, to assimilate it, to echo it in himself. This, the very quality and turn of his abundant energy, was the source of his frenzied passion for American details, of his need to reproduce them exactly for the substance of his art.
— Alfred Kazin, *On Native Grounds*

But scene by scene, character by character, Farrell's books are built by force rather than imagination, and it is the laboriously contrived solidity, the perfect literalness of each representation, that give his work its density and harsh power.
— Alfred Kazin, *On Native Grounds*

As novelists, Thomas Wolfe and James T. Farrell seem to have little in common. The prose style of one is implicitly a contradiction of the other's, and the scenes of their respective fictions, distinctive and inimitable, are shaped by very different aesthetic assumptions. And yet, novels as dissimilar as *You Can't Go Home Again* (1940) and *A World I Never Made* (1936) include some of baseball fiction's most evocative moments. It is a commonplace to remark that Wolfe and Farrell each loved baseball and a simple task to find significant depictions of the game in their respective works. For Farrell, baseball is one of the realistic details that give form and texture to the lives of his characters. Unlike other narrative elements — family, religion, work, money, sex — baseball affords Danny O'Neill a refuge from a tempestuous home, a recreation untroubled by the prejudices and infighting of his elders. For Wolfe, baseball is a metaphor of community and homecoming in a nation of displaced persons "whom a vast continent isolates, whom no tradition controls."[1] For both authors, baseball

[1]*Virginia Woolf, "American Fiction" (1925), p. 123, in "The Moment" and Other Essays (New York: Harcourt, Brace and Company, 1975), 113–127. The phrase appears in Woolf's appraisal of the importance of baseball in the fiction of Ring Lardner.*

proves to be inspiring, or at least invigorating; some of each man's best writing constructs an allusion or paints a scene of the game, its spectators, or its players. Despite their stylistic disparities, both authors have written long, integrated scenes that epitomize the realistic and impressionistic forms of the baseball allusion.

Farrell's place in this scheme is self-evident. Even if an afternoon at Comiskey Park brings young Danny O'Neill as close as he will ever come to the religious ecstasy that his Catholic devotions always withhold, the experience is reported with a factual accuracy that rivals the sports page. These baseball scenes hold more interest than the newspapers because the reader sympathizes with Danny O'Neill; by seeing baseball from Danny's ecstatic point of view, the reader feels the powerful appeal of an individualized consciousness apprehending an experience it loves. Farrell's simple sentences and documentary approach to the material render Danny's baseball experiences in seemingly unmediated form, as if the typewriter had taken down an anonymous dictation. In studiously unembellished prose, Farrell delineates Danny O'Neill's childhood and coming-of-age, recounts the vicissitudes of the boy's works and days, and traces, over the course of four long novels, Danny's early love for, youthful preoccupation with, and eventual loss of interest in baseball. In each stage, Danny's response to the game is a primary element of his characterization.

Thomas Wolfe's baseball interludes are more complex. Always intensely imagined, they fall variously along the continuum between realism and impressionism. Wolfe presents his "million memories of America" and baseball as realistic constructions of a singular fictive consciousness (Nebraska Crane) and, alternately, as images refracted within the omniscient narrator's hyperactive eye. The latter roves the continent as if it were America's collective vision; having gathered material, it is given a voice and invited to speak. Wolfe also uses baseball to flesh out characters, but even Nebraska Crane is most interesting when his remarks are read within the greater narrative context: the American experience as Wolfe imagines it. At times, Wolfe's immense frame of reference risks overwhelming specific scenes; he often writes of baseball on so grand a scale, so atmospherically, that it becomes a literary equivalent of abstract impressionism. And yet, whatever their mimetic register, the respective baseball allusions of Thomas Wolfe and James T. Farrell express major themes and, what is more notable, provide "objective correlatives"[2] of certain psychological states. Upon examination, the baseball allusions of these two very different writers show themselves faithful to both the texture and spirit of baseball, particularly as it was played and watched in the era the novels reflect.

In the baggy prose monsters of Thomas Wolfe, baseball often represents differing versions of the American Dream. Some episodes of the Dream exist only as a promise of a possible future, while others enter characters' lives by dint of

---

[2]"Objective correlative" is borrowed from T. S. Eliot's essay "Hamlet and His Problems" (1919), reprinted in The Sacred Wood (1920; reprinted, London and New York: Methuen, 1983), 95–103.

hard work brought over time to a successful conclusion — an ethic that in baseball defines the professional's devotion to his craft. In *You Can't Go Home Again*, George "Monk" Webber's happenstance reunion with his boyhood friend Nebraska Crane,[3] big-league ballplayer and star home run hitter, points out the difficulties of playing baseball as a paid professional even as it harkens back to the myth of baseball's rural invention. Nebraska is 31 years old and a veteran of ten major league seasons. Aware of the unsentimental laws of professional baseball, the aging athlete has made provisions to hold on to his piece of the American Dream after the cheering stops:

> "That's the way it is, Monk. You're good up there as long as you're good. After that they sell you down the river. Hell, I ain't kickin'. I been lucky. I had ten years of it already, an' that's more than most. An' I been in three World's Serious. If I can hold on fer another year or two— if they don't let me go or trade me — I think maybe we'll be in again. Me an' Myrtle has figgered it all out. I had to help her people some, an' I bought a farm fer Mama an' the Ole Man — that's where they always wanted to be. An' I got three hundred acres of my own in Zebulon — all paid fer, too!— an' if I git a good price this year fer my tobacco, I stan' to clear two thousand dollars. So if I can git two years more in the League an' one more good World's Serious, why —" he turned his square face toward his friend and grinned his brown and freckled grin, just as he used to as a boy —"we'll be all set."
> "And — you mean you'll be satisfied?"
> "Huh? Satisfied?" Nebraska turned to him with a puzzled look. "How do you mean?"
> "I mean after all you've seen and done, Bras — the big cities and the crowds, and all the people shouting — and the newspapers, and the headlines, and the World's Series — and — and — the first of March, and St. Petersburg, and meeting all the fellows again, and spring training —"
> Nebraska groaned.
> "Why, what's the matter?"
> "Spring trainin'."
> "You mean you don't like it?"
> "Like it! Them first three weeks is just plain hell. It ain't bad when you're a kid. You don't put on much weight durin' the winter, an' when you come down in the spring it only takes a few days to loosen up an' git the kinks out. In two weeks' time you're loose as ashes. But wait till you been aroun' as long as I have!" He laughed loudly and shook his head. "Boy! The first time you go after a grounder you can hear your joints creak. After a while you begin to limber up — you work into it an' git the soreness out of your muscles. By the time the season starts, along in April, you feel pretty good. By May you're goin' like a house a-fire, an' you tell yourself you're good as you ever was. You're still goin' strong along in June. An' then you hit July, an' you git them double-headers in St. Looie! Boy, oh boy!" [*You Can't Go Home Again* 64–65].

After a baseball career spent of necessity in America's cities, Nebraska wants only to retire to his farm, some three hundred acres in Zebulon, thereby returning to a facsimile of his own symbolic origins — Nebraska Crane is part Cherokee

---

[3]*Thomas Wolfe, You Can't Go Home Again (1940; reprinted, Garden City, NY: Garden City Books, 1942), 56–69. Quotations and references follow this edition.*

Indian — and gesturing at a passage home to baseball's fictive birthplace in the American countryside.[4] Nebraska is able, unlike George Webber, to "go home again," not merely because he plays baseball but because he has earned (and saved) enough money to secure a home for himself in advance of his need.[5] George, having recalled his meeting Nebraska four years ago in the Bronx, having seen him hit a home run and having read his name in the newspaper, thinks only of the excitement and adulation that to an outsider seem the whole of a major league player's life. Lacking the professional's concerns, unknowing of the demands that the game makes on the player, George thinks of spring training as a langorous dance in a bucolic landscape, and of the baseball season as a summer-long idyll.

Nebraska sets Monk wise with a firsthand report of the athlete growing old. The veteran player, now keenly aware that his playing days are (and have always been) numbered, worries about losing his roster spot as he regards his diminished physical prowess with failing confidence. The level of effort and proficiency required of a major league player, despite the stifling heat of high summer and the limitations of the body, seem suddenly to be slipping beyond the veteran's capabilities:

> "Monkus," he said quietly ... "you ever been in St. Looie in July?"
> "No."
> "All right, then," he said very softly and scornfully. "An' you ain't played *ball* there in July. You come up to bat with sweat bustin' from your ears. You step up an' look out there to where the pitcher ought to be, an' you see four of him. The crowd in the bleachers is out there roastin' in their shirt-sleeves, an' when the pitcher throws the ball it just comes from nowheres — it comes right out of all them shirt-sleeves in the bleachers. It's on top of you before you know it. Well ... you dig in an' git a toe-hold, take your cut, an' maybe you connect. You straighten out a fast one. It's good fer two bases if you hustle. In the old days you could've made it standin' up. But now — boy!" He shook his head slowly. "You cain't tell me nothin' about that ball park in St. Looie in July! They got it all growed out in grass in April, but after July first — " he gave a short laugh — "hell! — it's paved with

---

[4]*In* Seeking the Perfect Game: Baseball in American Literature *(New York: Greenwood Press, 1989), Cordelia Candelaria recognizes "Wolfe's unromantic delineation of the hardships ballplayers face" and "the physical and emotional pain" that attends their aging within the context of the game, yet insists that "Wolfe's allusions to [baseball] are, overall, eloquently pastoral" (Candelaria 54). In her formulation, "pastoral" serves as an all-purpose term to denote those "novelists who write nostagically [sic] about the sport [and] are markedly diffuse about it" and for whom "baseball embodies the finest ideals and possibilities of the prelapsarian, so-called the New World" (Candelaria 50). While it is true that much of Wolfe's allusive baseball might be called "pastoral," Nebraska Crane's accounts of spring training and the St. Louis summer are realistic and work-a-day, conveying neither a longing to recapture these moments (much less to revisit them) nor a "prelapsarian" freedom from work. Subsuming all of the allusive baseball in Wolfe's fiction under the "pastoral" label blurs the distinction between Nebraska's struggle to stay in the game for financial reasons and baseball as a recreative idyll.*

[5]*See Robert J. Higgs,* Laurel & Thorn: The Athlete in American Literature *(Lexington: The University Press of Kentucky, 1981), 127: "Wolfe ... made of [Nebraska Crane] the hero who could ... 'remain detached from the fever of the times' and, indeed, go home again. ... In Nebraska Crane this great, misunderstood American genius pointed the way back to our roots, and possibly to wisdom and salvation."*

concrete! An' when you git to first, them dogs is sayin', 'Boy, let's stay here!' But you gotta keep on goin'—you know the manager is watchin' you—you're gonna ketch hell if you don't take that extra base, it may mean the game. An' the boys up in the press box, they got their eyes glued on you, too—they've begun to say old Crane is playin' on a dime—an' you're thinkin' about next year an' maybe gittin' in another Serious—an' you hope to God you don't git traded to St. Looie. So you take it on the lam, you slide into second like the Twentieth Century comin' into the Chicago yards—an' when you git up an' feel yourself all over to see if any of your parts is missin', you gotta listen to one of that second baseman's wisecracks: 'What's the hurry, Bras? Afraid you'll be late fer the Veterans' Reunion?'" [*You Can't Go Home Again* 65–66].

Far from embellishing baseball as a pastoral diversion played at one's leisure, Wolfe chronicles in realistic terms the harried efforts of the professional player trying to maintain his livelihood for a few more seasons. The details of Nebraska's account are particularly effective, for they foreground several well-known hardships: the July heat in St. Louis; the diamond, once verdant and cool, having been baked as hard and dry as concrete; the blinding shirts of bleacherites that, for the batter, make each pitch an unnerving adventure. These obstacles to successful—in economic terms, profitable—play heighten Nebraska's sense of being watched, not by adulatory fans but by the critical eye of the manager and the appraising gaze of the sportswriters, who probe the players' weaknesses for stories. If any residue of the pastoral or lyric adheres to the passage, it is the impression the reader forms of Nebraska as a burdened beast, a man whose feet are barking dogs, who earns his bread with the sweat of his brow and fears that his body is falling to pieces. This imagery shifts when Nebraska running the bases becomes a train rumbling down a track, but the point remains the same: Baseball's movements are urgent and inescapably physical. The reader feels the heat and dust of Nebraska's dash into second base, the ache of stiff joints, the soreness of dormant muscles roused by spring training. Over the course of its long season, the game insists that the player perform as if he were unaffected by climatic or physical adversities. It is proof of Nebraska's equanimity, and of Wolfe's dexterous handling of the baseball material, that the humor of the ballplayer's wish rises unforced from the context: "'an' you hope to God you don't git traded to St. Looie.'"

As the spectator senses and the player knows all too well, the difference between excellence and failure is often paper-thin. The aging athlete, especially, plays very near the limit of his talent, tasks his waning skills to keep performance a level above mere competence so that he might keep himself in the game. For Nebraska, playing baseball is satisfying but difficult work, whereas retiring to his farm—a truly pastoral alternative—seems like "'the greatest life in the world!'" (*You Can't Go Home Again* 67). Many a professional ballplayer has shared Nebraska's sense of baseball as the hard job they love with fear and trembling. Some of them describe it in a language and tone similar to Nebraska Crane's, indicating the accuracy of Wolfe's description. Stanley Coveleski, a coal miner in his boyhood and a major league pitcher for 14 seasons (1912, 1916–1928), was inducted into the Hall of Fame in 1969, but, almost forty years after he last pitched, still spoke of baseball grimly, his love of the game compromised by a touch of occupational paranoia:

> I enjoyed playing ball. But it's a tough racket. There's always someone sitting on the bench just itching to get in there in your place. Thinks he can do better. Wants your job in the worst way: back to the coal mines for you, pal!
> The pressure never lets up. Doesn't matter what you did yesterday. That's history. It's tomorrow that counts. So you worry all the time. It never ends. Lord, baseball is a worrying thing.[6]

For all of the anxiety the game might cause, playing professional baseball is preferable to toiling in the Pennsylvania coal mines at a nickel an hour (*Glory* 118) — which is, in a sense, why Coveleski continues to find the pressure to perform daunting. It is not so much baseball that is "a worrying thing" but what will happen to him if he fails at baseball. Nebraska Crane can retreat to his tobacco farm when a younger player eventually replaces him, but Stanley Coveleski sees only a darker prospect, limned with soot.

His throwing arm was Coveleski's ticket out of the mines. Like him, many a boy of humble antecedents (including Mickey Mantle, who briefly swung a sledgehammer in the lead and zinc mines of northern Oklahoma, where his father worked for most of his life) has improved his fortunes and provided for his family by playing professional baseball. As a livelihood, baseball is an option for relatively few, but those with the requisite ability and the diligence to develop it can attain monetary success by playing the game. Wolfe sees in baseball the promise of a different kind of success, and plays a riff of glory on the tableau of one young dreamer "burning in the night":

> Or there, in the clay-baked piedmont of the South, that lean and tan-faced boy who sprawls there in the creaking chair among admiring cronies before the open doorways of the fire department, and tells them how he pitched the team to shut-out victory today. What visions burn, what dreams possess him, seeker of the night? The packed stands of the stadium, the bleachers sweltering with their unshaded hordes, the faultless velvet of the diamond, unlike the clay-baked outfields down in Georgia. The mounting roar of eighty thousand voices and Gehrig coming up to bat, the boy himself upon the pitching mound, the lean face steady as a hound's; then the nod, the signal, and the wind-up, the rawhide arm that snaps and crackles like a whip, the small white bullet of the blazing ball, its loud report in the oiled pocket of the catcher's mitt, the umpire's thumb jerked upward, the clean strike [*You Can't Go Home Again* 507].

Wolfe's descriptive language ("clay-baked piedmont ... tan-faced boy ... creaking chair") and poetic images ("faultless velvet of the diamond") transfigure a

---

[6]*Coveleski's remarks are quoted in Lawrence S. Ritter's indispensable oral history,* The Glory of Their Times: The Story of the Early Days of Baseball Told by the Men Who Played It *(1966; reprinted, New York: Vintage Books, 1985), 123; cited as* Glory.

moment that is essentially realistic. The scene, boys clustered at a firehouse, talking baseball and dreaming of fame, is as plausible as a Norman Rockwell painting. The immediate setting is rural, small-townish, yet gestures toward the city, the true arena of major league baseball. As a modern rendition of Every-boy setting off to seek his fortune, the movement from country to city reca-pitulates the familiar myth of baseball's rural birth and subsequent appropriation by urban entrepreneurs. The quality that distinguishes the scene, however, is not its embodiment of a theme but its enhancement of realistic details through language and sentence structure: the music of prose. Wolfe's long sentences, their regular rhythm and measured diction, heighten each ele-ment of the imagined moment: "The mounting roar of eighty thousand voices and Gehrig coming up to bat," places the reader not merely in the ballpark, but above it, gazing down on the scene entire, a composition of players, field, and grandstand that is a panoramic drama complete unto itself.[7]

Anecdotal accounts of many a small-town ballplayer's beginnings attest to the realism that underlies the transformative vision of Wolfe's tableau. Richard "Rube" Marquard, a major league pitcher for eighteen seasons, also tells a story of a firehouse where, as a rookie minor leaguer without a contract or a dollar in his pocket, he fell asleep beside a stove (*Glory* 7). Several years later, Marquard returns to that firehouse; unrecognized, he recalls the earlier scene:

> "Well, remember about three years ago you caught me sleeping back of that stove there?"
> "Oh, are you the kid from Cleveland that said he's a ballplayer?"
> "Yes. Remember me? My name is Marquard, Richard Marquard."
> "Of course. What are you doing here?"
> "I'm in the Big Leagues," I said. "I told you when I got to the Big Leagues I was coming out to visit you."
> "Well, I'll be darned," he said. "Who are you with?"
> "Why, I'm with the New York Giants."
> And boy, for years after that, whenever the Giants would come to Chicago I'd go out to that firehouse. I'd sit out front and talk for hours. The firemen would have all the kids in the neighborhood there ... all the families that lived around would stop by ... it was really wonderful [*Glory* 13].

Like Wolfe's artful prose, Marquard's simple diction describes a folksy scene. The pat questions and almost clichéd answers make Marquard's story absolutely recognizable — indeed, almost conventional — and epitomize its uncontrived charm. Some of Wolfe's images seem similarly "traditional," as if they have been fashioned from standard American archetypes. The boy's face like a "hound's," his "rawhide arm that snaps and crackles like a whip," "the small white bullet of the blazing ball, its loud report," conflate images of the woodsman hefting his axe, the hunter firing his rifle, with the actions of the baseball player at work

---

[7]*The urban setting of the boy's dream is New York City, the field Yankee Stadium; "Gehrig" is Lou Gehrig, Yankee first baseman, 1923 to 1939. See page 4 supra, note 2.*

with his own inimitable tools. The overall effect is one of Natty Bumppo's having been translated into the time and place of *The Natural*—which, in many ways, he is. The Georgia boy's baseball dreams, moreover, are inseparable from his native landscape, "the clay-baked piedmont of the South," where he has learned to field and hit and throw. Thus, the scene is local, literally grounded in what are plausibly the actual conditions of one boy's life "down home."

When Wolfe expands his field of vision — and the field he is envisioning — the baseball content seems to become more self-consciously symbolic rather than representative of what baseball is or can be in itself. In a long passage in *Of Time and the River* (1935), Wolfe articulates in epic terms the unity that baseball gives a heterogeneous people separated by an immense continent.[8] The energy of the prose is matched only by its excess, its hallmark ambition to capture and contain these open spaces and divergent lives. As the crowd watches Eugene's brother Ben operate the scoreboard in the newspaper office window, posting placards pitch by pitch, the raw physical distance between the game and these small-town spectators seems immeasurable. Wolfe's attempt to catalogue every topographical feature between Catawba and Boston has the effect of pushing the ball game toward the edge of the continent. Paradoxically, the hushed, expectant crowd, visualizing the action, watches Ben's scoreboard as attentively as it would watch the game itself:

> But now the crowd, sensing the electric thrill and menace of a decisive conflict, has grown still, is waiting with caught breath and pounding hearts, their eyes fixed eagerly on Ben. Somewhere, a thousand miles to the North, somewhere through the reddened, slanting and fast-fading light of that October day, somewhere across the illimitable fields and folds and woods and hills and hollows of America ... somewhere through the crisp, ripe air, the misty, golden pollenated light of all her prodigal and careless harvest; somewhere far away at the heart of the ... enchanted city of the North, and of their vision — the lean right arm of the great pitcher Mathewson is flashing like a whip. A greyhound of a man named Speaker, quick as a deer to run, sharp as a hawk to see, swift as a cat to strike, stands facing him. And the huge terrific stands, packed to the eaves incredibly with mounting tiers of small white faces, now all breathless, silent, and intent, all focused on two men as are the thoughts, the hearts, the visions of these people everywhere in little towns, soar back, are flung to the farthest edges of the field in a vision of power, of distance, space and lives unnumbered, fused into a single unity that is so terrific that it bursts the measures of our comprehension and has a dream-like strangeness of reality even when we see it.
>
> The scene is instant, whole and wonderful. In its beauty and design that vision of the soaring stands, the pattern of forty thousand empetalled faces, the velvet and unalterable geometry of the playing field, and the small lean figures of the players, set there, lonely, tense and waiting in their places, bright, desperate solitary atoms encircled by that huge wall of nameless faces, is incredible. And more than anything, it is the light, the miracle of light and shade and color — the crisp, blue light that swiftly slants out from the soaring stands and, deepening to violet, begins to

---

[8]*Thomas Wolfe, Of Time and the River (1935; reprinted, Garden City, NY: Sun Dial Press, 1944), 201–207. Quotations and references follow this edition.*

march across the velvet field and towards the pitcher's box, that gives the thing its single and incomparable beauty.

The batter stands swinging his bat and grimly waiting at the plate, crouched, tense, the catcher, crouched, the umpire, bent, hands clasped behind his back, and peering forward. All of them are set now in the cold blue of that slanting shadow, except the pitcher who stands out there all alone, calm, desperate, and forsaken in his isolation, with the gold-red swiftly fading light upon him, his figure legible with all the resolution, despair and lonely dignity which that slanting, somehow fatal light can give him. Deep lilac light is eating swiftly in from every corner of the field now, and far off there is a vision of the misty, golden and October towers of the terrific city. The scene is unforgettable in the beauty, intoxication and heroic feeling of its incredible design, and yet, as overwhelming as the spectacle may be for him who sees it, it is doubtful if the eye-witness has ever felt its mystery, beauty, and strange loveliness as did that unseen and unseeing audience in a little town [*Of Time and the River* 202–203].

Just as this moment is refracted within the consciousness of the omniscient narrator into a dozen or more discrete images, the people who watch Ben post the score visualize the game more keenly, with more imaginative involvement, than the "eye-witness" who sees it happen. The distant spectators are blind to the scene itself yet see it "at the heart … of their vision," feel "its mystery, beauty, and strange loveliness" as if endowed with preternaturally perceptive sight. In Wolfe's vision, baseball is a shared experience, a communal event that links Americans who are mutual strangers living in disparate regions of the country. The rapt intensity of the ballpark fans, "forty thousand empetalled faces," joined to the collective mind's eye of distant spectators, "unseen and unseeing audience" in small towns, creates the illusion of a collapsing landscape, the miles of mountains, valleys, and forests between Catawba and Boston being telescoped into one place and a single moment: the World Series, tenth inning, final game, October 16, 1912.[9]

The historical details of this moment interest Wolfe much less than the impressionist's tableau he can paint of it. Taken together, the elements Wolfe chooses to reiterate suggest less the observations of a baseball fan and more the perceptions of an artist evaluating a subject for his next canvas. Composition, perspective, color, and light all receive significantly more attention than the action on the field, which by the end of the passage seems suspended or forgotten. Wolfe's pictorial treatment renders certain details, such as faces in the crowded grandstand, the green and copper diamond, the players uniformed in white and gray flannel, as generalized components of a larger vista, a "scene [that] is instant, whole and wonderful." The result is an idealized blur of players and fans forever poised between pitches. Crouched, expectant, "on their toes," the players wait, frozen in the amber of Wolfe's interminable circumlocutions.

[9]*The New York Giants are playing the Boston Red Sox in Fenway Park. It is the eighth game (the second having ended in a tie) and the Giants are ahead, 2–1, in the bottom of the tenth inning. New York Giant ace Christy Mathewson, "Big Six," "The Christian Gentleman," faces star Boston batsman Tris Speaker, known as "The Grey Eagle" for his prematurely silver hair and preternaturally quick foot speed.*

Even as the prose strains to catch up with the fading sun, time and the ball game unwind as if before a crowd stricken with paralysis. Only the light finds motion, "the crisp, blue light that swiftly slants out from the soaring stands and, deepening to violet, begins to march across the velvet field and towards the pitcher's box," and the "Deep lilac light … eating swiftly in from every corner of the field," both of which mark time's decaying around the edges of the clock-less game. The light is beautiful and evanescent, a metaphor of athletic glory and its brevity — and a reminder that the sun does not always literally shine on victors. Mathewson, alone on the pitcher's mound and "forsaken in his isolation," is lit by "the gold-red swiftly fading light" as he prepares to pitch to Tris Speaker, who waits in "the cold blue of that slanting shadow." The "somehow fatal light" foretells Mathewson's defeat and makes it more poignant, as if the pitcher, "his figure legible with … resolution, despair and lonely dignity," performed a tragic role at the spot-lit center of a stage. The batter gestures in the dark margin, almost invisible as he awaits the pitcher's pitch, then defeats the reader's expectation by delivering the game-winning hit.[10] Suddenly, after subordinated clauses of anticipation and deferral, the game ends in a rush toward home:

> And suddenly, even as the busy figures swarm and move there in the window before the waiting crowd, the bitter thrilling game is over! In waning light, in faint shadows, far, far away in a great city of the North, the 40,000 small empetalled faces bend forward, breathless, waiting — single and strange and beautiful as all life, all living, and man's destiny. There's a man on base, the last flash of the great right arm, the crack of the bat, the streaking white of a clean-hit ball, the wild, sudden, solid roar, a pair of flashing legs have crossed the rubber, and the game is over!
>
> And instantly, there at the city's heart, in the great stadium, and all across America, in ten thousand streets, ten thousand little towns, the crowd is breaking, flowing, lost forever! That single, silent, most intolerable loveliness is gone forever [*Of Time and the River* 206–207].

[10]*Wolfe does not concern himself with giving an accurate account of the climax of the 1912 World Series. Speaker's "clean-hit ball," a single to right field in the bottom of the tenth inning, brought home the tying run and moved the winning run to third. What Wolfe omits, because Ben has no way of representing it on his scoreboard, is the dropped foul pop that Speaker hit on Mathewson's first pitch. With the ball in the air near the first base coach's box — "Any high school player could have caught it," reported sportswriter Fred Lieb — Mathewson, first baseman Fred Merkle, and catcher Chief Meyers (a Cahuilla Indian from California who attended Dartmouth College for a year) gave chase. The first baseman would normally make this play, but Mathewson called for the catcher — or Speaker yelled, "Chief! Chief!" to induce the slow-footed Meyers to pursue the ball. Merkle stood off as Chief Meyers tried to make a diving catch and had the ball glance off his glove. Having watched the botched play, Speaker shouted to Mathewson from the batter's box, "Well, you just called for the wrong man. It's gonna cost you this ball game!" On the next pitch, Speaker belted a line drive over Merkle's head, and the tying run scored. The Red Sox won the game and the Series when the next batter, Larry Gardner, lofted a sacrifice fly to right field. These gritty details resist assimilation by Wolfe's elliptical, picturesque account. See Noel Hynd,* The Giants of the Polo Grounds *(New York: Doubleday, 1988), 177–178; Charles C. Alexander,* John McGraw *(New York: Viking Penguin, 1988), 164–165; Paul Adomites,* October's Game *(Alexandria, VA: Redefinition, 1990), 12–13; and New York Giant center fielder Fred Snodgrass's account in* The Glory of Their Times, *109–111.*

The tone, nostalgic even before the winning run scores, becomes elegiac once the game is over, the season finished, the crowd dispersed. For Wolfe, the unities of baseball are preferable to the passage of chronological time, which he slows down so that the shared anticipation of the grandstand fans may last. Unlike Whitman's kinetic images of baseball, Wolfe's tableau aspires to a perfect and unchanging vision of a single, exquisitely composed moment. No wonder, then, that the privileged witness is not "him who sees it" but the "unseen and unseeing audience in a little town." Having not watched the multiform, sometimes complex action of the actual game, the distant "observer" can replay it on the enclosed field of his imagination without the contradictory testimony of visual evidence. A perfected aesthetic vision of a beautiful object need not be confounded or brought to grief by what one actually sees: Wolfe's slanting, rainbowed lights are more picturesque and appealing than the true autumn gloom of October 16, 1912, a "cold, bleak day" in Boston.[11]

Less given than Wolfe to poetic license, James T. Farrell uses baseball primarily to serve the end of narrative realism. In his long and often dispiriting Chicago-based novels, Farrell chronicles his love of baseball — especially of the White Sox — and the early influence the game had on him. Farrell's approach to fiction writing is essentially that of a documentarian, and his depictions of baseball follow this aesthetic. Realistic, unsentimental, almost journalistic, Farrell's allusive baseball is unencumbered by Wolfe's epic claims.[12] Whether in the novels recounting Studs Lonigan's surly youth and misanthropic young adulthood, or in the tetralogy devoted to the life and times of Danny O'Neill, baseball is part of a teeming cityscape: a recreative relief from stress and anxiety, to be sure, but without artfully wrought symbols or pictorial glamour. Danny O'Neill plays baseball and goes to White Sox games at (the original) Comiskey Park because, in Chicago during the early 1900s, baseball is the only game in town.

In Farrell's novels, baseball is what it is; allusions to it require little explication. When Danny O'Neill, some seven years old, attends a White Sox game with his brother Bill and cheers for star pitcher Ed Walsh, who hurls a no-hitter against the Red Sox,[13] the reader understands that Farrell has not fabricated the event. For confirmation, one need only turn to *My Baseball Diary* (1957), Farrell's collection of salient baseball memories from his fiction and his

[11]*Only 17,034 diehards turned out for the deciding game of what was a nip-and-tuck Series, which gives one an idea of just how foul the weather was in Boston (Hynd 176–177).*

[12]*Candelaria blurs the distinction between Farrell's allusive baseball and that of Wolfe by describing Farrell, the consummate prose naturalist and chronicler of urban hard times, as another "baseball pastoralist" (Candelaria 50). Contrasting the baseball of Studs Lonigan to the baseball of Danny O'Neill, Candelaria discerns prefigurements of their later lives: "Studs's petulance foreshadows his immaturity as an adult, while Danny's growing zest for the game is transmuted into enthusiasm for other life experiences, and represents the latter's finer sensibility" (Candelaria 51). Summing up, the critic asserts that for "Farrell the baseball trope is … simple. A character's boyhood love of the sport is a sign of health; indifference or hostility to it is a sign of dissolution and decay" (Candelaria 52–53).*

[13]*In chapter three of* A World I Never Made *(New York: The Vanguard Press, 1936).*

life[14]: "I waited over twenty years to write of Ed Walsh's no-hit game. And my account of it is part of my novel, *A World I Never Made*. Walsh pitched this game on August 27th, 1911, and I never forgot it. Down the years, I did not see another no-hit game pitched until Don Larsen hurled his perfect game in the 1956 World Series. Perhaps because I was a boy in 1911, Walsh's game excited me more than Larsen's" (*Baseball Diary* 45). The purpose of Danny's trip to Comiskey Park is twofold. First, it temporarily delivers the boy from the oppressive atmosphere of his home life. Out from under the jealous eye of his grandmother, freed of his Uncle Al's exacting discipline, Danny finds in baseball a restoration of spontaneous joy. Second, Danny's behavior at the ballpark, perhaps the only place where he lives from the center of his being, characterizes him as vividly as their raised voices and gossip characterize his contentious, hypocritical elders. Thus, although Farrell does not create Ed Walsh's no-hitter as a piece of fiction, he does re-create the scene at Comiskey Park on August 27, 1911, by showing it from Danny's perspective. The account is accurate, albeit necessarily selective, and designed to portray Danny as happy to be at the ballpark and sincerely concerned about the outcome of the game. Occurring early in the first of four novels that tell what amounts to Danny O'Neill's fictive biography, this baseball allusion provides the first substantive development of his character in relation to a world beyond the confines of a parochial Irish household. Left to his own preferences at Comiskey Park, Danny turns out to be an enthusiastic baseball fan and a staunch White Sox rooter:

> Scattered handclapping greeted Tris Speaker as he stepped into the batter's box and stood waiting, measuring off his swings while Walsh cupped his hands over the ball and held it before his mouth.
> "Put a lot of saliva on it for this boy, Ed!" a fan near Danny yelled in a booming voice.
> "Come on, you Bull Moose! Oh, you Ed Walsh, strike him out!" Danny shrieked in a high-pitched voice, causing men around them to watch him with amusement.
> "What do you think of that?" Danny breathlessly said to Bill amid his shrieks and cheers after Ed Walsh had retired the side by striking out Tris Speaker.
> "It's just luck when any pitcher whiffs Tris," Bill said, but Danny did not listen to him, because he eyed Ed Walsh striding off the diamond, dropping his glove on the foul side of the third-base line, walking with lowered head to the White Sox bench.
> "Come on, you White Sox, skunk them green!" he piped ... [*A World I Never Made* 35].

Walsh prepares to throw Speaker a spitball, in 1911 still legal in the major leagues.[15] This detail and its succinct depiction illustrate the quality of Farrell's baseball allusions. Unlike Wolfe, who uses baseball as a pretext for composing

---

[14]James T. Farrell, My Baseball Diary (1957; reprinted, Carbondale: Southern Illinois University Press, 1998).

[15]In 1921, the spitball became permissible only when thrown by seventeen "established spitballers" (Glory 123). Walsh would have been another of these, but he retired after the 1917 season.

impressionistic studies that are virtually still-lifes, Farrell simply reports the action of the game. Only Danny's response seems exaggerated, yet his "shrieks and cries" are a common element of the grandstand — especially when a seven-year-old baseball fanatic is sitting there. By representing baseball realistically — by putting the reader, as it were, in the seat beside Danny O'Neill — Farrell is able to dramatize baseball's effect on his protagonist — the point, after all, of sending Danny to Comiskey Park. Farrell, it seems, understands what Wolfe only intermittently guesses: that baseball itself does not mean anything until it is interpreted by an engaged audience. The observer's response might be intellectual, emotional, or both, but the game derives its significance from those who watch it. In comparison to Danny's individualized experience, broadly symbolic interpretations of baseball seem all-purpose, if not clichéd.

As the game approaches its climax, Danny's involvement becomes even more personal. Unable to root effectively enough to guarantee his hero's triumph — Walsh has one more batter to retire to complete the no-hitter — Danny resorts to a form of prayer. Still awed by Catholic orthodoxy, Danny silently negotiates certain matters of piety, hoping to strike a bargain with God:

> The last man. If God helped Ed Walsh get him out, he would never again try to miss Mass, or not do what he was told at home. He would try every way he could to be as good as his guardian angel, and never hurt God's feelings. A bounder. He held his breath. Amby McConnell had it, the throw to first base. Out! Whee! He stood up on his seat and gave all of himself in a last yell, as the applause and cheering boomed. The players hurriedly scuttled off the field, Walsh chased by fans who wanted to get near him [*A World I Never Made* 39].

Hellfire has proven to be an insufficient threat to lead Danny into moral rectitude, but the outcome of this ball game is a compelling inducement. Like all such promises, this one is forgotten after the final out, but Ed Walsh's achievement impresses Danny and for years afterward exerts a powerful influence. Asked by his aunt Margaret what he will do when he grows up, Danny replies, "'Gee, maybe be a baseball pitcher like Ed Walsh and pitch no-hit games'" (*A World I Never Made* 108). As the sectarian content of Danny's bargaining with God foreshadows, his dream of becoming a baseball player eventually places him in self-conflict regarding his supposed vocation for the priesthood. Ultimately finding that he possesses inadequate talent for professional baseball and a disposition unsuited to religious life, Danny becomes, in *My Days of Anger* (1943), a nascent writer and Marxist sympathizer. These developments, together with Danny's ongoing education and later employment as a gasoline station attendant, distance him from his earlier, all-consuming interest in baseball, which he remembers in *My Days of Anger* only sporadically, as part of his past.

The intervening novels of the tetralogy, *No Star Is Lost* (1938) and *Father and Son* (1940), record the salient formative events of Danny O'Neill's childhood and adolescence. Caught in a web of poverty, domestic violence, Catholic schooling, and personal awkwardness among his peers, boys and girls both, that often seems exaggerated to elicit the reader's sympathy, Danny finds many of his most fulfilling moments in baseball. As he grows older, Danny's own ball playing becomes the focus of the allusions; quite literally, Danny grows up with baseball, the level of his skills serving as an index of his maturation. The game he plays with Bill, for example, is stickball, a version of baseball known to city boys and baseball enthusiasts who lack enough players or open space for a regular game. Dispensing with bases, fielders, and the diamond itself, Danny and Bill reduce baseball to its essence: the confrontation between pitcher and batter:[16]

> Danny liked playing different kinds of ball games with Bill and pretending that these were big-league games. … [T]he game Danny liked best … was the one they played in the back yard with a ten-cent soft ball. They each represented a big-league team and batted according to that team's lineup, hitting right-handed or left-handed just as the real players in the lineup did. They played swift pitching and called balls and strikes. The home base was near the back fence so they didn't have to chase pitched balls that weren't batted at. The whole yard was plotted out and the game was played according to a complicated set of rules devised to make hits hard to get and to keep the score tight. Foul balls that went over the back fence or up on the greenhouses to the right were outs. Over the whole yard, there were only certain places where batted balls were scored as base hits. Over the back fence was a home run [*No Star Is Lost* 69–70].

The logic of this game, "played according to a complicated set of rules," is mimetic. Danny and Bill take it to be real to the extent that it is a plausible imitation of major league baseball. The rules of their own devising, like their physical impersonations of major league players, indicate the creativity involved in making the backyard ball game more like life. What is "real," however, becomes a complicated matter, for Danny's game, self-consciously constructed as a piece of mimicry, is intended to imitate not "real life" but another game — a *real* game, as the world reckons it, but a game nonetheless: a self-governing construct defined by rules. In relation to the real world, the significance of any game, as well as the validity of its rules, is conventional and inescapably fictive. The baseball played in the major leagues is considered real because the players are men instead of boys, and the stakes are not primarily the joy of winning and the disappointment of losing, or even the difference between pride and humiliation but, ultimately, money: the winner's and loser's shares of a substantial purse. To Danny, winning has nothing to do with money; it is a matter of accomplishment and pride. Seeing his chance finally to defeat his elder brother, Danny abandons the constraining pretense of mimicry — steps outside his characters, so to speak — and bends his will and entire being to lash out the base hit that will bring the winning run home:

> He had two chances, and [Jim] Scott and Buck Weaver, his batters, were right-handed.
> "Letting Scott, your pitcher, bat, or putting in a pinch hitter?" Bill asked.
> "He's batting," Danny said grimly.

[16]*In* No Star Is Lost *(New York: Vanguard Press, 1938), 69–72.

He waited. Instead of using the stance and swing of the players he was representing, he was going to swing as hard as he could to get a run in.

"Come on, pitch," Danny said while Bill dallied, pulling at his belt, looking at the ball.

"My catcher's coming out to have a conference with me," Bill said.

Danny liked going through all these pretendings, as if there were talks of players on the field and all that. But Bill was doing it now to get his goat. Bill always took a lot of time if Danny looked as if he might start a hitting rally.

"Come on, pitch!" Danny said impatiently while Bill continued to stall.

Bill walked away from the pitching box.

"I'm talking about what I'm gonna do with my infield," Bill yelled, grinning at Danny, knowing that he was making Danny nervous.

Danny stood swinging his bat, stamping his feet, asking himself if he could slam a couple of hits out now, anxious to have the game go on, losing his nerve and his confidence with every second Bill delayed.

Bill went back to the pitching box. He started winding up slowly. Now he had to hit [*No Star Is Lost* 71].

Danny is not exactly cheating, although his intentions violate the spirit of the game as he has designed it. One might argue that a ballplayer does, in a real game, put forth extraordinary effort at the critical moment. Danny, however, does somewhat more by resorting to means that are not, according to his own "complicated set of rules," properly a part of the available resources. Pride and a sense of accomplishment are as valuable to him as money is to the professional; to Danny, the game is real and defeating Bill counts. His personal stake outweighs his affinity for the elaborate structure of pretense (intended to enhance the game's reality) that impedes his effort to win. The allusion marks a rite of passage, a drama of sibling rivalry played out on an improvised field, and illustrates that baseball can reveal more about a character than how well he plays the game.

Another rite of passage, which introduces a boy to the company of men, also places Danny on a baseball field. Still young, Danny accompanies his Uncle Al to Washington Park for baseball practice with the latter's acquaintances. Danny is about eleven years old, which places him in the liminal state between childhood and adolescence: Too small and weak to stand in the outfield with the men and catch long flies, Danny waits closer in — implicity, closer to home — "and every so often the man hitting out the flies ... would bat him an easy fly or grounder" (*No Star Is Lost* 123). Danny recognizes his liminal status, especially when he muffs one of his chances:

Danny moved in on the ball to field it as if he were an infielder who was going to get off a quick throw and nail a man on a slow infield roller. The ball came bobbing along the grass. Danny grasped it. It dropped out of his hands. Just as if he'd made an error. Danny threw it underhanded along the ground. He was disappointed in himself. He stood now, hands on hips, and watched the man hit out a long fly, watched the ball sail outward in a curving arc, a small white pellet outlined against the enormous blue sky.

"I have it," he heard Uncle Al cry [*No Star Is Lost* 123].

Having failed to make the play deftly, as he believes an accomplished player would, Danny reverts to a child's gesture by throwing the ball "underhanded along the ground." His reaction is a sign of emotional immaturity and reiterates his physical error: the adult player knows that errors are sometimes unavoidable and, inevitably, a part of baseball. Danny, knowledgeable about the game to the point of holding his own in the talk about the Federal League (*No Star Is Lost*, 125–126), no doubt understands errors yet cannot accept them, for they confirm his callowness and underdeveloped abilities. In his impatience to "hurry up and get bigger so that he could play ball with bigger guys and men and catch flies with the men instead of being made to stay in here close" (*No Star Is Lost*, 123), Danny finds himself frustrated by the gap between a performative ideal and the reality of baseball.[17]

This frustration, familiar to every ex-adolescent ballplayer who once struggled to keep pace with bigger, stronger athletes, is complicated by an equally familiar ambivalence. Based on a fear of performance commingled with the desire to perform, this ambivalence makes baseball a worrisome pleasure. Danny notes his mixed wishes as he warms up his Uncle Al:

> Al threw the ball with an easy and unstrained overhanded motion. He was a southpaw, and after tossing the ball he spit into the glove on his right hand. Danny caught the throw, returned it. Al continued tossing them easy. Danny wished that he was a little bigger and that Uncle Al was a pitcher on a team, and that when Uncle Al pitched, he would catch him. He wished that he could catch everything Uncle Al threw just as Bill did. Uncle Al could pitch pretty good. He had a fast ball, and a curve. Bill thought so, too, and Bill often caught Uncle Al, warming him up in the back yard. He guessed that when Uncle Al was younger and played ball a lot, he must have been a pretty good pitcher.
>
> "I'm going to throw them faster now, Dan," Uncle Al said.
>
> "All right. I can catch them," Danny called back; he spat into his glove, wished that he had a catcher's glove on. But then, by catching hard ones with a fielder's glove, he would toughen his hands, and it would be good for him to learn how to catch them fast with a fielder's glove.
>
> Uncle Al wound up like a pitcher, swinging his left arm around in a circle twice, raising his right foot, and then he zoomed the ball at Danny straight and fast. His windup and motion were graceful. Danny caught the ball, returned it to him.
>
> "Good work, Dan," Uncle Al said.
>
> Danny set himself as Uncle Al wound up. He hoped that Uncle Al wouldn't toss them in too fast, and he hoped that he would. He hoped that he'd catch everything that Uncle Al threw at him, and he hoped that Uncle Al would burn them in, and

[17] *The Federal League, a third major league, was formed by competing interests on financial terms that were fairer to the players than those of the American and National Leagues. Federal League clubs signed untried young players, cast-off major leaguers, and, ultimately, current major league players whose contracts had expired but who were still bound to their respective teams by the Reserve Clause. In refusing to honor the Reserve Clause, the Federal League surely served its own interests, yet it also presented a serious challenge to a rule that gave the owners such leverage that their players were essentially powerless in negotiating salaries. Federal League players were guaranteed an annual 5 percent raise and could, after ten years' service, become unconditional free agents. The second provision became moot when the Federal League folded its tents after just two seasons, 1914 and 1915. See Harold Seymour, Baseball: The Golden Age (1971; reprinted, New York: Oxford University Press, 1989), 196–234.*

he was a little bit worried because he only had a fielder's glove on, and he was worried anyway because maybe Uncle Al would pitch them too fast. He tried to imagine himself a big-league catcher warming up somebody like Red Russell or Eddie Plank just before a game. He missed a pitch.

"You didn't watch. I signaled to you that I would pitch a drop that time," Uncle Al said.

"I missed it," Danny said; he turned and trotted to retrieve the ball.

He tried to wing it all the way on the fly to Uncle Al, but he didn't have enough power in his arm. The ball rolled to Uncle Al. Danny trotted back to where he had been standing, to continue warming up his uncle [*No Star Is Lost* 115–116].

Uncle Al is Danny's surrogate father, although Danny's biological father is alive through most of the tetralogy.[18] Jim O'Neill, a teamster who drives a wagon through the Chicago streets, is burdened by a family of young children and an ill-kempt, ever-pregnant, gossip-mongering, Catholic harridan of a wife. A man of little leisure and no peace of mind, Jim O'Neill is too harried to pay attention to his son and the boy's love of baseball. Uncle Al takes on this role just as he assumes responsibility for Danny's education and upbringing; baseball is one more endeavor, like verbal politeness and table manners, in which Uncle Al can correct his nephew's mistakes. The bleak realism of Farrell's fictive world is underscored by the absence of a true father-son game of catch, a baseball image that always risks being overwhelmed by sentimentality. In playing catch with Uncle Al, Danny is all business; like his uncle, he focuses on his performance and its results, which he measures against the standard he aspires to attain. At the same time, Danny compensates for his lack of ability by imagining himself as being better: as the catcher on a team for which his Uncle pitches, then as a major league catcher for pitchers like "Red Russell or Eddie Plank."[19] As if to heap indignity upon frustration, his day-dreaming prevents Danny from reading Uncle Al's sign, which causes him to miss a pitch. If one takes Danny's fantasies of competence as a form of fiction-making, his failure to catch Uncle Al's "drop" implies that creative thought is incompatible with playing baseball. The unfolding of Danny's baseball days in Washington Park, however, shows that the game serves him as a good companion during a difficult adolescence, and actually inspires an early example of his talent for converting life experiences into fiction.

By the time of *Father and Son* (1940), Danny O'Neill is nearing the end of

---

[18]*Jim O'Neill dies in chapter 52 of* Father and Son *(1940; reprinted, New York: World Publishing, 1947). Danny's response is self-regarding to the point of being cold-blooded: "A sudden thought came to him. He ought to know what he thought and felt. He might some day be a writer, and he ought to know and to remember how he felt at his own father's death" (*Father and Son *599).

[19]*The* Baseball Encyclopedia, *7th ed., edited by Joseph L. Reichler (New York: Macmillan, 1988), lists several pitchers with the surname "Russell," but none is noted to have carried the nickname "Red." "Reb" Russell pitched for the White Sox from 1913 to 1919 (*Baseball Encyclopedia* 2115). Eddie Plank, a Hall-of-Fame pitcher for Connie Mack's Philadelphia A's from 1901 through 1914, jumped to the Federal League (*note 17, *supra*) in 1915 and returned to the American League for the 1916 and 1917 seasons (*Baseball Encyclopedia* 2076).

grammar school (which carries him through the eighth grade) and beginning to consider his alternatives. Still enamored of playing professional baseball, Danny comes under the influence of a zealous nun, Sister Magdalen, who encourages him to examine his conscience for signs that God has called him to the priesthood. Again, Danny shows a curious ambivalence, both wanting and not wanting the call. Reluctant to disappoint Sister Magdalen but unwilling to renounce his own ambitions, he is caught between desires. As he passes through interludes of fervor and repulsion, Danny posits baseball as the only worthy alternative to taking Holy Orders. Contemplating the possibility that he might become "the first American saint" he asks himself, "Why should he feel his destiny maybe was to be Saint Daniel O'Neill of Chicago instead of a greater baseball player than Eddie Collins or Ty Cobb?"[20] (*Father and Son* 59). Loving baseball, trying to argue himself out of the priesthood, Danny imagines a complex destiny: "He could first be a baseball player, and never marry, and then, when his playing days were over, he could be ordained. But if he really had the call, he wouldn't always be fighting with himself this way. ... [H]e would want to be a priest. He wouldn't love Roslyn. He wouldn't be dreaming of being a baseball player the way he always did. Yes, he was convinced. He didn't have the call" (*Father and Son* 119). Danny's passion for baseball and his earnest but futile attraction to girls eventually outweigh the signs of piety; indeed, his life orbits around these worlds — baseball, girls, religion — and the triangulated conflicts that they incite throughout the first half of *Father and Son*. As if seeking the safety of home, Danny retreats to baseball when he feels uneasy around girls or rejected by his peers: "Yes, he'd felt as if he didn't belong at the party, and he'd told himself that he belonged on the ball diamond. Well, he was right. That stuff wasn't for him" (*Father and Son* 57). Later, when he is excluded from the social life of his contemporaries, Danny consoles himself with the thought that "soon he could be playing baseball every day in Washington Park and then he wouldn't even give them half a thought" (*Father and Son* 105). Baseball at these moments represents self-sufficiency, offers Danny a refuge from social expectation and embarrassment, affords relief from self-doubt. At no point during his adolescence does Danny demonstrate in social situations the confidence he feels on the ball field.

And yet, in a scene so acutely ironic it is almost cruel, Danny unwittingly places himself in an unpleasant, potentially dangerous position by going to the

---

[20]*Eddie Collins, a charter member of the Hall of Fame, was the White Sox second baseman from 1915 to 1926 and, along with Hall-of-Fame catcher Ray Schalk, a stalwart of professional integrity amidst the unseemly admissions of the Black Sox Scandal. Ty Cobb was the most famous and feared player of his era, most of which preceded the advent of Babe Ruth. For his smart and aggressive style of play, Cobb is a special favorite of Uncle Al, who recommends Cobb's intelligence to Danny as worthy of emulation. Not irrelevantly, Cobb was a very successful businessman and investor, a condition to which Uncle Al aspires but never quite achieves. The anecdotes of Cobb's reckless yet calculated style of play are almost endless; his reputation as "The Greatest Player of All Time" had already been established by 1910, before he had entered fully into the prime of his baseball career. See Charles C. Alexander's biography,* Ty Cobb *(New York: Oxford University Press, 1984).*

Washington Park ball fields alone. Finding that only "some little kids were playing" (*Father and Son* 113), Danny lingers, his mind wandering back to the priesthood. Without warning, he is accosted by a stranger, who engages Danny's attention by first mentioning baseball. This fellow's true interests reveal themselves, however, when he switches subjects with little sense or segue:

> "I see there's no baseball today," the man said, sitting down beside Danny.
> "It rained."
> "You like to play ball, don't you?"
> "Yes."
> "Don't you like the girls?"
> Danny noticed the strange expression in the man's eyes. To avoid meeting his gaze, Danny glanced off across the park and acted as if he had not heard the man's question.
> "How old are you?"
> "Fifteen."
> "Haven't you ever played hide the weenie with the girls out here at night? Lots of kids your age do."
> Danny didn't like the man talking to him like this.
> "You shouldn't blush. Don't you know it's nature?"
> He wanted to get away. He didn't like the look in the man's eye.
> "I got to go home."
> "Don't be in such a hurry," the man said, laying a restraining hand on Danny's arm. ...
>
> * * * * * *
>
> "Yes, Danny, I can't understand you," the man said.
> Danny smirked, confused.
> "You don't do anything to yourself?"
> "I don't know what you mean," Danny answered, but he did know what the man was talking about.
> "You must. All boys do it. Haven't you ever heard talk about whipping the dummy?"
> Danny felt that he must be red from ear to ear.
> He looked ahead, seeing the driveway that turned eastward and went past the refectory. Maybe the man would leave him there.
> "You don't mean to say that you don't know what I mean, Danny?" the man repeated, eyeing Danny closely.
> "Don't know what?"
> "What it means to whip the dummy? You do, you know that, now admit it."
> "Yes."
> "Well, don't you do it?"
> Danny looked at the man, puzzled, afraid. He'd once tried to find out what it was like when he was too young and couldn't do anything. But he hadn't ever really done it.
> The man suddenly grabbed Danny and felt his genital organs. Danny drew away. He blushed. He was afraid. He wanted to run and he was afraid. And what would this man say to the guys he played ball with? Gee, why had he ever come out to the park today to have this happen to him?
> "You're pretty big. You feel like you whip it."
> "I don't. I never did," Danny said, a note of protest and insistence coming into his high-pitched voice [*Father and Son* 113–116].

Without a ball game to fill his afternoon, Danny is easy prey for the middle-aged pederast. Having unnerved Danny with his passively aggressive demeanor, having embarrassed the self-conscious adolescent with inappropriate questions about girls and masturbation, the pervert maneuvers Danny into the false position of seeming to invite molestation. Frightened, shocked, so relentlessly diffident that he cannot strike his assailant or even run from him, Danny worries about the pederast's telling tales about him to his fellow ballplayers. The encounter is unnerving to read and Danny's mystified self-guilt painful to witness. Rather than censuring the pederast for his aberrancy and presumption, Danny perceives only his own sordidness, which he suffers in common with other human beings, "boys and girls and men and women and even priests and nuns ... because of the way they were made" (Father and Son 117). Incredibly, the scene continues for two pages beyond the excerpts given above. In length and content it stands in stark counterpoint to the recreational ball playing that Danny enjoys on the Washington Park diamonds; his "high-pitched voice" is a frightened, confused echo of his gleeful shrieks for Ed Walsh.

In addition to his anguish at being caught between natural sexual curiosity and Catholic sexual inhibition, the subtext of Danny's excessive forbearance toward the pederast involves the embryonic baseball career that he nurtures on these very fields: In the back of his mind, Danny thinks that the man might be a baseball scout. His thoughts when the pederast approaches him, read in the context of his hoping to find a ball game (and his having his baseball equipment in hand), imply that Danny assumes he is about to be "discovered":

> "Hello."
> The speaker was a man about fifty years old, with a mustache and red hair. Danny had seen him around here pretty often, and the man knew all the fellows who played down near this end of the park. Danny was pleased that the man recognized him and talked. The man must have seen him playing [Father and Son 113].

The illicit, outrageous nature of the discovery the pederast is ready to make (by playing a sexual ball game unrelated to any form of baseball known to Danny O'Neill) is incongruous to the setting of the Washington Park fields. Danny's mistaking the man for a baseball scout underlines his relative innocence and extreme naïveté even as it proffers an affecting example of his idealistic optimism (which is soon to sour). When one considers that Danny's baseball aspirations possess a seriousness that is devotional in its nature, and remembers that he consistently analogizes playing in the major leagues to the profound question of whether to take Holy Orders, the revelation of sexual perversity on a baseball field must strike one as a rude, profane surprise. In retrospect, however, it seems like an inevitable counterweight to Danny's ball playing, a sign of the world's refusal to allow the boy to play baseball "untouched" forever.

Later, and almost in a spirit of self-defense, Danny attempts to elude the grasp of adult concerns by trying to arrange his own "discovery." The letter he writes to Connie Mack,[21] which he hopes will insure an extended life in base-ball, is a charming bit of wish-fulfillment and an aesthetically satisfying link between Danny's baseball days and his future as a writer:

> Connie Mack was known above all other managers as the man to pick promising players off the sand lots and develop them into stars. Well, after receiving this let-ter, why shouldn't Connie send a scout out to Washington Park to look him over? And maybe the scout would see him on a good day and sign him up for a tryout with the Athletics a couple of years from now when he was old enough. Players had been signed up at fifteen before. There was the case of that pitcher, Hoyt. Proud of himself, he read the letter he'd just composed.

> *Mr. Connie Mack*
> *Shibe Park*
> *The Philadelphia Athletics*
> *Philadelphia, Pennsylvania.*

> Dear Mr. Mack:

>> *I am writing you this letter to tip you off about a kid named O'Neill who is to be seen playing ball in Washington Park in Chicago all of the time. He isn't ripe just yet because he is only fifteen or sixteen*

> That was a smart idea, to make out that the man who was supposed to be writing this letter didn't know too much about him, so it was best not to give his exact age.

>> *but he is coming along fast for his age, and he will be ripe soon enough and he looks like a real comer. If you look him over you can pick up a promising youngster now for nothing and he seems destined for the big show. I am a baseball fan and like to see kids get a chance, and take pride in pick-ing them. I picked some before and was a good picker. Years ago when George Mori-arity was playing on the sand lots of Chicago I picked him, and I think you must admit I picked a big leaguer then because Moriarity is a big leaguer. You can pick this kid up now for nothing and you will never regret it. He plays out in Washington Park all of the time, and you can send a scout out there to look at him and easily find out who he is.*
>> *I know you will not be sorry for this tip.*
>> *A baseball fan, a real one.*

>> *T. J. Walker*

> He was pleased and satisfied with his letter. All year he'd really felt that 1919 was going to be an important year for him. Maybe this letter might begin to prove that it was. He was smart to have thought up this idea [*Father and Son* 119–120].

Danny's stratagem is creative and resourceful,[22] but fails to achieve its intended result: No scout appears in Washington Park, looking for "a kid named O'Neill."

---

[21]*Connie Mack was still managing the Philadelphia Athletics when* Father and Son *was published in 1940. Mack managed the A's from 1901 to 1950, and the Pittsburgh Pirates from 1894 through 1896, making him the only seven-decade, two-century manager in the history of professional baseball* (Base-ball Encyclopedia *665–666).*

[22]*After having been released by his first minor league team, Ty Cobb wrote similar letters to sports-writer Grantland Rice. By varying his handwriting and signing nondescript names, Cobb, just seven-teen years old and playing semipro ball in Alabama, induced Rice to mention his name and standout play in Rice's syndicated newspaper column. Later that season, Cobb's original team asked him to return* (Alexander 18).

This disappointment links Danny to his peers; Farrell himself notes that "Of the thousands of boys who played baseball in Washington Park and dreamed or hoped to be discovered and rise to the rank of a big league star, Fred Lindstrom [of N. Y. Giants fame], to my knowledge, was the only one who succeeded" *(Baseball Diary* 259–260). In the end, Danny's baseball dreams come to nothing. Yet, his cunning letter foretells another kind of success, for it marks the consummation of another career; in certain circumstances, the best game of baseball one can play is the baseball one writes.

The letter to Connie Mack is Danny's first piece of fiction. It creates a persona, establishes a motive, and is designed to affect its reader. Its formal logic implicates its intended audience, for its resolution waits upon Connie Mack's response. In that sense, the fiction continues to evolve after the writer has set down his pen. One might argue that it is nothing but propaganda and misinformation, cute yet jejune and essentially dishonest. And yet, it says nothing more than what might be written in a thousand similar letters by "bird-dogs."[23] In any case, the gambit fails — although not necessarily because Danny's letter is unconvincing. For even if Connie Mack were to send a scout to Washington Park, Danny's performance on the diamond is the extratextual element that would determine his fiction's efficacy. In his case the performance is lacking. Despite several notable accomplishments, a few of which Danny recounts in a letter to Uncle Al (written immediately after the missive to Connie Mack; *Father and Son* 121), subsequent events indicate that no letter he could have written would have duped anyone into signing him to a professional contract. As an 18-year-old junior, Danny strikes out three times in one game with the bases loaded and realizes that, in spite of sporadic success — "two long doubles against Augustine, one of them with the bases full" and "a triple in another game" — "he just wasn't developing as a ballplayer" *(Father and Son* 232–233). Disgusted with himself, Danny achieves a level of self-knowledge that is painful but indispensable: "after kidding himself about his destiny, and having the nerve to think that he would be a star like Ty Cobb or Eddie Collins, he was a miserable failure" *(Father and Son* 233). In his senior year at St. Stanislaus, Danny does not turn out for baseball *(Father and Son* 510), marking the abandonment of his lifelong love. It is not clear what destiny will overtake him, but it will not arrive in baseball knickers and a flannel cap. The most that one can claim for Danny's literary juvenilia is its apparent promise that its author will find a vocation after baseball, outside baseball.

As his abilities ascend, then are eclipsed by those of truly talented players, Danny's interest in the Chicago White Sox seems to wane. He displays no enthusiasm for the 1917 championship team, which won the American League pennant

---

[23]*In* The Dickson Baseball Dictionary *(New York: Facts on File, 1989), Paul Dickson explains that, in baseball, a "bird dog" is a "Friend or associate of a scout who tips him off to high-schoolers and other young players with major league potential.... They are not paid, but occasionally one is given a small bonus for having spotted a boy who eventually becomes a major leaguer" (Dickson 56).*

and the World Series, and does not notice the great 1919 team that dominated the American League before losing the fixed World Series to the Cincinnati Reds. Of the aftermath of the Black Sox Scandal there is no word.[24] Danny's indifference to these events is surprising; that Farrell does not even register this indifference seems like a lapse, a conspicuous failure to unify this part of the narrative. Given Danny's rapture over the no-hitter that Ed Walsh pitched back in 1911, the absence of any allusion to the triumph and eventual disgrace of the White Sox is incredible. Then again, Danny has grown older. In *My Days of Anger,* he attends the University of Chicago, participates in high-minded discussions, begins seriously to write fiction; he patronizes brothels, contracts venereal disease, drinks liquor to the point of poisoning himself. The reader is invited to conclude that, having discovered a man's pleasures, Danny O'Neill no longer has any interest in a boy's game. This assumption seems to be borne out by his bitter retort to the question (asked in *My Days of Anger*), "'What is America?'" Danny "cut[s] in sarcastically" and, speaking from a personal disapointment more wounding than he will admit, offers his famously cynical summation: "'A nation of frustrated baseball players, delicatessen-store princesses, snobs and go-getters.'"[25] That simply, Farrell's angry young man says good-bye to baseball.

The baseball allusions of Thomas Wolfe and James T. Farrell stand as some of the most evocative in American fiction. From Nebraska Crane's gritty hardships on major league diamonds to the sandlot games of Danny O'Neill, baseball enlivens the novels of both authors, providing luminous details that attract the reader's attention again and again. The most notable quality of these allusions might well be the self-sufficiency of the material itself. Historical events, like Ed Walsh's no-hitter, possess their own rhetorical power, which the author releases by allowing baseball to be what it is within the fictive context: Players perform, the game unfolds, and the fictional characters watch and respond. The game itself neither invents nor confers meaning, for without a spectator to mark its progress, the game means nothing. Baseball does, however, afford the creative writer an opportunity to construct meaning. Noting Danny's responses to baseball, the reader infers why the game is important to the boy. Created scenes, like Danny's own ball playing or Nebraska Crane's description of baseball-as-work, are detailed and individualized. Emphasizing the actualities of play, these passages are realistic and convincing. The reader learns something about

---

[24]*Farrell registers his own reaction in "I Remember the Black Sox," which appears in* My Baseball Diary, *100–109. Summing up the effect of the Black Sox Scandal, Farrell writes, "My interest in baseball changed after this. For years I had no favorite team. I was growing up [Farrell was 'a boy of fifteen and a passionate White Sox enthusiast' at the time of the 1919 World Series (Baseball Diary 99)], and this marked the end of my days of hero-worshiping baseball players. Many fans felt betrayed. I didn't. I felt sorry. I wished it weren't true. I wished the players would have been given another chance" (Baseball Diary 108).*

[25]*James T. Farrell,* My Days of Anger *(New York: Vanguard Press, 1943), 309.*

baseball at the same time that he becomes privy to revelations of character. Finally, reimagined events, like the endgame of the 1912 World Series, allow the author to transpose anterior reality in ways that heighten its climactic drama, not to mention its pictorial grandeur. Such allusions are remarkable not because they alter the facts but for the way they enhance baseball's rhetorical potency within fictive contexts.

♦ *Five* ♦

"How to Live in It"
Synecdochic Naming and Hemingway's Baseball Games

Hemingway has expressed with genius the terrors of the modern man at the danger of losing control of his world, and he has also, within his scope, provided his own kind of antidote. This antidote, paradoxically, is almost entirely moral. Despite Hemingway's preoccupation with physical contests, his heroes are almost always defeated physically, nervously, practically: their victories are moral ones.
— Edmund Wilson, *The Wound and the Bow*

Many commentators have noted that physical contests are a distinctive element of Ernest Hemingway's literary work. Hemingway was drawn, in both his journalistic and his creative writing, to combative sports like hunting, fishing, and bullfighting, and distinguished these contests, which are fought to the death, from the games played by "the amateur sportsmen of America and England."[1] Hemingway did, however, find metaphorical potency in at least one of America's major games. In fictions from "The Three-Day Blow" (1925) to *The Old Man and the Sea* (1952), baseball provides the substance of many memorable allusions, several of which demonstrate a rhetorical technique that may be called "synecdochic naming." As practiced by Hemingway, synecdochic naming is the effect the author achieves when he "drops" the name of a real-life figure into a fictive narrative to serve a symbolic end. When it appears in an appropriate context — a context that cues the reader to release its unwritten significance — a synecdochic name functions as a complex metaphor, evoking both character qualities and a code of ethical values. In "The Three-Day Blow" and *A Farewell to Arms* (1929), synecdochic naming is likely to strike the reader as mere name-dropping, but the extraliterary associations of the synecdochic names extend the texts in surprising directions. In *The Old Man and the Sea*,

---

[1]*Ernest Hemingway*, Death in the Afternoon *(New York: Charles Scribner's Sons, 1932; reprinted, Norwalk, CT: Easton Press, 1990), 22. The pagination of the Easton Press edition matches that of Scribner's.*

the synecdochic name of a famous baseball player obviously carries more meaning than a slight topical reference or throwaway line; indeed, only the technique
of synecdochic naming can satisfactorily describe the rhetorical impact of "the
great DiMaggio," the nearly mantric phrase that Hemingway puts into the
mouth (and consciousness) of his Cuban fisherman. Whether an allusion uses
a synecdochic name for its particular associations, or engages more generally
the associations of baseball within American culture, its import becomes apparent when the reader identifies the historical referents of the baseball material,
then interprets the fictional context in terms of the expanded (baseball) trope.
Such an approach reveals the stories behind baseball allusions, which always
contain more meaning than meets the cursory eye. As Erich Auerbach wrote of
Old Testament figures and events, the allusions of Hemingway's baseball games
are "fraught with background."[2]

Heinie Zim and the Education
of Nick Adams

"The Three-Day Blow" (1925) includes a passage of baseball talk that places
a synecdochic name within a more complex allusion.[3] The result is an elaborate trope of emotional confusion and reticence that serves as a thematic epitome of the Nick Adams stories. To achieve this effect, the allusion combines
rumors of game-fixing with topical references to baseball players, as well as to
the National League pennant race of an uncertain year. One sign of the allusion's — and the story's — temporal context is Nick's response to the news that
the New York Giants have defeated the St. Louis Cardinals in both games of a
doubleheader:

> "That ought to cinch it for them."
> "It's a gift," Bill said. "As long as McGraw can buy every good ball player in the
> league there's nothing to it."
> "He can't buy them all," Nick said.
> "He buys all the ones he wants," Bill said. "Or he makes them discontented so
> they have to trade them to him."
> "Like Heinie Zim," Nick agreed.
> "That bonehead will do him a lot of good."
> Bill stood up.
> "He can hit," Nick offered. The heat from the fire was baking his legs.
> "He's a sweet fielder, too," Bill said. "But he loses ball games."

---

[2]Erich Auerbach, Mimesis: The Representation of Reality in Western Literature, translated by Willard R.
Trask (Princeton, NJ: Princeton University Press, 1953; reprinted, 1974), 11–12.

[3]"The Three-Day Blow," in In Our Time (New York: Charles Scribner's Sons, 1925; reprinted, Norwalk, CT: Easton Press, 1990), 39–49. Quotations from and references to "The Three-Day Blow" and
to "The End of Something" (In Our Time, pp. 31–35) follow the Easton Press edition and are cited as
In Our Time.

"Maybe that's what McGraw wants him for," Nick suggested.

"Maybe," Bill agreed.

"There's always more to it than we know about," Nick said.

"Of course. But we've got pretty good dope for being so far away" [*In Our Time* 41].

Having glossed the identities of Heinie Zimmerman and John McGraw, critics have ventured to date "The Three-Day Blow" according to hints in the baseball dialogue.[4] Unfortunately, the details of the boys' baseball talk are ambiguous; the year is almost certainly 1916, yet some elements seem to refer to 1917. In either case no one can establish definitive proof. To resolve the matter, one might begin with certain events of Heinie Zimmerman's baseball career, for these must be taken as logical markers of the story's temporal setting. Zimmerman, who won the Triple Crown in 1912 while playing third base for the Chicago Cubs, was traded to John McGraw's New York Giants in September of 1916 and retired from baseball late in the 1919 season amid rumors of game-fixing.[5] If the verisimilitude of the baseball talk is to be preserved, the story must be set within these years. The autumn of 1916 seems most reasonable because the boys speak of the Zimmerman trade as if it were a recent event. Moreover, the tone of the story and its extended reference to Nick's courting of Marjorie and their breakup (as well as the callowness of the conversation) seem to place it before Nick's being wounded in combat — and therefore before America's entry into the First World War.[6] Other points, however, cannot be reconciled

---

[4]*The following articles address the baseball dialogue in "The Three-Day Blow," either to date the story or to show that the tenor of the baseball talk is consistent with the prevailing themes of the Nick Adams stories, or both: George Monteiro, "Hemingway's Pléiade Ballplayers,"* Fitzgerald-Hemingway Annual *(1973): 299–301, and "Dating the Events of 'The Three-Day Blow,'"* Fitzgerald-Hemingway Annual *(1977): 207–210; Matthew O'Brien, "Baseball in 'The Three-Day Blow,'"* American Notes and Queries *16 (1977): 24–26; Howard L. Hannum, "Dating Hemingway's 'The Three-Day Blow' by External Evidence: The Baseball Dialogue,"* Studies in Short Fiction *21:3 (Summer 1984): 267–268; Kenneth G. Johnston, "'The Three-Day Blow': Tragicomic Aftermath of a Summer Romance,"* Hemingway Review *2:1 (Fall 1982): 21–25; Tim Summerlin, "Baseball and Hemingway's 'The Three-Day Blow,'"* Arete *4:2 (Spring 1987): 99–102.*

[5]*When Zimmerman was traded from the Cubs to the Giants, he was in the midst of a ten-game suspension for "laying down on the job," as the* New York Times *of August 12, 1916 phrased it; quoted by Charles C. Alexander in* John McGraw *(New York: Viking Penguin, 1988), 192. For a Midwest baseball fan like Bill, Heinie Zimmerman's reputation as a player who "loses ball games'" would precede the 1917 World Series.*

[6]*Kenneth G. Johnston maintains that the story is set in 1919 for the following reasons: Nick's regret about not being able to take Marjorie to Italy implies that he has already returned from the War; the talk of socks — "'Better take your shoes off,' Bill said. ¶ 'I haven't got any socks on.' ¶ 'Take them off and dry them and I'll get you some,' Bill said.... Bill came down with a pair of heavy wool socks. ¶ 'It's getting too late to go around without socks,' he said"* (In Our Time *40); the discussion of the pennant race; John McGraw's being able to "'buy'" all the players he wants; Heinie Zim; there being "'more to it than we know about'"; and Nick's wish "'to see the World Series.'" These elements, Johnston claims, form a complex and (it seems to the present author) exceedingly oblique pattern of imagery and allusion that refers to the Black Sox Scandal of 1919. Given that the baseball season has not yet ended, the fixed World Series has yet to occur. If one believes Johnston's thesis, the incidental details, baseball and otherwise, constitute an uncanny prefigurement of the event.*

to fit this frame. For example, Nick's remark that the Giants' doubleheader sweep of the Cardinals "'ought to cinch it for them'" indicates that the Giants are on the verge of winning the National League pennant — but in 1916, the Giants finished seven games behind the Brooklyn Dodgers. Nick must, therefore, be referring to the pennant-winning Giants of 1917, who finished ten games ahead of Philadelphia. And yet, Bill's ensuing complaint — that the World Series is "'always in New York or Philadelphia now'" *(In Our Time* 41)— becomes a *non sequitur* by 1917, when the Chicago White Sox finished first in the American League.[7] Readers aware of these indissoluble historical details are likely to conclude that Hemingway has conflated events of two different baseball seasons in this part of the dialogue.[8]

Despite a sense that the author has compromised the story's verisimilitude, the melding of details from two baseball seasons justifies itself when one examines the metaphoric content of the boys' dialogue and evaluates its rhetorical effects. As a matter of craft, the baseball talk gives the author (as well as the characters and the reader) an easy opening to a conversation that modulates, for Nick, into something worrisome and unfamiliar. As the first topic of discussion, baseball temporarily displaces the difficult main subject: Nick's breakup with Marjorie. Indeed, baseball substitutes as topic much in the same way that Bill substitutes, here and in the closing paragraphs of the preceding story, "The End of Something," as Nick's companion *(In Our Time* 35). In both stories, Nick is reluctant to surrender his boyish independence and the camaraderie of his male friend, yet uncomfortable in choosing Bill's companionship over Marjorie's. It is unclear whether Nick, on the cusp of juvenility and maturity, is simply experiencing some emotional growing pains or is truly frightened of the demands, both implied and explicit, of a heterosexual relationship. In the face of his uncertainty, possibly of his fear, Nick remains stoically distraught, reticent, confused. He knows that a new experience awaits his courage to confront it but withholds himself, believing that he has something crucial still to learn from his boy's life yet not knowing what it is.

In "The Three-Day Blow" the woman is more perfectly absent (they drink Bill's father's liquor instead of eating Marjorie's sandwiches) and the boys resort to a masculine redoubt for mutual edification. In this context, baseball becomes both an echo of their childhood and one of the clues they will need to decipher the riddles of the adult world, which they associate with knowing how to handle one's shotgun and one's whiskey ("'...dad only likes me to drink what's open. ... He says opening bottles is what makes drunkards'" [*In Our Time* 43]).

---

[7]*In 1917, the White Sox won the AL pennant by nine games (Baseball Encyclopedia 268); in 1918, the Chicago Cubs won the NL pennant by ten and a half games (Baseball Encyclopedia 270); in 1919, the White Sox won again, by three and a half games (Baseball Encyclopedia 276). Beginning in 1917, Bill has no reason to complain about New York and Philadelphia's monopolizing the World Series. See* The Baseball Encyclopedia, *7th ed. edited by Joseph L. Reichler (New York: Macmillan, 1988).*

[8]*George Monteiro seems to be alone in noticing the justness of this conclusion. See "Dating the Events of 'The Three-Day Blow,'" 210.*

Caught in the liminal state between adolescence and adulthood, Nick and Bill talk around "'that Marge business'" *(In Our Time* 46), discussing the baseball season in a tone of affected mastery, as if they were initiates of the game, confident of their knowledge but, again, uncertain of what the next level of expertise will require. Ironically, they discover in the language of baseball the terms to describe Nick's romantic misadventure, yet fail to recognize the metaphoric quality of their words.

Their conversation's high points — losing games, the baseball knowledge they do not have, the "bonehead" Heinie Zimmerman, the most compelling action's always taking place elsewhere — coalesce as a pattern of implication and double entendre that invites the reader to apply the boys' comments to the story's romantic subtext and to understand, even if Nick and Bill do not, that what they are uttering subtextually is an autopsy report of the dead love affair. Traces of this subtext are present in the allusion to Heinie Zimmerman (one of baseball's most prolific hitters), who lost his baseball career through dishonesty designed to serve immediate, perhaps chimerical, goals. Similarly, Zimmerman's "bonehead" play in the 1917 World Series, which is traditionally alleged to have cost the Giants the championship, is a transmutation of Nick's own "bonehead" emotional errors. Thus, "Heinie Zim" is this allusion's synecdochic name; the story's contemporary readers are likely to have remembered him, as well as the 1917 World Series and Heinie Zim's ignominious departure from professional baseball. These readers, moreover, are likely to have recognized Nick's naming Heinie Zim as a player made "discontented" and traded to McGraw's Giants as a sign of Nick's own discontent, which he seems, in "The End of Something," to have orchestrated (offstage) with Bill and which places him in the ethically illicit position of being Marjorie's jilting lover. Having lost the affection of a desirable young woman through his own mistakes and selfishness, Nick has relegated himself to an isolated cabin in the Michigan woods, drinking borrowed whiskey with another boy at the butt-end of summer. Having driven himself out of love's game, Nick may be said to have gone Heinie Zim one worse.[9]

---

[9]*Heinie Zim's World Series "error" is an often-told anecdote. In 1917, the New York Giants found themselves at a 3–2 disadvantage in a best-of-seven Series against the White Sox. In game six, White Sox second baseman Eddie Collins (see page 78 supra, note 20), keen of mind and fleet of foot, ended up on third base courtesy of two errors, one by Zim. With none out and another runner on first, the batter, Hap Felsch, bounced the ball back to the pitcher, Rube Benton. Benton fielded the ball, saw Collins caught off base, and threw the ball to Heinie Zim. With Collins trapped, Giants' catcher Bill Rariden moved up the line, took the throw from Zim, and chased Collins back toward third. When Rariden returned the ball to Zim, Collins dashed for home, which was unguarded. Collins ran, Zimmerman in hot pursuit, holding the ball in the fingers of his outstretched hand. In this fashion Collins crossed home plate with the game's first run, and the White Sox went on to win the game and the Series, 4–2. Manager John McGraw never blamed Zimmerman, insisting that first baseman Walt Holke should have covered home. The sporting press, however, lambasted Zimmerman for his "bonehead" play. The New York Times accused Zim of being responsible for "one of the stupidest plays that has ever been seen in a world series" (quoted by Summerlin 101). See Noel Hynd,* The Giants of the Polo Grounds *(New York: Doubleday, 1988), 206–207; and Paul Adomites,* October's Game *(Alexandria, VA: Redefinition, 1990), 18–19.*

The broader metaphoric content of the baseball dialogue becomes evident later in the story. After they have finished an open bottle of whiskey and started on an open bottle of Scotch, Nick and Bill begin drinking toasts to other topics of conversation, particularly fishing, which they both prefer:

> "It's better than baseball," Bill said.
> "There isn't any comparison," said Nick. "How did we ever get talking about baseball?"
> "It was a mistake," Bill said. "Baseball is a game for louts."
> They drank all that was in their glasses [*In Our Time* 45].

As they become intoxicated, Nick and Bill share an illusion of wisdom. Both boys try to act in a manner that is "consciously practical" (*In Our Time* 44), leading to the delusion that "Nothing was finished. Nothing was ever lost" (*In Our Time* 48). This notion assuages Nick's sense of hopelessness about his aborted romance, yet is as jejune as their talk of literature and as "consciously practical" as Nick's retrieving the dried apricots he has spilled on the kitchen floor. Their latent scorn for baseball is another symptom of this attitude and registers what they take to be a man's attributes: savvy, practicality, self-reliance. An awareness that "'There's always more to it than we know about'" may separate men from boys, but some men, those who are serious and worthy (according to Hemingway's macho code), set themselves apart by recognizing that baseball games and their outcomes depend on teams. Because one player's weakness or error can compromise the team's effort, baseball cannot achieve the unmediated revelations of character attained by the solitary fisherman or hunter.[10] Renouncing baseball reassures Nick and Bill that they are truly men, that, having ceased to be children, they have enough presence of mind to put aside boyhood's games. Their dismissal of baseball is a kind of posturing that is also, rhetorically, a sign of the anxiety and diffidence they intend to cover. Hemingway's own sporting preferences notwithstanding, Nick and Bill's sudden scorn for baseball makes their opinions about literature seem puerile and their valorization of fishing rather absurd. Despite their apparent certainty, neither books nor fishing has anything more (or less) to do with being a man than baseball. Ultimately, their macho posturing reveals the limits of the boys' knowledge and indicates the danger of their pretense — or delusion — of knowing more than they do.

Bill's notion that Nick "'might get back into it again'" (*In Our Time* 48) and Nick's ready acceptance of this idea testify that the boys judge sexual, or

---

[10]For an excellent discussion of Hemingway's attitude toward different kinds of sports and their relation to his fiction, see Christian K. Messenger, Sport and the Spirit of Play in American Fiction: Hawthorne to Faulkner (New York: Oxford University Press, 1981), especially 231–234, 237–240. See Wiley Lee Umphlett, The Sporting Myth and the American Experience: Studies in Contemporary Fiction (Lewisburg, PA: Bucknell University Press, 1975), 17–18, 59, 67–80. For a discussion of Hemingway's aesthetic responses to the bullfight, see Leverett T. Smith's The American Dream and the National Game (Bowling Green, OH: Bowling Green University Popular Press, 1975), 67–75.

romantic, relationships with the same prejudice they rely on to decide baseball's place in the hierarchy of worthy sports. In both cases, they merely guess at what a man does, how he might act or feel, what he seeks out or avoids. Nick and Bill both think that "'get[ting] back into it again'" is easy, as if love truly were a game that one could "get into" at will. Neither understands (or wants to believe) that the relationship can never be as spontaneous and unguarded as it once was, or that Nick, in rejecting Marjorie, has described a gesture he can never erase. "'There's always more to it than we know,'" Nick concedes, alluding to why baseball's smartest manager, John McGraw, might want a "bonehead"[11] like Heinie Zimmerman on his team, but also subconsciously referring to "'that Marge business,'" about which he does not know all he will eventually have to learn in order to function as lover or spouse. Indeed, Nick's responses to Bill's remarks about marriage—"'Once a man's married he's absolutely bitched. ... He's done for'" *(In Our Time 46)*—are silence—"Nick said nothing"—and the anxiety a boy might feel in the presence of his own ambiguous emotions: "'All of a sudden everything was over,' Nick said. 'I don't know why it was. I couldn't help it. Just like when the three-day blows come now and rip all the leaves off the trees'" *(In Our Time 47)*. Nick's vagueness is impressionistic and elemental, perhaps childish in its simple association of emotional crisis with the seasonal storms that betoken the onset of autumn. When Bill presses for an explanation, Nick reveals his confusion in a terseness that attempts to deflect responsibility for the romance's unhappy ending and bitter aftertaste. The distinction Nick tries to draw between his and Marjorie's general intention to get married and a formal engagement illustrates not only his confusion but also his reluctance or trepidation in committing himself in a serious, adult way to changing the terms and conditions of his life. The clearest sign of Nick's immaturity might be his professed ignorance that some promises, especially in affairs of the heart, are made implicitly rather than formally. Even Bill realizes that an unspoken mutual understanding can be as binding as a spoken pledge:

[11]*The term "bonehead" attained a wide usage well before the Zimmerman affair. In the heat of the 1908 pennant race between the New York Giants and the Chicago Cubs, Giant rookie (it was his first game in the majors) Fred Merkle, running from first base on a teammate's clean single to center field in the last of the ninth, failed to touch second base after the hit had apparently scored the winning run. Merkle, acting according to the custom of the day, veered toward the Giants' clubhouse, located above deep center field in the old Polo Grounds, when he saw the runner score and waves of Giants' rooters spilling out of the grandstand. Accounts of the play vary, but Cubs second baseman Johnny Evers claimed to have retrieved the ball from the center fielder and tagged second base before Merkle could return to the field. Home plate umpire Hank O'Day confirmed that Merkle had not touched second base and the president of the National League, Harry C. Pulliam, declared the game a 1–1 tie after nine innings, suspended by darkness and, if necessary to decide the pennant, to be replayed at the end of the season. When the Cubs and Giants finished in a tie for first place, the disputed game was replayed. The Cubs won. John McGraw defended his player, but the press castigated Merkle for committing an unforgivable "boner" and for being a "bonehead" guilty of a "bonehead play." Thus, when Bill calls Zimmerman a "bonehead," he might be using the term broadly to describe Zimmerman's performance on the field rather than referring to a specific incident. See Paul Dickson, The Dickson Baseball Dictionary (New York: Facts on File, 1989), 63–65; Hynd 147–149; and Alexander 133–134.*

"Weren't you going to get married?" Bill asked.
"Yes. But we weren't engaged," Nick said.
"What's the difference?" Bill asked judicially.
"I don't know. There's a difference."
"I don't see it," said Bill.
"All right," said Nick. "Let's get drunk."
"All right," Bill said. "Let's get really drunk" [*In Our Time* 48].

At this point, the reader is able to take the full measure of Nick's actions. It is not merely a girlfriend he has rejected, but a *de facto* fiancée to whom he has broken a promise, implicit or otherwise. Nick hopes to evade responsibility by insisting on a distinction that even Bill realizes does not exist, then abandons the problem in favor of a warm fire and more whiskey. Such creature comforts might be inducements to denial and a swift forgetting, and yet, lingering in Nick's consciousness, a sense of loss strains the bonds of goodfellowship and undermines the notion that Bill's cabin might serve Nick as a makeshift or surrogate home. Such a transference of Nick's implicit desire to move homeward is never more than metaphoric in "The Three-Day Blow." In any case, Bill's cabin is a counterfeit home, an empty construction or sign without import, despite the drying apricots, the blazing fire, the warm socks and plentiful liquor. By turning away from Marjorie, his prospective wife, Nick chooses to turn away from home and embark upon an extended sojourn — or boyhood — in a purely masculine world.

At story's end, Nick and Bill take the shotguns down from the rack and step outside. In the gale-force wind, Nick thinks that "the Marge business was no longer so tragic" and reassures himself with the thought that he can "go into town Saturday night" and, presumably, reconcile with the slighted girl. This notion, "a good thing to have in reserve" *(In Our Time* 49), indicates Nick's awareness of the error he has made. He can displace his anxiety temporarily by hefting a shotgun and looking for something to shoot, but soon the hunt will end — just as the daily adventure that is the spontaneous, unreflective life of a boy must be set aside for a man's attentiveness to domestic concerns. To be sure, Nick is unwilling to accept the kind of home life in which a man, according to Bill, finds himself "'absolutely bitched.'" At the same time, Nick is unwilling to lose Marjorie forever. Unable to choose a resolution, Nick settles for a fiction — that he "'might get back into it again'" — and stalks off on an impromptu hunt.

Instead of serving as a means of dating the story, the baseball dialogue functions primarily to underscore the manifest theme of initiation common to all of the short stories collected in *In Our Time* (see Summerlin 102). Subtly, with a sense of irony looming behind the words — the boys do not recognize the subtextual import of their remarks — the easy talk of baseball dramatizes the strategies of reticence and evasion that Nick uses to protect himself from pain. In this baseball allusion, Hemingway achieves the same kind of thematic and symbolic unity that marks his best fiction. Charting the education of Nick

Adams requires more than simply plotting his relative position on an arbitrary time line that the critic deems to run through every story, for the temporal component is less crucial to Nick's emotional maturation than the trouble he encounters and the language he invents to render traumatic experiences in intelligible forms. In this sense, Hemingway uses the baseball talk not primarily to place his characters within the scheme of chronological time but to locate them metaphorically on the continuum of their fictive careers. Nick and Bill are represented in their own time, just as the stories, read as a modulated but unified text that plays variations on its major theme, represent something of us in our time.

A Pitcher Playing for Boston

In *A Farewell to Arms* (1929), the baseball allusions bear an even stronger thematic relevance to the greater text. Despite seeming casual, almost offhand, these general, less history-bound baseball tropes achieve a powerful symbolic expression of ideas that anticipates the synecdochic effect of "the great DiMaggio" in *The Old Man and the Sea*. Unlike the allusions to Heinie Zimmerman and the New York Giants in "The Three-Day Blow," the allusions to Babe Ruth and the pennant races in *A Farewell to Arms* are temporally circumscribed and unambiguous. Using these apposite topical references, Hemingway locates Frederic Henry in time as if to underscore Henry's sense of being, as an American in Europe during the First World War, exiled in a foreign place:

> In my room at the hospital I undressed, put on pajamas and a dressing-gown, pulled down the curtains on the door that opened onto the balcony and sitting up in bed read Boston papers from a pile Mrs. Meyers had left for her boys at the hospital. The Chicago White Sox were winning the American League pennant and the New York Giants were leading the National League. Babe Ruth was a pitcher then playing for Boston. The papers were dull, the news was local and stale, and the war news was all old. The American news was all training camps. I was glad I wasn't in a training camp. The baseball news was all I could read and I did not have the slightest interest in it. A number of papers together made it impossible to read with interest. It was not very timely but I read at it for a while. I wondered if America really got into the war, if they would close down the major leagues. They probably wouldn't. There was still racing in Milan and the war could not be much worse.[12]

The throwaway line, "Babe Ruth was a pitcher then playing for Boston," gives the narration a touch of local color, a phrase one must use here with some irony because Frederic Henry is serving in Italy with the Italian Army. The allusion is, however, local to the time if not the places of World War I. The baseball details identify Frederic Henry as an American, which he seems himself to understate

---

[12]A Farewell to Arms *(1929; reprinted, New York: Scribner Paperback Fiction/Simon & Schuster, 1995), 136. Quotations and references follow this edition.*

by claiming uninterest in the baseball news even as he mentions it, as well as to figure him an isolated volunteer caught up in what is essentially a European war.[13] In terms of craft, Hemingway takes a minor gamble in using baseball to dramatize these elements of Henry's character. To remind the reader that Babe Ruth was, at the beginning of his career, a pitcher for the Boston Red Sox, risks introducing an inoperative allusion that achieves little except to signal Henry's awareness of a rudimentary piece of baseball history.[14] On the other hand, one might read the allusion as a foreshadowing of the evolution of Henry's military career; once a wounded hero, he becomes a deserter. The change from star pitcher to premier hitter, which Babe Ruth accomplished a decade before the 1929 publication of *A Farewell to Arms*, describes as unlikely and surprising a development, albeit without the problematic ethical questions. If this reading is valid, the metaphor is one of the more oblique Hemingway used. When one notices, moreover, that the allusion itself is not contiguous to the events but emerges in the process of Henry's retrospective narration — or during the time Hemingway was writing the novel — it seems that Babe Ruth's days as a Red Sox pitcher are merely a temporal marker — as if the First World War were not sufficient to establish the story's historical context.

    The residual baseball content of the passage is more illuminating. The year, of course, is 1917. The United States has declared war on Germany on April 6, but has not landed troops on the Continent until late June. With the baseball season approaching its end, Henry's remarks imply that the pennant winners have been all but mathematically determined. In 1917, the pennant races ended well before the final day: The White Sox won the American League pennant by

---

[13]*In 1918, with America a true combatant, the major leagues did, indeed, halt regular season play several weeks early. In truncating the schedule — they had decided before the season began to shorten spring training and play only 140 games (instead of 154, the regular number until 1961) — baseball owners bowed to the opinions of the editorial pages, particularly those of the* New York Times. *Labor Day, September 2, marked the end of the 1918 regular season, and the World Series opened on September 5, with Babe Ruth pitching a 1–0 shutout for the Red Sox. It is, however, not true that the major leagues were ordered by the President to suspend play. A White House letter of July 27, 1918, reported that President Wilson perceived "no necessity at all for stopping or curtailing the baseball schedule" (quoted by Harold Seymour in* Baseball: The Golden Age *[1971; reprinted, New York: Oxford University Press, 1989], 251). However, the "work or fight" order issued by Provost Marshal Crowder's office on May 23, 1918, did effectively end the season for many players, whom it obliged either to enlist or to find jobs in industries classified as "essential" to the war effort. Baseball owners appealed their business's classification as "nonessential" on the basis of its being the National Game and, so the argument went, indispensable to the morale of industrial workers, who depended on it to offset long working hours. Secretary of War Newton D. Baker rejected the appeal, and 227 major league players ended up enlisting. Others found industrial jobs, often in steel mills and shipyards, where they played baseball in company leagues. Nevertheless, players were free to stay with their teams until they were drafted, just as the teams were free to contrive rosters of bushers and over-the-hill veterans to complete a 154-game schedule. The owners chose the latter strategy during World War II. For an account of baseball during the First World War, see Seymour 244–255.*

[14]*Babe Ruth was a Red Sox pitcher from 1914 through 1919, then was sold to the Yankees and became a full-time outfielder. From 1915 through 1917, the Babe pitched in an average of 39 games a season, almost exclusively as a starting pitcher. In 1918 and 1919, Ruth split his playing time among the outfield, pitching, and first base* (Baseball Encyclopedia *1419, 2116); see also page 56* supra, *note 8.*

nine games over the Boston Red Sox (*Baseball Encyclopedia* 268), and the Giants clinched the National League title on September 24, outstripping the Philadelphia Phillies by 11 games (Alexander 201). One may, therefore, confidently identify the Boston papers as those of late August or early September. In light of the fact that Henry reads these papers in Italy after they have crossed the Atlantic by ship, he presumably gets the baseball news a week or two late; that he reads it at all despite its having, as he claims, no relevance, suggests that he is bored and merely kills time until Catherine comes on duty. Still, he reads it and little else from the Boston papers, as if baseball must recall even to an estranged American the atmosphere of his homeland. Happily, this baseball allusion does not conspire with the sentimental hankering many Americans living abroad feel for home, which typically expresses itself in rhapsodies about mountains, rivers, and plains of amber grain. The passage's chief effect is its portrayal of character: a wounded man disgusted by war who turns for relief to a neutral subject, a game that is both graceful and intense and, when well-played, aesthetically pleasing. It hardly needs to be said that Frederic Henry reads the baseball news because it is wholly unrelated to Europe's entangling animosities and distant from the mayhem of the trenches. The point bears reiteration because it dramatizes Henry's evolving disengagement from the war and presages the separate peace that he manages to negotiate for himself in the later course of events. Thus, his brief escape into baseball is a metaphoric foreshadowing of what will become Frederic Henry's farewell to arms.

The fact that the baseball news catches his eye indicates that Henry might be more homesick than he realizes and more than he — or the tone of the novel — will admit. He does not miss the provincial preoccupations of his countrymen ("the news was local and stale"), nor do America's preparations for its impending plunge into the maelstrom concern him, except to make him happy that he is not "in a training camp." The baseball news, "not very timely" at best and at worst superfluous during a war, is a modest consolation, a sign that the life he has left behind in America continues despite the war's interrupting the continuities of peace. Baseball provides continuity for those who pay attention to it, creating a pattern by which the days from April to October align themselves. Frederic Henry, exiled and displaced, reads the irrelevant baseball news at the tail end of a season that he has observed intermittently across a several-thousand-mile-absence, and in that act expresses more poignantly than his pared-down language suggests a need to rediscover a pattern of continuity and coherence amidst war's tumult. His love affair with Catherine Barkley temporarily establishes such a pattern, even implies a happy homecoming, until that figure is shattered by Catherine's untimely death.

When Catherine dies, Henry articulates the import of her death in unexpected terms that express his anger more forcefully than his mute melting away into the rain. Understanding that this death will open an unmendable fracture in his life, Henry concludes that fate is random and war without conscience, that life itself defies notions of justice and fair play. In keeping with Hemingway's characteristic laconic intensity, Henry's language at this anguished moment describes the inequity of events in a few declarative sentences and one remarkable idiomatic phrase:

> Now Catherine would die. That was what you did. You died. You did not know what it was about. You never had time to learn. They threw you in and told you the rules and the first time they caught you off base they killed you. Or they killed you gratuitously like Aymo. Or gave you the syphilis like Rinaldi. But they killed you in the end. You could count on that. Stay around and they would kill you [*A Farewell to Arms* 327].

The expression "caught off base" is an ordinary phrase of baseball's lexicon, yet it becomes richly suggestive when Frederic Henry uses it to describe the invisible malevolence that seems to have forced Catherine's death. Henry sees Catherine as a reluctant participant in the war, which he depicts as a haphazard, dangerous "game" with vague, infrequently enforceable, often disregarded rules. As a game, war is distinctly unplayful, more an elaborate ritual of execution nearly Kafkaesque in its dispassionate victimization of combatants and civilians alike. As one caught off base, Catherine is revealed as an unskilled player who is quickly "put out" in a game she does not understand, just as those who are more adept at playing the game (Aymo; Rinaldi) are eventually "put out" after what one assumes is a trial of prolonged suffering. Parenthetically, it is worth noting that Catherine is an Englishwoman whose ignorance of baseball would leave her as uncertain of the meaning of Henry's baseball trope as she would be of the necessity of *not* being caught off base.[15] Her ignorance of baseball, for which she can hardly be blamed and ought not to be held accountable, underscores Catherine's essential innocence in relation to the malevolent or indifferent forces that are, in Frederic Henry's ontology, immanent in the cosmos and inimical to human aspirations. It seems as if both kinds of

---

[15]*In* Hemingway: The Writer as Artist *(Princeton, NJ: Princeton University Press, 1972), Carlos Baker notes Hemingway's use of the baseball trope: "Living now seems to be a war-like game, played 'for keeps,' where it is to be tagged out is to die. Here again, there is a moral implication in the idea of being caught off base — trying to steal third, say, when the infield situation and the number of outs make it wiser to stay on second. ... One trouble, of course, is that the player rarely has time enough to learn by long experience; his fatal error may come in the second half of the first inning, which is about as far as Catherine seems likely to go. Even those who survive long enough to learn the rules may be killed through the operation of chance or the accidents of the game. Death may ... come 'gratuitously' without the slightest reference to 'the rules'" (Baker 100). Baker's commentary is slightly muddled by his perceiving a "moral implication" in an ill-conceived play. Trying to steal third with none or two out might be poor baseball strategy, yet it hardly compromises the state of a man's soul. To quibble further, to be thrown out trying to steal a base is not the same thing as to be caught off base. The latter is a mistake of inattention or imperfect judgment — a result of not reacting quickly enough (or of overreacting) to the flight or location of the ball. A runner thrown out stealing usually has committed no mistake other than that of believing his skills equal to his aggressiveness. He is tagged while off base, but one describes him as "thrown out stealing," or "thrown out trying to steal." When a base runner is picked off by the pitcher or catcher, or falls for the hidden ball trick, one says that he has been "caught off base." To say that Catherine has been caught off base is to suggest a confluence of persecution and/or duplicity (on the part of the "game") and poor judgment (on her part). To confuse "caught off base" with "thrown out stealing" is to lose Henry's sense of Catherine as a passive victim, no more complicit in having aggressively shaped her fate than she is blameworthy for not having avoided it.

knowledge are accessible only to men — perhaps only to American men, for baseball is the source of the metaphor — although in the end men survive only nominally better than women.

Catherine, however, is especially disadvantaged on both counts:

> "They won't get us," I said. "Because you're too brave. Nothing ever happens to the brave."
>
> "They die of course."
>
> "But only once."
>
> "I don't know. Who said that?"
>
> "The coward dies a thousand deaths, the brave but one?"
>
> "Of course. Who said it?"
>
> "I don't know."
>
> "He was probably a coward," she said. "He knew a great deal about cowards but nothing about the brave. The brave dies perhaps two thousand deaths if he's intelligent. He simply doesn't mention them."
>
> "I don't know. It's hard to see inside the head of the brave."
>
> "Yes. That's how they keep that way."
>
> "You're an authority."
>
> "You're right, darling. That was deserved."
>
> "You're brave."
>
> "No," she said. "But I would like to be."
>
> "I'm not," I said. "I know where I stand. I've been out long enough to know. I'm like a ball-player that bats two hundred and thirty and knows he's no better."
>
> "What is a ball-player that bats two hundred and thirty? It's awfully impressive."
>
> "It's not. It means a mediocre hitter in baseball."
>
> "But still a hitter," she prodded me.
>
> "I guess we're both conceited," I said. "But you are brave."
>
> "No. But I hope to be."
>
> "We're both brave," I said. "And I'm very brave when I've had a drink" [*A Farewell to Arms* 139–140].

In this conversation, Henry insults Catherine's sense of what it means to be brave through a sarcasm ("'You're an authority'") that suggests a kind of residual disrespect, even resentment. He does not believe that any woman, even one who continues to serve as a nurse in a combat zone after already having lost her fiancé to a mortar shell, can know anything of bravery; she does not, after all, fire a rifle from a trench or charge pell-mell across No-Man's Land. Courage, like war and baseball and the soul's grave pain, is, Frederic Henry apparently believes, negotiable only in the language of men. He emphasizes this point tacitly in the baseball analogy, which he uses in part because he knows that Catherine will not understand it and he will be able to explain it to her. Making her ask what it means to be a .230 hitter is equivalent to making her admit that she understands neither the language of men nor the defining qualities of their world. Slyly, Henry attempts to discredit Catherine's understanding of bravery by revealing her ignorance of baseball. And yet, it is uncertain whether he convinces anyone but himself.

To her credit, Catherine understands Henry's simile of the .230 hitter after he explains it — and better than he might like. However, just as Catherine cannot initially comprehend the baseball metaphor, so too does she fail to perceive Henry's self-disgust with his own lukewarm conviction and unremarkable efforts. She does not, judging from Henry's account, appreciate the disappointment and longing a man feels when he comes to realize that he is only modestly endowed (with bravery; with athletic skill; with intelligence) and cannot increase by one iota his portion of the talents and attributes he can imagine possessing in glorious abundance. Henry covers his dread about the possible consequences of his mediocre bravery with the analogy of a .230 hitter, a characterization that, like every comparison of the non-player or fair amateur to the professional athlete, is nominally self-denigrating but subtly self-aggrandizing — as Catherine shrewdly perceives ("'But still a hitter'") and Henry, "prodded," sheepishly admits: "'I guess we're both conceited.'"

The shrewdness and courage that Catherine can justly claim to possess by the end of the novel are not enough to save her, Henry believes, because no amount of skill or savvy can keep her (or anyone else) from being caught off base. Everyone will register an "out" sooner or later because the nature of the game demands it. Indeed, "they" have designed the terms of participation in a way that requires ultimate capitulation; to modify a line from *The Sun Also Rises*, "they" help you neither to understand the game nor to know how to play it. This view of life as an abusive, murderous game that is lost before play even begins is closer to Hemingway's opinion of football than baseball, yet baseball supplies the apposite metaphor of being caught off base to describe Catherine's ethical position (as an unwed pregnant woman) in relation to the conventional morality of Anglo-American culture, circa 1917.[16] The metaphor might seem "homely and unbookish" to some readers, a figure of speech that might "naturally occur to any young American male at a comparable time" (Baker 100), yet its evocation of a game suggests that Catherine Barkley has been victimized by a punishment egregiously disproportionate to her lapse. Indeed, to a judge who shares Frederic Henry's frame of reference (which claims that "Abstract words such as glory, honor, courage, or hallow were obscene beside the concrete names of villages, the numbers of roads, the names of rivers, the numbers of regiments and the dates" [*A Farewell to Arms* 185]), any conventional notion of chastity is likely to seem so thoroughly irrelevant in wartime as to constitute a form of vulgarity. Charged with the bitterness that Henry feels in the first shock of grief, his conclusion that a person will be killed for being caught off base is a hyperbolically sardonic rejoinder that shifts responsibility from Catherine to an

---

[16]*Hemingway was suspicious of all team sports, but especially disliked the inequitable brutality sanctioned by the football rules. See Messenger 238: "His description of football in* The Torrents of Spring *made explicit his distaste. ... The football center ... performed his work and within the rules was blasted on every offensive play. Thus for Hemingway, football incorporated a terrifying aspect of rules and games: the rules were always set in his opponent's favor. The man opposite him could strike a blow before Hemingway could set himself and without a defense, Hemingway's sportsman felt foolish and stripped of weapons — a quintessential victim."*

anonymous "they" who become, finally, the taskmasters of an inequitable game. "They" compel a doomed performance based on a perfunctory statement of the rules, then exact excessive retribution when the player, who has no true chance to succeed, commits a routine error. Thus, Frederic Henry's baseball metaphor powerfully expresses his disgust with the nameless and pervasive conspiracy that has demanded Catherine's death.

The Great DiMaggio and Others

Hemingway's most extensive use of the baseball allusion appears in *The Old Man and the Sea*. Literary criticism has tended to divide the baseball content of this novel into two unequal parts: Santiago's invocations of "the great DiMaggio" while at sea, and the more specific baseball talk between the old man and the boy. Almost invariably, critics seize upon the allusions to Joe DiMaggio, whose name is familiar to all baseball fans and to most other Americans, as the repository of meaning. The baseball talk of Santiago and Manolin, perhaps because it is highly topical and allusive, typically receives short shrift even from commentators at some pains to establish the significance of the baseball material.[17] To be sure, each reiteration of "the great DiMaggio" demonstrates the expressive efficiency of synecdochic naming; the apostrophe that identifies the famous player provides both Santiago and Hemingway with a simple, coherent formula of professional expertise and committed effort in the face of adversity.[18] However, the baseball dialogue of Santiago and Manolin, whether or not it alludes to Joe DiMaggio, is equally significant in developing the novel's major themes.[19]

It is baseball as much as fishing that has come to define the relationship between Santiago and the boy, which one may describe as that of surrogate father and son. Similarly, the baseball talk dramatizes the dynamic of teaching and learning whereby apprentices develop into seasoned masters. Finally, Santiago's recourse to baseball, particularly his soliloquy of "the great DiMaggio"

---

[17]Exceptions are James Barbour and Robert Sattelmeyer, "Baseball and Baseball Talk in The Old Man and the Sea," Fitzgerald-Hemingway Annual (1975): 281–287; and Richard A. Davidson, "Carelessness and the Cincinnati Reds in The Old Man and the Sea," Notes on Contemporary Literature 1 (1971): 11–13.

[18]The Old Man and the Sea (New York: Charles Scribner's Sons, 1952), 18, 23, 75, 107, 114, 116. Quotations and references follow this edition and are cited as Old Man.

[19]In "The Sham Battle Over Ernest Hemingway," in Western Review 17 (Spring 1953): 234–240, Ray B. West contends that the baseball content is "unsuccessful — because not integrated into the story. Imagine ... how many footnotes would be necessary in order to prepare an edition for a French or a German, and you will see the most obvious objection..." ("Sham Battle" 240). It seems that West would have preferred Hemingway to have either omitted the baseball talk and "the great DiMaggio" or to have embedded identifying glosses in the text. For obvious reasons both alternatives are wrongheaded, yet not as mistaken as the critic's assumption that a writer is responsible for the ignorance of his (foreign) readers.

during his trial of isolation and pain, is an expression of his need for something that is reliable, predictable, familiar: a psychic or metaphoric sense of what home means, especially to a character whose own home is threatened. By inscribing the story's major themes in the baseball material, Hemingway infuses events with a spiritual coherence that arrays ordinary details in a pattern of meaning. Thus, the requirements of the story's formal realism are to a great extent satisfied by Hemingway's successful integration of the baseball allusions. The dialogue with Manolin and the invocations of "the great DiMaggio" are hopeful gestures of solidarity and *sympatico,* words spoken on a level of discourse above that of common small-talk. Given Santiago's precarious hold on life and his epic battles against marlin and sharks, the imagined figure of his baseball idol aspires to a symbolism that is almost mythic. DiMaggio's accomplishments and abilities are an inspiration, and Santiago's appeals to him a kind of prayer.

As an established master of his trade, Santiago figures to Manolin as role model and bearer of vocational knowledge. In conversations with the boy, the old man speaks as father and teacher. Baseball, the game Manolin might play instead of fishing the true Gulf, seems to exist on the periphery of their lives yet preoccupies their talk despite (or because of) chronic difficulties that are too embarrassing for Santiago to admit and too distressing for Manolin to name. The old man has insufficient food and is bereft of even the tools of his trade, privations that his fictious references to a "'pot of yellow rice with fish'" (17) and a cast net emphasize:

> There was no cast net and the boy remembered when they had sold it. But they went through this fiction every day. There was no pot of yellow rice and fish and the boy knew this too.
> "Eighty-five is a lucky number," the old man said. "How would you like to see me bring one in that dressed out over a thousand pounds?"
> "I'll get the cast net and go for sardines. Will you sit in the sun in the doorway?"
> "Yes. I have yesterday's paper and I will read the baseball."
> The boy did not know whether yesterday's paper was a fiction too. But the old man brought it out from under the bed.
> "Perico gave it to me at the *bodega,*" he explained.
> "I'll be back when I have the sardines. I'll keep yours and mine together on ice and we can share them in the morning. When I come back you can tell me about the baseball."
> "The Yankees cannot lose."
> "But I fear the Indians of Cleveland."
> "Have faith in the Yankees my son. Think of the great DiMaggio" [*Old Man* 17–18].

Santiago and Manolin are involved in a conspiracy of reticence designed to obfuscate an ancient fear. Death hovers near Santiago; its signs are poverty, hunger, and 84 fishless days. The interest he takes in baseball, particularly the pennant races, is a temporary relief from worry, a distraction from the desperate situation that his life has become. Given his suffering, one might expect

Santiago to regard baseball as frivolous, a waste of time; the fact that he does not, that he considers the game important in its own way, might suggest delusion, even a form of insanity, were he not able to examine the dire circumstances of his life with lucidity and self-possession.[20] As a diversion, really as the only form of leisure he can afford, Santiago reads about baseball in the newspaper and talks about the game with Manolin to remind himself that he has not lost everything, that this part of his life retains the pleasure it has provided in the past. In its history, in the day-to-day unfolding of its season, baseball is a pleasure to which Santiago can look forward, a comfort on which he can look back. It is a part of the future that is neither implicitly threatened nor manifestly doomed, as well as a part of the past that, because of the reflective conversations with Manolin, enjoys continuity with the present. Baseball's temporal plasticity makes it a steady companion for Santiago, who is in many ways being defeated by time. Indeed, the game's symbolic content offers Santiago hope; baseball's long season, its cyclical return in the juvenescence of the year, is implicitly one of revivification. Santiago does not have the luxury of resorting to abstractions in trying to understand his life, but the reader is at liberty to imagine that, through baseball, the old man may metaphorically postpone death. The game's clockless scheme and counterclockwise movement symbolically indicate Santiago's resistance to temporal limits and the decrepitude that time's passing incurs. The baseball season, like the season of the big fish, will eventually end, then return again. The self-conscious fictions of the cast net and the pot of rice and fish are prideful lies, prevarications that cover Santiago's fear of death, but yesterday's newspaper with box scores and game stories is real: a small, good thing that imparts solace and helps the old man complete the effort of living into the next day. These fragments he has shored against his ruins.

To argue that baseball preserves Santiago's life is not, however, merely to extend a fanciful metaphor beyond its plausible limits, for baseball truly does help to keep the old man in touch with the boy. His bond with Manolin keeps Santiago alive; it is his one abiding source of human companionship and, indispensably, his only dependable source of food. Manolin has been Santiago's apprentice. Now a fisherman in his own right, he works, on orders from his natural father, from another boat, but Santiago continues as his mentor by educating the boy in the important subject of baseball. Understanding Santiago's predicament, Manolin initiates their baseball talk as a way of honoring his teacher. And yet, what "honoring" amounts to in this case is caretaking. Manolin brings food to Santiago, buys him beer, catches sardines to bait his lines; he spends time with the old man, talks to him, encourages him. In the effort to preserve Santiago's life, Manolin feeds his adoptive father in body and spirit. The reciprocity of their relationship finds poignant yet unsentimental expression in the dinner

---

[20]For example, after he has killed the marlin, Santiago ponders the ways of life and death, and recognizes that his labor alone does not sustain him: *"everything kills everything else in some way. Fishing kills me exactly as it keeps me alive. The boy keeps me alive, he thought. I must not deceive myself too much"* (Old Man 117).

they share with talk of baseball. The clean, simple give-and-take of eating and conversation dramatizes a friendship that affects the sensibilities like love:

> "Your stew is excellent," the old man said.
> "Tell me about the baseball," the boy asked him.
> "In the American League it is the Yankees as I said," the old man said happily.
> "They lost today," the boy told him.
> "That means nothing. The great DiMaggio is himself again."
> "They have other men on the team."
> "Naturally. But he makes the difference. In the other league, between Brooklyn and Philadelphia I must take Brooklyn. But then I think of Dick Sisler and those great drives in the old park."
> "There was nothing ever like them. He hits the longest ball I have ever seen."
> "Do you remember when he used to come to the Terrace? I wanted to take him fishing but I was too timid to ask him. Then I asked you to ask him and you were too timid."
> "I know. It was a great mistake. He might have gone with us. Then we would have that for all of our lives."
> "I would like to take the great DiMaggio fishing," the old man said. "They say his father was a fisherman. Maybe he was as poor as we are and would understand."
> "The great Sisler's father was never poor and he, the father, was playing in the big leagues when he was my age."
> "When I was your age I was before the mast on a square rigged ship that ran to Africa and I have seen lions on the beaches in the evening."
> "I know. You told me."
> "Should we talk about Africa or about baseball?"
> "Baseball I think," the boy said. "Tell me about the great John J. McGraw." He said *Jota* for J.
> "He used to come to the Terrace sometimes too in the older days. But he was rough and harsh-spoken and difficult when he was drinking. His mind was on horses as well as baseball. At least he carried lists of horses at all times in his pocket and frequently spoke the names of horses on the telephone."
> "He was a great manager," the boy said. "My father thinks he was the greatest."
> "Because he came here the most times," the old man said. "If Durocher had continued to come here each year your father would think him the greatest manager."
> "Who is the greatest manager, really, Luque or Mike Gonzalez?"
> "I think they are equal."
> "And the best fisherman is you."
> "No. I know others better."
> "*Qué va*," the boy said. "There are many good fishermen and some great ones. But there is only you" [*Old Man* 22–25].

Despite the master-apprentice subtext, the tone of their dialogue is neither pedagogic nor tasking. The quality of initiation, of the man revealing secrets and explaining subtleties to the boy, removes the element of one-upmanship; the chiding is gentle, almost indulgent, their purpose not to prove points but to discover truth. As in every true dialogue, an exchange occurs: Manolin learns and helps the old man live; Santiago finds shelter against despair. Baseball opens a clean, well-lighted space beyond poverty and hunger, beyond fear, beyond all pain, a space where friends share encouragement, reassurance, praise.

In their baseball dialogue Santiago instructs Manolin in a man's wisdom, as if the game were part of tribal custom or cultural lore rather than the national pastime of a foreign land. One piece of knowledge that he wishes to impart is that of finding one's own best figure of inspiration and acting as a witness of the great man's deeds. Santiago assumes this role in relation to Joe DiMaggio (although he witnesses DiMaggio's feats only through the newspaper) and tacitly hopes that Manolin will follow this example by choosing him (Santiago) as the subject of professional reverence. They approach the matter by short, linked questions: Who will win the pennant? Who makes the difference? "'Who is the greatest manager...?'" "'And the best fisherman is you.'" Santiago declines the boy's praise with proper humility — "'I know others better'" — for the true professional is self-effacing, especially before an acolyte. And yet, the old man is gratified by Manolin's judgment because he believes he has earned it. The dialogue unfolds beautifully, moving within a fluent exchange to a statement of heartfelt veneration. "'There are many good fishermen and some great ones. But there is only you,'" the boy tells the old man, placing him apart from all others, affirming that he is unique. In his praise Manolin speaks more literally than he knows, for on the true Gulf in his small boat, Santiago is truly alone. He understands that he can teach Manolin about respect and emulation only through the example of his actions, yet is compelled, ironically, to perform his exemplary feats on the solitude of the sea. In his fight with the marlin, amidst heroic fatigue, Santiago seeks a witness as much as he longs for help: "'I wish I had the boy. To help me and to see this'" *(Old Man* 52).[21] Despite his isolation and Manolin's absence, Santiago's respect for "the great DiMaggio" and Manolin's prior fishing experiences with the old man seem to have coalesced for the boy into a compelling model of heroic action and witnessing.

The conversation's father-and-son subtext, expressed in every line, establishes a pattern of surrogate paternity that clarifies the dialectical relationship of the old man and the boy, as well as that of Santiago and "the great DiMaggio." Thinking of DiMaggio's father, a San Francisco fisherman, Santiago regards the famous ballplayer as a spiritual son: He might "'take the great DiMaggio fishing,'" that is, initiate him in the ways of the father, which the son might come to understand. It is not surprising, therefore, that Santiago regards DiMaggio's father with respect, for the elder DiMaggio's vocation makes identification not only possible but easy. In this way, Santiago can figure in his own imagination as the proud father of his own hero. And yet it is not the father but the son who is "the great DiMaggio," the celebrated athlete who, in terms of success as the world reckons it, stands in relation to the father as Aeneas does to Anchises.[22]

[21]*See* Old Man *49, 55, 57, 62, 68, 91.*

[22]*Having come of age in the Trojan War, having wandered for years afterward in search of a home, Aeneas ultimately figures as the father of a new civilization, uniting the Latins and the Trojans and becoming the founder of Lavinium, the city that becomes Rome. Anchises, father of Aeneas, is a Trojan prince and a paramour of Aphrodite. He does not figure in any of the important myths of either the Greeks or the Romans.*

When Santiago defeats the marlin, he tells himself, "'I think the great DiMaggio would be proud of me today'" (Old Man 107), as if his first concern were to fulfill a father's expectations. Similarly, after killing the first shark, he reconsiders his job-well-done as if he were hoping to win a father's praise: "I wonder how the great DiMaggio would have liked the way I hit him in the brain?" (Old Man 114). The reversal of the father-son relationship that is implicit in this language is prefigured in the paternal solicitude with which Manolin attends to the old man's welfare. So, too, has Manolin matured as a fisherman while Santiago has struggled through three luckless months, suggesting that the son has supplanted the father in his traditional role.[23] The apparent supremacy of sons engages that aspect of the American Dream (not wholly irrelevant to the story of this Cuban fisherman) that holds out the promise of filial betterment. By climbing upon his father's shoulders, the son will stand taller, see farther, come that much closer to touching the sky.

The comments about Dick Sisler, however, reestablish certain Old World ideas (also pertinent to the novel) about paternal dominance; that Santiago first mentions Dick Sisler (the son) and Manolin expands the allusion's scope by referring to "'the great Sisler's father'" is much to the point of a dialectic. Dick Sisler, although a major league player and an obviously memorable home run hitter, did not equal the accomplishments of his father, George Sisler, who was elected to the Hall of Fame in 1939.[24] Of all statistics, perhaps the most telling one in the present context is longevity: George Sisler played in the major leagues for sixteen years (1915–1930); his son, Dick, played for eight years (1946–1953). This allusion confirms two crucial truths: that Santiago lives in a dusty twilight years beyond the best of his time, and that if much is taken, much abides, that the strength of El Campeón has waned but the heroic temper and proud heart endure. Santiago is not ready to surrender, much less to die; he is unwilling to yield his place to any son. His vital memories, of which he dreams at night, are signs as eloquent as the tropes of baseball and paternity; indeed, these memories tend even to undermine the claims one can make for the baseball material. Once a boy before the mast of a ship bound for Africa, Santiago is not impressed by George Sisler's having played in the major leagues at Manolin's

[23]Santiago might be regarded as a dying fertility god, a symbolic association that becomes important in Malamud's The Natural. Manolin is a kind of acolyte who witnesses the old god's loss of critical power — in this context, the power to bring forth nourishment from the fickle, indifferent sea (la mer, as Santiago thinks of it). As a dying fertility god, Santiago's condition is ameliorated by Manolin and the enthusiasm they share for baseball; like his dream of lions on an African beach, baseball and Manolin renew the old man's vitality.

[24]The elder Sisler's nickname was "Gorgeous George," but the son was a larger man (6'2" 205 lbs. to 5'11" 170 lbs.) and hit home runs about twice as often — including four home runs in two days while playing winter baseball in Cuba, from December 1945 to February 1946, before starting his career in the major leagues. Dick Sisler led the Cuban League in home runs that winter and belted one ball over 500 feet and completely out of Tropical Stadium, which Santiago calls "'the old park.'" The next day, Sisler hit three home runs and became famous in Cuba, even garnering a gold medal from the government. See Samuel E. Longmire, "Hemingway's Praise of Dick Sisler in The Old Man and the Sea," American Literature 42 (March 1970): 96–98. See also Baseball Encyclopedia 1462.

age.[25] Manolin, for his part, does not gainsay the old man's sense of himself as superior to the elder Sisler, who was merely playing a "boys' game" while Santiago was watching lions on beaches of African white and gold. Curiously, Santiago was "'too timid'" to approach the son, Dick Sisler, with an invitation to go fishing because the younger man's prowess in hitting a baseball reduced the fisherman's self-confidence to diffidence and awe — a response that aligns him with Manolin, a boy, also "'too timid'" to presume an intimacy of an athletic hero.

The other baseball names, John McGraw and Leo Durocher, Adolpho Luque and Miguel Angel Cordero (Mike) Gonzalez, introduce the idea of professionalism by juxtaposing American and Cuban managers. McGraw and Durocher, both famous managers in the National League — and, in different eras, of the New York Giants — visited Cuba during the off-season to manage teams of American major leaguers in exhibition games.[26] McGraw, his attention divided between baseball and horse racing (and other forms of gambling), impresses Santiago only as an imperfect model of professional commitment, despite his success. Further, McGraw's reputation as a gambling man (he owned, with Giants' owner Charles A. Stoneham, the Oriental Racetrack and the Cuban American Jockey Club, as well as the Casino Nacional, all in Havana [Seymour 389]) and loutish brawler precludes Santiago's esteem.[27] Leo Durocher, known as a fighter, gambler, and an obnoxious if entertaining (to some; not umpires) loudmouth of the ball field, as a player known as "The All-American Out," as a manager known as "Leo the Lip," is a baseball descendant of John McGraw and is

[25]*George Sisler broke into the majors at the age of 22 (Baseball Encyclopedia 1462), which suggests either that Manolin (or Hemingway) has a mistaken notion of the elder Sisler's precocity or that both Manolin and Santiago have entered their own "man's world" much later than is implied. Whether Manolin is the adolescent he seems or the 22 of George Sisler's major league debut is never clarified.*

[26]*As a rookie minor leaguer, 16-year-old John McGraw visited Cuba for the first time as a member of Al Lawson's 1890 American All-Stars and became a favorite of the Cuban fans, who dubbed him "el mono amarillo" ("the yellow monkey") because of his size, speed, and uniform (the All-Stars wore yellow). As a manager, McGraw first brought the New York Giants to Cuba in November of 1911 for a four-week, twelve-game series against the Havana Reds and Almendares. McGraw returned to Cuba for part of the off-season nearly every year (Alexander 17–19; 183, 189, 195, 203, 227, 233, 239, 253, 276), usually for a vacation that included gambling.*

[27]*See Alexander's John McGraw, 71–72, 105, 126, for McGraw's love of betting on the ponies, and 216 for his purchase of the Oriental Racetrack complex, "which included ... a casino, restaurant, and small hotel." Alexander also recounts a story about McGraw in Cuba that may well account for Santiago's dislike ("'he was rough and harsh-spoken and difficult when he was drinking'"): During a 1911 game pitched by the Almendares' José Mendez, a black Cuban and a national hero for frequently defeating American teams, McGraw offended the fans at Tropical Stadium ("'the old park'") by shouting, "as loudly and irreverently as possible" (Alexander 160), "Who is that guy?" in the customary silence that fell as a sign of respect from the Cuban fans when the 5'10", 150-pound pitcher took the mound. Mendez was touched for a two-run triple in that inning and lost the game to Christy Mathewson (who called Mendez "a great pitcher"). Later (about 3:00 A.M. the next day), after a party in a Havana restaurant, McGraw and umpire Cy Rigler were menaced by a group of Cubans wielding a knife — they were still upset by McGraw's antics and by his argument with Almendares catcher Miguel (Mike) Gonzalez in the previous game. Rigler managed to disarm the Cubans, but he and McGraw were taken into police custody. Far from dismissing the charges, the judge levied a fine of $20 apiece and ordered both men to publish an apology in the Havana* Post, *an English-language newspaper, for "any disrespect they may have appeared to show toward Cuban baseball or the Cuban people" (Alexander 159–160).*

equally unlikely to have won Santiago's respect.[28] Conversely, Adolfo Luque[29] ("The Pride of Havana") and Mike Gonzalez[30] were both native-born Cubans who played in the major leagues and returned to Cuba as managers, where they were renowned for their knowledge of the game. Because baseball acuity is in its essence a matter of responding shrewdly and effectively, in terms of using both players and game strategy, to the ongoing process of any particular game and to the long series of games that constitute a season, it is impossible to measure; like interpretative reading, managing a baseball team demands conscientious attention to the present context, as well as inventive responses to the opportunities and challenges that the context offers. Adolfo Luque and Mike Gonzalez manage within a context that Santiago and Manolin understand and can appraise for themselves, and so the two Cuban stars vie for the unofficial title of "greatest manager."

To Santiago, however, the greatest player and most profound inspiration is Joe DiMaggio. Hemingway's prominent use of DiMaggio in *The Old Man and the Sea*, like his broader use of baseball in the novel, has drawn a variety of responses. Some critics judge the baseball material ineffective, even distracting, and describe its effect on the conversations between Santiago and Manolin in the novel's first movement, before the old man rows "out too far" *(Old Man* 133), as trivializing and bathetic. Similarly, Santiago's invocations of "the great DiMaggio" tend, for these readers, to diminish the fisherman's stature as a code hero engrossed in a life-and-death battle with marlin and sharks.[31] Other critics,

[28]*Durocher, then the manager of the Brooklyn Dodgers, held spring training in Havana during February and March of 1947. By Opening Day he had been suspended for the entire season by Happy Chandler, then the commissioner of baseball, for allegedly consorting with gamblers. Other than having spent some weeks the previous autumn living in George Raft's house, Durocher maintained that he was innocent of any wrongdoing. Once, then–NL president Ford Frick fined Durocher $100 and suspended him for five days for "prolonged argument and conduct on the field tending to incite a riot."* See Gene Karst and Martin J. Jones, Jr., Who's Who in Professional Baseball *(New Rochelle, NY: Arlington House, 1973), 270–275, and* Nice Guys Finish Last, *Durocher's autobiography with Ed Linn (New York: Simon & Schuster, 1975).*

[29]*On their 1911, tour McGraw's Giants were beaten by a diminutive right-hander from the Havana Reds named Adolfo Luque (Alexander 159). In 1914, Luque, a white Cuban, began a major league career that would last 20 seasons (Baseball Encyclopedia 1968).*

[30]*Miguel (Mike) Gonzalez was among the first Cubans to play in the major leagues. As a coach and scout for the St. Louis Cardinals, Gonzalez, to whom English remained foreign, struck upon the telling "Good field, no hit" to summarize a ballplayer's talent (Baseball Encyclopedia 1001–1002).*

[31]*In 1953, Ray B. West opined that the baseball talk is essentially fatuous and ineffective: "American sports are not capable — at least, not yet — of carrying the mythological burden Hemingway puts upon them" ("Sham Battle" 240). Several years later, West strikes a similar note in his comments on Mark Harris's* Bang the Drum Slowly *(1956): "How much more [than baseball Harris's novel is about] depends, in part, upon how one views the possibility of baseball to convey that larger and more universal world that it is designed to image. As symbolic hero (and despite Hemingway's use of Dimaggio [sic] in* The Old Man and the Sea), the baseball player is at least once removed from the bullfighter, who is not merely playing a game but is facing possible death each time he steps into the ring." See Ray B. West, "Six Authors in Search of a Hero," Sewanee Review 65:3 *(Summer 1957): 498–508. For other disparaging opinions of DiMaggio's presence in the novel, see Robert G. Davis, "Hemingway's Tragic Fisherman," in the* New York Times Book Review *(September 7, 1952), 20; and Claire Rosenfield, "New Worlds, Old Myths," reprinted in* Twentieth Century Interpretations of The Old Man and the Sea, *edited by Katherine T. Jobes (Englewood Cliffs, NJ: Prentice-Hall, 1968), 50–52.*

however, recognize the special rhetorical effect of Santiago's repeated allusions to "the great DiMaggio."[32] Of these, some read the novel as a drama of personal metamorphosis: Beginning as an individualistic, isolated, and prideful code hero, Santiago passes through a three-day ordeal that transforms him into a Christly fellow who is acutely sensible of the necessity of human solidarity and the inevitable interdependence of all living things.[33] Constructing this model obliges the critic, in the course of summarizing the historical background, to place special emphasis on the idea of DiMaggio as the consummate team player, the man who "'makes the difference'" because the whole effect of his effort is much greater than the sum of his separate statistics.[34] As an individual performer of great talent and impeccable steadfastness, playing always for the success of the team, "the great DiMaggio" is read as a simplistic analogue of what becomes Santiago's own ethos of selflessness and altruism.[35]

Santiago's inveterate striving against death, however, renders him implausible as a figurement of Christ. He is an uncooperative martyr, perhaps because anything like a martyr's cause is absent. An alternative scenario, also adumbrated with exemplary thoroughness since the novel's publication, depicts

---

[32]*In "The Great Santiago: Opium, Vocation, and Dream in* The Old Man and the Sea," *Fitzgerald-Hemingway Annual (1976): 230–242, Samuel S. Baskett offers a strong contextual reading of the DiMaggio allusions that presupposes their seriousness. Christian K. Messenger posits a familiar triangular relationship among Santiago, DiMaggio, and Hemingway, in which each figures as an analogue of the others in terms of a professional's completing his work despite injury; see* Sport and the Spirit of Play in American Fiction, *291–296. In "Santiago, DiMaggio, and Hemingway: The Ageing Professionals of* The Old Man and the Sea," *Fitzgerald-Hemingway Annual (1975): 273–280, George Monteiro uses newspaper accounts of DiMaggio's return to the Yankee lineup in June 1949, following off-season heel surgery and a spring-long recuperation, to establish DiMaggio as an inspiring performative figure; cited as "Ageing Pros." David Halberstam recounts DiMaggio's dramatic reappearance in* Summer of '49 *(New York: William Morrow, 1989), 141–145, 148–149. Barbour and Sattelmeyer focus on the conversations of Santiago and Manolin in "Baseball and Baseball Talk in* The Old Man and the Sea" *(see note 17, supra). In* Ernest Hemingway: A Reconsideration *(University Park: Pennsylvania University Press, 1966), Philip Young notes the effect of baseball in the novel: "Baseball works a charm on the pages of this book. The talk about it is vastly real, it gives a little play to the line when unrelieved tension would be dangerous, and the sober conversations about it, which Santiago conducts with himself and with the boy, are delicious in their own right" (Young 130). In* The American Dream and the National Game, *Leverett T. Smith examines the legend of Joe DiMaggio constructed by the popular press, including the early "autobiography"* Lucky to Be a Yankee *(1946), to evaluate the symbolic effectiveness of "the great DiMaggio." In Smith's account, DiMaggio emerges as the consummate professional who plays at his work (and works at his game) with an amateur's love (Smith 84–100). In* The Sporting Myth and the American Experience, *Wiley Lee Umphlett offers a relatively straightforward reading of the relationship between Santiago and DiMaggio, stressing the value of performance despite pain and the necessity of endurance despite hardship (Umphlett 79–80).*

[33]*See Clinton S. Burhans, Jr., "*The Old Man and the Sea: *Hemingway's Tragic Vision of Man," American Literature 31 (January 1960): 446–455, especially 447, 452–453.*

[34]*Joe DiMaggio played from 1936 to 1942, then from 1946 through 1951 (like many others, he lost the 1943 through 1945 seasons to World War II). Of the 13 pennants contested during DiMaggio's playing career, the Yankees won ten; of ten World Series, the Yankees won nine (Baseball Encyclopedia 907–908; 2749–2764).*

[35]*Burhans emphasizes DiMaggio's role as a "'team player'— one who always displayed his individual greatness as part of his team, one to whom the team was always more important than himself" (Burhans 451).*

Santiago as unchangingly the prideful, combative code hero of Hemingway's fiction.[36] In this reading, Santiago's association with Christian motifs does not transform him into a limpid sentimentalist unmanned by the tenets of abject love and humility but rather plays off the *suggestion* of Christ against the always-withheld affirmation of Christ's symbolic incarnation in the Cuban fisherman. The effect is a rhetorical paradox: simultaneously implying the paradigm and denying it "sanctifies a non-Christian ethos."[37] According to this model, the imagery that constructs Santiago as an archetype of the persecuted Christ equally projects a secular contest or passion, such as that of a prizefighter tasked by the law of the ring: Kill or be killed. Not incidentally, this dictum is also Nature's foremost law. Deciding that Santiago retains "the pride and self-esteem of the fighter and killer" (Wittkowski 7), the critic concludes that "the fighter-in-the-ring model subsumes the Christ model" (Wittkowski 16). In such a scheme, Santiago's regard for Joe DiMaggio becomes a combatant's respect for the prowess of a formidable peer. Santiago's is a respect raised nearly to the level of adoration because the professional deportment of "the great DiMaggio" makes him, among all players, unique (Wittkowski 4).[38]

More to the point are Hemingway's specific allusions to DiMaggio as the injured athlete, the player of extraordinary ability and technical expertise who is, in relative terms, handicapped by physical debility and age. The parallel of ballplayer and fisherman is evident. Santiago analogizes DiMaggio's performance despite pain to his own endurance during the bad streak of 84 barren days, and so is heartened that, as he tells Manolin, "'The great DiMaggio is himself again'" *(Old Man* 23). For himself, Santiago believes that now that the big fish of September have come, he, too, will return to form and become once again *El Campeón* of the true Gulf. Nearly enfeebled by age and malnourishment, thought "definitely and finally *salao,* which is the worst form of unlucky" *(Old Man* 9), Santiago continues "cheerful and undefeated." With Manolin's encouragement, he finds that "His hope and his confidence had never gone. But now they were freshening as when the breeze rises" *(Old Man* 14). Abiding ability and unrelenting will—"'I know many tricks and I have resolution'" *(Old Man* 25)—embolden him to continue, to use every resource of courage, perseverance, and skill to capture the marlin and resist the sharks. Santiago proves that his confidence is not delusive and that his selection of DiMaggio as the locus of ideal performance is neither unthinking nor specious. The ballplayer is not a factotum used to suppress an old man's fear in the midst of a death-dream; he is an icon that inspires strength exactly because Santiago believes, with a

[36]*Philip Young defines the Hemingway code hero in* Ernest Hemingway: A Reconsideration, *96–97.*

[37]*Wolfgang Wittkowski, "Crucified in the Ring: Hemingway's* The Old Man and the Sea," *16, translated by Veysey and Wells, in* The Hemingway Review *3:1 (Fall 1983): 2–17.*

[38]*In a footnote, Wittkowski contradicts Burhans's explication of the DiMaggio allusions: "DiMaggio, after all, was famous as a 'team player.' Nothing, however, in the text calls that to mind. Here the accent is placed on the uniqueness of the champion, and not, as Burhans would like, on the solidarity and interdependence among people" (Wittkowski 4, n. 9a).*

kind of unjustifiable faith, that some occult spiritual kinship links him to his hero, this ballplayer whom he has never met.[39]

A word of baseball history makes the relationship that Santiago imagines between himself and Joe DiMaggio more intelligible. In 1949, Joe DiMaggio missed the Yankees' first 65 games (a streak not unlike Santiago's 84 fishless days, both of which stand in tacit contradistinction from DiMaggio's unmatched run of success: his 56-game hitting streak of 1941[40]) because of burning pain in his right heel, which had been operated on for bone spurs in November, 1948. He hobbled around on crutches through much of the spring and into summer, but when he began playing again on June 28, 1949, the pain had disappeared (Halberstam 44–45, 122, 141–143). When Santiago reiterates his concern about the bone spurs — despite reassuring Manolin earlier that "'The great DiMaggio is himself again'" *(Old Man* 23) — he either does not realize or has forgotten, in the extremity of his own hardship, that DiMaggio's pain is gone. It might be that Santiago refers to the 1948 season, in which DiMaggio played 153 of 154 games, almost all of them in acute pain (Halberstam 43). Still, DiMaggio's infirmity was · remediated by surgery and convalescence. Without underestimating the severity of his injury or the suffering he endured throughout the 1948 season to fulfill his professional obligations — or the frustration and sense of uselessness he felt in sitting out the first third of the 1949 season (Halberstam 122, 127–128) — one must conclude that DiMaggio's debility was temporary and, even in relative terms, short-lived. Santiago, dreaming of lions on the beaches of a long-gone youth, is headed toward death even as he strives grimly against it. No surgery can deliver Santiago from his suffering; for him, convalescence is impossible. Isolated on the true Gulf, the taut line cutting into his palms and across his back, Santiago requires a hero who is larger than life, defies pain, succeeds despite injury:

> I must have confidence and I must be worthy of the great DiMaggio who does all things perfectly even with the pain of the bone spur in his heel. What is a bone spur? he asked himself. *Un espuela de hueso.* We do not have them. Can it be as painful as the spur of a fighting cock in one's heel? [*Old Man* 75]
>
> ******
>
> Do you believe the great DiMaggio would stay with a fish as long as I will stay with this one? he thought. I am sure he would and more since he is young and strong. Also his father was a fisherman. But would the bone spur hurt him too much? "I do not know," he said aloud. "I never had a bone spur" [*Old Man* 75–76].

---

[39]*It is not possible to say, as Cordelia Candelaria does in* Seeking the Perfect Game: Baseball in American Literature *(New York: Greenwood Press, 1989), that "Hemingway wrote about baseball as he wrote about other physical endeavors such as hunting, fishing, boxing, and bullfighting" (Candelaria 55) and approach the truth about Hemingway's baseball allusions. The critic's discussion of* The Old Man and the Sea *is cursory at best: Candelaria sums up the baseball content with the remark that "Santiago/Hemingway's view of baseball crystallizes the pastoral view into a touchstone of perfection and hope against even debilitating odds" (Candelaria 55). The all-purpose "pastoral" neither successfully characterizes Santiago's oceanic trial nor accounts for the Cuban fisherman's unique relationship to baseball, Manolin, and the inspirational figure of "the great DiMaggio."*

[40]*See Michael Seidel,* Streak: Joe DiMaggio and the Summer of '41 *(New York: Penguin Books, 1988), for a detailed contextual history of DiMaggio's charmed 56 games.*

Santiago's imagination supplies the image of Joe DiMaggio, practically crippled by pain, performing with innate grace and power the fine, difficult skills of baseball.[41] Whether he forgets or underestimates the extent of DiMaggio's recovery, the distortion serves Santiago's need more completely than could any merely accurate representation of the facts, a paradox he himself seems to understand. Indeed, the fiction of an ongoing injury might well be Santiago's self-conscious creation, given his earlier statement, "'The great DiMaggio is himself again'" (*Old Man* 23). Reconciling his apparent knowledge of DiMaggio's recovery to Santiago's remarks about bone spurs, one is left with the impression that Santiago constructs his own version of an incompletely healed DiMaggio who simultaneously "'is himself again'" in the splendor of his performance if not in the soundness of his body. In light of Santiago's own physical pain, it is not surprising that any reports he might have read over the past two or three years about DiMaggio's bone spurs would have stayed in his mind, or that he would have permanently incorporated this injury into the image he conceives of his hero. For Santiago's needs of comparison and identification, DiMaggio must be scarred; for aesthetic purposes, perhaps as a bit of facile symbolism, it is fitting that the exemplary athletic hero be impaired by a modern version of the Achilles's heel.

Thus, the approximation of DiMaggio's standing in his profession at age 34 (in 1949) to Santiago's own plight counts for much in the latter's imagination and inspires the fisherman's hero worship of the ballplayer. It hardly needs to be said that this approximation is purely metaphoric; indeed, Santiago's apparent indifference to (or ignorance of) Joe DiMaggio's material affluence threatens to diminish the analogy's potency and even endangers the reader's regard for the Cuban fisherman — and for the author who proposes a baseball player earning $100,000 per season as the spiritual *confrère* of a man without even a pot of rice.[42] The incongruity between the socio-economic status of Joe DiMaggio, baseball's best center fielder on baseball's greatest team in America's

---

[41]In "*The Interior Stadium*," *Roger Angell conveys his sense of DiMaggio's extraordinary skills: "Joe DiMaggio batting sometimes gave the same impression — the suggestion that the old rules and dimensions of baseball no longer applied to him, and that the game had at last grown unfairly easy. I saw DiMaggio once during his famous hitting streak in 1941; I'm not sure of the other team or the pitcher — perhaps it was the Tigers and Bobo Newsom — but I'm sure of DiMaggio pulling a line shot to left that collided preposterously with the bag at third base and ricocheted halfway out to center field. That record of hitting safely in fifty-six straight games seems as secure as any in baseball, but it does not awe me as much as the fact that DiMadge's old teammates claim they never saw him commit an error of judgment in a ball game. Thirteen years, and never a wrong throw, a cutoff man missed, an extra base passed up. Well, there was one time when he stretched a single against the Red Sox and was called out at second, but the umpire is said to have admitted later that he blew the call" (The Summer Game 288). "The Interior Stadium" appears in Angell's The Summer Game (1972; reprinted, New York: Ballantine Books, 1989), 281–293.*

[42]*George Monteiro quotes a* Time *magazine article of April 25, 1949, that pegs DiMaggio's salary at $90,000 ("Ageing Pros" 274). Monteiro argues that the baseball talk refers "to events from two consecutive seasons. Their remarks on team competition relate to the 1950 season ... but their references to DiMaggio pertain to events of the previous [1949] season" ("Ageing Pros" 273). Of DiMaggio's salary, the press reported it variously as $90,000 and $100,000. See The DiMaggio Albums, vol. 2, edited by Richard Whittingham (New York: G. P. Putnam's Sons, 1989), 568–569, 572, 575, 590.*

most famous city, and Santiago's threadbare obscurity in an island fishing village risks severing the skein of metaphoric associations that unites them. Today, in the pall of cynicism that descends on the average spectator when he regards the professional athlete, in many cases absurdly young, who is enriched to a degree beyond imagining for playing a game, it is easy to consider Santiago's veneration of the monied baseball player implausible or grotesque. The material differences of their respective worlds make DiMaggio's empathy problematic, yet emphasize Santiago's self-confidence and pride, as if these qualities could raise the fisherman — as they do, by novel's end — to the status of athletic exemplar in the reader's mind (see Baskett 235). The key to understanding Santiago's respect is the recognition that it originates in his admiration of difficult tasks accomplished with grace and seeming ease. Unlike petty Jason Compson, who resents every dollar of Babe Ruth's fabulous salary, to Santiago all questions of money are mooted by the aficionado's appraisal of the professional's performance: its skill and style, its efficiency of movement, its purity of line. Mindful of the standard of authentic action to which he conforms his own fishing practices — which in precision and rectitude approach the coherence of a systematic aesthetic — Santiago responds to DiMaggio's athletic ethos with no reference to his salary, a tenth of which would to him be a king's treasure. And yet, Santiago's respect embodies more than the dilettantish appreciation of the aficionado. It includes the artisan's acknowledgment of a fellow tradesman worthy of emulation, as well as the solitary combatant's measuring himself against the standard of mental and physical toughness he discerns in the athlete's gritty resolution to "play hurt."

Santiago responds to "the great DiMaggio" as both artist and artisan,[43] working perforce in a different medium but allied nonetheless by what Santiago takes to be, and what the reader is intended to recognize as, similarities of temperament and attitude. The quality of this response is most important, for it indicates not only the rightness of DiMaggio as Santiago's idol but also the viability of Santiago's preoccupation with and use of baseball — as a game, as an idle diversion, as a sustaining fiction within the greater context of his life's grim truth. Santiago does not, for example, permit baseball to interfere with the business of fishing. Rich people afloat in leisure boats may listen to baseball games on radios, but Santiago cannot afford such luxury, in any sense of the word. While he is fishing he must concentrate on his craft: tracking the fish, hooking it, bringing it in. To do the job correctly and well, Santiago must devote to it the undivided attention of his mind and body. Thus, it is "no time to think of baseball" but "to think of only one thing. That which I was born for" (43–44).

---

[43]For Santiago's artistry, see Old Man 33–35, 48, 106–107. The fisherman, like the baseball player, is an artist in terms of his performance when he displays a high level of technical expertise combined with physical grace. "Artisan" might seem like a more appropriate appellation, yet the aesthetic quality of baseball's "work" has long impressed spectators: In the nineteenth century, players who showed especially polished skills were known as "artists." See Harold Seymour, Baseball: The Early Years (1960; reprinted, New York: Oxford University Press, 1989), 61.

For Santiago, who is no sport fisherman, a radio broadcasting baseball is a temptation, a self-indulgent mitigation of work with play. Even thinking of baseball is inappropriate and counterproductive; such day-dreaming will be paid for in lapses of attention and possibly error or accident (Baskett, 234). And yet, the old man must fight his own thoughts, which tend to wander to the game. After Santiago has hooked the marlin and begins the battle to subdue it, he yearns, in his undemonstrative way, for the company of baseball during the work to come:

> I wonder how the baseball came out in the grand leagues today, he thought. It would be wonderful to do this with a radio. Then he thought, think of it always. Think of what you are doing. You must do nothing stupid.
>   Then he said aloud, "I wish I had the boy. To help me and to see this" [Old Man 52].

Santiago moves inevitably from baseball to Manolin, his only companions, but the boy is absent and the game little more on the true Gulf than the opiate of a coward or fool. In its proper place, on the Terrace with Manolin, over dinner or beer, baseball is a safe harbor from the day's hardships; to his psyche, baseball is as rejuvenating as any home Santiago has. To give himself over to its pleasures while at sea, however, would be to approach his work in bad faith. A committed professional, Santiago refuses to compromise the purity of the hunt with extraneous pleasure — even if, in doing so, he might assuage the rigors of exile with the comforts of home.

Conversely, Santiago's invocations of "the great DiMaggio" are neither dodge nor distraction. Santiago steadies his will by summoning his hero, who can, he imagines, withstand all pain and accomplish any feat. Thus, DiMaggio's importance to Santiago depends less exclusively on his being a baseball player and equally on his being, by reputation and in fact, the professional's professional and the son of a fisherman. This confluence of attributes, bolstered by Santiago's love of baseball and that, having forsaken conventional religion, he draws inspirational exemplars from the game, allows "the great DiMaggio" to become a touchstone of commitment.[44] The fame of the historical Joe DiMaggio

---

[44]*Leverett T. Smith touches on the similarities that Santiago perceives between himself and DiMaggio in a way that makes their respective physical feats both necessary and amoral: "The thematic climax of the book comes when the old man makes a statement of the essential nature of his contest with the fish. He has been meditating on the possibility that his action may have been sinful. 'Do not think of sin,' he tells himself, "…there are people who are paid to do it … you were born to be a fisherman as the fish was born to be a fish. San Pedro was born to be a fisherman as was the father of the great DiMaggio.' The implication here is that people who were born to be something live in a fundamentally different universe than those who are merely paid to do something. DiMaggio here is connected with those who are born into their professions. This quality enables one to transcend the workaday world where sin is inevitable. … Essentially the distinction is between the world of work and the world of play, a public world and a private one. The professional ethic here includes the peculiar morality of play. The concept of sin does not cover the situation. Both opponents have played the game in the correct manner and this is what gives the situation meaning" (Smith 98–99). The notion that certain "natural" professionals are exempt from conventional moral categories (in their work/play) is vexing until one remembers that every profession has its own ethical code that is itself conventional and normative.*

enables Hemingway to make his name a synecdoche for an artist's or artisan's fidelity to his craft, for perseverance during a trial of endurance despite the diminution of native powers by injury and age. The famous player does not need to appear in uniform and hit a fastball out of Tropical Stadium to evoke the qualities that even contemporary readers, most of whom are too young to have seen him play, still contemplate with awe. Just the name — just "the great DiMaggio"[45] — is sufficient.

[45]*This encomium has become standard English since* The Old Man and the Sea, *yet David Halberstam reports that after DiMaggio belted his fourth home run in three games against the Red Sox in June 1949, a biplane flew over Fenway Park "trailing a banner that said: THE GREAT DIMAGGIO" (Halberstam 149).*

PART II

♦ *Proem* ♦

The Baseball Novel
Writing a Good Game

If baseball is a Narrative, it is like others — a work of imagination
whose deeper structures and patterns of repetition force a tale, oft-told,
to fresh and hitherto-unforeseen meaning. But what is the nature of the
tale oft-told that recommences with every pitch, with every game, with
every season? That patiently accrues its tension and new meaning with
every iteration? It is the story ... of going home after having left home, the
story of how difficult it is to find the origins one so deeply needs to find.
— A. Bartlett Giamatti, *Take Time for Paradise*

To write a successful baseball novel for an adult audience, the author must fashion a version of the game that is much more self-contained and complete than even the most meaningful of baseball allusions. As the commentary of Part I illustrates, the evocative power of baseball derives not simply from the game and the reader's knowledge of it but from the context — the greater fictional world — in which the allusion appears. Similarly, the best baseball novels depend less extensively on a contrived superstructure — the concoction of teams and pennant races, the recitation of play-by-play — than many readers (and some writers) seem to assume. Like all successful fiction, a well-written baseball novel demonstrates originality, or at least ingenuity, in essential elements of the novelist's craft: believable yet surprising characters whose thoughts, motivations, and actions are rendered in a distinctive (better still if it is inimitable) narrative voice. If such a novel seems more than "literary" fiction to be driven by a profluent plot — the elaboration of a compelling yet plausible story — that impression proceeds from the causal nature of baseball itself. Like any game, baseball cannot escape its own serial unfolding, the self-perpetuating dialectic of action-reaction that continues until the moment play ends. Like the movement away from and back to home, a profluent plot is a feature that all baseball fictions share.

Admittedly, some stories are better — more compelling and plausible — than others. The failings of many baseball novels — dull, trifling plots; absurd characters — are not, however, inevitable results of fictions constructed around baseball but rather the by-products of authorial miscalculation. Unsure not of their material but of their attitude toward it, most baseball novelists commit several cardinal errors: not approaching their subject matter with any serious intention; not regarding their characters as "real"— as credible representatives of human psychologies, behaviors, emotions, etc.; not presuming that the fictive lives of these characters are (or can be made to seem) meaningful and important. As if these derelictions were not sufficient to undermine the literary quality of their respective works, many baseball novelists weaken the genre further by seeming to assume that they are writing not for literate adults but for children.

Given the origins of the baseball novel, this error is understandable (although not excusable). Before Ring Lardner's sustained-narrative breakthrough, *You Know Me Al* (1916), baseball was confined to third-rate novels and, more relevantly, to boys' dime novels and weekly pulp magazines. Baseball had, indeed, supplied much of the subject matter of juvenile and pulp fiction since the late nineteenth century, when Gilbert Patten's stories of prep school and collegiate hero-athletes began to appear in *Tip Top Weekly*. The Frank Merriwell series, published under Patten's "Burt L. Standish" pseudonym, ran from 1896 to 1915, despite Patten's having turned the writing over to others in 1912. These same Frank Merriwell stories appeared in book form from 1900 to 1933.[1] As popular as these and similar entertainments were, they could by their nature serve only to devalue the literary currency of baseball.

Other writers attempted baseball fiction after Lardner, but with few exceptions — notably *The Sun Field* (1923), by Heywood Broun, and Lucy Kennedy's historical novel, *The Sunlit Field* (1950)— these books were conceived and written as juvenile amusements (see Oriard 337, n. 5).[2] Unfortunately, this legacy of "juvenile amusement" seems to be the one that most baseball novelists have claimed as their own. Such an outcome is surprising: Given the example of Ring Lardner, why would an aspiring writer choose Gilbert Patten or Zane Grey as his model? Surely, it cannot be the case that later authors did not perceive the differences separating boys' baseball tales from the narrative and rhetorical sophistication of *You Know Me Al*, to say nothing of the manifest unlikeness of Frank Merriwell and Jack Keefe. If one were to speculate, one might conclude that it was simply a matter of intended audience; conceiving the appeal of their baseball fictions as being limited to boys, many writers might have imitated the circumstantial plots, implausibly heroic actions, and happy endings of their

---

[1]The Merriwell books were not novels but merely the original stories reissued in a new format. See Oriard, Dreaming of Heroes *(Chicago: Nelson-Hall, 1982), 27–28, 307; and 29–36 for the prototypical elements of the genre. See Messenger,* Sport and the Spirit of Play in American Fiction *(New York: Columbia University Press, 1981), 165–171, 178–179 for details of the Frank Merriwell series.*

[2]For commentary on The Sun Field, *see Oriard 181–183 and Candelaria,* Seeking the Perfect Game *(New York: Greenwood Press, 1989), 31–32. For remarks on* The Sunlit Field, *see Messenger,* Sport and the Spirit of Play in Contemporary American Fiction *(New York: Columbia University Press, 1990), 346–347; cited as CAF.*

popular precursors to ensure themselves a similar vogue. Alternatively, it could be that Lardner's accomplishments in the genre led, ironically, to its diminishment. Lardner's achievement in baseball fiction was unprecedented and might have discouraged imitators who lacked his keen ear for vernacular speech and his ability to write revealingly in the mode of comic realism; having become so well known to so large an audience, Lardner's work proved inimitable.[3] Also, because comic realism seemed, judging from Lardner's example, to define the tonal parameters of the genre, serious writers (Hemingway, Fitzgerald, Faulkner, et al.) are likely to have regarded baseball as too frivolous to supply the subject matter of literary art.[4] Historically, the economic and social tribulations of the Great Depression and the Second World War worked a change on the prospective audience for baseball stories (and sports fiction of all kinds), for adults involved in life-and-death struggles could hardly find the contrived conflicts of the playing fields to have a justifiable demand on their attention.[5] Thus, the prejudices of America's finest writers conspired with the urgency of historical circumstances to banish America's National Game to the margins of the nation's fiction. The result is the allusive baseball explored in Part I, which authors played after the success of Ring Lardner and before the fresh examples of Bernard Malamud and Mark Harris.

With the publication of *The Natural* (1952) and, a few months later, of *The Southpaw* (1953), baseball proved itself as usable subject matter in American novels aspiring to the condition of literary art. Both of these books are first novels, suggesting that a sense of baseball's literary fitness walked abroad in the land — or haunted the hallways of untenured academia. Of *The Natural*, Malamud reports that most of the writing occurred during his early academic employment:

> During my first year at Oregon State, I wrote *The Natural*, begun before leaving New York City. Baseball had interested me, especially its comic aspects, but I wasn't able to write about the game until I transformed game into myth, via Jessie Weston's Percival legend with an assist by T. S. Eliot's "The Waste Land" plus the lives of several ballplayers I had read, in particular Babe Ruth's and Bobby Feller's. The myth enriched the baseball lore as feats of magic transformed the game.[6]

[3]*Lardner himself disdained the notion that his baseball stories were serious literature and generally mocked such assumptions (Messenger 108, 110). See also CAF 336.*

[4]*See pages 37–38 supra, for Fitzgerald's appraisal of Lardner's baseball fiction; see Messenger for the* "strong high culture-popular culture split fostered through modernism" *that* "simply deemed" "certain subjects ... unacceptable for sustained treatment in serious fiction" *(CAF 336).*

[5]*See Oriard 56–57 and CAF 335–336. Conversely, Wiley Lee Umphlett notes that baseball and other sports fiction thrived in the pulp magazines and serials of the 1930s, and offered an escape from real troubles and concerns (Umphlett 41). See Umphlett's* "Formulaic Sources of the American Sports-Fiction Tradition: The Code of Quality Performance in Juvenile Sports Fiction" *in* The Achievement of American Sport Literature: A Critical Appraisal, *edited by Wiley Lee Umphlett (Madison, NJ: Fairleigh Dickinson University Press, 1975), 25–45.*

[6]*Quoted by Mark Harris in* "Horatio at the Bat, or Why Such a Lengthy Embryonic Period for the Serious Baseball Novel?" *reprinted in* Aethlon *5:2 (Spring 1988), 1–11; cited as* "Horatio."

The Natural shows the traces of its author's early development and mature education, as Malamud himself attests: "Baseball players were the 'heroes' of my American childhood. I wrote *The Natural* as a tale of a mythological hero because, between childhood and the beginning of a writing career, I'd been to college" (quoted by Messenger, *CAF* 335). About *The Southpaw* Mark Harris has been similarly flippant, once characterizing the book as "facile realism in a facile style."[7] On a note of less self-deprecation but greater iconoclasm, Harris claims that his first three "baseball books are written out of a rebellion against formal language."[8] Years later and in another forum, Harris affirms the seriousness of his purpose in writing a baseball novel, a seriousness he believes has also inspired Malamud:

> One thing we deeply shared was our self-consciousness about what we were doing: we were insisting we were creating literature just as earnestly as Ring Lardner, forty years earlier, was insisting that he was NOT creating literature. I was at the time of the publication of *The Southpaw* a graduate student at the University of Minnesota, and I certainly did not want my professors to think of me as frivolous. Therefore I claimed a literary standing for my work which was above the old-time Baseball Joe sentimentality. If anybody wanted to know where my inspiration came from, it came from Huckleberry Finn, so widely respected in the English Department, not from Baseball Joe or even from Ring Lardner ["Horatio at the Bat" 9].

Harris's awareness of his precursor is evident throughout *The Southpaw*, from the "Special Warning to All Readers!!!" to the vernacular idiom of the narrator-protagonist. The realistic literature that Harris saw himself creating through baseball subject matter differed from Malamud's project, which concerned the adaptation of some of Western culture's most familiar myths to the history and phenomenal reality of baseball. This divergence of authorial intentions accounts not only for the obvious dissimilarities of *The Natural* and *The Southpaw*, but also for each work's seminal status in the baseball fiction genre. *The Southpaw* and the later installments of the "Author" Wiggen tetralogy represent the most extensive adaptation yet of baseball to the novel's requirements of formal realism and may be said to have established the standard for the realistic baseball novel. Conversely, *The Natural* embellishes its realistic surface with magical effects to create a narrative that is overtly symbolic, or "mythic," and that constitutes the genre's first major rendition of magical realism (which subsequent authors, notably W. P. Kinsella, have extended into the realms of fantasy). Earlier, *You Know Me Al* defined the tone and substance, and explored many of the narrative possibilities, of baseball fiction cast in the form of comic hyperbole. More recently, Robert Coover's *The Universal Baseball Association, Inc., J. Henry Waugh, Prop.* (1968) borrows deftly from the three earlier works to contrive a book that is unlike its precursors and sets the standard for metafictional

[7]Mark Harris, Best Father Ever Invented *(New York: Dial Press, 1976).*

[8]"Mark Harris: An Interview," *19, by John Enck,* Wisconsin Studies in Contemporary Literature *6:1 (Spring-Summer 1965): 15–26.*

treatments of baseball. Coover's novel might be the genre's most original, but each of these books is a seminal text that has influenced later baseball fictions.

Whether or not it recounts the playing of games or focuses on players and the progress of a season, a baseball novel either manifestly or implicitly describes a pattern of exile and homecoming that is, in terms of narrative structure, analogous to baseball's definitive movement away from and back to home. The protagonist may or may not come safely home, yet the story always retains the possibility of reunion. In novels that complete the pattern in logistic as well as thematic terms, the protagonist, usually a baseball hero, does return to a specific place that figures as the site of a prior triumph. In *The Southpaw*, Henry Wiggen's initiatory adventures come to a satisfying conclusion when the young ballplayer returns to his hometown and to the people — Pop, Holly, Aaron — who have prepared him to navigate the exile of his rookie season in the major leagues. Separated from home by the demands of professional baseball, "Author" Wiggen discovers that working at the game, which he has hitherto only played, alienates him from his innocent beliefs and cherished dreams. To affirm his sense of self and reclaim his original values, Henry must pitch and, later, write his way toward understanding and self-knowledge, both of which he attains through Holly's guidance. In *The Natural*, Roy Hobbs is locked into a scenario of hubristic failure and early death. Conceived as a once-and-future Knighterring, Roy briefly inhabits a luminous present of athletic pre-eminence, then is quickly cast into a premature exile that foretells the outcome of his truncated baseball career. Homeless, Roy tries to recapture the tranquillity of his boyhood, yet fails to escape either his tumultuous present or his own chronophobia. Driven by ambition to live forever in the timeless present of a hero, Roy cannot help slipping into ordinary chronicity; his time having expired, the future closes down before him. Distanced from his better self, lacking the (self)knowledge that might lead him home, Roy Hobbs is doomed to permanent exile. The most inventive variation on the theme appears in Robert Coover's *The Universal Baseball Association,* the wry yet pathetic story of J. Henry Waugh and his invented game of baseball. This novel directs the reader's attention to its own fictiveness by foregrounding the "virtual reality" of its protagonist's game-within. Even as it alerts the reader to the context-dependent meaning of novel and game, *The Universal Baseball Association* engages the ambiguous distinction between phenomenal reality and textual fictionality to suggest that the worlds about which one reads and writes — the playing fields of the mind — can become more "real" than the quotidian banality of real life. By novel's end, J. Henry Waugh retreats from his real world to enter wholly the fictive universe of his game, thereby coming home to the UBA in a way that consigns him to exile even as it confines him within his apartment. Henry Waugh's exile within the very space of home is a paradox that suggests, finally, that "home" is less a matter of physical space than it is of psychology: a sense of well-being, a rationally disposed frame of mind. Conceived along these lines, "exile" is not merely nor necessarily physical wandering but mental rootlessness and drift. In extreme forms, as in the case of J. Henry Waugh, the exile of the mind involves self-alienation, possibly schizophrenia. A milder form of this malady contributes to the marginal delusions of Ring Lardner's busher, Jack Keefe. Despite his best efforts to create a home and live tranquilly at its heart, Jack never quite arrives at a home that equals his conception of what it should be. By writing to "friend Al" about his oft-reiterated wish to come home to "that yellow house across from you," Jack sustains himself with a fiction that he believes is real, always assuming or hoping that a devoutly anticipated homecoming is the next impending success of his "big league" life. Ironically, even as he waits upon its threshold, Jack decides that home is where the heart is but that the action is elsewhere, and chooses to embark on an extended, self-imposed exile instead of coming home.

◆ *Six* ◆
A Portrait of the Ballplayer as a Young Man
Busher Keefe's Dramatic Monologues

> *[Lardner] makes no attempt to get at the primary springs of human motive; all his people share the same amiable stupidity, the same transparent vanity, the same shallow swinishness; they are all human Fords in bad repair, and alike at bottom. But if he thus confines himself to the surface, it yet remains a fact that his investigations on that surface are extraordinarily alert, ingenious, and brilliant— that the character he finally sets before us, however roughly articulated as to bones, is so astoundingly realistic as to epidermis that the effect is indistinguishable from that of life itself.*
> —H. L. Mencken, "Ring Lardner"

Jack Keefe is the boastful young baseball player of Ring Lardner's epistolary novel, *You Know Me Al* (1916). Over the course of several seasons in the minor and major leagues, Jack writes many "letters home" to his friend, Al Blanchard. He recounts games, describes his relations with players and coaches, and tells of his life off the field. As protagonist and narrator, Jack is, as one might expect, the center of attention; his exploits are the narrative action, and his voice is the voice of the story. Jack's dual role of character-narrator is also the main source of humor, for his words and his behavior are often starkly at odds. The result is an inadvertent (self)portrait of the ballplayer as a young man, an unintentional revelation of personality that recalls the great self-betrayals of "My Last Duchess," "The Bishop Orders His Tomb at Saint Praxed's Church" and other of Robert Browning's dramatic monologues. By his own unwitting admissions, "busher"[1]

---

[1] *In defining "busher" The Dickson Baseball Dictionary (New York: Facts on File, 1989) notes Lardner's usage: "The term was given a boost with the publication of Ring Lardner's novel* You Know Me Al*.... The word busher is key to the book (Keefe has a fight with one of his girlfriends because he thinks she called him one)..." (Dickson 78). The pejorative sense of "busher" derives from the ignorance of the busher on and off the field.*

121

Keefe is an obstinate *naïf* given to a rhetoric of self-aggrandizement and motivated by solipsistic conceit. Whether he truly believes that he is endowed with
wisdom, which he seems unlikely ever to possess, or merely pretends to know
more than he really understands, Jack does not learn from his mistakes because
he does not recognize — or is unwilling to admit — that he has made any. Lardner dramatizes the inherent humor of Jack's "know-it-all" myopia by embroiling
him in the complexities of big-city society, including what one may loosely call
"romances" with modern urban women.[2] As these situations move toward comic
impasse, Jack's aggrieved self-justifications add detail to his self-portrait, indicating that behind the arrogance of Lardner's "natural" — or, as at least two critics have identified him, Lardner's "primitive"[3] — a bewildered young man is adrift
in an inhospitable world. Finding "big league" life both harsh and alienating, Jack
continually lays plans to return to his hometown, yet is prevented by circumstances
from doing so. Diverted by the comedy of his romantic trials, puzzled by the
discrepancies between his own estimation of his abilities and the assessments of
others, readers seldom note Jack Keefe's homeward gestures or question how the
absence of a true home exacerbates the callow pitcher's imprudences and errors.

   Critics have made much of Busher Keefe's narrative voice.[4] The achievement of devising Jack's "bush league" language, its ungrammatical lucidity as
remarkable as its malapropian eloquence, is sufficient to place Lardner with
Mark Twain as a recorder of vernacular speech (see Candelaria 26). In its punchy
rhythms and comic tone, Jack's voice generates humor easily, often without the
speaker's knowledge. In an overtly comic situation, its effect can be hilarious:

> FRIEND AL: Coming out of Amarillo last night I and Lord and Weaver was sit-
> ting at a table in the dining car with a old lady. None of us were talking to her but
> she looked me over pretty careful and seemed to kind of like my looks. Finally she
> says Are you boys with some football club? Lord nor Weaver didn't say nothing so
> I thought it was up to me and I says No mam this is the Chicago White Sox Ball
> Club. She says I knew you were athaletes. I says Yes I guess you could spot us for
> athaletes. She says Yes indeed and specially you. You certainly look healthy. I says
> You ought to see me stripped. I didn't see nothing funny about that but I thought
> Lord and Weaver would die laughing. Lord had to get up and leave the table and
> he told everybody what I said.[5]

[2]*Wiley Lee Umphlett notes Jack Keefe's inability to adapt to the urban ethos and his failure to conform
his expectations of and behavior toward others to the usages of city life. See* The Sporting Myth and
the American Experience *(Lewisburg, PA: Bucknell University Press, 1975), 89–100.*

[3]*David A. Jones and Leverett T. Smith, Jr., "Jack Keefe & Roy Hobbs: Two All-American Boys," 121, in*
Aethlon *6:2 (Spring 1989): 119–137. This article attributes Jack's failures to his inability to learn the
values of society, then to internalize them in a way that would govern his behavior.*

[4]*Cordelia Candelaria summarizes several critical reactions to Jack Keefe's idiomatic language in* Seeking the Perfect Game: Baseball in American Literature *(New York: Greenwood Press, 1989), 26–27.
See also Donald Elder,* Ring Lardner *(New York: Doubleday and Co., 1956), 121–124.*

[5]*You Know Me Al, as reprinted in* Ring Around the Bases: The Complete Baseball Stories of Ring
Lardner, *edited by Matthew J. Bruccoli (New York: Charles Scribner's Sons, 1992), 16–17. Quotations
from and references to* You Know Me Al *follow this text.*

This paragraph might be the novel's funniest moment, both for sheer comedy of situation and the absence of anxiety that darkens later events. The voice of the plainly spoken, crudely mannered rube attains its proper register from the outset and maintains a perfect pitch. Some commentators describe this language as "wise-boob," but in the busher's case the term does not aptly characterize the speaker or his patois: "wise-boob" speech "signifies control, self-discipline, and quick intelligence."[6] Jack Keefe can hardly be said to speak as a "wise-boob," in "the polished idiom of professionalism" (DeMuth 75), or to possess the sense and sensibility of Mark Twain's more cunning narrators,[7] but his language does express significant aspects of his inner life. F. Scott Fitzgerald alludes to the expressive power of Keefe's voice when he reckons that while Lardner "wrote within that enclosure [of baseball subculture] the result was magnificent: within it he heard and recorded the voice of a continent."[8] Indeed, Jack's suppressed emotions bleed through the gauze of colloquial rhetoric in a way that reminds some readers of the stream-of-consciousness narratives of James Joyce and Virginia Woolf.[9] Recent critics claim that the voice of Jack Keefe is representative of a (then) lately ascendant middle class, as well as a rendition of a provincial mind circumscribed by rustic conditions and limited alternatives (Messenger 112, 124).[10] Lardner himself avers, in a preface written for the 1925 Scribners' edition of *You Know Me Al*, that Jack Keefe was modeled not after a baseball player but after a certain "Jane Addams of Hull House, a former Follies girl."[11] This disclaimer, half modesty, half comic derision, is offered with the deadpan facetiousness typical of Lardner's resistance to being thought a serious literary artist. It also implicitly mocks the question: Anyone interested enough to ask about models for Jack Keefe would have known that Lardner had covered baseball for years as a Chicago sportswriter and knew dozens of athletes. That Keefe is a composite of these acquaintances

[6]*James DeMuth*, Small Town Chicago: The Comic Perspective of Finley Peter Dunne, George Ade, and Ring Lardner *(Port Washington, NY: Kennikat Press, 1980), 75.*

[7]*See Messenger,* Sport and the Spirit of Play in American Fiction *(New York: Columbia University Press, 1981): "[Lardner's] narrators ... lacked the breadth of humanity that characterized so many of Twain's narrators. Whole areas of human pathology which Twain ... exposed were closed to Lardner, the student of surface manners" (Messenger 124).*

[8]*Fitzgerald, "Ring" (1933), 36, reprinted in* The Crack-Up, *edited by Edmund Wilson (New York: New Directions, 1956), 34–40. See pages 37–38 supra for Fitzgerald's opinion of baseball as Lardner's formative aesthetic.*

[9]*Maxwell Geismar,* Ring Lardner and the Portrait of Folly *(New York: Crowell, 1972), 91.*

[10]*See also John E. Hart, "Man As Thing: Ring Lardner's* You Know Me Al," South Dakota Review *23:1 (Spring 1985): 114–122, for a discussion of Jack Keefe as a figure of "the average American" (Hart 121) who becomes, in Emersonian terms, "a thing" (Hart 120). In* Dreaming of Heroes *(Chicago: Nelson-Hall, 1982), 88–95, Michael Oriard reads Lardner's "baseball players as rural naturals impossibly confused by their urban environments" and notes Lardner's satiric treatment of "the most important sociological development of his time — the migration of Americans from small rural communities to the urban metropolis" (Oriard 88).*

[11]*This preface is not included in* Ring Around the Bases. *It appears in a paperback reprint of* You Know Me Al *(New York: Vintage Books, 1984), 17–18. References to this preface are cited as Lardner.*

seems a reasonable assumption, especially when one learns that Lardner assisted more than a few semiliterate ballplayers in writing a letter home.[12] Lardner, too impatient or uninterested to explain, or enjoying a chance to tease his readers — "a reply would have stopped the boys and girls from guessing, and their guesses have given me many a thrill" (Lardner 17) — does not proffer the relevant information. In a similar spirit, Lardner contrives an absurd acknowledgment to demean his mastery of American vernacular speech, as well as his baseball knowledge: "The writer wishes to acknowledge his indebtedness to Mayo brothers, Ringling brothers, Smith brothers, Rath brothers, the Dolly sisters, and former President Buchanan for their aid in instructing him in the technical terms of baseball, such as 'bat,' 'ball,' 'pitcher,' 'foul,' 'sleeping car,' and 'sore arm'" (Lardner 18). Like the disinformation about Jack Keefe's "original," this piece of self-effacement chides any reader unaware of the on-the-job training that fitted the author to become, without any assistance from critics — those guessing "boys and girls" — the innovator of Jack Keefe and his dicey verbal skills. Lardner's point is that Jack Keefe is drawn from no single extratextual original, that the busher's (self)portrait is a collage of traits and eccentricities, a collection of character fragments that exists only in his letters to Al. Busher Keefe is the sum of what he writes, a moving picture of concatenated word-cells. His words and deeds often strike the reader as cartoonish, as if, in reading his letters, one were perusing an extraordinarily well-developed comic strip. In articulating the language, Lardner breathed life into the character.

The busher is remarkable for his boastfulness, ignorance, and solipsistic conceit, which he displays throughout the novel. As a young athlete, Jack does not ponder his vulnerabilities — he might not be aware that he is vulnerable, for a sense of invincibility is the signal delusion of many a player at the beginning of his career. Anxiety, doubt, melancholy, all of the afflictions of the spirit usually associated with a contemplative personality, seldom darken Jack Keefe's brow unless he is reacting to a specific setback. Only when his situation is plainly desperate, when he is abandoned by his wife or out of cash or shipped down to the minors, does the busher admit to being worried or scared. At such junctures, Jack writes a letter that presents his version of events, along with self-exculpatory explanations, and states his fears to the extent that he is able to articulate them. However, even ordinary letters, some of which read like offhand notes written to apprise Al of that day's happenings, convey hints and tokens of Jack's suppressed anxieties.

The first letter, which Jack writes while still in Terre Haute with a "bush" team, relays the happy news "to all you good pals down home" (7) that the White Sox have purchased his contract. As the busher looks forward to joining his first

---

*See C. Kenneth Pellow, "Ring Lardner: Absurdist Ahead of His Time," 111–112, in Aethlon 6:2 (Spring 1989): 111–118; James Diedrick, "Ring Lardner's 'New' Journalism," 111, Arete 3:1 (Fall 1985); Ring Lardner, Jr., The Lardners: My Family Remembered (New York: Harper & Row, 1976), 84–85; and Elder 123.

major league team, he writes as if to reassure himself that he will confidently negotiate the passage into the arenas of "big city" and "big show":

> Well Al it will seem funny to be up there in the big show when I never was really in a big city before. But I guess I seen enough of life not to be scared of the high buildings eh Al?
> I will just give them what I got and if they don't like it they can send me back to the old Central and I will be perfectly satisfied [7].

Jack sounds as diffident here as in any of his letters, although he tries to mask his uncertainty with a clichéd joke about a rube's bent-neck awe of skyscrapers. Jack does not think of himself as a rube, but he does have a small-town boy's pride about going home if he does not make the grade. Despite the confidence that he overstates in every letter, Jack has already imagined the possibility of not being good enough for the "big leagues." Behind an antic mask, he whispers an appeal for encouragement — and for sympathy before the fact of a failure he senses might be imminent.

If he fails, Jack intends to return to "the old Central," his baseball "home," presumably to become a career minor league pitcher. Baseball is Jack's profession; he must play it wherever he is paid to do so, but the game, especially in the minor leagues, is as much a lifestyle as a job. The long season requires teammates, players and coaches alike, to live and travel together for half the year or more, in effect substituting a band of brothers for a family, a ballpark and clubhouse for a home. Minor league players, "bush leaguers," are usually very young, often just 18 years old, and have left their parents and homes for the first time.[13] Jack never refers to his parents or to a familial home, nor does he ever call the White Sox "family" or Comiskey Park "home." The first omission suggests the severity of Jack's isolation, and the latter indicates his estrangement from his peers. Jack does not comment openly on these deprivations, but their effects on him are evident. Indeed, because Jack never mentions them in his letters to Al, the reader assumes that the busher has neither parents nor a permanent home. He remains connected to his hometown through Al; his letters testify to Jack's need not just of a friend and confidant but also of reassurance that, in a certain place, among certain people, he is known and welcome.[14] Thus, Jack asks Al to "Write and tell me all the news about home" (11); in another letter he refers to Al and the boys' coming to Chicago to see him pitch, and adds, "Thanks for the papers" (19), presumably Bedford's local press. By its nature,

---

[13]Two baseball nonfictions convey a powerful sense of what it feels like to be a young minor leaguer. Pat Jordan's A False Spring (1975; reprinted, New York: Simon & Schuster, 1988) is the bittersweet memoir of a gifted pitcher whose pursuit of baseball fame ended prematurely and with mysterious suddenness. Roger Kahn's Good Enough to Dream (Garden City, NY: Doubleday, 1985) is the author's account of his brief ownership of the Elmira Blue Sox, a team in the New York–Penn League. Kahn constructs vivid portraits of the Blue Sox players, each of whom is young and, despite considerable skills, unlikely to reach the majors.

[14]Umphlett reads Al's role as that of confidant and father figure, and Jack's nearly compulsive letter-writing as being in itself a symptom of insecurity (Umphlett 91, 94).

regular communication signals Jack's desire to belong to a stable social context of some kind: a hometown, a team, a family.

Given Jack's difficulty in truly becoming a part of the White Sox, this desire seems not merely poignant but sad. In the busher's era (and for decades thereafter), established players regarded rookies as interlopers who meant to steal their jobs. Coolly received and often abused by a more or less unified front of veterans, rookies suffered all manner of indignity, from simple ostracism to finding their bats sawed in half and their uniforms tied in knots, to being heckled in practice and even run off the field.[15] If the newcomer endured the hazing and performed well in spite of it, acceptance would evolve among the veterans. Evaluated within this context, the busher's know-it-all attitude and intractability — he skips the first workout, threatens to punch teammates and even the manager — can only prove counterproductive.[16] Perhaps the most telling sign of Jack's insecurity (it is not too much to call it fear) is the dismissiveness with which he writes of his teammates. It is not clear whether Jack broadcasts these opinions or confines them to his letters, but he does belittle everyone from rookie pitcher to established star: "My roommate is Allen a lefthander from the Coast League. He don't look nothing[17] like a pitcher but you can't never tell about them dam left handers" (11). Allen later becomes part of Jack's extended family (in "The Busher's Honeymoon"), but Jack never regards him as brother(-in-law) or friend. Even well-intentioned advice from future Hall of Fame pitcher Ed Walsh[18] elicits a defensive response. Told that he has been tipping off his spitball, Jack thinks that he has "got Walsh's goat with my spitter" (12) and ascribes the senior pitcher's remarks to jealousy. When Walsh offers to teach Jack how to conceal the slip-pitch, Jack's reply (to Al: he does not repeat the answer he has made to Walsh) betrays his insecurity: "I guess Al I know how to cover it up all right without Walsh learning me" (12). The truth is that Jack cannot cover up anything, least of all his need to have his talent praised. He infers envy from Walsh's constructive criticism yet is too disingenuous — or too dim-witted — to fabricate envious remarks and (mis)attribute them to Walsh. Similarly, when

[15]*Ty Cobb's rookie experience seems to have been particularly hellish. See Charles C. Alexander's account in* Ty Cobb *(New York: Oxford University Press, 1984), 38–40, 42–43, 45.*

[16]*Jack's behavior on the baseball field indicates to most readers that, as a ballplayer, he is a negative example of the qualities Lardner prized. Leverett T. Smith identifies the valued attributes as "shrewdness and the ability to learn" and Jack Keefe as "the antithesis of these qualities." By contrasting Lardner's depiction of Keefe to his praise of Ty Cobb and Christy Mathewson (in two nonfiction articles, "Tyrus: the Greatest of 'Em All" and "Matty," both published in 1915), Smith argues that "Lardner is in this sense conservative, wanting not to change the ideals of the community of professional sports, but to reassert their values." See* The American Dream and the National Game *(Bowling Green, OH: Bowling Green University Popular Press, 1975), 110–126.*

[17]*The construction "He don't look nothing" is Keefe's. Because it would serve only the most pedantic of points to note each of the busher's grammatical and spelling errors (and riddle the text with [sic]s), I must ask the reader to trust me. If in doubt, consult the Bruccoli text of* You Know Me Al.

[18]*Ed Walsh was an expert spitball pitcher with the White Sox. See pages 72–73 supra.*

Collins,[19] whom Jack describes as one of the team's best hitters, tells the busher, "You got some fast ball there boy ... I don't want to hit against you when you are right" (12), Jack does not hear the sarcasm or realize that his own success in that day's intrasquad game (it is spring training) is due to the regular players' working themselves gradually out of their winter indolence. Kid Gleason, at this point "a kind of asst. manager to Callahan"[20] (10), tries to set the busher wise: "Don't believe what he tells you boy. If the pitchers in this league weren't no faster than you I would still be playing ball and I would be the best hitter in the country" (12). Jack reports Gleason's admonishment, but only the reader gets the point.

Jack's fidelity in reporting the words of others seems paradoxical, given his basic unreliability, but his selective accuracy is essential; without it, the reader would have no standard against which to measure the busher's skewed perceptions. Selective accuracy is, indeed, a formal constraint of first-person narration and might be its most telling deficiency. Because any first-person narrator is always potentially unreliable, all first-person narrations must find a way to relate some information truthfully; otherwise, the story will not cohere. By portraying Jack as too insecure about his own standing to counterfeit his teammates' remarks, Lardner reserves a small, crucial portion of reliability for the busher. Likewise, Jack's inability to detect sarcasm, as well as his general imperceptiveness of jokes and gibes, allows Lardner to present such comments, or to have Jack report them, as if at face value. The result is Jack's obliviousness to the joke his own narration plays on him. To be sure, he tries to impart his own "spin" to his teammates' words — in this sense, Jack is always throwing curveballs at the reader — but these falsifications practically announce their presence, each one a transparent example of the megalomaniac cutting off his competitor's head to make himself appear taller.

When Jack is the one cut down to size, as he is by the end of "A Busher's Letters Home," he is unwilling, having enjoyed his short run in "the big show," to return to the bush leagues. Written less than a month into the season, the final letter reveals Jack as a heartbroken, sulking boy even as it provides an unsentimental ending to the story of how his dream has (apparently) died. In his meeting with White Sox owner Charles Comiskey, at which Jack learns that his contract has been sold to a team in the Pacific Coast League, the busher's pain is palpable but unspeakable:

> Then he patted me on the back and says Go out there and work hard boy and maybe you'll get another chance some day. I was kind of choked up so I walked out of the office.

---

[19]*"Collins" is Shano Collins, White Sox outfielder/first baseman from 1910 to 1920 and a career .264 batter on a light-hitting team (pre-1915). See* The Baseball Encyclopedia, *7th ed. edited by Joseph L. Reichler (New York: Macmillan, 1988), 851. Eddie Collins (see page 78 supra, note 20) did not join the White Sox until 1915 (Baseball Encyclopedia 849).*

[20]*James Joseph "Nixey" Callahan managed the White Sox in 1903 and 1904 and from 1912 to 1914. Kid Gleason became manager in 1919 (Baseball Encyclopedia 647, 656).*

I ain't had no fair deal Al and I ain't going to no Frisco. I will quit the game first and take that job Charley offered me at the billiard hall.

I expect to be in Bedford in a couple of days. ... I am going to rest and lay round home a while and try to forget this rotten game. Tell the boys about it Al and tell them I never would of got let out if I hadn't worked with a sore arm.

I feel sorry for that little girl up in Detroit Al. She expected me there today.

Your old pal, JACK.

P.S. I suppose you seen where that lucky lefthander Allen shut out Cleveland with two hits yesterday. The lucky stiff [24].

Confronted for the first time with the little death of athletes, Jack tries to deny it in a burst of self-pity and a claim of having been wronged. The sense that the best of his life has slipped away virtually immobilizes him with grief, as if he were reacting to the loss of a loved one. Whether from arrogance or shame (the PCL is Allen's former circuit), or the belief that his chance is forever lost, Jack resorts to a prospect of home: to hiding from the loud world, to taking up an ordinary life and small job like the other homeboys, to forgetting. His general obtuseness notwithstanding, Jack is saddened most of all for the future it now seems he will never know. He must give up his provisional home in Chicago and fledgling "romance" with Violet, "that little girl up in Detroit," not to mention the life of a professional baseball player. The chance to see the nation's great cities, to play before thousands of fans, to showcase his talent in public forums is lost. All of Jack's rue, jealousy, and melancholy longing is contained within the terse, apparently ancillary yet perfectly eloquent "P.S." Lardner's timing and control here are impeccable.

In the Pacific Coast League, Jack is farther from home than ever before. This exile, professional baseball's equivalent of university rustication, is marked by another rejection that is intimately related to the busher's standing in the game. Upon learning of Jack's demotion to the minor leagues, Violet jilts him. To Jack, this act is a sign that Violet "is just like them all Al. No heart" (26). Her "Dear John" postcard informs her would-be suitor that she "[has] no time to waste on bushers" (26). Jack's reaction is telling, for he takes greater offense at Violet's contradicting his sense of his professional status than he does at her ending their romance: "What do you know about that Al? Calling me a busher. I will show them" (26). Jack's romantic disappointment blends with his sadness at having been sold by the White Sox, as his grammatical conflation "I will show them" (rather than "her") attests. The expression "No heart" and Jack's umbrage at being called a busher sound like an athlete's bitterness toward a team that has given up on him. Admittedly, these locutions come to Jack spontaneously; he knows sporting language best and readily uses it to represent affairs of the heart as well as of the diamond. To the extent, however, that his language implicitly analogizes the broken romance and his faithless team, it is evident that Jack's hectic romantic life shadows his baseball odyssey.

The advent of a new romance, therefore, signals a change in the busher's baseball fortunes. After a two-month suspension of his letters home, Jack abruptly writes that he is engaged to be married. His fiancée is Hazel Carney, "some queen, Al — a great big stropping girl that must weigh one hundred and sixty lbs." (26). The reader might presume a common explanation for Jack's silence — that he is writing letters to his fiancée instead of to Al — except that he has met Hazel in San Francisco and spends almost all of his evenings with her (27). The implication, significant if not surprising, is that Jack stops writing letters home when he senses an opportunity to prepare a home of his own. The clownish ease with which the busher tumbles into a "proposal" of marriage infuses the patent comedy with a yearning that is keenly felt, if never stated:

> Night before last she asked me if I was married and I tells her No and she says a big handsome man like I ought to have no trouble finding a wife. I tells her I ain't never looked for one and she says Well you wouldn't have to look very far. I asked her if she was married and she said No but she wouldn't mind it. She likes her beer pretty well and her and I had several and I guess I was feeling pretty good. Anyway I guess I asked her if she wouldn't marry me and she says it was O.K. I ain't a bit sorry Al because she is some doll and will make them all sit up back home [27].

Little romance is involved in this affair. Far from home, toiling anonymously in a bush league, Jack takes on Hazel as if in reflex. His behavior is not so much spontaneous as it is spasmodic, his emotions less a matter of ambivalence than inchoateness. Although he hardly knows what he is doing and can barely guess at what he needs, Jack is certain that he wants to bring his new wife to his old town. To return to Bedford, however, Jack must take a detour through Chicago and the other American League cities, for only in "the big show" can he earn the money required for marriage and homecoming. Again, baseball and romance converge, as if Jack cannot have one without the other, or both were expressions of a single desire. When the White Sox recall him a month later, the busher is, in essence, retrieved from exile and his homeward course correctly oriented.

Jack's progress, however, is subject to many adjustments and one deflection that threatens to change its path. As if returning to the majors implied repletion of all kinds, Jack enjoys success in baseball and, by the end of "The Busher Comes Back" (Chapter II), in romance as well. On the diamond, he pitches winning games against the Philadelphia Athletics and, more tellingly, the Detroit Tigers (whose potent lineup has embarrassed him in April and precipitated his demotion to the minors). The second victory, in which Ty Cobb gets the only hit — "a scratch single that he beat out. If he hadn't of been so dam fast I would of had a no hit game" (30) — renews Violet's interest in Jack (she lives in Detroit and has seen him pitch). While Violet protests that she has never called him a busher (31–32), Jack receives a letter from Hazel that reports her October arrival and asks for $100 for traveling expenses and new clothes (32). Jack sends $30 to Hazel and, because it fits his self-conception, believes Violet's revision; he sends her his New York address (the White Sox are on the road) even as he claims that he will keep his distance because of his impending marriage (33).

As if to belie his words with an action nearer his heart, Jack writes a postcard "to poor little Violet" (38), a gesture he advertises as sympathetic but which his own situation reveals as defensive: "I don't care nothing about [Violet] but it don't hurt me none to try and cheer her up once in a while. We leave here Thursday night for home and they had ought to be two or three letters there for me from Hazel because I haven't heard from her lately. She must of lost my road addresses" (38). It is difficult to tell whether Jack secretly prefers Violet or if he is merely hedging his bets like the most cynical — or unconfident — of gamblers; his "it don't hurt me none" shimmers with ambiguity. An earlier letter from Violet seems to evoke genuine emotion from Jack, although his sympathy resolves itself in conceit: Her letter "pretty near made me feel like crying. I wish they was two of me so both them girls could be happy" (35). In the upshot of events, it seems that Jack would rather marry Violet but can find no way to clarify his shifting feelings. This incapacity recurs later in the novel and renders Jack virtually powerless in his relationships with women.

The significance of Jack's being on a road trip during this period of flux should be obvious, and the letters from Hazel that are *not* awaiting him in Chicago ought to be taken as a sign that Jack's homeward movement will be forestalled even as he anticipates its completion. Jack heightens the comic irony of this situation by asking Al, in the same letter that reports his fiancée's silence, to rent "that yellow house across from you" (38) so that he, Jack, might bring his new bride home. "Oh you little yellow house" (44) becomes the summation of Jack's hopes, just as "Oh you Violet" (21) carries similar connotations earlier in the story, before Jack imagines a specific form or location for his desires. Perhaps the most ironic of these events is Jack's elation at receiving a letter from Hazel that tells him not when she will arrive in Chicago but that she has jilted him to marry a prizefighter named Kid Levy (40). Now Jack can revise his own story, asserting that Hazel "was no good and I was sorry the minute I agreed to marry her" (40). Read in context, this statement encapsulates the paradoxes at play in Jack's narration: Having asked Hazel, after a fashion, to marry him, Jack first writes that he "ain't a bit sorry" (27) even though (it turns out) he is, yet is prepared to keep his word until Hazel provides the basis on which he can contradict it. And yet, contradicting himself reveals what seems to be his true desire: to marry Violet, who has "got Hazel beat forty ways" (40). Inevitably, Jack's updated intentions entail additional revisions of the written record: The earlier breakup with Violet "seems like a dream," a "misunderstanding," for now Jack cannot believe — and cannot afford to admit — that his prospective fiancée has ever called him a busher. Having reconstructed his recent past, Jack completes the pattern by fabricating a future: "I know Violet will be perfectly satisfied if I take her right down to Bedford. Oh you little yellow house" (40).

The adaptability of Jack's affections, however, is defeated by circumstance. When he learns that Violet is already engaged to another player, Detroit pitcher Joe Hill, Jack's spirit fails. He has little enthusiasm for pitching the final game of the Chicago city series against the Cubs, and winning the series and the extra money seem like matters of small importance. Most significantly, he tells Al to try to cancel the lease on the yellow house; lacking a wife, Jack feels that coming home is meaningless. His distress is real yet seems excessive — he hardly knows Violet — and the reader tends to doubt the profundity if not the sincerity of his sadness. The combination of hyperbole and true woe yields a mixed tone: "maybe I will go to Australia with Mike Donlin's team. If I do I won't care if the boat goes down or not. I don't believe I will even come back to Bedford this winter. It would drive me wild to go past that little house every day and think how happy I might of been" (41). Jack's impulse to join an exhibition tour to Australia indicates that he would like to travel as far from Bedford as possible, as if a self-imposed exile were the only possible response to an abortive homecoming. His purported "death-wish," here plainly a bit of melodrama, foreshadows the excesses that characterize the balance of the novel. In his next letter Jack reports that he has had "a couple of high balls before breakfast" to offset a bad dream about Violet (42). In the ensuing chapters, Jack displays increasingly self-destructive behavior, including a winter-long abuse of beer and liquor. Alcoholism is one threat at least from which baseball and its training regimen help to protect the busher.

The effect of marriage on Jack's life finally becomes real when he suddenly weds Florrie, sister-in-law of his spring training roommate, Allen. Having met Florrie in Chicago while waiting for Hazel and having judged that "she ain't much for looks" (30), Jack later decides that "She is O.K. Al" (43) after she comes to Comiskey Park to watch him pitch. For all of his contradictions, Jack consistently forms his opinion of women — and everyone else, for that matter — primarily according to their appreciation of his athletic talent. This response is Jack's half of a dialectic that posits an owner who pegs players' salaries, buys, sells, and trades players without consulting them, signs and releases players based on their performances and his own needs or whims. Having learned to value himself as professional baseball values him, Jack becomes complicit in his own reification and susceptible to thinking of others in similar terms. Florrie, like Violet before her, is a gauge to measure Jack's baseball status: "Florence knows a lot about baseball for a girl and you would be supprised to hear her talk. She says I am the best pitcher in the league and she has saw them all" (43). Having found a woman who confirms his self-image, Jack can do nothing except marry her and so fix her judgment for all time — or until his playing days are over. Jack attempts to elide a lingering reservation through one of his uniquely misquoted aphorisms: "[Florrie] maybe ain't as pretty as Violet or Hazel but as they say beauty isn't only so deep" (43). Typically, the Keefeism emphasizes what it intends to downplay; typical, too, is the form in which Jack announces his engagement: "When I come home to Bedford I will bring my wife with me" (43).

From the moment he and Florrie agree to marry, Jack looks forward to living in the yellow house. Many of his letters alert Al to their imminent arrival; one letter even pinpoints their train as the noon departure from Chicago and requests that Al "ask Ben Smith will he have a hack down to the deepo to meet us" (108). In another apposite "P.S.," Jack arranges for a home-cooked meal of "spair ribs and crout" to greet their arrival (108). These plans, like all of Jack's intentions to come home, are repeatedly deferred and finally cancelled. Curiously, the competing interests that prevent Jack's return to Bedford are the compromises of married life. Prepared to come home after the close of the Chicago city series (which the White Sox and Cubs formerly played every October), Jack marries Florrie on October 15 and writes two days later that his homecoming will be delayed so that Florrie can visit awhile with her sister, Marie (46). By October 22, Jack finds his return postponed again, this time ostensibly by Marie, who wants Florrie to stay until she and her husband, the left-hander Allen, have set up housekeeping in their winter quarters (47). Obviously, the reasons for postponement are becoming rather slight. Jack, concerned about the $10-a-month rent he is paying on the yellow house, extracts a promise from Florrie that "she would not stay no longer than next Saturday at least" (47). Jack's substitution of "at least" for "at the latest," not to mention the double negative, reduces his version of Florrie's promise to its opposite even if the timetable is clear in his own mind. Two days later, Florrie apparently has managed to change Jack's mind so completely that he believes he is thinking for himself. On October 24, Jack writes that he and Florrie will "stay a week or two" in the Allens' "spair bedroom." This arrangement satisfies Jack because he anticipates that "it won't cost nothing" (47). Florrie clearly has played Jack's concern about saving money off his desire to winter in Bedford, where she has no intention of living. Behind the scene of Jack's letters, Florrie manipulates the situation by degrees and succeeds in keeping them in Chicago all winter, eating too much, drinking too much, spending their money too quickly. Her technique, another means by which Lardner creates humor, implicates Jack in the project of his own deception. By November 2, Jack has his mind changed again; he has rented "that flat across the hall from the Allens" and will not come home except for a Christmas visit (49). Predictably, Jack asks Al to try to cancel the lease on the yellow house (50), underscoring the loss of what would have been the newlywed's first home. In its stead, Jack lives in furnished rooms rented only until spring. As Christmas nears, Jack does invite Al and Bertha to visit them in Chicago—a visit that Florrie does not welcome—but his plans to return to Bedford for the holidays never materialize.

This process, in which stated intentions are continually revised and desires repeatedly thwarted, traces a pattern of deferral in which Jack is a pawn shuttled hither and yon by a hand whose touch he never feels. To the extent that Florrie is the prime mover of Jack's life, the joke of which he is the brunt subjects him to an irony that he recognizes only later, in the extremity of his frustration. For marriage conventionally assumes the founding of a home, and it is, in part, for the sake of a home that Jack has married. Although he tries to impersonate a "citified" sophisticate in his letters to what one assumes is his equally bumptious friend, Jack remains a small-town boy whose responses to life are governed, when he acts free of undue influence, by traditional assumptions. Living in a pricey Chicago apartment is not a version of home that is familiar or congenial to him. Marriage, in which Jack has invested so much suppressed emotion, is proving to be a disappointment. But that is the busher's fate for having wed an opportunistic Baseball Annie.

Having chosen his bride neither wisely nor too well, Jack compounds his error during the off-season, when the reins that professional baseball holds on his proclivity for dissipation have been dropped. Overeating and habitual drunkenness are the beginning of Jack's troubles, which culminate in what seems to be the premature end of his baseball career. As their gluttonous winter winds down and spring training approaches, Jack realizes that he has spent his earnings on rent and groceries, restaurant checks and bar tabs, and cannot afford to take Florrie to the White Sox camp in California. Unwilling to leave his wife alone in Chicago (Marie is making the trip), Jack regrets not having established a home in Bedford; when Al offers to host Florrie until Jack returns with the team, Florrie refuses to go (55–57). Other stratagems, which include asking Comiskey for a higher salary and trying to jump to the Federal League,[21] fail to raise the necessary cash and leave Jack without a spot on any major league roster. Unable to find his bearings, seemingly incapable of acting without making another mistake, Jack writes, "I am worried to death Al.... Maybe I will go out and buy a gun Al and end it all and I guess it would be better for everybody. But I cannot do that Al because I have not got the money to buy a gun with" (60). The humor of Jack's fuddled thoughts partially cloaks his desperation, which deepens when he learns that Comiskey has sold him to Milwaukee, a minor league team. In the wake of this news, Florrie abandons him; like Violet, she presumably has no time to waste on bushers. Alone in Chicago, flat broke and with debts still to pay, Jack asks Al, who has already lent him $100 to cover the rent and grocery bill, for train fare back to Bedford (63). Al sends $25 and Jack, with no one to hinder him and no place to be after his "honeymoon" ends, finally goes home.

Obviously, no letters are necessary while Jack is in Bedford. After he returns to Chicago (the sale to Milwaukee having been deemed invalid by league president Ban Johnson), Jack is restored to his place on the White Sox but remains separated from his wife. Comiskey placates the busher by giving him a three-year contract, which is a comfort—"I am sure of my job here for 3 years and everything is all O.K." (71)—despite its freezing his salary at $2800. Jack either does not understand that Comiskey is exploiting his insecurity or does not care because the deal, unfavorable in monetary terms, seems to promise him an identity within a social context. Estranged from his wife, alienated from his in-laws and friendless outside Bedford's town limits, Jack turns to baseball. When

[21]*The Federal League began in 1913 as a minor league and was a major league in 1914 and 1915. It accepted many of the majors' cast-off players, so Jack's attempt to jump is predictable. See Harold Seymour,* Baseball: The Golden Age *(1971; reprinted, New York: Oxford University Press, 1989), 199–234; and page 76 supra, note 17.*

he joins the White Sox in spring training, his tone changes; whether or not they are glad to see him back, the busher is genuinely happy to belong to this makeshift family.

The most influential member of Jack's baseball family is Kid Gleason. Before Jack's marriage, and again after he returns to the team, Gleason is Jack's mentor and, in a combative way, a surrogate father. Gleason instructs the busher on and off the field during his rookie season, teaching him how to field bunts and back up third base as well as steering him away from high-priced bars and city women. In New York (about a month before his marriage), Jack notices many women, presumably prostitutes, whom he "would of liked to of got acquainted with but [Gleason] wouldn't even let me answer them when they spoke to me" (35). Although Kid Gleason helps Jack navigate the urban labyrinth, the busher never learns to recognize its perils. When they meet "a couple of peaches" and Jack is swept up as if caught in a whirlpool, it is Gleason who must pull him out of the vortex: "[Gleason] says Go home and get some soap and remove your disguise from your face. I didn't think he ought to talk like that to them and I called him about it and said maybe they was lonesome.... But he says Lonesome. If I don't get you away from here they will steal everything you got. They won't even leave you your fast ball" (35). Most of Gleason's savvy eludes the busher, but Jack manages to benefit in spite of himself. When they meet in Los Angeles for spring training, the tone of their relationship resumes. Their banter sounds good-natured even if the jokes always work at Jack's expense, their humor a sign of the optimism of spring baseball. The most admirable feature of Lardner's composition here is the distinct yet unsentimental reminder of Jack's marital misfortunes. As if to depict the rough love of this baseball family, Lardner has Kid Gleason mock the busher; he greets Jack as "'the old lady killer,'" which Jack, with his characteristic obliviousness, takes as a straight compliment: "He ment Al that I am strong with the girls..." (72). To Jack's claim of being in playing shape, Gleason retorts, "'Yes you look in shape like a barrel'"; when Jack says that his weight is up because "'my mussels is bigger,'" Gleason replies, "'Yes your stumach mussels is emense'" (72). Undeniably, Kid Gleason's teasing is double-edged. He touches the sore spots of Jack's infelicitous marriage and ballooning physique as if to administer a balm, but the wounds are too fresh not to sting. Jack's acknowledgment that Gleason is "a little rough" (72) refers to Gleason's habit, which one suspects is only half-playful, of "hitting [Jack] in the stumach" (77), but here Jack winces at a different kind of pain. He does not admit that Gleason's gibes hurt, but the reader apprehends Jack's melancholy despite his reticence. Gleason is the nearest thing Jack has to a father figure, yet never offers the busher more than an antagonistic friendship. Indeed, the paternal quality with which he monitors Jack's training habits — he tries to restrict Jack's consumption of food and beer so that the busher will lose weight — is cynically compromised, for it proceeds from the pitcher's value to the team and Gleason's own duties as a member of its management, rather than from any heartfelt personal concern.

Still separated from Florrie on Opening Day and uninterested in reconciliation, Jack devotes himself to baseball, displacing frustration and loneliness with the demands of competition. This evasion proves unsuccessful and its climactic gesture indicates the fragility of Jack's ego. When he confronts Violet's husband, Joe Hill, in a game in Detroit against the Tigers, Jack suffers a spasm of virtual madness that is only slightly predicated on the game situation. After striking Jack out with the bases loaded — and with Violet watching from the grandstand — Hill taunts the busher: "I don't want nothing more of yourn. I allready got your girl and your goat" (81). If one reads Jack's words at face value, his rage is literally blinding; he takes the mound, "so mad I could not see the plate or nothing," and promptly loads the bases (81). When Hill steps in to bat (it is the bottom of the tenth inning of a scoreless game), Jack's repressed emotional life reasserts itself:

> But when I seen this Hill up there I forgot all about the ball game and I cut loose at his bean.
> Well Al my control was all O.K. this time and I catched him square on the fourhead and he dropped like as if he had been shot. But pretty soon he gets up and gives me the laugh and runs to first base. I did not know the game was over till Weaver came up and pulled me off the field [82].

Ironically, Jack exercises more control over the baseball than he does over his behavior. Then again, his act is almost mindless, so the instinctive accuracy of the beanball is poetically just. The extremity of his reaction to Hill's taunt, however, suggests that Jack is emotionally distraught, and possibly mentally ill. Apart from a sense of offended vanity, Jack is not truly hurt over having "lost" Violet, nor is it the first time he has failed to hit with runners on base. The insult is personal, to be sure, but by the standards of the time relatively tame. What upsets Jack is its subtext: that Hill and Violet have a happy home while the busher has botched his own marriage. The implicit sense of this innuendo— that Jack is a loser — provokes the busher into what can only be described as homicidal rage. Before he recounts having thrown at Hill's head, Jack writes, "If I had of had a gun I would of killed him deader than a doornail" (81). This threat might be just bluster, but Jack insists that his fastball would have killed Hill if he had had his usual strength.[22] "And how could a man go to 1st base ... if he was dead which he should ought to have been..." (79). Free of remorse, lacking better judgment, Jack reacts with instinctive aggression, hoping to kill his rival as if the murder would improve his own life.

In the aftermath of these events, Jack's life turns for the better. He and Florrie reunite, Jack having learned that she is about to give birth, and again take up temporary residence in the Allens' "spair room" (149). At this point, Florrie's earlier flight begins to seem like a pretense or stratagem; when one discerns that

---

[22]Kid Gleason has been monitoring Jack's diet and limiting his portions, which leaves the busher, by his own estimation, "½ starved to death" (82).

she dupes Jack into accepting an unwarranted fatherhood, her motive in marrying him seems morally culpable. Ironically, the son that Florrie presents as Jack's own becomes his life's greatest joy and the occasion (in "The Busher's Kid") of Jack's most affirmative, least self-centered utterances. These letters, certainly Jack's finest moments, are generally less humorous than most of *You Know Me Al*, for the irony of little Al's paternity is too exploitative of Jack's newly realized compassion to seem funny. Similarly, the events that fill the second half of "The Busher's Honeymoon" display too much of Jack's stupidity to be taken as innocently comic. The reader is less amused by the playing out of human folly than disturbed by the busher's chronic imprudence and its consequences.

The birth of little Al seems to complete the Keefe family circle, but the signs say that something is amiss. Although Florrie has been absent only three months, Jack is unaware of her pregnancy until she tells him just two weeks before the baby is born. Unless an unpregnant Florrie is quite fat (so that the pregnancy does not show until the final trimester), Jack's ignorance is inexplicable, an opacity of the plot; no man is that dumb or unobservant. The most that one can say in his defense is that Jack is not — and has not been — paying attention. Given his enthusiastic response to the baby's imminent arrival, he seems also to have forgotten the date of his marriage — or the time frame of human gestation — along with his bad feelings. Perhaps the real measure of Jack's happiness lies in his almost forgetting his monetary troubles in the first flush of new fatherhood: "I am still paying the old man $10.00 a month for that house ... which has not never done me no good. But I should not worry about money when I got a real family. Do you get that Al, a real family?" (86). Luckily for Jack, he is oblivious to the vulgar trick that Florrie and her brother-in-law have played on him. Lardner does not allow any suspicion of the baby's illegitimacy to whisper through Jack's narration, but he does supply hints: Florrie insists on naming the boy Allen, "which Florrie thinks is after his uncle and aunt Allen but which," Jack assures Al, "is after you old pal" (85–86); and little Al is, according to the doctor (and to Jack's displeasure), left-handed.[23] Jack never reads these signs and the truth of little Al's paternity is never explored, much less resolved, but a simple reckoning of dates reveals that Jack has been hoodwinked. He and Florrie marry on October 15 (43, 45), and little Al is born on June 16 (85–86), suggesting that Florrie is at least one month pregnant when she and Jack marry. The baby might be premature, but no evidence of this appears in Jack's letters. The probable explanation is that Florrie and Allen, "the lucky stiff" (24), have engaged in a conspiracy of the flesh and that Florrie, desperate to conceal her wrong from her sister Marie, has foisted herself on the slow-witted Keefe, an easy patsy. This scenario might also account for their overly intimate living arrangements: After Florrie and Jack reunite they share

---

[23]*Handedness is impossible to determine in infants, so it might be that the doctor, if he is not merely joking, is part of the conspiracy to taunt Jack and make him look foolish. If he does so at the instigation of Florrie and/or Allen, perhaps one or both of them are sending the impercipient busher a hint about little Al's true paternity.*

the Allens' apartment for the remainder of the season, just as the Allens have lived with them for most of the previous winter (55–56). It might be that what the busher never knows will never hurt him, but the likely circumstance of little Al's bastard birth, with its background of adultery and nominal incest (by marriage), is an ironic undermining of Jack's home.

By denying Jack even an evolving suspicion that little Al is not his biological son, Lardner exposes the busher as a quintessential fool; by withholding any tell-tale sign that would place the matter beyond ambiguity, he perpetrates a minor literary crime. The reader is left with the author's coyness and an uneasy sense that it has made him a secondary fall guy, Busher Keefe's unwitting fellow dupe. This feeling is intensified by the novel's epistolary form, which implicates the reader by nominally casting him as Jack's "friend Al" and, therefore, dumb-by-association. The busher, it seems, is trapped in a sham family and ersatz home, while the reader, apprehending the near-perversity of the situation, is certain of little beyond his own misgivings. When Jack displays vigilant concern for little Al, the reader feels something like embarrassment on Jack's behalf; Lardner should be ashamed, one almost decides, to make his protagonist such a hapless ass.

The busher's obtuseness and the reader's guilty knowledge are redeemed, surprisingly, by Jack's better sensibilities. Although he is hopelessly inept in caring for the child (98–99), Jack's obsessive interest in little Al betokens a change in his solipsistic conceit. His demeanor in the penultimate chapter, "The Busher's Kid," might be no more remarkable than that of any normal, responsible parent, but nothing prior to little Al's birth suggests that Jack will mature into a normal, responsible adult. To some extent, Jack's eagerness to show off his son is an uncunning means of self-aggrandizement — a strategy familiar to most parents. It is as if Jack understands his own shortcomings for the first time and looks to little Al to redeem them. Indeed, he is so eager for Kid Gleason to see little Al that, in anticipating the visit, Jack's expectations almost outstrip his pen: "I am glad he is comeing because he will think more of me when he sees what a fine baby I got though he thinks a hole lot of me now.... I will tell you what he says about little Al and I bet he will say he never seen no prettyer baby but even if he don't say nothing at all I will know he is kidding" (91). Jack can never escape the quality of his performances, for they define his baseball competence and invite the professional judgments of Kid Gleason and others. In "The Busher's Kid," however, he begins to understand that life involves more than the ability to throw a baseball and that his standing as a father depends on criteria other than his won-lost record. Jack's impulse to "get the game over with quick so as I can get back here and take care of little Al" (90) signals this realignment of priorities. Jack seems to have learned how to place his family before baseball; the game is his livelihood, but it means nothing without a greater good to nurture. Jack senses these values even if he cannot articulate them, writing instead another revealing "P.S.": "Babys is great stuff Al and if I was you I would not wait no longer but would hurry up and adopt 1 somewheres" (90).

The "P.S." testifies to Jack's enthusiasm about his new family and indicates that little Al would be (as he is) a happy addition even if the busher knew that the child is not his own. Its peculiar circumstances aside, this is the life Jack devoutly wishes to possess.

As a pitcher, Jack excels during this period. Although his family lacks its own home — he, Florrie, and little Al are still living with the Allens — having a wife and son seems to raise Jack to a level of performance he has never previously attained. Predictably, Jack's exalted conception of his own prowess and his concomitant disparagement of his teammates' efforts continue. The games he wins reflect his abilities, whereas the ones he loses have been "throwed away behind me" by poor fielding (91). Still, Jack professes not to care about his record, for "I am not the kind of man that is allways thinking about there record and playing for there record while I am satisfied if I give the club the best I got and if I win all O.K. And if I lose who's fault is it. Not mine Al" (91). Critics like to point out that Jack Keefe does not change during the course of his letters, that his "busher" characterization is emendable neither by education nor experience. Any alterations of his character are usually taken to be fleeting and superficial.[24] Although the advent of little Al foregrounds those elements of Jack's persona that make him a neurotic parent — impulsiveness, abrupt swings of mood and behavior — Jack's other "busher" traits — ignorance and boastfulness among them — remain intact. He is a more effective pitcher but still has the demeanor of a loutish boor. Kid Gleason confirms this impression in "Along Came Ruth," a Jack Keefe baseball story set at a later date than any chapter of *You Know Me Al*.[25] In "Along Came Ruth," Gleason is more personally concerned with Jack's private life than any of the novel's chapters reflect. After another episode of irrational play on the diamond and abusive behavior at home (Jack has accused Florrie of being romantically involved with her business partner), Gleason upbraids the busher:

> "Well," [Gleason] says "I was over to see your little wife last night and I have got a notion to bust you in the jaw." So I asked him what he meant and he said "She sported your kids wile you was in the war and she is doing more than you to sport them now and she goes in pardners with a man that's O.K. and has got a wife of his own that works with him and you act like a big sap and make her cry and pretty near force her out of a good business and all for nothing except that you was born a busher and can't get over it" [193].

Gleason sets the matter right and preserves the Keefes' marriage — a service he performs more than once — but Jack does not assimilate the offered wisdom.

[24]*This judgment, generally supported by the narrative and by Jack's predictable responses when faced with a new or difficult situation, is implicit in nearly all of the criticism that addresses the issue. See Maxwell Geismar,* Writers in Crisis: The American Novel, 1925–1940 *(Boston: Houghton Mifflin, 1942), 10; Candelaria 28–29; DeMuth 75; Oriard 91–93; Hart 117–120; Jones & Smith 132–134.*

[25]*"Along Came Ruth" is a Jack Keefe baseball story printed in the* Saturday Evening Post *several years after the publication of* You Know Me Al. *See Bruccoli's note in* Ring Around the Bases *(179) and note 30 infra.*

Parenthetically, the game that Jack loses through this latest interlude of reflexive rage also registers the ascendancy, in 1919, of Babe Ruth and the transformative effect of his home run hitting. Ruth hits a first-inning, three-run homer on Jack's final pitch of that game, but Jack notices only the inherent contradiction that he believes is responsible for his undoing: "a man can't pitch baseball and have any home life and a man can't have the kind of home life I have got and pitch baseball" (193).[26]

Due, perhaps, to nothing more complicated than his ignorance of life's little compromises (and despite the compromises in which he himself traffics), Jack concludes that sustaining a marriage, a home, and a father's responsibilities conflicts with the demands of professional baseball. If his baseball career must, indeed, be pursued at the expense of his home life, or vice-versa, this conflict becomes apparent long before the busher faces Babe Ruth. In "The Busher's Kid," Jack forbids Florrie to attend the city series even though he is slated to pitch because he will not trust little Al's safe-keeping to any stranger. Believing that Florrie is with little Al, Jack pitches shutout ball for seven innings. Then he sees Florrie and Marie in the grandstand and demands to be removed from the game (101). Manager Callahan orders him to the mound, but the busher cannot concentrate on pitching, so worried is he that little Al might be "dying right now and maybe if I was home I could do something" (102). After Jack loads the bases and Callahan takes him out, the neurotic father leaps into street clothes and runs straight home, where he finds an adolescent babysitter looking after his son (102). Jack is appalled; the girl is fourteen and has "no babys of her own! And what did she know about takeing care of him? Nothing Al" (102). The deception leads to a fierce argument, which melts away after Kid Gleason counsels Florrie in private. They tell Jack that the matter is resolved, that he can go to the ballpark and pitch and "give the club the best I got" (103). Jack, assuming that Gleason has convinced Florrie to stay home with the baby, pitches well, and the White Sox win. As if to reward himself, Jack plans an off-season far from the ballpark's madding crowds, during which he plans to "stay home and play with little Al" (104). The only apparent impediment to his realizing this intention is his not having a home to which he can bring his family. Jack wants to come home to Bedford, but Florrie consistently vetoes this move. Jack believes that he must "leave her have her own way about something" after she has missed

[26]*In "The Battle of Texas," Kid Gleason helps to save the Keefes' marriage by casually thwarting Jack's dalliance with a certain Miss Krug, "a swell heiress from St. Louis" (166), who drives her own automobile and with whom Jack keeps sporadic company during his first spring training after returning from France (where he has served briefly in the trenches; having been wounded in the left arm, he is sent home) and becoming the father of a second child, a girl (168–171). Although Jack mentions Florrie and the children in his letters, it is Gleason who pointedly alludes to them in Miss Krug's presence. Jack's duplicity and disappointment are clear: "Well of course they won't be no more picture shows for Miss Krug and I and of course it don't make no differents to me as I was going to tell her about me being married and everything and her and I was just good friends and liked to talk to each other but its haveing [Gleason] cut in on my private affairs and try to run them that makes me sore and he must think this is the army the way he acts" (174). Gleason intervenes before adultery is consummated, but Jack's protestations indicate that the girl has charmed him.*

the city series, so a Bedford homecoming seems unlikely. Jack's disposition changes dramatically, however, when he learns that Florrie has deceived him again: She has hired a nurse with some of the $50 that the White Sox have paid her to stay home and has gone to every game. In reaction, Jack decides to take little Al to Bedford and leave Florrie behind — an unconventional and, given the era's assumptions about the necessities of motherhood, infeasible plan. The idea marks the extremity of Jack's determination to impress his will upon his personal life but turns out to be nothing more than a threat made in anger. Committed to founding a home that matches his conception of what a home should be, Jack patches up his marriage and writes that he wants to renew the lease on the yellow house "because Florrie has gave up and will go to Bedford or anywheres else with me now" (107–108). Jack seems just a train trip away from his long-sought arrival.

And yet, circumstances collude with the busher's malleable nature to divert the final passage. Now it is baseball itself that lures Jack Keefe farther from any real or imagined home he has ever had. Offered the opportunity to join the 1913-1914 around-the-world exhibition tour staged by Charles Comiskey and John McGraw — and constantly cajoled by McGraw himself to participate — Jack virtually renounces his interest in a home apart from the camaraderie of athletes.[27] Given his hitherto persistent desire for family life, this behavior is paradoxical. The sense of paradox intensifies when one notes that Jack, who claims to look forward to bringing his family to Bedford and spending the winter with "Bertha and [Al] and the rest of the boys" (109), initiates his own outward movement. Jack postpones his return in the first letter of "The Busher Beats It Hence," choosing to pitch in the final exhibition game before the teams leave Chicago. Pride and other inducements lead him to join the tour, which takes him to Mississippi and Texas, across the southwest to San Diego, north to San Francisco, Oregon, and Washington, then to Canada and, eventually, Japan. The earlier trials of his domestic life suggest that Jack does not lose much by this delay; when one learns that he asks Florrie "did she care if we did not go to Bedford for an other week and she says No she did not care if we dont go for 6 years" (110), one understands that Jack postpones only a renewal of familiar tumult. Florrie's predisposition to be miserable in Bedford outweighs her concern about Jack's absence. To avoid the former, she first assents to Jack's accompanying the tour as far as Vancouver, which will keep her in Chicago for an extra month (113). When

---

[27]Organized by Comiskey and McGraw, this tour occurred during the 1913-1914 off-season along the lines sketched by Keefe in "The Busher Beats It Hence." For the historical details, see John McGraw, by Charles C. Alexander (New York: Viking Penguin, 1988), 173–177. As Keefe reports, McGraw was short of able-armed pitchers because several Giants hurlers chose to stay home. As a stop-gap, McGraw borrowed a young White Sox pitcher, recently acquired from the Western League, who pitched so effectively that McGraw did try to buy his contract. This pitcher was Urban "Red" Faber, who started the next season with the White Sox, pitched for them for twenty years, and was elected to the Hall of Fame in 1964. Coincidentally, the first Jack Keefe baseball story appeared in the Saturday Evening Post on March 7, 1914, the same day that baseball boosters treated the returning players to a welcome-home banquet. See Walton R. Patrick, Ring Lardner (New York: Twayne, 1963), 42.

Florrie finally accedes to the entire tour, it seems as if Jack has shrewdly parlayed his wife's revulsion for a Bedford winter into an all-expenses-paid trip around the world for himself. However, the busher's ingenuous language — and Florrie's alacritous consent — signal that Jack blunders in spite of himself into a fulfillment of what have become his revised wishes. For despite his real concern for wife and child, Jack now desires neither to be homeward bound nor bound to a home.

For the first time, Jack understands that "home" is a circumscribed place of sharply defined relationships. Its possibilities of exploration and excitement are modest, the opportunities it offers for novelty few. As he weighs familial obligations against his nascent desire to visit foreign countries and play baseball for new fans, "to go a round the world and see every thing they is to be saw" (117), Jack realizes that a long winter on home ground with wife and child is prospectively less interesting than an extended exile. Jack seems to guess that being at home will subject him to frustrations that might not be balanced by domestic comforts, and avail him of a serenity that is at best suppositional. Conversely, exile in this instance promises to be fulfilling in its own right. The reader perceives that the others want Jack along as witless comic relief — McGraw tells the uncomprehending busher, "I like to be a round with boys that is funny and dont know nothing a bout it" (115) — but Jack, to his credit, recognizes that Bedford is not the limit of the world: "I guess the boys in Bedford would not be jellus if I was to go. ... [S]ome of the boys down home has not never been no futher a way then Terre Haute" (117). In wishing his conscience and volition free — Florrie at first forbids his departure (110) — Jack is willing to rewrite his story yet again, if he only could: "Well Al it is to late now to cry in the sour milk but I wisht I had not never saw Florrie untill next year and then I and her could get married just like we done last year only I dont know would I do it again or not but I guess I would on acct. of little Al" (118). Although his resolve wavers (he admits on the eve of sailing, "I would give all most any thing I got Al to be back in Chi with little Al and Florrie" [126]), Jack embarks on his self-imposed exile, reaching back even as he departs to touch once more the home he is leaving. Fearing that he might perish at sea, Jack instructs Al to see that Florrie collects the insurance money and then to establish her in a home in Bedford, for "she can live there a hole lot cheaper than she can live in Chi and besides I know Bertha would treat her right and help her out all she could. All so Al I want you and Bertha to help take care of little Al untill he grows up big enough to take care of him self and if he looks like as if he was going to be left handed dont let him Al but make him use his right hand for every thing" (127–128). Even as he removes himself, Jack sets forth plans for the home he has always wanted but at which he has never quite arrived. To some extent, his prospective absence is, to him, almost moot, provided that he can insure the stability of his family, which only now tenuously coheres after much time and great trouble. The well-being of his wife and child genuinely concerns Jack and proposes that he has, in this important respect, matured from a heedless busher into a cognizant if unevenly attentive family man. Ironically, Jack's impulse to move homeward persists even as the distance of his outward journey lengthens; circumnavigating the globe is, perhaps, but the prelude to a future homecoming. Readers tend to forget that Jack writes to "friend Al" during the around-the-world tour and again when he serves in France during World War I. Of the additional stories, five relate the vicissitudes of the busher's baseball days in his inimitable voice and reiterate his concerns about family, money, and home. The final set of letters, subsumed under the topical title "The Busher Pulls a Mays,"[28] chronicles the decline and eventual eclipse of Jack's baseball career. He is traded at last to the Philadelphia Athletics, a team that, in 1919, can be said to have been composed entirely of bushers.[29] Having drunk and pitched his way off the pennant-winning White Sox, Jack finds himself consigned to another, seemingly permanent, exile. The confident bluster he enlists to put a bright face on his decline is the same sophomoric boasting and swagger once more recycled. From his experiences, Jack Keefe seems in the end to have learned nothing; from witnessing the busher's megalomania, the reader learns that the solipsistic personality, especially when combined with an athlete's arrogance of the body, is capable of uncovering inexhaustible resources of self-vindication. Read in the order of their periodical publication,[30] the eleven Jack Keefe baseball stories depict only a modest development of their main character, whom they delineate in firm, bold lines. Busher Keefe might not change in most ways, but the heartfelt attention he devotes to little Al describes a significant improvement on the self-centered personality that dictates his initial letters home. This evolution, slight though it is, distinguishes Jack from what E. M. Forster defined long ago as a "flat" character.[31] Although Lardner's busher never rounds into full verisimilitude, the inadvertent self-portrait that coalesces as his letters home accumulate does display both the high definition of idiosyncratic traits and the critical obliviousness of the self's own foibles that distinguish the most memorable of Robert Browning's dramatic monologues.

[28]The "Mays" of the title is pitcher Carl Mays. In 1919, disgruntled over the weak support of his Red Sox teammates and discouraged about the team's chances of winning the pennant, Mays walked out in midseason and went home to Pennsylvania. The complicated series of rule-breakings, clandestine deals, and judicial decisions that sent Mays to the Yankees is told by Mike Sowell in The Pitch That Killed (New York: Macmillan, 1989), 26–58.

[29]In 1919, the Athletics finished last for the fifth consecutive year. They won 36 games, lost 104, and did not have in their starting lineup even one player from the pennant-winning team of 1914. Even their winning pitchers of 1914 had been sold to other clubs (Baseball Encyclopedia 251, 258, 264, 268, 271, 275).

[30]Donald Elder's account of how Lardner's "busher" stories came to be published in the Saturday Evening Post is quite informative; see Elder 113–124. The first six stories appeared serially from March 7, 1914, to November 7, 1914, and were published in book form in 1916 as You Know Me Al. Later Jack Keefe stories dealing with baseball subjects or having a baseball context ran in the Saturday Evening Post on the following dates: (1) "Call For Mr. Keefe!" March 9, 1918; (2) "The Busher Reenlists," April 19, 1919; (3) "The Battle of Texas," May 24, 1919; (4) "Along Came Ruth," July 26, 1919; and (5) "The Busher Pulls A Mays," October 18, 1919.

[31]In Aspects of the Novel (1927; reprinted, New York: Harcourt Brace Jovanovich, 1955): "Flat characters were called 'humorous' in the seventeenth century, and are sometimes called types, and sometimes caricatures. In their purest form, they are constructed round a single idea or quality: when there is more than one factor in them, we get the beginning of the curve towards the round. The really flat character can be expressed in one sentence" (Forster 67–68).

◆ Seven ◆
"Only Connect"
The Tragicomic Romance
of Roy Hobbs

The romance, which deals with heroes, is intermediate between the
novel, which deals with men, and the myth, which deals with gods.
—Northrop Frye, Anatomy of Criticism

Since its publication almost fifty years ago, Bernard Malamud's first novel
has been the object of so much critical attention that a recent commentator has
remarked, "*The Natural* lives to be interpreted—or did before it was interpreted to death."[1] It is regrettable that the book's mythic content should have
caused its demise after having vouchsafed it a kind of vogue among academi-
cally-trained readers, but this fate is, perhaps, poetically just. Its hero, Roy
Hobbs, is similarly undone by mythic forces, which initially lend him the figure
and substance of a superhuman athlete capable of miraculous feats. Like the
heroes whose legendary exploits his own performances shadow, Roy seems to
be part divine. Humble origins, however, and an ordinary character (as well as
a peasant's name) indicate that Roy's heroic pretensions are a sham; in the end,
he is revealed as little more than the defeated knight of a modern romance. His
story begins as a comic melodrama of the American Dream, then swiftly turns
into a cautionary tale about the self-destructive nature of hubris. The balance
of the narrative depicts Roy trying to live correctly in his "second life," which
Iris Lemon describes as "the life we live with after" our first life of critical learning.[2] In his second life, Roy attempts to claim everything he believes he has lost
through the "accident" of fifteen years before, not the least of which are the
badges of athletic valor: a column of estimable statistics set down beside his

[1]*Christian K. Messenger,* Sport and the Spirit of Play in Contemporary American Fiction *(New York:*
Columbia University Press, 1990), 336. Cited as CAF.

[2]*Bernard Malamud,* The Natural *(1952; reprinted, New York: Farrar, Straus and Giroux, 1989), 158.*
Quotations and references follow this edition.

name in the record book and public adulation as "'the best there ever was in the game'" (33).

More important, however, than fame, more important than women and money, are the time and space of home. Having hardly possessed a home, having lived most of his life with no sense of being "at home," Roy seeks not a place but a way of living that will return him to the serene self-sufficiency that he remembers as the best part of his boyhood. Estranged from this youthful plenitude by dislocation and abandonment, Roy struggles to return to time past, to being the boy he once was and recapturing the boy's feeling of contentment and well-being. In this sense, home for Roy is a state of inner peace—a state of mind and soul—rather than a physical location. His final baseball season recounts Roy's quest for such peace and how that quest goes wrong. Perhaps the most tragic aspect of the Natural's career is that Roy recognizes how to return home but fails to commit himself to the actions that would lead him toward reunion. Unable to accept the finitude of his existence, unwilling to deny or even stem his appetites, Roy Hobbs learns nothing from his first life and so relives its mistakes in his second. His journey ends with the beginning of another exile, suggesting that Roy is condemned to repeat the cycle of pain and doom thereafter. The story one hopes will end happily resolves itself as the tragicomedy of a failed hero.

To appreciate the nature of Roy's thwarted quest, one must approach *The Natural* not simply as a novel but as a Romance. According to Nathaniel Hawthorne, one of the genre's foremost practitioners, the Romance takes shape in the author's darkened study suffused with moonlight.[3] Spilling through a window, "falling so white upon the carpet, and showing all its figures so distinctly," moonlight can render the familiar room "a neutral territory, somewhere between the real world and fairy-land, where the Actual and the Imaginary may meet, and each imbue itself with the nature of the other."[4] The light's peculiar cast causes a slight skewing of ordinary vision that transforms the commonplace into something unfamiliar. A book written to capture such a vision is a Romance, which differs from a Novel in its representation of reality, or mimesis. The Novel intends "a very minute fidelity, not merely to the possible, but to the probable and ordinary course of man's experience"; the Romance enjoys "a certain latitude" of style and substance, and presents "the

---

[3]In *"Malamud's Unnatural* The Natural" *in* Studies in American Jewish Literature 7: 2 *(1988): 138–152, Ellen Pifer uses Hawthorne's remarks on Romance to explain the narrative's "'unnatural' landscape, the deliberate design ... a network of seemingly magical events, interlocking images, linguistic motifs ... [that distance] the reader from the novel's setting and characters" (138). Pifer argues that Malamud "[grafts] postmodernist techniques to a deeply rooted moral vision" to propose that, despite the ambiguities of human perception, the individual's moral sense is innate and, therefore, always accountable for the behavior it permits (151).*

[4]*Nathaniel Hawthorne,* The Scarlet Letter *(1850), reprinted in* Nathaniel Hawthorne, Novels (Fanshawe, The Scarlet Letter, The House of the Seven Gables, The Blithedale Romance, The Marble Faun), *edited by Millicent Bell (New York: Literary Classics of the United States, 1983), 149. Quotations and references follow this edition and are cited parenthetically by title and page number.*

truth of the human heart" with an admixture of "the Marvellous," according to the author's "choosing and creation" (*Seven Gables* 351). Although "it must rigidly subject itself to laws" (*Seven Gables* 351), the Romance is not expected by its readers to be completely plausible. One might consider it a heightened or more obviously "artificial" form of prose fiction. In foregrounding the archetypal nature of its characters and infusing events with symbolic meaning, the Romance tries not to be "like life" but larger than life: more colorful and exciting, more lavishly given over to heroic or magical deeds, more resonant with awareness of the great issues at stake. In a Romance, strange events occur; physical laws are often suspended. Action is not limited to the necessary, inevitable, or merely surprising but incorporates the melodramatic and symbolic while maintaining the narrative's aesthetic coherence.[5]

The Natural presents readers with a particular challenge, for it is not a "pure" Romance but a composite of Romance and Novel.[6] The book mixes the significant detail, colloquial language, and characterization of a Novel with the symbolic content and magical events of a Romance. Because the action conforms more to a mythic template than to the demands of verisimilitude, the magical trumps the realistic at moments of crisis or impasse. This varied mimesis troubles many readers; some, expecting the representation of reality to be consistent, find the book silly or tedious. Admittedly, if mimetic and tonal consistency are taken to be definitive of the formal realism of the Novel, then *The Natural* cannot seriously be considered a novel at all. Its mimetic shifts are often abrupt and occasionally startling, and the reader might legitimately feel disoriented from chapter to chapter or even from one paragraph to the next. Individualized characters just slightly more distinct than caricatures or types gesture within a loosely knit allegory, intermittently re-enacting ancient rituals in a realistic context. Magical effects compromise verisimilitude and heighten the symbolic quality of fictive events. To make sense of the narrative, one must

---

[5]See Richard Chase, The American Novel and Its Tradition *(Garden City, NY: Doubleday and Co., 1957): "[T]he romance, following distinctly the medieval example, feels free to render reality in less volume and detail. It tends to prefer action to character, and action will be freer in a romance than in a novel, encountering, as it were, less resistance from reality. ... In American romances it will not matter much what class people come from, and where the novelist would arouse our interest in a character by exploring his origin, the romancer will probably do so by enveloping it in mystery. Character itself becomes, then, somewhat abstract and ideal, so much so in some romances that it seems to be merely a function of plot. The plot we may expect to be highly colored. Astonishing events may occur, and these are likely to have a symbolic or ideological, rather than a realistic, plausibility. Being less committed to the immediate rendition of reality than the novel, the romance will more freely veer toward mythic, allegorical, and symbolistic forms" (Chase 13).*

[6]See Northrop Frye, Anatomy of Criticism: Four Essays *(1957; reprinted, Princeton, NJ: Princeton University Press, 1973), for the separableness of the Romance and its continuity with the Novel: "The prose romance, then, is an independent form of fiction to be distinguished from the novel and extracted from the miscellaneous heap of prose works now covered by that term. ... "Pure" examples of either form are never found; there is hardly any modern romance that could not be made out to be a novel, and vice versa. ... It may be asked, therefore, what is the use of making the above distinction, especially when, though undeveloped in criticism, it is by no means unrealized. ... ¶ The reason is that a great romancer should be examined in terms of the convention he chose"* (Anatomy 305).

read it on its own terms, according to its own "given": as a prose romance that selectively utilizes certain elements of the Novel, according to its author's judgment.[7]

As a novelistic romance, *The Natural* is generally read as a retelling of the regeneration myths of Western culture. Critics soon noticed the interpenetrating renditions of fertility paradigm, Arthurian legend, and Jungian archetype that crowd its narrative, and assiduously combed the pages of Sir James Frazer's *The Golden Bough* (1890–1915), Jessie Weston's *From Ritual to Romance* (1920), and T. S. Eliot's "The Waste Land" (1922) to identify the archetypes that Malamud transposes into images of modern America.[8] As its title indicates, Malamud's version foregrounds the hero, whose arrival in a desiccated land seems to portend a season of new birth: a greening of the fields and the spiritual redemption of the people. Baseball serves as an acculturating device that translates the myths of, respectively, Osiris, Demeter, the Grail quest heroes, and Christ for a twentieth-century American audience, and thereby enables the author to invest a modern artifact (the game of baseball and its long season) with ancient meaning.[9] In this construction, the contemporary significance of Malamud's transformative vision remains the final item of debate, for the Passion of Roy Hobbs, unlike that of the martyred gods and exemplary heroes whose trials he recapitulates, is unredemptive. Malamud emphasizes the old god's death and downplays the advent of the new god, whose appearance a reader of legend or myth would expect to inspire celebration — and narrative focus. At this crux, the story follows a novelistic mode; as if obsessed with the demise of its (anti)hero, the narrative pursues Roy Hobbs into a figurative grave with Wonderboy, shattered talisman of his natural

---

[7]*Some critics disagree. See Gerry O'Connor's "Bernard Malamud's* The Natural: 'The Worst There Ever Was in the Game'" *in* Arete 3:2 *(Spring 1986): 37–41, for a "realistic" approach to* The Natural.

[8]*Earl R. Wasserman's seminal article, "The Natural: Malamud's World Ceres" in* The Centennial Review of Arts and Sciences 9: 4 *(1965): 438–460, is the earliest complete discussion of these sources and their respective impacts on the novel. Wasserman's explication is so thorough that subsequent efforts to uncover analogues and allusions are obliged to acknowledge its precedence and then address minor items.*

[9]*Malamud's choice of baseball truly seems a "natural" when one considers that baseball's ultimate origin is the ball-and-stick rituals performed annually in ancient Egypt. These rituals, part of the fertility rites overseen by the priest-kings, involved a mock combat in which opposing sides would vie for possession of and eventually dismember an effigy of Osiris, then ceremoniously bury the pieces in a gesture intended to restore the vital spirit to the dormant land. The head of the effigy acquired special significance because it was believed to be the most powerful part of the human body and consequently became a symbol for the spirit of fertility generally associated with Osiris. The object of the ritual combat became to capture the head of the god and return it safely to his temple — to bring it "home." See Cordelia Candelaria,* Seeking the Perfect Game: Baseball in American Literature *(New York: Greenwood Press, 1989), 7–14. See also Robert W. Henderson,* Ball, Bat, and Bishop: The Origin of Ball Games *(1947; reprinted, Detroit: Gale Research, 1974). Modern baseball recapitulates many of these ancient patterns, especially that of seasonal rebirth, growth, maturity, and demise, the climactic passages of the Fall Classic now splendidly lit by harvest moons. Malamud seems well aware of baseball's Egyptian origin, for the description of Roy Hobbs's body indicates that the ballplayer is a modern incarnation of the dismembered Osiris: "Investigation showed he had no appendix — it had long ago been removed along with some other stuff. (All were surprised at his scarred and battered body.)" (192).*

prowess, then devolves to a full stop, truncated and unredeemed by the dying god's "many bitter tears" (237). In a sense, Malamud has it both ways, but even the new god's premature arrival (the season is October, not April) and the pathos of Roy's defeat cannot obviate the sense of a pessimistic ending. Critics have proposed various explanations for this resolution: the obdurate selfishness of the modern hero; the corrupt society whose debased values the hero assimilates and enacts; the inadequacy of the athlete, no matter how gifted, to serve his culture as a true hero; the template of myth and legend and the completion of its fixed pattern that preordains the hero's demise.[10] *The Natural* invites this kind of analysis, requires it in fact. Before attempting a broader discussion, one is virtually obligated to review the story from the perspective of the myths and archetypes that form so large a part of its critical legacy.

Endlessly allusive, elaborately patterned, *The Natural* demonstrates that baseball's "rules and realities,"[11] as Jacques Barzun has described them, can supply both subject matter and metaphor in a self-consciously "literary" work. Roy Hobbs, a naïve athlete with heroic aspirations who springs from America's rustic West, enjoys in his youth a brief baseball triumph played in an interstice of time. In an impromptu contest, Roy strikes out the American League's best hitter with three magical pitches, thereby winning the adulation of Harriet Bird, cryptic classicist and student of mythology. Lured by desire into conversation with Harriet, Roy unknowingly reveals the self-centered hubris that must disqualify him from serving his culture as a legitimate hero.[12] The veiled femme fatale judges the Natural to be a false idol, unworthy of adulation, and executes her verdict by shooting Roy with a silver bullet. Consigned to a fifteen years'

[10]*These views, in whole or in part, can be found in the following works:* Candelaria, Seeking the Perfect Game; Messenger, Sport and the Spirit of Play in Contemporary American Fiction; *Michael Oriard,* Dreaming of Heroes: American Sports Fiction, 1868–1980 *(Chicago: Nelson-Hall, 1982); Wiley Lee Umphlett,* The Sporting Myth and the American Experience: Studies in Contemporary Fiction *(Lewisburg, PA: Bucknell University Press, 1975); Wasserman, "Malamud's World Ceres"; David A. Jones and Leverett T. Smith, "Jack Keefe & Roy Hobbs: Two All-American Boys" in Aethlon 6:2 (Spring 1989): 119–137; Robert Shulman, "Myth, Mr. Eliot, and the Comic Novel" in Modern Fiction Studies (Winter 1966-1967): 395–403; Jonathan Baumbach, "The Economy of Love" in Kenyon Review 25:3 (Summer 1963), as reprinted in Modern Critical Views, edited by Harold Bloom (New York: Chelsea House Publishers, 1986), 21–36; Frederick W. Turner, "Myth Inside and Out: Malamud's The Natural" in Novel 1:2 (1968): 133–139; Daniel Walden, "Bernard Malamud, An American Jewish Writer and His Universal Heroes" in Studies in American Jewish Literature 7:2 (1988): 153–161.*

[11]*Jacques Barzun's famous line, "Whoever wants to know the heart and mind of America had better learn baseball, the rules and realities of the game," appears in* God's Country and Mine *(1954).*

[12]*See Norman Podhoretz, "Achilles in Left Field," Commentary (March 1953): 321–326: "Malamud would like us to think that his hero's defect is a classic case of hubris, [but] his failure to make the sense of pride concrete ... is a tip-off that he no more believes in the tragedy of pride than we do. ... Appetite, nothing more, is Roy's tragic flaw" (326). Podhoretz argues that* The Natural *is a failed tragedy (325). See also Harvey Swados, "Baseball à la Wagner: The Nibelung in the Polo Grounds," in American Mercury 75:346 (October 1952), as reprinted in Critical Essays on Bernard Malamud, edited by Joel Salzberg (Boston: G. K. Hall and Co., 1987), 23–25. Swados focuses on themes of tragic heroism, hero-worship, and the effects of the lingoistic prose style; he, too, judges the book a failure.*

wandering in the wilderness,[13] Roy is finally restored to the baseball diamond by what seems to be poetic justice cooperating with time. A reborn rookie at age 34, Roy is vouchsafed a single season on earth. He brings rain to a dry land, transforms defeat into victory, collects life-enhancing hits, suffers killing strike-outs, and leads the Knights toward the goal most prized: the league pennant. Alternately tested and tempted by the life-giving and death-dealing avatars of the archetypal Mother (*Mater Magna* and *Mater Saeva*, respectively [Wasserman 448]), Roy's life pivots on a final decision. At his moment of truth, the Natural succumbs to the same self-centered impulse that has caused his first death. He takes the Judge's bribe money to throw the playoff game without understanding that it is blood money, and that it is his own blood that will be shed in pursuit of the bitch-goddess of success, Memo Paris, "a whore" (235). At the moment of public crisis, Roy realizes his transgression but, having repented too late, fails to connect with the decisive pitch. His personal life parallels his baseball performances and similarly deteriorates despite (or because of) his overreaching ambition to "make it big." Like the climactic swing-and-miss, Roy does not "connect" with the characters he most needs to know, particularly Iris Lemon, and understands at his career's end that he is the once-and-future victim of his own nature. The reader's corresponding insight is that Roy Hobbs cannot elude the logic of his temporal existence. Striving always to regain lost time and return to the younger, better self whom he believes he has left in the distant past, as well as to catch up with his destiny of baseball glory, Roy is unable to live in a finite present in which his ambitions are compromised by age. Having seen the best of his time before he begins, the Natural never enjoys a fruition of love, family, or home. Emblematic of a fertility god but desperate to resist the progress of the seasons, Roy Hobbs is a sterile icon.

At every moment of fear, soul-searching, or self-doubt, Roy reveals his concern with time. Even before Harriet Bird inflicts the gunshot wound that initiates the exile of his first life, Roy is aware of the temporal disjunction that has already placed him behind his time. Looking out the window of the eastbound

---

[13]Wiley Lee Umphlett states that Roy "spends fifteen years in the bush leagues before making the big time" and that "Roy's years as a minor leaguer are integral to interpreting and understanding the meaning and interrelationship of the two major divisions of the story" (Umphlett 158). To be slightly more precise, Roy's "fifteen years in the bush leagues" are not "integral" to understanding anything because they have not occurred. As Roy tells Pop Fisher, he has recently returned to baseball and has been playing with the Oomoo Oilers, a semipro team. Before that, Roy was a high school ballplayer but, by his own account, has not played professional baseball (what Pop calls "organized baseball") prior to joining the Knights (The Natural 48). Thus, the natural has never been a busher. Roy does not provide a detailed account of what he has been doing between the day Harriet Bird shot him down and the day he picks up baseball again, but his prowess as a hitter makes an extended bush league rustication incredible. The shape of Roy's life during the lost fifteen years — literally, his "buried life" — may be inferred from several allusions to the trouble he's seen; see The Natural, 52, 120–121, 156–158. Like Jay Gatsby, Roy's past is an enigma to his casual admirers, who are more than willing to script his history themselves; see The Natural, 103–104, and The Great Gatsby, edited by Bruccoli (New York: Cambridge University Press, 1991), 36, 40–41, 49, 52–53.

train, Roy sees dawn breaking yet knows that time has already been lost: "somewhere near they left Mountain Time and lost — no, picked up — yes, it was lost an hour, what Sam called the twenty-three hour day" (12). Roy is able to anticipate the break of day without a timepiece (9) yet is incapable of telling time as a clock measures it. Having entered the tick-tock of ordinary chronology when he boarded the train, Roy's temporal progress proves to be swift and virtually unchecked; apart from the pause during which he vanquishes the Whammer, the train carries Roy steadily away from his origins (in both time and distance) with every minute's mile. Insofar as it expresses these dimensions of the time-space continuum, the image of the speeding train neatly embodies Roy's temporal dilemma: He must be on the train (in the stream of time) to reach his destination (the majors), but the logic of such travel will inevitably bring him to the end of his time. Having ridden these rails, Roy eventually will be obliged to disembark.

The power of this image becomes evident during Roy's "second life," his season with the Knights. Upon his arrival, Roy sits in the Knights' dugout, trying to rest from his journey. He knows that he is fifteen years late; haunted by the specter of a train that is always in motion, Roy feels that he still has a distance to go, that although his body is motionless, his mind and inner being still travel "on the train that never stopped ... through towns and cities, across forests and fields, over long years" (47). The author's expression of this sentiment sets the tone of Roy's impatience, which never completely subsides. Acutely aware of his own belatedness, Roy is unreconciled to time's passing. His anxiety to retrieve the time he has lost is so intense that the present, no matter how gratifying, seems intolerably belated; to Roy, any success he enjoys should have come much, much sooner. Despite his great feats as a hitter, accomplished in merely a matter of weeks, Roy feels dissatisfied with the present and eager for the advent of a more wondrous impending day: "He was gnawed by a nagging impatience — so much more to do, so much of the world to win for himself. He felt he had nothing of value yet to show for what he was accomplishing, and in his dreams he still sped over endless miles of monotonous rail toward something he desperately wanted. Memo, he sighed" (91). It is as if his destiny had unfolded without him, if such a thing were possible, yet were still within reach, so hot is his desire to catch up. Roy's urgency is pervasive, affecting everything he does and says, even constructing the future as something, a time, a place, a person, that is endlessly deferred and ever unattainable. As time continues to slip away, as he watches everything he should already have "[won] for himself" pass beyond his grasp, Roy veers into panic and dread. At the first nadir of his second life, the batting slump that sets in shortly after his night ride with Memo, Roy fantasizes about escape. Chronic failure has brought the rebuke of the fans down on him, and his own frailty — intermittent physical weakness and his refusal (which is really a form of pride) to give up Wonderboy — leaves him without resources to endure it. At this juncture, Roy imagines the ever-traveling train as a means of escaping from his present suffering and returning to a home that he knows does not exist. Awaking alone in the locker room, Roy tries to tell the time by his wristwatch; its being "past midnight" (139) suggests not only the loss of the present (now just-passed) day but also the imminent end of Roy's belated baseball season. At such a moment it is understandable that Roy yearns for human companionship and the safety of home: "He longed for a friend, a father, a home to return to—saw himself packing his duds in a suitcase, buying a ticket, and running for a train. Beyond the first station he'd fling Wonderboy out the window. (Years later, an old man returning to the city for a visit, he would scan the flats to see if it was there, glowing in the mud.) The train sped through the night across the country. In it he felt safe" (139). Even without the wristwatch Roy would know that the hour is late, the day spent, that his own time is quickly wasting. Showing and feeling his age, Roy experiences something like a midlife crisis, his distress evoking a proleptic vision of himself as an old man revisiting the scene of his present undoing. His desire for "a home to return to" is poignant, given his lifelong itinerancy, and appropriately vague; he approaches this home by train but never arrives. Roy's vision of going home is one of an endlessly suspended animation: a train hurtling across the dark continent with himself inside it, feeling a sense of shelter. Implicitly an image of temporal regression (as the train travels westward, Roy will regain the hours he has lost fifteen years ago), the imaginary train ride suggests that the process of moving homeward is almost as desirable as home itself. Home might turn out to be illusory, a bit of wishful thinking, so Roy finds comfort in making the search and believing in it. Yet, as he realizes in the next moment, for Roy even the journey is impossible—but not only for the reasons he assumes.

Home is inaccessible to Roy because his sense of it is identical to his sense of himself as he was as a boy. More than parents or a family, more than any region or town, Roy's point of origin is his boyish self dwelling not so much within time as amidst a natural landscape set in an eternal past.[14] Malamud establishes this trope in "Pre-game," the book's self-contained parable of prefigurement, and returns to it thereafter. Roy, gazing from the train window during his initial journey, imagines a primal scene that displaces traditional notions of home and family. As if it were real, Roy sees a "bone-white farmhouse with sagging skeletal porch, alone in untold miles of moonlight, and before it this white-faced, long-boned boy whipped with train-whistle yowl a glowing ball to someone hidden under a dark oak, who shot it back without thought, and the kid once more wound and returned" (9). Roy's impulse to recall the temporal space of home evokes an image of hauntedness and compulsion. What is presumably a father-son game of catch transpires in front of charnel-house or sepulchre, automatic hands throwing and catching a radiant ball without apparent joy or sense of communion. The father is invisible, the

---

[14]See Umphlett 163: "The sense of aloneness that was a unique part of his lost boyhood is an essential part of the real quest of Roy Hobbs."

boy a ghost-figure, implying that the vision is substanceless, a graphic halluci-nation or dream of fear. Roy shuns this unreal vision, aware that it is, in some emotional or psychic sense, metaphorically accurate, "a way … of observing himself" (9). The scene is not a memory but a sight of pre-memory, an image of what Roy believes must be true about his unremembered home, given his current homelessness. The most telling detail is the "train-whistle yowl" that accents the thrown ball, for this sound effect links the lost scene of play to the journey of "the train that never stopped" (47). Taken together, these elements make Roy's ghostly vision the essential metaphoric expression of the Natural's antagonistic relationship to time, as well as the emblem of his desperate effort to dissolve that conflict in baseball. The vision is unique — it never reappears, and Roy does not revisit either the "bone-white farmhouse" or the game of catch — but its thematic content is reprised many times throughout *The Natural*.

Thus, Roy's conception of home is not grounded in a specific house nor dependent on other characters. Indeed, his idea of being "at home" is solitary, yet not lonely, and matches the disposition of an introspective mind with the "uncivilized" man's way of living in the moment, as if Huck Finn were a stu-dent of Emerson's writings. Like Huck, Roy Hobbs recoils from civilized ver-sions of home life, preferring self-sufficient freedom in natural environs. As if he can foretell at the outset everything that will befall him, Roy leaves his rus-tic origins with trepidation. He seems to know that his movement through time, toward civilization, will culminate in a permanent estrangement from his nat-ural home. Watching from the train, Roy feels the onset of melancholy as he notices land and sky receding, blending into indistinctness. Once lost, his sense of place seems irrecoverable, as if the place itself has disappeared. The past seems to collapse behind him, his vistas closing down like a door swinging shut on a fading day (22). Roy himself feels homeless, a man who comes from nowhere on his way to a vaguely threatening future, as if the train were headed into a storm. It is a classic case of homesickness, which seems paradoxical, given Roy's own sense of homelessness. At this early juncture, before his exile (which begins after he is shot), Roy's melancholy seems overstated; as far as the reader can tell, home exists only as a vision of a whitened sepulchre and as "somewhere, a place he knew was there" (22). Neither offers much hope of reunion. Indeed, Roy's early misgivings (9–10, 22–23) almost lapse into the sentimental or mor-bid, as if he fears that homesickness might become chronic and end in death.

Roy's premature, perhaps excessive melancholy at having "lost the feeling of a particular place" (22) indicates the true nature of what he considers his home. His attraction to natural landscapes and his sense of contentment within them places the matter beyond any doubt. By day, the train window affords Roy a view of forests and hills, then a level woodland that, in most of the ways that mean anything, has given Roy his only true sense of home. The woodland is "the only place he had been truly intimate with in his wanderings, a green world shot through with weird light and strange bird cries, muffled in silence that made the privacy so complete his inmost self had no shame of anything he thought there, and it eased the body-shaking beat of his ambitions" (22–23). Vague, practically unlocatable, this version of home has nonetheless lent Roy a sense of well-being and self-sufficiency, a feeling of safety, all of which he lacks during his baseball career. It is a telling detail, and one that foreshadows his frustration and failure, that Roy ponders returning home so soon after having left it. He has yet to transcend his liminal status as an untested pitcher — his initiation into athletic glory is shortly to follow — yet he feels an impulse to return to boyhood, as if sensing the imminence of Harriet's silver bullet, as well as the inevitability of his final defeat.[15]

Although he evokes his younger self several times during his season of sin and expiation, Roy does not derive constructive knowledge from it. All he possesses of this boyish Natural is a modest collection of images, all so familiar and summarily recollected that the "boy-Roy" figure seems little more than one of American culture's many clichés. Roy conceives one such cliché when, newly arrived in the major leagues, he finds the professional baseball scene to be something other than what he has expected: strange, faintly hostile, overtly profane, essentially disappointing. Roy considers simply walking away, "jumping back on a train, and going wherever people went when they were running out on something. Maybe for a long rest in one of those towns he had lived in as a kid. Like the place where he had that shaggy mutt that used to scamper through the woods, drawing him after it to the deepest, stillest part, till the silence was so pure you could crack it if you threw a rock" (52). Confronted with the quotidian realities of baseball, Roy sees the past beckoning. His alternatives are to play the role of the Natural or devolve to the cliché of a boy and his dog. The landscape is an ancient wood, the time an indefinite past, and his mother and father are absent: not much of a home, but the only inkling of home that Roy can recall. His parents are absent because he seems hardly to have known them.[16] His mother was "'a whore. She spoiled [his] old man's life'"; his father was "'a good guy but died young'" (185), who, Roy tells Harriet, installed him in a series of orphan homes, retrieving him during the summer to teach him baseball (32). Still, Roy does not blame his parents for the strange predicament his life has become, just as he does not yearn to go back to being their son or to any orphan home. Self-invented and self-driven, Roy is a simple fellow, a true Natural. He wishes to return home only to recover the boy he was before something changed powerfully within: "Sometimes he wished he had no ambitions — often wondered where they had come from in his life, because he remembered how satisfied he had been as a youngster, and that with the little he had had — a dog, a stick, an aloneness he loved ... and he wished he could have lived longer in

[15]Wiley Lee Umphlett attributes Roy's ultimate failure to a conflict of native innocence, "as suggested by the novel's recurring references to the forest and his lost boyhood, and the confrontation of experience that the challenge of his goal demands" (Umphlett 158).

[16]As a child, Roy seems to have lived first with his grandmother and then in various orphanages (32); his father, claims Sam Simpson, was a semipro ballplayer "who wanted awful bad to be in the big leagues" (35–36).

his boyhood" (117). This "old thought" (117) visits Roy anew as he and Memo drive through the woods in Roy's new Mercedes-Benz. Both the setting and the companionship are cues for the thought to recur; his lost self haunts the woods' moonlit stillness, and "Memo" is a phonic and graphic substitution for "memory." Roy's overmastering attraction to Memo begins in "the act of love" (77) and continues because "she was a truly beautiful doll with a form like Miss America" (166), but in symbolic terms it tells the reader that Roy is in thrall to memory, which he (erroneously) believes will sustain his athletic potency. To Roy, possessing Memo means recapturing the promise of his youth. He pursues her, yearns for her, ultimately forgoes his only real chance of redemption by committing his future to Memo(ry), a visible form and symbol of the past.

Roy's error becomes obvious on that night's wild ride. Having previously summoned the boy-Roy image and envied its simple inner life and generative solitude, Roy translates the image into a desire for home. As if time, his own unconscious, and the earth itself were conspiring to afford him a glimpse of his own soul, Roy is visited by a sign that his better self still lives, wandering the night like a wraith. With Memo driving fast without lights (memory cannot see what lies ahead), the night's dappled shadows and ghostly light reveal an embodiment of the past. Just as Roy is wishing he could return to a home, he glimpses

> in the moonlight a boy coming out of the woods, followed by his dog. Squinting through the windshield, he was unable to tell if the kid was an illusion thrown forth by the trees or someone really alive. After fifteen seconds he was still there. Roy yelled to Memo to slow down in case he wanted to cross the road. Instead, the car shot forward so fast the woods blurred, the trees racing along like shadows in weak light, then skipping into black and white, finally all black and the moon was gone [122–123].

Roy shouts for light. Memo does not respond, so he turns on the headlamps himself. Memo screams, wrenches the steering wheel, and Roy feels the impact of the car's hitting something, he is not sure what. He tells Memo to stop, that they have run someone down, but Memo refuses, her face as white as the moon. When Roy claims that they must have hit a person because he has heard a human groan, Memo replies, "'That was yourself'" (123). Roy, however, cannot remember having made a sound. Despite the scene's apparent terror, it matters less whether the boy is "real" (an independent character) or a projection of Roy's psyche than that Roy sees the figure, recognizes it, and apprehends that Memo has run it down, not merely intentionally but heedlessly and with seeming vengeance. It seems paradoxical that Memo would attempt to expunge Roy's memory of himself, yet she needs him, on another level of mimesis, to serve her own practical ends. Knowing or guessing that his sense of his better self is the only independent strength Roy has, Memo tries to destroy it so that he will become more the Natural at her behest and, as idiot, simpleton, or fool submit ever more compliantly to her demands. And yet, novelistic realism only tints this scene, for Memo's responses are surpassingly odd if judged by the standards of verisimilitude: she acts by turns like zombie, murderess, and hysteric (123). It might be that, like another American bitch-goddess, Daisy Fay, of an earlier American fable, *The Great Gatsby*, Memo is literally "a bad driver" *(Gatsby* 138). And yet it is Roy who wrecks the Mercedes (124) and, in his death agonal, wounds Iris Lemon with a foul ball purposively struck in anger (223–224). No doubt Nick Carraway would call both of them dangerous for the way they conduct their respective lives, yet such a judgment would be irrelevant to their emblematic roles. Memo's behavior, like Roy's vision of the boy, is shaped not by the criteria of verisimilitude but by the story's symbolic rationale. Even the landscape of moonlight and woods and "trees racing along like shadows in weak light" indicate that this scene is the medium of a Romance.

As Hawthorne would have it, the actual and the imaginary meet on the road that night, and "each imbue[s] itself with the nature of the other." Thus, when Roy returns to what he believes is the scene of the accident, he finds neither a broken body nor sign of injury. Quite simply, he mistakes the mimesis of the event. Like the sportswriters who debate how Roy has been able literally to knock the cover off a baseball (79), Roy tries to understand a magical event through the logic of tangible evidence. Because the story includes several banal acts of magic, like Roy's plucking an egg from Memo's bosom and spilling silver dollars from Gus's nose (112–113), events like the coverless baseball unraveling into center field ought to be called preter-Natural. The truth of what happens on the road that night, like the explanation for what happens to the baseball Roy flays on the first day of summer, is not reducible to the terms of causal realism. The narrative offers a few false hints — the sportswriters' debate about the type of swing necessary to shear the cover off a baseball, Roy's scanning the newspapers for reports of a hit-and-run accident (131) — then quickly forgets them. Despite one sportswriter's experiment with "a hard downward chop" that "[splits] the horsehide" (82) and Roy's finding no news of a vehicular manslaughter, all explanations are inconclusive and become, after a point, misleading. Malamud is either anxious about orchestrating conjunctions of "the Actual and the Imaginary" and ostensibly attempts to mitigate their strangeness, or is subtly teasing the reader with bogus possibilities that underline the monumental irrelevance of interpreting preter–Natural events according to the standards of causal realism.

Many of the book's major episodes possess this preter–Natural quality and can be satisfactorily understood only as a conjunction of "the Actual and the Imaginary." Roy's meeting with Iris Lemon, which initiates the countermovement to his death-dance with Memo, is such a moment. When Iris appears, Roy is still caught in the grip of death, figured as an extended batting slump, and is desperate for release. He steps to the plate in Chicago, an unconfident pinch hitter dreading repeated failure and, having promised to hit a home run for a dying boy (Pete Barney), sick at heart at what failure now might mean. The pitcher, Toomey, gets two quick strikes on Roy, and then Iris intervenes. When she stands up, the fans try to hoot her down, but she ignores them and waits. Catching sight of her, Roy apprehends that "her smile was for him. Now why would she do that for? She seemed to be wanting to say something, and then it flashed on him the reason she was standing was to show her confidence in him. He felt surprised that anybody would want to do that for him. At the same time he became aware that the night had spread out in all directions and was filled with an unbelievable fragrance" (147). Hooting at Iris to sit down, like assuming that she is "mixed up about the seventh inning stretch" (145), is to approach this scene with a stubbornly realistic imagination. By the same token, the game's being played at night despite the fact that night baseball did not come to Wrigley Field until 1988 is irrelevant to the moment's symbolic accuracy. What matters is that Iris transforms the night through her act of faith. The moment coheres: The pitcher throws; Roy swings, connects; the ball streaks through the pitcher's legs, flies over the second baseman's glove, rises "through the light and up into the dark," finally soars skyward "like a white star seeking an old constellation" (147). Literally a "star-shot," Roy's home run saves Mike Barney's son and establishes the crucial link between Roy Hobbs and Iris Lemon.

Having saved the Natural from an untimely death (it is still summer), Iris presides at his confession of his past mistake and witnesses his return to power and grace. Vouchsafing himself the recompense of reunion that the game has lately withheld, Roy crashes four consecutive home runs in a single contest against the Pirates (the Knights' archrival) and enjoys four unhampered passages around the bases and back to home (177). A few games later, Roy continues his assault on time by hitting a line drive that shatters a clock on an outfield fence (178): "The clock spattered minutes all over the place, and after that the Dodgers never knew what time it was" (178). In the a-temporal aftermath, Roy collects fourteen consecutive hits, fully regaining what he has languished without during the devastating slump, "the special exercise of running the bases … the gloating that blew up his lungs when he crossed the plate" (132). Touching home plate inspires Roy as with the breath of life, as one might expect of an impatient exile seeking home. Then, too, his counterclockwise movement around the diamond figuratively undoes time, as if he were retracting the unwinding hours. For Roy, time and its deferral or extension is the essence of the game despite the fact that, within baseball's clockless parameters, time itself is comparatively powerless. Baseball's temporal space is similar to an eternal present, for any inning, any game, can in theory last forever. Play continues until a certain level of failure is reached, regardless of the elapsed time, so Roy can assuage his chronophobia by achieving perfect competence. If the Knights score runs and make no outs, inning and game will never end, time will (seemingly) not expire, and Roy Hobbs will find compensation for the years he has lost. Although he does not articulate these ideas, Roy does understand one way in which baseball mitigates the horror of time's passing and provides the player with the means to a modest immortality: "'if you leave all those records that nobody else can beat — they'll always remember you. You sorta never die'" (156).

With Roy restored to himself by Iris's intervention and the Knights on the verge of clinching the pennant, this baseball romance seems destined for the generic end of all Romance: homecoming, reunion, reconciliation, marriage.

The Natural swerves, however, from this generic ending, for Roy cannot stay the homeward course. The beguilements of Memo(ry), as well as Roy's inability to reintegrate the boy-Roy contentment into his adult psyche, dictate that he will miss his chance to connect with Iris, the only character who can teach him how to live apart from his baseball vainglory and the stultifying demands of his animal appetites. It is truly the whiff of a lifetime, and it precludes Roy's arrival at home. It might be most accurate to say that Roy convinces himself to reject Iris until accepting her is too little, too late to redeem his accumulated errors. Just as these errors are his responsibility despite the archetypal patterns that tend to decree them (see Pifer 151), so is Roy complicit in formulating his own demise by subscribing to a definition of self that engages all of the terms of solipsistic and mythic pretension. At the heart of this self-conception is Roy's belief, at once desperate and pathetic, in his own permanent youthfulness. At its simplest, Roy's clinging to boyhood is his most direct way of denying the passage of time, and is inscribed in his playing, at 34, the boy's game. On another level of abstraction, Roy's continual recourse to the boy-Roy image expresses his desire to return home, even if the home he envisions exists only in his mind and is, for all practical purposes, inaccessible. This conception of home is, moreover, essentially boyish. Solitary, self-indulgent, and sterile, it constitutes a shirking of responsibility, a shrinking from challenge, and as such is useless to a man. As one might expect, Roy's insistence on remaining boyish and thinking of himself in boyish terms culminates in his inability to conceive a mature image of home. This failure, in turn, finally undermines the only relationship that can grant Roy the opportunity of a fruitful homecoming.

Iris Lemon, mother at 16 years of age and grandmother by 33 is an embodiment of repletion, a human cornucopia of life-wisdom and life itself. After she restores the hero to his natural abilities, Iris tries to emend Roy's limited notion of the meaning of his achievements. She reminds Roy of the boys who regard him as a hero and role model, not just as a baseball player but also as a man, and tries to dissuade him from investing the statistical achievements of the diamond with inordinate value (156). Roy imperfectly understands her counsel; he recognizes in Iris a cessation of his suffering at the hands of women but not that his suffering is an index of his lack of self-knowledge (157–158). Similarly, Roy responds naturally to Iris's naked beauty yet will not reconcile himself to her special intercourse with time. In word and deed, Iris synthesizes "the life we learn with and the life we live with after that" (158). In body she manifests a fecundity that is both youthful and mature: "From above her hips she looked like a girl but the lower half of her looked like a woman" (162). Knowing or sensing that what Memo withholds out of niggling self-interest Iris gives freely in grace and joy, Roy feels "never so relaxed in sex" until Iris tells him that she is a grandmother (163). Repulsed almost to the point of physical withdrawal, Roy continues in a way that transforms what began as an act of love into rape.[17] Iris knows that she will become pregnant if their intercourse is unprotected and tries to ask Roy if he is using a prophylactic. The Natural refuses to be interrupted in the midst of his pleasure: "he shoved her back and went on from where he had left off" (163). Roy uses Iris to gratify the sexual desire that Memo thwarts, then rejects the older woman because the circumstances of her life remind him too intimately of his own relatively advanced age (to be playing the boy's game) and the passing of his season on earth. Although Iris pleases him in body, Roy ignores her essential self and its wisdom; he defers reading her letter and focuses instead on what he views as her "symbolic" meaning, which confronts the Natural with the simple fact of his own mortality. To Roy, accepting Iris as his mate seems not fitting and proper but equivalent to resigning himself to grandfatherhood, a status he considers proof of decrepitude. Roy rejects this conception of himself, for "he personally felt as young and frisky as a colt. That was what he told himself as the train sped east, and ... he fell into a sound sleep and dreamed how on frosty mornings when he was a kid the white grass stood up prickly stiff and the frozen air deep-cleaned his insides" (165). Roy's insistence on his own virility, like the image of the train and the dream of his younger self, ought to be familiar by now, and their relevance to his attitude toward Iris should be self-evident. Roy is 34 years old, an age that marks him as Iris's rightful mate and a mismatched paramour of Memo, but his maniacal fear of submitting to time's irrevocable scheme tears him from the embrace of (grand)mother and wife and delivers him again into the hands of the bitch-goddess. Considering the relatively late stage at which the above reiteration occurs, one concludes that Roy Hobbs will remain forever behind his time even as he chases it. One can hardly read these lines as anything other than a sign that Roy will never disembark from "the train going nowhere" (157) nor free himself from an emotionally fascistic Memo(ry).

Indeed, Roy acts almost compulsively on the basis of chronophobia and conjugal delusion. To the extent that he is aware of these flaws but unable to correct them, Roy's failures seem sympathetic, and the reader feels more acutely the conclusion's unhappy effect. The case, however, is more precisely that Roy has a clear sense of his delusions and anxieties but does not attempt to subdue them in any way that would require him to control his appetites for sex, money, or food, or to surrender his obsessions with youth and time. Even when he suspects the truth or is confronted with a sign of it, Roy turns back to his phobias and presumptions, believing that he can, by sheer force of will, wrest error into

---

[17]*When Roy recalls this moment, his language indicates that the rough culmination ("him banging her") of the act is discontinuous with its romantic, even sentimental prelude: "he remembered her pretty face and the brown eyes you could look into and see yourself as something more satisfying than you were, and ... Iris swimming down in the moonlit water searching for him, and the fire on the beach, she naked, and finally him banging her. For some reason this was the only thing he was ashamed of, though it couldn't be said she hadn't asked for it" (187).*

the outward shape of rectitude. This process is displayed most dramatically when, at a late stage of events, Roy envisions a tableau of an idyllic home life:

> His heart ached the way he yearned for [Memo] (sometimes seeing her in a house they had bought, with a redheaded baby on her lap, and himself going fishing in a way that made it satisfying to fish, knowing that everything was all right behind him, and the home-cooked meal would be hot and plentiful, and the kid would carry the name of Roy Hobbs into generations his old man would never know. ...
> It later struck him that the picture he had drawn of Memo sitting domestically home wasn't exactly the girl she was. The kind he had in mind, though it bothered him to admit it, was more like Iris seemed to be, only she didn't suit him [179–180].

Having centered his vision of home on Memo, Roy quickly realizes which part of the picture does not fit its frame and who should take Memo's place. Roy's insight, as accurate as it is, does not effectively bring him any closer to wisdom, for he neither alters his behavior nor revises the terms of his ambitions. Roy's vision here is conventional, another permutation of the American icons he adopts throughout the narrative, yet it might liberate him from the enticements of ego and the gratifications of his monstrous appetites, to say nothing of his fear of death, if he could share it with the right partner. The image of Roy as the Natural restored to the land and its elemental pursuits promises a more auspicious future than the figure of the athlete greedy for success, trapped on the train whose destination recedes at its approach. Most of all, the possibility of a child evokes the crucial exchange of vital power from father to son (or daughter) that is traditionally associated with the generational continuities of baseball and the progress of its seasons. And yet, despite these procreative signs, Roy's vision is delusional, occurring as it does within a parenthesis of present longing for a sterile woman with a "sick breast" (124). Roy thinks of Memo as a trophy and of possessing her as the compensation due him for the time and rewards (of money, pleasure, and fame) that he has lost, but this conception, like Roy's visualizations of the sepulchral farmhouse and the boy and his dog who haunt the woods, is finally substanceless. The bracketed "Memo" of the quoted passage is a clarifying substitution for the less-definite "her" that appears in Malamud's text; the essentially anonymous pronoun suggests that Roy half-expunges his dream girl even as he tries to force her involvement in his self-indulgent vision. Memo's virtual absence here, in the image of a home designed to enshrine her, will strike the attentive reader as an irony that operates at Roy's expense, for it is Iris Lemon who has already anticipated Roy's image of a prospective home in her own moment of inspired foresight.

While Iris and Roy are swimming in Lake Michigan, Roy dives underwater and does not surface for some time. When his disappearance has lasted so long that it feels like abandonment, Iris recalls her original motivation in connecting with him: that she wanted to share his life because he was "a man who had suffered." In the next moment, Iris envisions a future that seems to her already lost: "She thought distractedly of a home, children, and him coming home every night to supper. But he had already left her..." (160). Iris's instincts about Roy are correct. As surely as he might have established a home with her, so too does he abandon her before this process can properly begin. Iris's faith sustains her, however, and her sympathetic vision of home inscribes Iris as a real presence in Roy's life despite his reflexive impulse to exclude her. Iris's "fat letter" bulging in his suit pocket provides a reminder so weighty it is almost like companionship (165). This letter, which tells of Iris's efforts to be a good mother to her illegitimate daughter and to provide the child with a home in spite of having been banished from her father's house, is very much the example of "how to live" that Roy has sought. He chooses, however, not to read the letter until he has already taken bribe money to throw the playoff game. Iris's profession of faith reaches Roy too late.

Iris subsequently re-enters Roy's life, but her second coming is similarly belated. Too late to teach Roy "how to live" in his second life, Iris reappears soon enough to complete the displacement of Memo that begins when Iris first stands up for Roy at Wrigley Field. When Roy sees Iris again, long after the episode at the lake, he feels "an odd disgust for Memo. It came quickly, nauseating him" (225). Now, after having injured her with a foul ball he has struck intentionally and in malice (to silence the imprecations of Otto Zipp), Roy finally participates in Iris's vision of home and understands the redemption he would find there. Learning that Iris is pregnant, Roy accedes completely, his gestures a sign of his commitment: "he kissed her mouth and tasted blood. ... He kissed her hard belly, wild with love for her and the child" (225). Unfortunately for Roy Hobbs, his time is already past and his future will remain unfulfilled, as Iris apprehends when she likens him to her first seducer/rapist, the father of her daughter (225). In spite of her eerie sense of recapitulated abuse, Iris is ready to forgive Roy and accept him as her husband. Roy's transgressions, however, have already placed him beyond the practical limits of forgiveness. The Natural has sold out to the Judge's money and Memo's sex, prostituting himself for superficial rewards and violating a culture's chief claim on its heroes: the integrity of their trials. The possibility of reconciliation vacates the Gethsemane of the enclosed green field; "home plate [lies] under a deepening dusty shadow" even as Roy perceives the metaphysical stakes of this baseball game and his performance in it: "A hit, tying up the game, would cure what ailed him. Only a homer, with himself scoring the winning run, would truly redeem him" (230). Desperate for redemption, Roy watches a fog of memory gather around the young relief pitcher sent in to strike him out, just as he vanquished the Whammer in that golden moment when the train briefly stopped and Roy Hobbs achieved a performative ideal commensurate with his natural abilities. Now an old god who has outlived his time, a false hero who has betrayed his acolytes, Roy is bereft of both preter-Natural and ordinary power. At the end, he is a decrepit Natural on the verge of exile, an exhausted ballplayer able only to gesticulate feebly in the descending gloom.

Failure and death are a common ending of modern novels. The implicit presupposition is that such a resolution more closely resembles real life, as most of us presumably experience it, than the "old-fashioned" happy ending, which has come to seem like a falsification or contrivance of fiction fit only for children, cowards, and fools. Yet only the most unregenerate cynic would claim that life always turns out badly, and only the most alienated critic would insist on a catastrophic finish. Most readers can imagine a measure of hope, a glimpse of a new day replete not necessarily with grace but with a chance to find or create a sense of grace amidst suffering. One need not be immature or craven or weak of mind to see the beauty of such a vision. Something like it ought to be possible for Roy Hobbs, despite the appointed completion of the mythic pattern that tends to force his defeat (*CAF* 338–340). If Roy is to be held responsible for his failures and transgressions (Pifer 151), so too should he be allowed to remediate them, or at least to exercise freedom of choice (and a free will) as he attempts to mend his ways. To deny Roy a meaningful possibility of personal reformation is to diminish his stature, to make him less like a man (to say nothing of a hero) and more like a clay figure shaped and manipulated by his author's determined hands. Even if one claims that Roy is not intended to be a realistic character in a realistic novel, but rather an archetypal figure in a prose romance, the mixed genre of *The Natural* suggests that the generic ending of Romance — homecoming and marriage — is as valid for the story as the irony and despair of its endgame. Either way, the protagonist ought to have an effective option that would enable him to escape what seems to be a predestined doom. Instead, Roy Hobbs understands only one regrettable truth and envisions only a grim future: "I never did learn anything out of my past life, now I have to suffer again" (236). The epigraph to *Howards End* — "'Only connect'" — pertains literally to the beaten hero of Bernard Malamud's baseball romance and to that hero's thwarted quest. At his life's decisive moments, Roy Hobbs must "only connect" — with Iris Lemon, with the two-strike pitch — to avoid reliving a desultory exile, to confer on his performances a meaning that transcends the rough beauty of the baseball diamond, to enter a future free of the burden of ancient suffering. Roy's inability to connect in crucial situations condemns him to re-enact, in a more public arena and at greater length, his earlier triumph over the Whammer and ensuing ignominy at the hands of Harriet Bird. Whatever else they might signify, these missed connections resist the conventional movement of Romance toward reunion and precipitate a tragic ending. Roy Hobbs strives mightily for self-vindication, trying to undo in a single-season career the fatal error of his youth. Gesturing repeatedly homeward to define an image of himself apart from baseball, Roy is powerless either to attain the conventional notion of home that he mistakenly conceives at the heart of its absence, or to recuperate the semblance of his younger self that haunts him from the shadows of a forest, in the spaces of a dream.

♦ *Eight* ♦
The Game's the Thing
Adventures of Henry Wiggen

> There, in the struggle of a boy to establish himself over hostile powers, in the discovery of menace when confronting life on one's own terms — there is the true meaning of a "boy's book"; it explains why boys can read The Adventures of Huckleberry Finn *as boys and then grow up to read it as an epic of life that adults can identify with. The great epic, the tale of the wandering hero triumphing over circumstances — this is the stuff of literature that a boy is nearest to, since every initiation into the manhood he seeks must take the form of triumphing over an obstacle.*
> — Alfred Kazin, *An American Procession*

By "mythifying" baseball, Bernard Malamud recuperated its symbolic content for the American literary imagination. Several months after *The Natural* appeared, Mark Harris demonstrated that baseball itself, the game as it is played on the diamond, could provide the context for a realistic novel. In *The Southpaw* (1953), Harris rejects simplistic characters of the Frank Merriwell variety, as well as the formulaic plots of juvenile baseball stories. By the same token, *The Southpaw* shuns allegorical reconstructions of the fertility myths that are immanent in baseball's scheme of seasonal play and neglects the metaphors of "eternal presentness" inscribed in its counterclockwise movement, all of which Malamud enlists to fabricate — or solicit — artistic legitimacy. Eschewing both the facile moralizing of "boy's books" and the calculated arcaneness of Malamud's mythifications, Harris portrays a true-to-life pitcher playing baseball that is recognizably real. The author renders plausible events in colloquial language and enlivens the narrative with homespun yet clever humor. The result is a realistic fiction that is both particular and representative: Henry Wiggen's personal, or "inside," story reveals the baseball player as a man and dramatizes his effort to uphold the "home truths" that define his character in contradistinction to the exigencies of his time.

To enhance verisimilitude, author Mark Harris writes "left-handed," as one may say, in the persona of his titular southpaw. Henry Wiggen poses as "author" of *The Southpaw* and the three ensuing novels (by the second book, Henry is nicknamed "Author" by his teammates) that chronicle his baseball career.[1] By allowing Henry to narrate his own story in his own maladroit language, Harris creates a narrative that reads like an autobiographical *Bildungsroman*. Within the fictive world, Henry Wiggen figures as both writer and player, and authors a book that is both an "inside" story of major league baseball and the story of a young man's formative experiences — his initiations or, as Henry refers to them late in the novel, his "crisises."[2] As Henry conceives it, his book is the true account of his rookie season and of the years of preparation that have made it possible. His motive in writing is neither money nor vainglory (such as might inspire Roy Hobbs), but truth: to correct the distortions of sportswriter Krazy Kress, who, as Henry claims in the Dedication, has maligned him in a newspaper column. Beginning with this premise, Mark Harris creates a credible novel of initiation that describes the education of a baseball player. In this sense, *The Southpaw* is a distinctly American example of the *Bildungsroman,* for its hero develops into an artist of the diamond as well as of the pen. As they evolve along these lines, Henry's baseball "crisises" from boyhood to the major leagues cohere as a series of lessons in "how to live." Henry's behavior in baseball contexts, how he meets or evades the challenges posed by living and playing the game, describes the essential problem of *The Southpaw:* How can Henry Wiggen perform as a professional athlete yet retain his personal values as an honest and compassionate man?

In thematic terms, Henry's task is to undertake the professional venture and all of its attendant temptations yet to remain faithful to the values he has learned from Pop, Aaron, and Holly. Henry's baseball career superficially involves a journey away from his hometown, for he must travel to distant cities in order to play the professional game, but this nominal exile is much less traumatic than the conflict Henry perceives between the imperatives of professional competition and the "home truths" that Holly espouses and upholds. In the effort to win at any cost, Henry confronts demands that make his amateur, "innocent" baseball ethos, which he has learned from his father, a contradiction or obstacle. The solution, as Henry's "inside" story testifies, is for the southpaw to test, appraise, and reaffirm his values by learning from the positive (Holly, Pop, and Aaron) and negative (Sam Yale, Dutch Schnell, and Patricia

---

[1]*The other novels are* Bang the Drum Slowly by Henry W. Wiggen, Certain of His Enthusiasms Restrained by Mark Harris (1956); A Ticket for a Seamstitch, Henry W. Wiggen, but polished for the printer by Mark Harris *(1957); and* It Looked Like For Ever *(1979). The four novels were not planned as a tetralogy, as Norman Lavers explains in* Mark Harris *(Boston: Twayne, 1978), 58–59. Of the second novel, Harris himself opines, "I think I may very well have been anxious to repeat. In a way that book is a rewrite of an earlier book. I may have been doing something that would come easy, and I liked it, and I had fun with that language." See John Enck, "Mark Harris: An Interview," 21, in* Wisconsin Studies in Contemporary Literature 6:1 *(Spring-Summer 1965), 15–26.*

[2]*Mark Harris,* The Southpaw by Henry W. Wiggen, Punctuation freely inserted and spelling greatly improved by Mark Harris *(1953; reprinted, Lincoln: University of Nebraska Press, 1984), 343. Quotations and references follow this edition.*

Moors) relationships that define his engagement with baseball and with life. For Henry, baseball is the point, and in the novels Mark Harris has written in the voice of the ballplayer, the game is the thing: It can inspire and disappoint, reveal frailties, showcase talents, "catch the conscience" like the play within *Hamlet* that the Prince of Denmark stages to expose the perfidy of the King. Playing the game, living the life of a professional pitcher committed to his craft, Henry acquires a knowledge of how to compete without neglecting the promptings of his conscience or violating the standards of his better self. With the guidance of Holly Webster and through the clarifying process of authorship, Henry Wiggen translates baseball savvy into life-wisdom and formulates a response to the question of "how to live."

One might pose this question in simpler terms and ask whether Henry Wiggen can imagine himself independent of his game; even as a boy, Henry seems interested only in baseball. His only friends are Holly Webster, a girl his own age, and her ancient uncle, Aaron Webster, a scientist in charge of the Perkinsville Observatory. When Henry and Holly are children, Aaron tries to bring them together by sparking a mutual interest in the natural world. Aaron points out the phases of the moon, the geology of the landscape, the genealogies of plants and animals, but Henry notices little of what the scientist presents. Motherless since the age of two, raised by a father who "inexplicably" abandoned his own pitching career on the threshold of the major leagues ("in despite of the fact that Pop had all the makings of a great" [16]),[3] Henry fixes on baseball and takes the game to the center of his being; baseball is the thing the boy will become: "No, there was only 1 thing I was fond of, not moons nor rocks nor leafs nor trees nor bugs nor books nor baby birds, nor least of all Holly Webster. Only baseball. And the older I growed the greater my interest become" (25). At first, the game is a solitary personal invention: "I pitched about 5,000 games of baseball against the back of the house with a rubber ball. I had a regular system" (24). Henry does not mention playing baseball with friends until he reaches high school and seems to have no childhood companions other than Holly, his next-door neighbor in Perkinsville, a small town "about halfway to Albany" in New York's Hudson Valley (13). Henry does not remember his mother, but she has contributed symbolically to his literary avocation by giving him the middle name of Whittier, "because she was a fan of a

[3]*In* Seeking the Perfect Game: Baseball in American Literature *(New York: Greenwood Press, 1989), Cordelia Candelaria judges this detail a "mystery," for Harris introduces it "early in the story and apparently forgets about it because we never do learn, here or in the remaining three books, why Pop gave up his promising career" (Candelaria 88). Norman Lavers remarks that "We are made to feel he quit on some personal principle, that despite the obvious tremendous cost to himself and his family, when the time came, he chose for his own integrity" (Lavers 43). In another context, Mark Harris indicates why no explanation is offered: "I write. Let the reader learn to read. ... I resist, as true novelists do, the injunction (usually a worried editor's) to be clearer, to be easier, to explain, if I feel that the request is for the convenience of the reader at the expense of craft" ("Easy Does It Not" in* The Living Novel *[1957], edited by Granville Hicks, as cited by Wayne C. Booth in* The Rhetoric of Fiction, *2d ed. [Chicago: University of Chicago Press, 1983], 90). As the reader will discover near the end of this chapter, Pop has quit professional baseball for a simple reason, as Henry himself suggests in* The Southpaw.

poet by that name" (17).[4] This muted influence provides the only counterbalance to Henry's love of baseball, which translates the poetic symbolism of his middle name into the diligence he brings to reading every baseball book in Perkinsville's public library. Limited as it is, Henry's early reading prepares him for the writing he will do about baseball.

Before discovering the baseball stacks, which hold a series of "How To" books covering all nine positions, as well as the baseball fables of "Sherman and Heyliger and Tunis" (34) and the fiction of Ring Lardner, Henry "had begun to think there wasn't any books worth spending time on" (31). He resists the efforts of the public schools to educate him, concluding of high school, "It struck me as all a waste of time, and nothing took, or at least if it took it done so in such a way I never noticed" (29). He tries to muster some interest in Aaron's books, but promising titles like "'Giants in the Earth,'" which he "thought at first might have to do with baseball," and "others such as books with the word 'Yankee' in the title, and 'Reds' and 'Senators' and such ... turned out to be something else": "a dud" (31). To Henry, books are either dull or useful in a practical way. In preadolescence, he reads in their entirety only Pop's baseball scrapbook and a slim volume on sex education that Aaron lends him (when Henry is ten) to explain why Holly will not "get a baby" from Henry's having kissed her (27–28). Other attempts to get Henry reading prove futile:

> [Aaron] would have a book such as "Moby Dick" concerning the white whale, and we begun to read it together, Holly and me, and we never come to the whale so I give it up. And there was "Huckleberry Finn" that begun "You do not know about me without you have read a book by the name of "The Adventures of Tom Sawyer","" and I told Aaron that was a dirty trick to start a book that you no more opened then the writer was telling you to read still another as well. He just laughed, though probably I flung the book at him [25].

This inauspicious start does not quite ruin Henry as a reader, for he does become interested in fiction through baseball. The boy's baseball tales that he finds commingled on the library shelves with Lardner's stories (which are not his favorites) mark the beginning of his focused, if unexceptional, reading life. Later, when he is traveling the major league circuit, Henry chooses to "ride the lobbies" of the hotels and read "quarter murders" (280, 35) to avoid his teammates' bickering. His childhood reactions to *Moby-Dick* and *Adventures of Huckleberry Finn* notwithstanding, Henry's impatience with fiction is not the materialist's quarrel with its rhetorical artifices and narrative strategies, but the athlete's reluctance to respect — or entirely trust — any experience that is not a performative

---

[4]*John Greenleaf Whittier (1807–1892) was a native of Massachusetts and a Quaker. A poet first and last, he became an active Abolitionist and newspaper editor and also wrote prose fiction. Technically flawed and usually sentimental, his poetry is not often read today. Whittier was short on formal schooling; he was influenced mainly by religion and the books he read as a boy. See* The Oxford Companion to American Literature, *5th ed., edited by James D. Hart (New York: Oxford University Press, 1983), 823.*

confrontation. In the books he reads, Henry wants potboiling, cliff-hanging action, blended with baseball if possible and delivered in the circumstantial plots of tales like "Double Curve Dan, the Pitcher Detective" (1888)[5] and the sixteen "Sid Yule" books by a "fellow name of Homer B. Lester" (34), all of which he reads with alacrity.[6] No wonder, then, that Henry tires of Ishmael's musings long before the last three "Chase" chapters, even if his setting aside *Huckleberry Finn* after the first sentence is surprising.[7]

Not surprising, however, is Henry's preferred literary genre: baseball nonfiction. His favorite book is the "autobiography" of Sam Yale, Henry's pitching idol on the New York Mammoths. Purportedly written by the ballplayer but actually ghosted by fictive sportswriter Krazy Kress, *Sam Yale — Mammoth* is the book that fires Henry's passion for reading by connecting so exactly to his dream of becoming a major league pitcher. Henry reads *Sam Yale — Mammoth* for the first time in the library, "crouched there on my knees" (32).[8] He eventually steals the book because he does not have a library card and reads it repeatedly thereafter. He believes every word of its fatuous advice and clichéd rectitude, and does not notice the all-purpose prose. This text becomes for Henry a normative guide, an early answer to the question of "how to live." The book so predominates in Henry's consciousness that he razors out the picture of Sam Yale and "the inspiration he had wrote" and folds them into his wallet with another talisman of success, "a picture of Pop in his Scarlets uniform" (33). The theft of the book is dishonest, its defacement selfish and jejune; as a whole, Henry's appropriation of *Sam Yale — Mammoth* represents the crude beginning of his own literary creation: He borrows (or steals) from his precursor.[9] As Henry writes his own book, he evaluates his early idolatry of Sam Yale, as well as his interest in boy's baseball stories, and dismisses their respective influences as a poet might deny the influence of prior poets on his own

[5]*George Jenks wrote three Double Curve Dan stories for Beadle's* Dime Base Ball Player *between 1888 and 1890. See Christian K. Messenger,* Sport and the Spirit of Play in American Fiction: Hawthorne to Faulkner *(New York: Columbia University Press, 1981), 102–103, for a plot synopsis.*

[6]*From the plot summary that Henry gives of the standard "Sid Yule" baseball novel, it is obvious that Mark Harris knows the genre well. See* The Southpaw, *34–35; Messenger 166–171; Michael Oriard,* Dreaming of Heroes: American Sports Fiction, 1868–1990 *(Chicago: Nelson-Hall, 1982), 27–52; and Harris's "Horatio at the Bat, or Why Such a Lengthy Embryonic Period for the Serious Baseball Novel?" in Aethlon 5:2 (Spring 1988): 1–11.*

[7]*Later, Henry claims to have read* Huckleberry Finn *"and could not see much sense in plowing through again.... I would say it is a waste of energy to read a book once, let alone twice" (134).*

[8]*At least one critic has noticed Henry's posture at this moment and likened it to prayer. See Christian K. Messenger,* Sport and the Spirit of Play in Contemporary American Fiction *(New York: Columbia University Press, 1990), 332. Cited as CAF.*

[9]*I have adapted this term (in a simplified sense) from Harold Bloom's* A Map of Misreading *(1975; reprinted, New York: Oxford University Press, 1980), 10–11, 18–20. Unlike a "strong poet," who can no more "choose his precursor, any more than any person can choose his father" (Bloom 12), Henry has chosen Sam Yale for obvious reasons. The fact that he has made his choice consciously might explain why Henry feels none of the anxiety in the presence of his model that a strong poet suffers in repressing or denying the influence of his precursor.*

verse. As if to assure the reader that he has outgrown boyhood's callow creduli-
ties, Henry hints at the lessons that life and baseball have taught him since boyhood: "Such corny crap as that is all behind me now. I ain't even interested in
Sad Sam Yale no more. You spend a long period with a fellow and he stops being
a hero all of a sudden. Sam ain't all he is cracked up to be. But I didn't know it
then. I wasn't but a kid" (35). These remarks, a kind of practical disclaimer, portend that Henry's continuing education will allow experience to supplant "inspiration" as the measure of truth. Indeed, once he achieves professional standing,
Henry proves to be as keen a student of his colleagues' failings as he has been
of his father's expertise.[10] The influence of *Sam Yale — Mammoth* is emended by
experience, but other, nontextual lessons turn out to be consistently persuasive.

In a practical sense, Henry learns baseball from Pop, who teaches him the
game in terms of pitching. Henry and Pop share baseball in a way that becomes
trite in many subsequent stories of fathers playing catch with sons, but in *The
Southpaw* the trope is fresh. Pop is the star pitcher of the Perkinsville Scarlets,
a local semipro team, and his son reveres him as a hero of the diamond. Henry
internalizes the wisdom Pop imparts about pitching, refining his control and
strategy in the simulated games he pitches in a field near home (Pop plays
catcher with a custom-made left-handed mitt). From an earlier time, when he
was too young to play the game himself, Henry recalls having participated vi-
cariously in the games Pop pitched for the Scarlets: "The earliest thing I remember was Sundays in summer, going out in the morning with Pop to look at the
sky. If it looked like a good day he would twirl his arm around a few times, and
he would say, 'Son, I am going to pitch 3-hit baseball today,' or if there was a
little nip in the air he would say he would pitch a 7-hitter. Pop was a good hot-
weather pitcher. He was great in any weather, but better in hot" (19). The
preparatory ritual he shares with Pop gives Henry an early sense of himself, and
of himself in relation to baseball. The serene confidence with which Pop contemplates that day's game is one of the qualities that Henry learns as a child
and carries with him to the major leagues. Success is not in doubt, although its
extent depends in part on circumstances like weather. The gestures are familiar, their intricacies performed with practiced surety, as if they were choreo-
graphed. To the degree that a respectful intent has established this ritual and its
repeated enactment, Pop and Henry's pregame routine defines an approach to
baseball that is almost sacerdotal. As Pop suits up, Henry looks after the equipment, a job he takes as a conferral of honor and a sign of his own worthiness:

> Then he would say, "Hank, my glove," and that was me. I always carried Pop's glove,
> and I was proud to do it. Sometimes he would let me oil it. It had that leathery oily

[10]*Leverett T. Smith argues that Mark Harris, like Hemingway, "includes a romantic ideal which must
be overcome before maturity is attained" and that the "romantic ideal" of baseball is "embodied in a
book, which is a parallel of Henry's own:* Sam Yale — Mammoth.*" See Smith's* The American Dream
and the National Game *(Bowling Green, OH: Bowling Green University Popular Press, 1975), 100. Sam
Yale — Mammoth and* The Southpaw *can hardly be called "parallel," however, for the latter overtly
rejects not only the "romantic ideal" of baseball but also* Sam Yale — Mammoth *and Sam himself.*

smell which is 1 of the best smells I know. Then he would get his shoes, and sometimes he would let me carry them, though not always. ... The spikes on the shoes
were bright and silver, not all run down like you see on seedy ballplayers that don't
care how they keep themselves up. Every year Pop bought new shoes, which is what
any self-respecting ballplayer will do. You have noticed how these straggley semipro clubs wear run-down shoes. But not Pop. Nor me [19].

Pop's example makes a strong impression, for Henry's recollections are sensory
and detailed. In this fashion, Henry learns respect for the game: how to wear
the uniform, how to care for glove and shoes, even how to approach a ballpark
and how to enter it. Nurtured in the art of baseball, Henry learns that it grants
special status to those with the skill, luck, and industriousness to, in Roy Hobbs's
words, "'get in the game.'"[11] The rewards of a professional player are obvious,
but to Henry the personal compensations count for more. To be "inside" that
select circle is a greater good than money, which he does not associate with
baseball until he is pitching in a pennant race. Before dollars become the point
of the game, when play is not utilitarian but sought in its own right as a pleasure and a challenge, Henry feels the pure excitement of being "inside": "Pop
would walk in his stockings in through the private gate that was only for players and relations. As a kid it always give me a great thrill to go in any park
through the player gate. It made me feel important — made me feel like I was
somebody" (20). As he recalls the education that Pop has given him, Henry
remarks that "These thrills wear away with the passing of time" (20), as if to
disclaim his youthful response to the simple pleasures of baseball. Essentially
an amateur's regard, the innocent attitude of his boyhood is easy to maintain
while Pop dominates the opposition; however, on a day when Pop is knocked
out of the box, Henry "cried for 2 innings. I was ashamed, but I was very small"
(22). Just as he writes from a place beyond the boy's thrill, so does Henry no
longer feel the child's anguish. "Author" Wiggen may revisit these emotional
extremes in writing, but he cannot restore within himself the sensibility of the
boy who has felt them. As a star pitcher, the southpaw is definitively "inside"
and quickly outgrows the thrill of being there.

Henry discovers, however, that he can recuperate his earlier relation to
baseball by writing about it; writing his "inside" story makes the thrill recoverable. When "Author" Wiggen recaptures the moment in which he first visu-
alized himself actually on a pitching mound in the major leagues, the reader
perceives that reconstructing the image allows Henry to feel the emotion as if
he were (re)living it. When he is 16 years old, Henry travels with Pop to New
York City for Opening Day at Moors Stadium. Watching a young relief pitcher,
Henry concludes, "'Why, Pop, pitch for pitch I am the equal of him'" (57). Pop
agrees, and later Henry imagines himself at the splendid center of the "big towns
and big parks, and there would be 30,000 people and my name on 30,000 score-
cards and the music and the singing and the cheering, and I would touch my

---

[11]*Bernard Malamud*, The Natural *(1952; reprinted, New York: Farrar, Straus and Giroux, 1989), 32.*

hat when they cheered, and I would wind and rear and fire and they would see, and they would know an immortal when they seen 1, and I dived back on the bed and pounded the pillow, and I shouted again, 'Thunder, thunder, thunder, and THUNDER,' and I felt better" (57). This passage (re)creates an image that has previously existed only in Henry's mind: the moment when he takes his place at the center of the diamond and is publicly recognized for what he privately believes himself to be. The completeness of Henry's optimism and the clarity of his vision make him impatient for a future that seems immanent in his present life; the shouts of "thunder" seem to announce the advent of a new god, "an immortal." In this case, the writing process creates "reality" from what has only been a fragment of optimistic visualization. The moment exemplifies an accomplished novel's virtual reality, which is always in some way a heightened or intensified version of what one takes to be the mundanely real.

Such moments of heightened reality illustrate the intimate relationship between baseball and writing that is evident throughout *The Southpaw*. The two disciplines merge in Henry's description of Pop's pitching mechanics. Although Henry states that "Pop had all the makings of a great" (16) and repeats this judgment several times, the extent of Pop's ability and Henry's admiration of it become fully present to the reader only when Henry turns his newly "mastered" craft of writing to a representation of his father's baseball artistry:

> I have seen many a pitcher, but there's few that throw as beautiful as Pop. He would bring his arm around twice and then lean back on 1 leg with his right leg way up in the air, and he would let that left hand come back until it almost touched the ground behind, and he looked like he was standing on 1 leg and 1 arm and the other 2 was in the air, and then that arm would come around and that other leg would settle down toward the earth, and right in about there there was the least part of a second when his uniform was all tight on him, stretched out tight across his whole body, and then he would let fly, and that little white ball would start on its way down the line toward Tom Swallow, and Pop's uniform would get all a-rumple again, and, just like it was some kind of a magic machine, the split-second when the uniform would rumple up there would be the smack of the ball in Tom's mitt, and you realized that ball had went 60 feet 6 inches in less than a second, and you knowed that you seen not only Pop but also a mighty and powerful machine, and what he done looked so easy you thought you could do it yourself because he done it so effortless, and it was beautiful and amazing, and it made you proud [20–21].

The second-person pronouns notwithstanding, Henry writes to himself as the implied audience of this passage as much as he pitches it to the reader. As well as being a practical demonstration of "how to pitch," Pop's motion is an exhortation for Henry to attain a comparable standard of power and grace, to function symbiotically as literal man and figurative machine, to embody the substance of the tradesman in the form of the artist. Except for its prose framing, Henry's rendition of Pop's pitching mechanics might be called poetry in motion, for it is the kind of thing writers have in mind when they allude to the aesthetic quality of baseball. In spite of "Author" Wiggen's poor grammar and limited resources of metaphor and imagery, the precise attitudes of balletic limbs, the astute timing device of Pop's stretched-tight uniform rumpling up as the ball strikes the catcher's glove, do resemble the leisurely yet explosive fluidities of pitching. It is doubtful that Henry has learned to write about baseball in this manner from reading "Sid Yule" books. Rather, his early acquaintance with poetry has imparted to him a certain sensitivity to the modulations of the written line, which correspond to the balance and rhythm of Pop's windup and delivery.

Given his preferred reading material, it seems out of character for Henry to take an interest in poetry, but the terms of his introduction to it suggest otherwise. Holly reads poems to Henry during the early stage of their courtship, as if taking it upon herself to improve his "book learning" beyond what is available in juvenile baseball novels. With Holly at Silver Creek, "the most peaceful place you will find anywhere" (62), Henry responds to the sensation of *dolce far niente* and the undercurrent of sex as well as to poetry, pleasures that seem indivisible as Holly proffers them:

> There was Shakespeare and Marble and Champion and Johnson and Dunn and Milton something and Browning and Yates, and I am not ashamed to say that I took to it pretty well, for I would lay there with my head in her lap, and she would read to me with 1 hand whilst rubbing my temples with the other. Some of them poets have really got a knack of making words into music, for it soothed me and made the air smell sweet, and it made ripples run up and down my spine [63].

Henry spells the names as if Donne were playing second base and Yeats center field, but his appreciation of poetic language suggests that his mother's middle-naming him "Whittier" has been a bit of prescience once removed. Henry even tries to "whip out a poem or 2 on my own hook," then translates Holly's critique into terms he understands: "she read them and said they was minor league but showed promise. She said if I stuck at it I might amount to something some day" (63). These locutions liken authorship to pitching, which one might regard as inevitable, given Henry's preoccupation with baseball. Then, too, he is still learning both trades; in every art, talent must be shaped by practice and discipline to attain a finished form worthy of its raw potential. At the same time, the effort of writing his own book has taught "Author" Wiggen to respect Holly's claim that being Babe Ruth is not exactly the same thing as being Shakespeare: "She says any lunkhead can play baseball but he has got to be something special to write a poem" (63).

Holly's judgment is pointed, for Pop's tutelage ends once Henry graduates to the professional ranks, whereas the lessons that she teaches the southpaw are just beginning. Besides introducing him to sex and poetry, Holly reveals Henry to himself, shows him that he is a man before and after he is a ballplayer. Only through Holly's exegesis does Henry understand that he differs from his teammates, that he is "'a southpaw in a starboarded atmosphere'" (307), and that his left-handedness is as temperamentally defining as it is distinctive of his ability to pitch in the major leagues. Throughout the process of Henry's maturation, Holly acts as caretaker of the man who suffers the demands of his profession and teacher of the mind that re-creates the story of its evolving awareness. In guiding Henry as he writes the "inside" version of his young life, Holly performs a service as crucial to the making of *The Southpaw* as Pop's teaching Henry the subtleties of pitching. Henry needs help in completing the jump to manhood, and Holly Webster, literally "the girl next door," becomes wife, friend, and mentor in "how to live."[12]

In the book's early chapters, Henry discovers that mastering narrative prose requires more effort than he has ever expended in learning how to pitch. As he admits, Henry's limited abilities have been made more rarefied (and highly valued) by being applied consistently to one purpose. The expertise required to pitch in the major leagues tends to foreclose other possibilities of personal development and leaves Henry in the position of a stunted expert, the man who has perfected a single skill that depends on its unique context for meaning and value and that proves useless to its possessor outside his field:

> Give me a baseball in my hand and I know where I am at. Give me a piece of machinery and I may be more or less in the dark. Give me a book and I am lost. Give me a map and I cannot make heads nor tails, nor I could no more learn another language then pitch with my nose. But give me a baseball and I know where I am at, and I fired down to Fielding twice, 2 blazing fast balls, and then I changed up and throwed him a jughandle curve that he went for like a fool ... [205].

Even linked to a performance that validates it, this self-assessment is the downside of Henry's extraordinary confidence and technical mastery. Perhaps the most significant knowledge that Henry must acquire is how to excel between the diamond's white lines while simultaneously transcending its circumscribed contexts. Intuitively, the reader knows that Henry approaches this wisdom by writing his book. The work of writing — the gathering of relevant facts, the thoughtful appraisal of material and its coherent deployment, most of all the evolving awareness, which accrues only during the process of actually setting words down on paper, of what one is trying to say and why — provides the opportunity for Henry to examine his life and articulate its meaning. Henry might be impelled to write his "inside" story for personal, even selfish reasons, but the book he produces exceeds his original intentions because Holly serves as its muse. The standards of behavior and the personal values that she communicates to Henry give the book a reach and depth it is not likely to have possessed had it been written by an untutored athlete working alone.

As far as style is concerned, Holly's advice helps to mitigate some of the beginner's standard mistakes. It can, however, impart neither eloquence nor

---

[12]*The remarks pertaining to Holly are developments of points adduced in the following: Candelaria 85–86; Oriard 144; Lavers 42, 44. Surprisingly, Christian K. Messenger does not discuss Holly's role as teacher despite emphasizing "The Education of Henry Wiggen" as the manifest theme of* The Southpaw *(CAF 331–333).*

grace to Henry's rough-and-ready prose. The closing paragraphs of the first chapter indicate both the efficacy of Holly's lessons and the limits of their impact; the last paragraph may be taken as their epitome: "That's it. Those are the folks and also the end of the chapter. Holly says try and write up 1 thing and 1 thing only in every chapter and don't be wandering all over the lot, and then, when the subject is covered, break it off and begin another" (18). As a teacher of writing, Holly gives sound instruction: Define the subject, focus on its major points, organize the material. Without any evidence that she herself is a writer and has distilled these insights from the practice of her craft, one concludes that Holly is an attentive habitual reader who abstracts the principles of successful narration from the books she loves. In this way is she able to supply the literary deficiencies of "Author" Wiggen, who, like Huck Finn, is an improvisational author, unaccustomed to his medium and trusting to instinct in matters of grammar and structure.[13]

At the heart of the "trouble it [is] to make a book"[14] is language, questions of which Henry adjudicates in ad hoc fashion. In a prefatory "Special Warning to All Readers," which underlines Harris's sense of Mark Twain as a precursor and *Adventures of Huckleberry Finn* as a literary model for *The Southpaw*,[15] "Author" Wiggen indicates the assistance he has received in framing his book's language, which some of its pre-publication readers consider "filthy and vulgar." Pop wants Henry to "blank in the filthiest and the vulgarest," especially "the 'f——s'," to "'protect the women and the children,'" but Aaron reveals the fecklessness of substituting dashes for letters that every reader knows how to rewrite. Henry consents to "blank in" the offending words "for Pop's sake" and abjures blame "for whoever blanks it out again" (7 [unnumbered]). The debate widens in chapter 11-A, which addresses novel theory and issues of craft. Pop, Aaron, and Holly listen as Henry reads the first 12 chapters, then discuss the narrative's flaws and agree that "number 12 is too long" (106). What follows is an impromptu seminar on the author's selection of material, compression of time, and narrative method (telling versus showing), to which Henry initially responds with defensive sarcasm and simplistic logic. Point by point, Holly,

---

[13]*In* It Looked Like For Ever, *Henry's retirement notice in a national magazine notes "one of his rules of writing: 'If you do not know how to spell a word make your very best guess at it'" (34).*

[14]Adventures of Huckleberry Finn *(1889), as reprinted in* Mark Twain: Mississippi Writings, *edited by Guy Cardwell (New York: Literary Classics of the United States, 1982), 912; cited as* Huck Finn.

[15]*Twain's "NOTICE" to* Huckleberry Finn *warns the reader against finding "motive," "moral," and "plot" in the narrative (*Huck Finn *619), and the famous "EXPLANATORY" informs the reader that the "shadings" of American dialectical speech have been done "pains-takingly, and with the trustworthy guidance and support of personal familiarity with these several forms of speech" (*Huck Finn *620). Harris's allusion to Twain's preambulatories prepare the reader for the vernacular narration and episodic structure that follow, as well as invite comparison to* Huckleberry Finn. *Critics have picked up Harris's hints by noting the similarity between Huck's raft trip down the Mississippi and Henry's travels around the circuit of major league cities. For a remarkable critical consensus, see Messenger CAF 332; Candelaria 85, 89; Lavers 37; Oriard 138–139; and Robert Cochran, "Bang the Drum Differently: The Southpaw Slants of Henry Wiggen," 156, in* Modern Fiction Studies *33:1 (Spring 1987): 151–159.*

Aaron, and Pop convince the fledgling author that much of what he has written is extraneous and other sections merely dull. The upshot is Henry's discarding chapter 12 and writing instead a detailed account of its critique and
dismantling, which appears as metafictional commentary in chapter 11-A. Henry
comments on the writing of *The Southpaw* throughout the novel but never as
extensively as here.[16] His point — and Harris's — is that a lot more effort goes
into the composition of a thoughtful book, much of it stained with a sense of
failure, than any reader can know. All of this hidden work, the psychological
and physical toll that extended writing exacts from a writer, is every book's
"inside" story. "Author" Wiggen emphasizes this idea in the first half of *The
Southpaw,* then devotes the second half to the "inside" story of his rookie season and the invisible toll that it has demanded of him and his teammates.

Henry pays for his baseball tuition in a currency of disillusionment and
alienation. These psychic consequences are, perhaps, inevitable, for an initiation seldom seems worthwhile or fully educative without such a cost. As the
season unfolds and Henry attains his baseball dreams one by one, the "thrills
wear away" so that by the time he pitches in the All-Star Game, "it seemed like
there was getting to be no dreams left, only the Series" (237). The season's second half proves to be more tasking, however, and as the pennant race heats up,
professional realities intrude upon Henry's "innocent" baseball dreams. His
experiences among his teammates and on the field bring Henry to a series of
crises, and his responses suggest that he is as temperamentally unfit to continue
as a professional baseball player as he is physically capable of becoming, as he
has always believed, "an immortal." His ascent into awareness is dispiriting and
often painful. The thrill of being "inside" dissipates; tension, cynicism, and
selfishness settle upon the southpaw like real weight. Henry moves slowly toward
these attitudes, but the deportment of manager Dutch Schnell and several veteran players, as well as the prevarications of Krazy Kress and Mammoths' owner
Patricia Moors, finally shock the southpaw into a new dispensation.

Among the first of Henry's disillusionments is his discovery that Sam Yale,
the veteran pitcher whom he has long regarded as a role model, is nothing like
the abstemious paragon depicted in *Sam Yale — Mammoth,* his ghostwritten
autobiography. This knowledge comes to Henry from Mike Mulrooney, his minor
league manager, just prior to the southpaw's departure from the Queen City Cowboys. Before Henry leaves to join the Mammoths in New York, Mike corrects
Henry's assumptions about the profane, hard-drinking, womanizing Sam Yale:

> "Do not listen to a single word said by Sam Yale. Do not play cards with him. Do
> not drink with him. Do not lend him money nor borrow any. If you see him with

---

[16]*On page 255, "Author" Wiggen reprises the debate on language and reminds the reader of the "Special Warning." Now, Red Traphagen weighs in with his opinion against Pop: "'Do you not want Henry
to write a true book so as to explain everything that happened just like it was? Why, a book about baseball without no swearing would be like 'Moby Dick' without no whale or 'Huckleberry Finn' without
no Huck.'" Besides being repetitive, this cameo moment works hard to situate* The Southpaw *within
the traditional canon of American fiction.*

a woman put that woman down in your book as a tramp, for if she is not a tramp at the start Sad Sam will make her 1. Everything that Yale touches will turn to shit. Except only 1 thing, and that is a baseball. When he is pitching you must glue your eyes to him and never take them off. You must learn to watch him and never listen to him, and you will learn much about baseball and much about life" [118].

In effect, Mike tells Henry that Sam Yale can teach him how to pitch but not how to live, except by negative example. The same is true of all the Mammoths. Even Red Traphagen, the Harvard-educated catcher, "'the smartest ballplayer in baseball today'" (118), is flawed: "'He does not believe in God. ... A ballplayer must believe in God'" (119). Mike tells Henry to write down and study everything that Red tells him on the field but otherwise to ignore him. Henry discovers that Red is intelligent, cynical, and rebellious, totally unenamored of baseball, its players, and its fans.[17] Henry's encounters with Sam Yale confirm Mike's assessment. Disillusioned and radically cynical, Sam has learned that the material prizes for which he strives (money, sex, fame) are unfulfilling and short-lived. After Sam reads Henry's copy of *Sam Yale — Mammoth,* he offers an analysis of the book that effectively summarizes his attitude toward life:

> "You get so you do not care. It is all like a ball game with nobody watching and nobody keeping score and nobody behind you. You pitch hard and nobody really cares. Nobody really gives a f— what happens to anybody else." He looked very sad, exactly like he looked in the picture in my wallet.
> "*Sad* Sam Yale," I said.
> "I ain't sad," he said. "I just do not care. I just play for the money I do not need and fornicate for the kicks I never get. Some day there will not even be the kicks. If I was to write a book they would never print it. It would be 5 words long. It would say, Do Not F —— With Me. I would send it to every church and every schoolhouse and tell them to hang it up over their door. It will not get you anywheres in life. But it is the best you can ask for *out* of life. The best you can hope is that everybody else will just leave you alone. This book is all horseshit" [238–239].

Sam's nihilism obliterates even the rough pleasure of competition and culminates in his own alienation. This harsh "philosophy" sounds as false as its opposite extreme, the callow platitudes and vacuous advice offered up in his spurious autobiography. And yet, by the time the season ends, Henry has aligned himself with Sam's perspective. Having started with an attitude that sacrifices personal relationships to the professional's icy credo that "old friendship cannot matter ... Only the game matters" (167), Henry claims at the lowest ebb of emotion, "'I play baseball for the kicks and the cash only'" (337).

Henry's adopting Sad Sam's kicks-and-cash cynicism as his philosophy of

---

[17]In The Southpaw, *Red refuses to stand for the National Anthem after Opening Day (204) and calls the fans "sheep" (203); in* Bang the Drum Slowly *(1956; reprinted, Lincoln: University of Nebraska Press, 1989), Red has retired from baseball to teach college English but returns to help the Mammoths win the pennant despite believing that baseball is another opiate of the masses: "'baseball is stupid, Author, and I hope you put it in your book, a game rigged by rich idiots to keep poor idiots from wising up to how poor they are'" (*Bang the Drum Slowly 207).

life is a symptom of his exile. At this point, Henry is not only far from home but seems to have forgotten that home exists. He has discarded or neglected most of his personal values, those "home truths" that Holly tries to call to his attention and that, if he could uphold them, might help him avoid some mistakes and mitigate his sense of alienation. All that Henry really needs to remember is the one true thing that Holly imparts to him just before he leaves home: "Then she give me the best advice anyone ever give me concerning baseball and how to play it. She said, 'Henry, you must play ball like it does not matter, for it really does not matter. Nothing really matters. Play ball, do your best, have fun, but do not put the game nor the cash before your own personal pride,' and I said I would. I loved her and would of said most anything…" (135). "If he were able to apply Holly's advice to the dilemmas that vex him, Henry would possess all the wisdom he would ever need. It is simple wisdom, after all — Holly merely reminds Henry of his true priorities and that he must keep them intact — but personal values are easily overwhelmed by the hurly-burly of professional competition. Then, too, Henry seems strangely uncertain of his values despite having internalized them long ago. This paradox is, in part, a result of Henry's limited self-conception, for he has no strong sense of identity apart from baseball. The rules of the game are clear to him and the terms of competition are ones he knows intuitively, but when these norms conflict with his personal values, Henry instinctively relies on the ethos of the competitor to shape his conduct. As a basis of action, the professional's code — "Only the game matters" — is exactly the opposite of Holly's advice. To Holly, Henry is and must remain a man, a moral human being, whether or not he is a baseball player. Her counsel is intended to resolve, or to pre-empt, any conflict that might arise between trying to win the game and Henry's "'personal pride'" (135).

Henry, however, burns with the fever of competition and thinks primarily of victory. He is a highly talented, professionally trained athlete; like a soldier, he has been taught to achieve one goal by the best possible means. He is not encouraged to question the worthiness of victory, to express dissent, or to reflect on the state of his soul. He does sense, however, that something is wrong and, as the season unfolds, discovers that certain elements of professional competition undermine the thrill of being a major league pitcher. The most acute and prolonged of Henry's trials is the pain in his back, a physical wound that objectifies his internalized trauma. Having pitched a 16-inning, complete game victory, Henry feels a "crick," which he has noticed "before … but never like this" (260). Expecting the "crick" to fade with treatment and rest, Henry has x-rays taken when it gets "no worse but no better" (265). He becomes impatient with the doctor's conclusion that, the x-rays showing nothing, the pain is probably psychosomatic. Despite Henry's protests that "If I say I have got a pain in my back I have got 1, and it is in my back and not in my mind" (284), the x-rays cannot photograph psychological stress. Although this wound is temporary, it is a real consequence of Henry's overwork (at the direction of Dutch Schnell) and a sign of his growing alienation from baseball. The condition is not debilitating, but it is compromising; the pain prevents Henry from pitching with his usual confidence and effectiveness. The "crick" is also, with poetic justness, the proximate cause of Henry's most notorious personal failure.

Pitching in relief with the tying run on second base, Henry feels the "crick" and watches the batter smash two hanging curveballs into the left-field stands, narrowly foul. Desperate not to lose, Henry cheats. He throws a spitball half out of opportunism, half out of fear:

> ... I felt of my face, and it was wet like I was fresh out of the shower, and I ... tugged at the peak of my cap with my thumb and first finger, and with the other fingers I took the sweat of my brow and rubbed it along my fingertips, and then, with my fingers still wet, I throwed the curve.
>
> That is what you call a spitter. It is outlawed from baseball. ... [Y]ou can kill a man with a spitter if you hit him right. You do not have it under full control. All this I knowed, and I did not care. I did not wish to kill Tubs Blodgett, but my curve was not breaking on account of my back, and I throwed quick before I had time to think about consequences, and the curve broke big and sharp, for my fingers was slimy and wet, and Tubs swang and missed, striking out and ending the inning. Red whipped it down towards third, like he was making a play on Chickering coming down from second, and George never even reached for the throw but left it roll to the outfield, for the rolling dried it off, and Boston stormed from their dugout and beat their chest and raged and swore and howled and stamped their feet, for it was plain to all that I had throwed a spitter. ... I was all a-tremble, knowing that I done wrong according to the rules and could of been suspended and might of killed Tubs Blodgett besides [298].

Henry's depiction of the spitball reveals a misapprehension,[18] presumably on the part of his "editor," Mark Harris, yet the point is made: With the connivance of his teammates (to expunge the evidence), Henry throws an illegal, dangerous pitch and ends up saving the game. Holly witnesses the spitter on television and subsequently accuses Henry of forgetting that baseball "'really does not matter,'" and worse: "'you are losing your manhood faster then hell,'" Holly admonishes him, "'and becoming simply an island in the empire of Moors'" (306). As Holly sees it, cheating to win a baseball game is a prostitution of personal integrity; the end cannot justify the means because the end is not — or should not be — of comparable value to Henry.[19] Ethical theory aside,

[18]*A little knowledge is a dangerous thing: To throw a curveball, the pitcher wants dry fingers and a ball with high seams to pull down on, so that he can impart a tight, fast spin (at about a 45-degree angle to the ground) that will make the curve break "big and sharp." The spitball, a different pitch entirely, is thrown with the index and middle fingers wet against the baseball, between the seams, and riding lightly to create as little friction as possible, so that the thumb pressing upward at the instant of release makes the ball squirt from the fingers like a watermelon seed. The spitter looks like a fastball until it reaches the batter, when it abruptly drops because of the extreme topspin (perpendicular to the ground) created by the top fingers exerting almost no pressure while the thumb presses up and the arm whips down. The spitter is difficult to control, but any pitch can kill a batter if it "hit[s] him right."*

[19]*Leverett T. Smith reads Holly as a touchstone of wisdom: "Holly sees baseball as an island of cleanness in a corrupt world, a place where innocence and integrity are still possible. She is trying to revert Henry to his original view of baseball, this time unromanticized" (Smith 102).*

what upsets Holly most is that the Henry she has known since childhood is changing into another creature altogether: a man who identifies himself so thoroughly with the "organization" that he imposes its implicit orders on himself. At no other point does Henry so closely imitate the ethos of Patricia Moors, or stray so far from his personal values. The spitball he throws at a decisive moment, like the "crick" in his back, is a symptom of his estrangement from the young man who has responded vitally to the poetry Holly has read to him. Caught in the pressure of a pennant race, only sporadically in touch with home, Henry does not recognize his exile for what it is. He knows only that he is wounded and turns for relief to an expedient "out" that seems justifiable, if dishonest.

Despite some trepidation at what might have happened if the spitball had slipped the wrong way, Henry defends his chicanery as disreputable means in the service of legitimate ends. This argument essentially asserts that the stakes of being a professional are unlike those of being a pitcher for the Perkinsville Scarlets and that Henry's values have shifted accordingly. For an afternoon's pitching, Pop "got 25 [dollars] ... in the early days, 50 and 75 and as much as 100 in later years" (23); in a major league pennant race, the monetary consequences are much more serious. Now, "'Things are tight.... Terrible tight. Every pitch is cash, Holly. Big cash. Not only my cash but the cash of all the boys. It is a brick house for Coker Roguski's folks and a new start in life for Hams Carroll's little girl. This is for keeps. This ain't playground baseball'" (306). Holly has stated that she does not care how much money Henry earns or whether he is "'a New York Mammoth or a Perkinsville Scarlet ... so long as he is a man'" (305–306), but Henry cannot reconcile her small-town integrity to the mercenary imperative of big-time baseball. To justify his cheating, Henry cites the monetary realities of professional play, in effect meeting Holly's question "'Is it worth it, Henry?'" (306) with the professional's only possible rejoinder: It has to be. This implicit answer intensifies the reader's sense that baseball is no longer just Henry's form of self-expression but a job he does as an employee in "'the empire of Moors.'" Yet, Holly does not want Henry to renounce his ambition and quit the game. It is, she believes, not baseball but the calculating minds, avaricious spirits, and small, embittered souls of certain men (and at least one woman) who corrupt the thrill and beauty of pure play: "It is a grand game. I love to see it, and I love to hear you talk about it. It is a beautiful game, clean and graceful and honest. But I will be damned if I will sit back and watch you turn into some sort of a low life halfway between a sour creature like Sad Sam Yale and a shark like Dutch Schnell" (307). Holly's life-counsel, like Mike Mulrooney's professional advice, is for Henry to resist emulating the personalities he encounters among the ballplayers, to learn baseball from them but to create his own model of athletic excellence joined to personal integrity. The key to achieving this synthesis is an attribute that he has possessed innately all along: Henry must follow his "southpaw" nature, on the diamond and especially in life.

In the lexicon of baseball, to be a southpaw means simply to be left-handed,[20] but in a culture populated by and designed for right-handed predominance, to be left-handed is implicitly to diverge from the norm. In terms of character, a "southpaw" is openly different, out of step, irregular — a nonconformist who stands up to the stratagems and expediencies of Patricia Moors, the macho bullying of Dutch Schnell, the prevarications of Krazy Kress. Holly's role is really quite simple. She reveals Henry to himself, tells him who he is and to be true to his left-handed nature:

> "You are a lefthander, Henry. You always was. And the world needs all the left-handers it can get, for it is a righthanded world. You are a southpaw in a starboarded atmosphere. Do you understand?"
> "Sure I understand," said I. "I am not such a stupid goon as you might think."
> "Exactly," she said [307].

Just in case Henry does not understand quite well enough, Holly offers a few well-chosen metaphors to help him think about how he must distinguish between professional obligations and his own moral imperatives. At this point the narrative veers toward a sentimentality that would be excessive if the narrator were not a 21-year-old trying to describe how the woman in his life, worldly wise beyond her years and beyond him, has used his hand as the objective correlative of his sensibility and her love of it:

> "I hold your hand," she said, "and your hand is hard, solid like a board. That is all right, for it must be hard against the need of your job. On a job such as yours your hand grows hard to protect itself. But you have not yet growed calluses on your heart. It is not yet hard against the need of your job. It must never become hard like your hand. It must stay soft.
> "In most places of the world hardness is a mark of credit. I do not believe that. I believe the best hand is the soft hand, the best heart is the soft heart, the best man is the soft man. I want my old soft Henry back, Henry the Coward Navigator" [307–308].

Physical strength and ability, a resolute will, a competitive attitude impervious to sentiment or compromise are qualities that enhance Henry's performance on the baseball field but that are ambiguously applicable to ordinary human relationships. To Holly, attributes like compassion, tolerance, and generosity, all of which Henry imperfectly possesses, are at least equally important to how he conducts his life. All of her insight into Henry's nature, all of the wisdom she conveys, prepare Henry to navigate his separate confrontation scenes with

---

[20]*The etymology of the term "southpaw" offers an excellent example of the dialectic between language and the anterior world that creates it and is in turn (re)created by it. In* The Dickson Baseball Dictionary *(New York: Facts on File, 1989), Paul Dickson provides this explanation: "[Southpaw] derives from the 'fact' that ballparks were once laid out with home plate to the west which meant that a left-handed pitcher faced the west and threw with his southern limb. This westward orientation kept the sun out of the batter's eyes and out of the eyes of the customers in the more expensive seats behind home plate during an afternoon game" (Dickson 366).*

Dutch Schnell, Krazy Kress, and Patricia Moors, which are crammed into the novel's final 25 pages (when the pennant race reaches its climax, a lot of energy spins tumultuously free). Henry cannot assimilate Holly's metaphors readily enough to save himself from every error, but he does maintain his personal integrity in the face of external pressure and considerable temptation. In the crucial tests that occur near the end of the book, Henry demonstrates what he has learned — or what he has remembered, or been reminded of — about being his own man and serving no false master. These episodes provide a fitting, somewhat antagonistic close to Henry Wiggen's baseball education.

The rapid development of these conclusive events might explain Henry's apparent descent into selfishness, cynicism, and greed, yet his own failures of character conspire, ironically, with athletic success to accelerate the downward spiral. In the second-to-last game of the season, Henry pitches masterfully for eight innings despite the pain in his back and is on the verge of clinching a tie for the pennant. With three outs still to get, he knows that "1 way or another in the next 10 or 15 minutes the pressure would be off for good — off *me* at least — and that was something to look forward to" (318). In the ninth, with the crowd roar "beating against me like it was a solid thing, like waves in a genuine ocean" and feeling the noise as stress "in my back from knob to knob, from the back of my neck to the base of my spine" (321), Henry retires the first two batters and then delivers his final pitch:

> I do not know if I could of throwed another. I pitched it in noise and pain that I will never forget, letter-high and hard, the full wind and the full pump and the full motion, and he swang, and the wood on the ball made a thin slim sound like a twig you might break across your knee, and the ball went upwards and upwards, almost straight up, halfway down the line between home and third, and Red called, not that you heard him but that you seen his mouth move, and the ball hung in the air and then fell, down through the lights, Red weaving, dancing first 1 way and then the next, his big mitt waiting, and then it hit, soundless ... [321].

The pop-up ends the game and, Henry assumes, his part in the pennant race. To his consternation, that evening's paper reports that he will pitch the final game if it will decide who wins the pennant. Henry hears this rumor on the radio, reads it again in other newspapers, "and every time I seen it or heard it it was like somebody stuck a knife in my back" (325). During the team meeting before the penultimate game, just before the Mammoths take the field to try to make the point moot by winning, Henry renounces his responsibility in case they lose. Before anyone actually tells him that he will pitch the deciding game — no one knows if one will be necessary — Henry tells his teammates, "'Naturally I doubt that we could possibly lose today. But if by some miracle we do I doubt that I could pitch tomorrow if my life depended on it'" (326). This announcement is not only egregiously premature and self-serving, it is ill-timed: The pressure on the other players is great enough without forcing them to take the field absolutely certain that, in case of dire need, they have no (pitching) ace-in-the-hole. Dutch Schnell tries to mitigate this impression without promising Henry that he will not be called on to pitch, but when Henry backs his manager into a corner the result is an exchange of verbal spars that escalates until Dutch notes that "'we would pull it out so long as we had no quitters and nobody dragging their feet amongst us'" (327). This remark and the silence that answers it tell Henry that Sam Yale's selfish attitude is correct, that everyone serves only himself and befriends another only if that other serves his interest, too. Henry has acted no better — it is a credit to him that he tells this tale on himself — and seems annoyed that his teammates will not excuse him for it. Realizing that he must dispel the deleterious atmosphere he has created, angry that he must defend himself after already having done his best, Henry incriminates his teammates' tacit selfishness even as he sarcastically recants his own selfish announcement:

> "Okay. I am glad to know the score. Sam told me it would take me 15 years to find it out, but I have found it out in 1. I am 15 times as smart as Sam. Piss on you, Sam," said I to Sam. "Piss on the whole lot of you. Pitch me tomorrow. Pitch me *today* for all of that."
> Something snapped in my back. I did not give it a thought at the time, but I remembered it afterwards.
> "Pitch me any old time," I said, "but do not call me a quitter or tell me I am dragging my feet. We won 96 ball games through yesterday and 26 of them was mine. On a staff of 9 pitchers plus Crane tell me who dragged their feet and who did not" [328].

Henry has a valid point: He has borne his share of the burden, and then some. But statistics do not, as he claims in another context, tell the whole story; a pitcher might have credit and blame assigned to him, but each victory and loss belong to the team. Henry knows this, but what he perceives as an undercurrent of abuse sweeps him into outrage. Dutch's readiness to pitch him on one day's rest, even in an all-or-nothing game, tells Henry that the Mammoth "organization" is ready to use him up to accomplish its own ends, all of which are finally reducible to the making of profits. For money, the "organization" is willing to risk impairing Henry's talent by making him vulnerable to permanent injury (just as for the "big cash" Henry has thrown a spitball at the risk of killing an opposing batter). "When the team wins, everyone wins" is another professional platitude, but if the effort of winning destroys a player's career he is likely to end up asking Holly's question: "'Is it worth it?'" (306). This conflict is always at the heart of the relationship between the athlete and his team, but having to confront it in such bald terms nearly extinguishes Henry's sense of himself as a "team player."

When the Mammoths succeed in clinching the pennant in that penultimate game, Henry feels the pain leaving his back one vertebra at a time, its descent matching the fly ball's fall from the sky, "hitting the lowest knob at the moment the ball snuggled in Scotty Burnses glove, and out through my spine — gone I do not know where and do not care. But gone, and for good and ever" (331).

As he comes to realize what his body has been trying to tell him for the past three months, Henry's mood sours. The scene at the Moors's victory party strikes his critical eye as an emblem of venial sin and moral hypocrisy. Teammates he has always known to despise each other now drink toasts and converse affably, revealing the essential falseness of relationships based on nothing but mutual self-interest and the expectation of success: "Oh, winning heals many a wound in the flesh! And I could not help thinking, 'What if we lost? What if 6 games between April and September had went the other way? What then?'" (335). Henry realizes that his own "wound in the flesh" has healed in the warmth of victory, but other wounds, psychic and emotional analogs to the "crick," remain. As if he were feeling these intangible wounds more acutely now that his physical duress has ended, Henry becomes indignant and fractious. Having walked out of the party, he takes issue with Krazy Kress, actual author of *Sam Yale — Mammoth,* for the falsities that book has perpetuated:

> "That book was a pack of lies," I said.
> "I would not say that," said Krazy. "I thought it was a good book and read it several times myself."
> "It is horseshit," I said. "Sam says so himself."
> "Then why did he sign his name to it?" said Krazy.
> "Why, he *wrote* it," I said.
> "He did not," said Krazy.
> "Well then," said I, "whoever wrote it certainly piled up the horseshit thicker and faster. I could write a better book then that lefthanded. Furthermore, if I ever wrote a book I would write it myself and not hire some lug to do it for me. Why does not somebody write 1 decent book about baseball, Krazy? There never been a good book yet."
> "There been dozens of good books," said he.
> "There has been only fairy tales," I said.
> "It is a fairy tale game," he said. "You are 21 years old, Henry, and you have very few brains in your head except with a baseball cap on. Yet you will draw upwards of 10,000 this year for 40 afternoons of work. Is that not a fairy tale game?"
> "40 afternoons," I said. "That is all *you* seen, Krazy. The pain in my back you never seen" [336].

Henry does not dispute Krazy's pejorative remark about his intelligence, seizing instead on the "40 afternoons" of performance that are the only visible signs — to Krazy and to the fans — of Henry's existence. Henry cites his three-month backache, which has at times caused him to alter his pitching motion at the risk of ruining his arm, but he could mention as well the rest of his "inside" story: the 5,000 games of solitary baseball pitched against the side of the house, the countless practice sessions with Pop, all of the "crises" he later enumerates for Patricia Moors, even the books he has not read and the poetry he has not written, all in favor of becoming a highly adept specialist in an esoteric trade. Physically, every pitch costs Henry something because of the strain it puts on his arm and shoulder, which will not always be supple and strong, yet every pitch has already cost him in terms of time spent and "crises" endured and opportunities passed by. He will pitch hereafter, he says, "'for the kicks and the cash only,'" as if to liquidate this outstanding debt, if he can.

For some, the money and the glory never balance the ongoing pressure and sense of other losses, and this inequitable exchange is why Pop gave up professional baseball with all the world before him. Sensing that he did not have the steeliness and grit of a professional competitor, Pop quit rather than go through the motions of an impossible performance: sustaining over a long season the "perfect pitch" of physically difficult, emotionally exhausting athletic virtuosity. Pop has forgone the rewards to spare himself the backache. He has chosen a quiet life at home — a kind of inverted, permanent exile that distances him from professional baseball but allows him to live at peace. This answer to the question of "how to live" is the right one for him; the personality that is happy living in a backwater like Perkinsville, driving the school bus and pitching semipro ball, is not a personality suited to the pitching mound in Moors Stadium and the glare of transient fame. The best Pop can do is to prepare his son for the professional arena by teaching him the mechanics and logic of the discipline he himself practices in relative privacy. Pop cannot teach Henry how to live with the win-at-all-costs imperative of the majors nor how to endure the pressure of a pennant race, because he has not endured these "crisises." Pop never explains why he has retreated from baseball because this knowledge would burden his son with doubt, which could undermine the resolve that Henry must sustain to achieve his ambition.[21] Even without this psychological handicap, Henry, himself a thinker of "left-handed" thoughts, apprehends the true motive of Pop's "mysterious" withdrawal: "The exact story ... is still not clear in my mind and probably never will, though after last summer I can actually see where a man might do what Pop done" (16).

The outcome of Henry's unguarded conversation with Krazy Kress is a newspaper column that depicts the southpaw as callous, privileged, and colossally selfish, a monster of calculating self-regard. In the "Dedication" to his book, Henry claims that he has written *The Southpaw* so that "the 100,000,000 boobs and flatheads that swallowed down whole the lies of Krazy Kress ... would have my side of the story, which is the true side, and not Krazy's, which is more or less of a lie from start to finish" (5 [unnumbered]). Henry excerpts Krazy's version, which also purports to be the "inside" story, and prints it as part of his narrative. The article castigates Henry for the "impudence and arrogance and downright orneriness" (339) that he displays at the triumphant end of the pennant race, but the true dispute between Krazy Kress and Henry Wiggen concerns the latter's well-established pacifism and its corollary, his refusal to join a baseball tour of Korea to stage exhibition games for American troops. Weary from the long season and feeling especially cynical after witnessing its climactic

---

[21]Henry has inherited Pop's uncompetitive nature in his own constitutional inability to tolerate aggression, as manifested by what Aaron calls his "Coward Crouch" (36–38). This trait does not compromise Henry's ability to pitch in the majors, but it does disqualify him from participating (in any way) in the Korean War.

hypocrisies and exploitative meanness (325–335), Henry must rely on his modest verbal skills to formulate an answer to Krazy's importunate requests that he participate. "Leave us forget Korea" refers only to the tour, which Henry prefers not to discuss. A literal quotation would have been "'Leave us forget Korea and the girls,'" the latter feature one of Krazy's inducements. Krazy truncates the sentence, distorts its sentiment,[22] and quotes it out of context, presumably to make a better story of Henry's throwaway remark. In his column, Krazy uses the misquotation as a conceit and affects a chiding tone, an air of offended patriotism, to portray Henry as a snot-nosed boy who plays baseball while soldiers his age are dying in combat (339–343).

The immediate repercussion of Krazy's article is a final piece of evasion: Patricia Moors, the young, rich, beautiful owner of the Mammoths, with whom Henry has desired to "fornicate" since spring training, typewrites two responses, one an apology and admission of "guilt," the other a denial of every charge, and asks Henry to sign the one he prefers because "'This is the kind of a rhubarb that brings on a crisis for the organization'" (343). Henry refuses to sign either statement. By now he fully possesses the terms of his independence and states his position in a way that brings into focus a key element of his "inside" story:

> "I am not worried about crisises," I said. "I am through with them. I been through 1,000 crisises since I was a kid — high-school ball, Legion ball, semi-pro tryout, my first semi-pro game, camp games at Aqua Clara, my first games at Q. C., my first relief job with the Mammoths, Opening Day. How many crisises is a man supposed to go through? Does there not come a time when a man must simply say that nothing is so important that he must forever fight against crisises? No, I will not sign them, neither of them, neither apologizing nor denying."
>
> "Yet could you not at least keep these thoughts to yourself?" she said. ... "It is the organization that must be kept pure and free from scandal. You are a part of the organization."
>
> "I am a part of nothing," I said [343].

Henry's principled refusal to sign either of Patricia's prepared responses, like his opposition to the Korean War, marks him as a nonconformist caught up in an age of conformity; in his left-handed attitudes, Henry is implacably at odds with the prevailing right-wing *Zeitgeist*. His upbringing, his ability to pitch a baseball, his exalted position on the mound, all contribute to Henry's unwillingness — his temperamental incapacity — to become, or even to feign the obsequiousness of, an organization man. The "crisises" that he enumerates for Patricia Moors remind the reader that Henry's baseball trials, enacted in a public forum, exert personal effects that spectators neither see nor understand. Yet these hidden effects influence Henry's behavior when each new crisis comes along. This scene is integral to Henry's book, his self-justifying reply to Krazy

---

[22]Earlier in the season, when Henry tries to explain why he will not participate in the exhibition tour, he is careful to discriminate his loyalties from his oppositions. When Krazy asks, "'Ain't you behind the boys over there?'" Henry replies, "'I am behind the boys ... but I am against the war'" (239–241).

Kress's hatchet job, just as it serves Mark Harris's purpose of dramatizing the transformation of Henry Wiggen from the rookie who wants to "fornicate" with Patricia Moors to the man Holly Webster consents to marry.

In the course of denying any debt of loyalty owed to the "organization," Henry demonstrates that he no longer desires to incur a new debt, particularly one on which Patricia will be certain to collect. Henry reminds Patricia of some old business between her and one of the ballplayers that has involved, in effect, an exchange of sexual favors for money. Ugly Jones, the Mammoths' shortstop, has been a holdout during spring training, asking $2000 more than the team was offering. In an innuendo so plain it stops just short of being a declarative sentence, Ugly lets his teammates know that he has signed without getting the $2000 because he and Patricia have spent a long night together in a motel room. Patricia's own imprudent behavior tends to confirm Ugly's claim. Having become drunk-sick at her own party, Patricia tells Henry, "'For having his sense below his belt it cost Ugly 2,000' ... and she laughed in a most hysterical way" (162). Now Ugly Jones is laid up in the hospital with a broken jaw, which he has suffered in a skirmish during the season's second-to-last game, and no one from the team visits him. In reprising the rumor of Patricia's mercenary sexuality, Henry sharpens the distinction between himself and his teammates:

> "Have you paid a visit to Ugly Jones that you screwed out of 2,000 dollars 1 fine night in Aqua Clara?"
> "Who has made such a statement?" said she.
> "It is common knowledge," I said.
> "It ain't true," she said.
> "And you would behave towards me in the same way if you thought it would keep me in line," I said. "But I have learned a lot this year. I remember what you said of Ugly 1 night in Aqua Clara. You said his brain was down below his belt. But mine ain't."
> I believe I hit home with that, for I know very well that there was nothing, neither money nor her own self, that Patricia would not part with to smooth the path of the organization. It was her club that her father give her, her baby, her precious thing, and she would keep it rolling at any cost. I admired her for that, and I said so to her face, saying also that there was a time when for the touch of her flesh I would of done anything, said anything, apologized 300,000 times to the newspapers for what I said to Krazy. But living and hearing and seeing learned me that if I was to be a man — a *man* like the kind of a man Holly Webster wished me to be — I was best off at a far distance from Patricia [344].

One thing Henry learns is that Patricia is the quintessential organization (wo)man, willing to prostitute herself to lower costs. As he correctly senses, staying close to her can lead only to his becoming an organization man — or thing, because after his usefulness is exhausted he will be discarded.[23] Coming from

---

[23]*As indeed happens some 19 years later, when Henry, pushing 40 and having demonstrably lost his fastball, is released by Patricia Moors and the Mammoths. The "organization," amid self-validating claims of being a family, declines even to give Henry a chance to be its manager. See* It Looked Like For Ever, *6, 10–11.*

a sophisticated narrator, Henry's plain statements of truths realized and lessons learned would be considered artless, too overtly directed by the author. Coming from Henry, such remarks seem appropriate, even necessary — especially near the end of his story — but these insights would probably elude him if he were writing without Holly's guiding sensibility. Whether one judges it to be contrived or inevitable, this moment of self-awareness defines the wisdom that Henry Wiggen discovers through his experiences in baseball, on and off the field.

Having survived all the "crisises" of his first season in the majors, Henry returns home to Perkinsville. No welcoming committee greets him, no brass band plays for him, no holidays are declared in his honor. Henry's hometown rooters have read Krazy Kress's allegations and believed enough of them so that even in Borelli's Barber Shop, where Henry used to listen to the World Series on the radio, they have removed the picture of Henry in his Mammoth uniform and left the wall bare. Finding the battery in his car dead, Henry begins to walk home in the rain, but the mawkishness of such a homecoming is averted when Pop, Aaron, and Holly meet him en route. Despite such anticlimax in the wake of his success, Henry enjoys a fulfilling homecoming that culminates in his marriage to Holly, who helps him evaluate his recent passage. Henry claims to believe that "'when the dream comes true it falls flat on its face'" (348), a conclusion that indicates his newly acquired awareness of the absurd gap that separates our idealizations of how the world ought to be and our shocked discovery of what the world actually is. Holly, in turn, sums up his accomplishments, which she sees as "'a year of great victory,'" in a way that marks her as Henry's able muse, the special prospective reader who alerts Henry to the "inside" story that is more important and more worthy of being told than the baseball statistics that he believes represent the sum of his achievement. Holly supplies an epitome of the story that the statistics cannot show, which sounds very much like the story of the book Henry writes:

> "What they do not show is that you growed to manhood over the summer. You will throw no more spitballs for the sake of something so stupid as a ball game. You will worship the feet of no more gods name of Sad Sam Yale nor ever be a true follower of Dutch Schnell. And you will know the Krazy Kresses of this world for the liars they are. You will never be an island in the empire of Moors, Henry, and that is the great victory that hardly anybody wins any more" [348].

Just as she guides him in life, so does Holly direct Henry's apprentice authorship by articulating the themes of his book and defining an attitude with which he can approach them. Most importantly, Holly encourages would-be "Author" Wiggen to tell his "inside" story or risk its being co-opted and falsified. Although she will not let him dedicate the book to "the 100,000,000 boobs and flatheads" that have believed Krazy's distortions, she does validate his having written it.

Henry's final interview with Krazy Kress, in which he alludes to doing the writing himself, might strike the reader as self-serving, for Henry is left-handed to begin with and has by this point all but finished his baseball book. Yet the stories, biographies, and reportage of baseball that precede *The Southpaw* generally conform to Henry's opinion of them (if one grants that *The Natural* is an adult version of the "fairy tale" with a horror-story ending—that is, a myth).[24] To this extent, *The Southpaw* is baseball fiction's watershed text. Just as Roger Angell's baseball journalism set the standard for that genre in the early 1960s,[25] and Roger Kahn, with *The Boys of Summer* (1972), and Robert Creamer, with *Babe: The Legend Comes to Life* (1974), established the tone and style of serious baseball biography,[26] so does *The Southpaw* initiate the realistic tradition of the baseball novel and define the benchmark of its verisimilitude. At the same time, the novel's major themes are sufficiently foregrounded to represent more general concerns: personal independence and the subjugation of the self, political nonconformity and patriotism, the nexus of money and sex. These issues and others tend to place the book firmly in its historical context (the early 1950s), yet hardly in a way that limits its relevance. It might be that Henry Wiggen begins his baseball career more innocent of the ways of the world than most present-day ballplayers, but his experiences remain compelling if one appreciates the southpaw's rustic, almost isolated childhood and unsophisticated demeanor. Most persuasive are the lessons Henry learns, for this education is manifestly the product of firsthand experience. Henry's journey through the majors during his rookie season is a series of adventures that reveal human frailty in many guises. Fear masquerades as anger or resentment; selfishness and egotism dress in a baseball uniform to look like professionalism and team spirit; vanity and petty pride dissemble themselves behind a grimace of competitiveness. The problem of how to live in this world without enslaving one's self to its dictates tasks Henry Wiggen throughout *The Southpaw*, for the wisdom of "how to live" is elusive. Adversity often proves to be its own object lesson, but experience becomes usable wisdom only after its truths are distilled by the protagonist's guiding spirit, who becomes, poetically, his wife. What remains amidst the detritus of winter is for Pitcher Wiggen to turn Author and write his own revivifying book in expectation of spring. For as Edmund Wilson said of Ring Lardner, if he "has anything more to give us, the time has now come to deliver it."[27]

[24]*The major exception is Ring Lardner's* You Know Me Al *(1916), which is nothing like a fairy tale.*

[25]*Roger Angell's first volume of baseball essays,* The Summer Game, *appeared in 1972, collecting occasional articles he had written for* The New Yorker *during the previous ten years. The earliest dated piece, "The Old Folks Behind Home," is from March 1962.*

[26]*Prior to these books, baseball biographies were usually written along the lines of* Sam Yale—Mammoth. *One conspicuous exception is Ty Cobb's autobiography,* My Life in Baseball: The True Record *(Garden City, NY: Doubleday and Co., 1961). This book, co-authored with Al Stump, was compiled while Cobb was dying of cancer. It represents its subject and his baseball career with essential, albeit selective and self-justifying, accuracy.*

[27]*Edmund Wilson, "Ring Lardner's American Characters" in* The Shores of Light *(New York: Farrar, Straus and Giroux, 1952), 97.*

♦ *Nine* ♦
Writing Baseball
J. Henry Waugh's Game-Within

Choosing life in an artifact, people agree to live in a state of similitude.
— A. Bartlett Giamatti,
Take Time for Paradise

Baseball is Life. The rest is just details.
— popular tee-shirt aphorism

In *The Universal Baseball Association, Inc., J. Henry Waugh, Prop.* (1968), Robert Coover transcends the narrative realism of *The Southpaw,* the mythic allegories of *The Natural,* and the comic monologues of *You Know Me Al* to write about an all-engrossing game-within. No other baseball novel is so concerned with the dialectic of text and life and how these forms of experience can seem equally (un)real to author, character, and reader. Cunningly devised as a fiction-within-a-fiction, the novel dramatizes the consciousness of its protagonist, J. Henry Waugh, in relation to his imaginary yet "life-like" Association. Living within the world of the game, Henry discovers that baseball can, indeed, become virtually the whole of one's life, and its details the subject of obsessive attention. As he plays, however, Henry hopes for something more than winners and losers: a transcendent meaning that will raise the game to the level of art. This desire, in the form Henry conceives it, is one that the game happens to thwart. In response, the proprietor destroys the UBA-as-game, reconstructing it as history, novel, and ritual. This mimetic evolution ends with the game and its player's coming home to a self-absorbed isolation, an exile from everything outside the invented world. As a story of creative energy gone awry, *The Universal Baseball Association* questions the presumption that literary meaning is or can be the product of authorial intention attaining self-selected ends, and proposes that "perfection [isn't] a thing, a closed moment, a static fact, but *process.*"[1] As a parable of one man's despair at the disjunction of ideal and

---

[1] The Universal Baseball Association, Inc., J. Henry Waugh, Prop. *(1968; reprinted, New York: New American Library/Penguin, 1971), 212.*

reality, the game-playing career of Proprietor Waugh demonstrates that the fictions by which one lives are one's only support in confronting "the terror of eternity" (238).

A tour de force of wit, comic pathos, and rhetorical ingenuity, *The Universal Baseball Association* brilliantly exploits its main narrative artifice of a fiction-within-a-fiction. The greater fiction is the third-person narrative that tells the story of J. Henry Waugh, a 56-year-old bachelor accountant, and his estrangement from life. Moving through a world of impoverished relationships, employed by a small accounting firm, Waugh spends much of his off-work time playing, with expertise and commitment, a multiform and ever-evolving baseball game of his own invention. Thanks to its proprietor's capacious imagination, the UBA truly is a game-within, impeccably realized and inimitable. Like a deeply felt, fully rendered novel, the UBA possesses so persuasive a virtual reality that its players often seem to have an autonomous existence; taken together, these fictive lives constitute the novel's microfiction.[2] The illusion that characters like Damon Rutherford, Jock Casey, Fennimore McCaffree, Barney Bancroft, Paul Trench, Hardy Ingram, et al. exist apart from Henry's consciousness is evidence of Robert Coover's literary artistry. By representing all of the characters as if they occupied the same plane of reality within the macrofiction, the author demonstrates that they are all equally (un)real. The greater game, then, is Coover's; he is the author of Waugh's existence, instigator of its crises, and ultimately the creator of the Universal Baseball Association — although Coover as *primum mobile* remains necessarily inscrutable to his "Prop."[3] The fact that Proprietor Waugh figures as the author of the UBA and nominal creator of its players indicates merely that he has been made so by a greater master.

To say that the UBA and its proprietor are mutually dependent can hardly be counted a great insight, for the Association is, within the macrofiction, obviously a projection of Henry's mind. The reader, noticing that individualized players (as well as game action and uproarious off-field antics) appear as vividly as Henry Waugh, is led to ask which of the interpenetrating worlds is the "real" one. This is a trick question begged by the fiction-within, for neither the interior world of the UBA nor Henry's outside life as a bachelor accountant is anything more than a series of images created by words. This point should be self-evident, but the UBA often seems demonstrably more real than its proprietor, especially during the intervals of Henry's nominal absence. Even then,

---

[2]See Roy C. Caldwell, Jr., "Of Hobby-Horses, Baseball, and Narrative: Coover's Universal Baseball Association," 162–163, in Modern Fiction Studies 33: 1 (Spring 1987): 161–171.

[3]In Seeking the Perfect Game (New York: Greenwood Press, 1989), Cordelia Candelaria notes Coover's authority: "Henry is but the 'Prop.,' the proprietor, yes, but also a stage prop, an object lacking any power or control" (Candelaria 123; see 128). In Playful Fictions and Fictional Players (Port Washington, NY: Kennikat Press, 1981), Neil Berman judges Henry to be "as much a part of his own game as his players, and ... Henry and the Association are parts of a larger game being played by still another god figure — Robert Coover" (Berman 93).

when he seems to have been subsumed, the UBA exists as a projection of its inventor's consciousness. Just as he plays the game on his kitchen table under the sun of a 100-watt lightbulb, imagining the sights, sounds, and smells of the ballpark, so does Henry imagine the words, thoughts, and lives of his players. In the UBA, baseball is set in motion by three dice, which define the outcomes on highly detailed, interactive charts, but it is the mind of its proprietor that brings the Association to life. The results of the dice-throws are based on the interplay of probability and statistics, but these results acquire meaning only as they are appraised and recorded by J. Henry Waugh. Each UBA player is ranked as an Ace, Star, Regular, or Rookie, yet each player lives in his creator's mind as a distinctive personality who is more important than his statistical profile. From the opening scene, the UBA appears in such keen detail that it supersedes the macrofiction that is ostensibly designed to encompass it, yet the logic of fictional narrative finally denies it an autonomous presence, no matter how separable it might seem from its proprietor. Without doubt the UBA is the central reality of Henry Waugh's inner life; his consciousness roves among its personas as his mind navigates the involutions of the game. Yet the UBA exists purely within Henry's omniscience of it; if Henry stops thinking about the game, it disappears. Even in chapter eight, when the microfiction of UBA activity has wholly displaced the macrofiction and the proprietor himself has been erased, J. Henry Waugh must be present in mind, if not in name or body, to cogitate the Damonsday ritual in its superfine complexity. Inevitably bound by the macrofiction and its narrative logic, Henry is always the author of the UBA even if he scripts it for an audience of one: himself.

To say that Henry Waugh has created the UBA and administers its affairs is not, however, to claim that he is, in all ways and at all times, its master. Indeed, the UBA exercises a discernible psychological influence on its proprietor and visibly affects his behavior. The UBA is Henry's frame of reference in his encounters with the outside world, informing his perceptions of and responses to job, acquaintances, and surroundings. Henry even thinks in the language of baseball, creating metaphors from the game's vernacular that illustrate its adaptability to literary purposes. With the co-authorship of Hettie Irden, a neighborhood B-girl with whom he occasionally dances the old dance, Henry translates sexual intercourse into a run around the bases that makes both acts humorous and exciting (33–35). His goal — their shared goal — is "home," not as a domestic establishment but as culmination, climax, and focal point of a sexual exchange. Playing baseball's symbolic association with the rejuvenation of nature off Henry and Hettie's spirited coupling on the dark side of middle age, this moment is the happiest Henry shares with another character. It is playful, comic, cutely erotic, and ends with the sly double entendre of a run-down play — what Henry calls "a hotbox":

> he's around third! on his way home! but they've got him in a hotbox! wow! third
> to catch! back to third! hah! to catch! to pitch! catch! pitch! catch! pitch! Home,

Henry, *home!* And here he comes, Hettie! He's past'em! past'em! past'em! he's bolt-
ing for home, spurting past, sliding in — *POW!* Oh, *pow,* Henry! pow pow pow pow
POW! They laughed softly, hysterically, flowing together. She let go her grip on the
ball. He slipped off, unmingling their sweat. Oh, that's a game, Henry! *That's* really
a *great* old *game!* [34–35].

Seldom has an author used exclamatory phrases and italic type so poignantly.
By being funny, inventive, and thrilling, this sexual interlude convinces the
reader that the UBA pervades Henry's life. The game's nomenclature and
imagery so predominate in his imagination that he analogizes sex, which from
a male perspective generally emphasizes the telos of orgasm, to a sequence of
play-by-play, which typically describes process without reference to its (un)fore-
seen end. For Henry, for any man, sexual climax is not only foreseen but anticipated. This simple truth accounts for the passage's equation of male orgasm
with "home" and lends the baseball metaphor its wry sexual resonance: Having touched all the bases, the player scores. Rhetorically, this analogy suggests
a relationship among baseball, sex, and home that describes the tenor of Henry's
life at the same time that it indicates its insufficiencies. As the reader soon discovers, Henry's revivifying intimacy with Hettie is a rare pleasure. Henry has
a home, it is true, but his apartment is a desolate place. Apart from the UBA,
infrequent visits by Hettie, and a single, misconceived episode with Lou Engel,
Henry is companionless at home. To an extent remarkable for its perfect intro-
version, the baseball game that he has invented is the form and substance of
Henry's life; it is his "home" and only steady partner, the secret sharer of his
joy and sorrow. To the reader, the UBA figures as Henry's imaginative escape
from his job at Dunkelmann, Zauber & Zifferblatt, as well as a relief from an
ugly urban world (Henry recognizes that "Some people would look on his game
... as a kind of running away" [140]). To Henry, the UBA is a forum of athletic
achievement and sexual prowess, a scene of male camaraderie and paternal
affection, a source of artistic inspiration and the medium of its expression: a
simulacrum of a life and what Henry's ideal life might include.[4]

For all of the energy he devotes to it, to the degree that it preoccupies him,
the UBA might be a novel in progress and Henry a writer composing his supreme
fiction. Read along these lines, *The Universal Baseball Association* becomes a
rendition of artistic failure, the story of a writer's breakdown as his fiction over-
whelms his efforts to refine it, as if veering off into its own undisciplined telling.

[4]*In* The Joy of Sports *(New York: Basic Books, 1976), Michael Novak argues that "Play, not work, is
the end of life," that "Work ... must be done" but that "Play is reality. Work is diversion and escape"
(Novak 40). Like Novak, Coover inverts the traditional hierarchy by representing Henry's play as more
"real" than his work, thus challenging the reader's presumption that work is "reality" and play "diversion and escape." Henry himself is certain of the boundaries between work and play yet refers to the
UBA (early in the novel) as "work," as if to legitimize the demands it makes on his time: "the work,
or what he called his work, though it was more than that, much more, was good for him" (5–6; see
26–27, 155, 164). The distinction is clear to Henry, but communicating the UBA's special quality remains
a problem (164–165, 179–199). Like Damon Rutherford, whom Henry thinks of as its embodiment, the
UBA begins and ends as a "self-enclosed yet participating mystery" (9).*

The UBA, however, is a game; its aleatory[5] elements are indifferent to Henry's desire to embody his intentions in the outcomes of play. Eager for the UBA to express the meaning that he believes is immanent within it, Henry compromises the game's integrity by attempting to script its events as if play were premeditated. When the UBA begins to express its proprietor's sense of meaning — or when Henry begins to believe that it does so — it becomes something other than a game: history or novel, the story of his life as Henry would write it. When, as one might expect, the game does not conform to his expectations, Henry perceives the influence of a counter-intention. Eventually, Henry abandons the UBA-as-game and forces its ludic framework to bear the weight of his desires. The circumstances of this transformation suggest that Henry's drive to discover meaning compels him to reject play's processes, which are unpredictable and finally meaningless, in favor of the (presumably) controllable process of novel-writing.

Henry authors the UBA beyond having devised the game in an indefinite pretexual past and keeping its records thereafter. As a practical matter, he generates players for the annual rookie draft, an act of creation analogous to a writer's contrivance of fictional characters. Later, Henry's efforts as the Association's most versatile writer (to complement his role as its quintessential player) manifests itself in the folk ballads that he composes in the persona of Sandy Shaw (36), and in the Book, an ongoing 40-volume text that he writes from the perspective of the game-within. The Book of the UBA contains "Everything ... worth keeping": player statistics, newspaper articles, "seasonal analyses [and] general baseball theory" (55), all authored by J. Henry Waugh. To lend the Book verisimilitude, Henry varies his prose style. He records simple facts in succinct sentences, resorts to "the overblown idiom of the sportswriter" in composing game stories, and ventriloquizes an eloquent, possibly elegiac voice for ruminative essays and memoirs (55). Subject matter is not limited to baseball material, for the Book includes "tape-recorded dialogues, player contributions, election coverage, obituaries, satires, prophecies, scandals" (55–56). Although Henry writes consistently within the fictive universe of the UBA, referring neither to the game's artifice nor his own role as proprietor, his emotional life does transpose itself to the pages of the Book: "His own shifting moods, often affected by events in the league, also colored the reports, oscillating between notions of grandeur and irony, exultation and despair, enthusiasm and indifference, amusement and weariness. Lately, he had noticed a tendency toward melancholy and sentimentality" (56). Realizing that a box score omits important details and that a player's performance is more than the simple sum of his statistics, Henry devises the Book to "take counsel with himself" (55) and provide a comprehensive accounting of the UBA. His facility in an encyclopedic variety of genres enables him to document the Association in a protean work as diverse as the inventory of any newspaper stand, effectively

---

[5]*"Aleatory" refers to outcomes that depend on chance or a throw of the dice.*

serving as a complete popular literature of the fictive world. The Book is the most obvious example of Henry's authorial role and reflects both a writer's relationship to a work-in-progress and, more importantly, a man's variable disposition toward the phases of his life. Henry's changeable attitude toward the game reports, the "shifting moods" of "exultation and despair" and so forth, indicate that his response to the UBA includes more emotional depth than a mere spectator's momentary exuberance or chagrin.

Henry's personal investment in the UBA, already considerable, becomes excessive in relation to the players, whom he inspires with the breath of life.[6] As Henry conceives it, the most important aspect of framing a new player involves the author's task of significant naming. Henry brings a seriousness of intention to this work, for players' names "[give] the league its sense of fulfillment and failure, its emotion" (47). Inscribing a notion of fulfillment in the UBA indicates that Henry approaches the game as an evolving story with an inherent telos, rather than as an elaborate but basically idle diversion, play for its own sake. Like a writer gleaning material from the world and transmuting it into fiction, Henry plays riffs on the cues offered by his immediate surroundings. On his way home from work, Henry waits in the rain for a traffic light to change and sees everywhere the stuff of which names are made:

> A policeman in a slicker stood stoically in the thick of the traffic, blowing his whistle and jerking his arms like a base coach urging a runner on. The light changed to green and Henry crossed over to his bus stop. Green. Slicker. Cop. Copper Greene. Might try it. Have to jot it down when he got home.
> Everywhere he looked he saw names. His head was full of them. Bus stop. Whistlestop. Whistlestop Busby, second base. Simple as that [46].

The formulation of names demonstrates Henry's authorship at the same time as it illustrates the interpenetration of the UBA and his quotidian world. The process is dialectical: The policeman's gestures evoke a baseball image in Henry's mind, which in turn transposes selected details of the tableau into potential names. His imagination discards "policeman" as unamenable to naming and substitutes "Cop," which the green traffic light shifts into color. In the next permutation, the policeman's whistle pinch-hits for "Bus" to yield "Whistlestop," and so forth. Presented as a display of mental agility, the act of naming reveals Henry's authorial intention at work, for the names he chooses express his sense of who a new player is and what he will become in the UBA.[7] This process is so mysterious as to elude explanation, yet Henry is certain that "name a man and you make him what he is" (48). A player's later development might — and often

---

[6]*Many critics regard J. Henry Waugh as a God-like creator and discern in his initials (JHW) a sign of the Hebrew Yahweh. See Berman 87–102; Candelaria 127–128; Michael Oriard,* Dreaming of Heroes *(Chicago: Nelson-Hall, 1982), 235–240; Arlen J. Hansen, "The Dice of God: Einstein, Heisenberg, and Robert Coover" in* Novel *10 (Fall 1976): 49–58.*

[7]*See Berman 89–90.*

does — contradict the content or intention of his given name, but "the basic stuff is already there. In the name. Or rather: in the naming" (48). The parallel to a writer's work is evident: The author conjures fictive names from those of his past and present acquaintances, the newspapers, the telephone book, and then the characters go on to independent lives in spite of their impressed monikers. Henry Waugh extends the consequences of naming by having convinced himself of a mystical relationship between a player's name and his fate: "Names had to be chosen ... that could bear the whole weight of perpetuity" (47). Henry's insistence on this point is a sign that he resists phenomena, however slight, that disrupt the intelligible pattern of cause and effect. When a player's development does not fulfill the promise of his name, Henry adjusts the worldly order with a nickname or explains the disjunction through emendations of the UBA's never-ending story, as set down in the Book. These revisions seem persnickety, even obsessive, and prove the relentlessness of Henry's insistence that the UBA reflect a larger meaning. Thus, when a son of Brock Rutherford (a great pitcher, "Hall of Fame, of course" [8]) is ready to appear, Henry conceives of him as Brock Jr.; when Brock Jr. fails as a pitcher, his manager returns him to the minor leagues to become a first baseman (31). After the boy washes out a second time, Henry's search for alternatives leads him to reconstitute Brock Jr. as the prospective father of a ball-playing son (159–160). As extended as this scenario seems, it is readily assimilated by the capacious fictive world. Henry may rewrite the UBA, but only within the parameters he has previously established; his intentionality is flexible yet limited. However, when Henry tries to confer meaning on the career of Brock Jr.'s younger brother, Damon Rutherford, the imposition undermines the UBA's ludic structure and sets in its place the aesthetic construct of a novel.

Although initially masked, signs of novelization are visible from the outset. *The Universal Baseball Association* begins *in medias res*, near the end of Damon Rutherford's perfect game, which seems to Henry to promise "A new day. A new age" (30). The opening paragraph does not pause to explain the premise or introduce characters. Coover, *il miglior fabbro*, forgoes reassuring gestures, such as placing Henry in time and space or defining his relationship to the UBA, in favor of casting the reader directly into the action: "Bottom half of the seventh, Brock's boy had made it through another inning unscratched, one! two! three! Twenty-one down and just six outs to go! and Henry's heart was racing, he was sweating with relief and tension all at once, unable to sit, unable to think, *in* there, *with* them! Oh yes, boys, it was on! He was sure of it! More than just another ball game now: *history!* And Damon Rutherford was making it. Ho ho! too good to be true!" (3). Swept up in a whirl of images and racing thoughts, the reader is suddenly involved, as if he has joined Henry at the ballpark on a summer afternoon.[8] Feeling the energy, riding the crest of

---

[8]*Richard Crepeau, among others, notes the opening paragraph's "virtual reality" and its uncanny power to lure the reader into repeatedly mistaking the action for a real baseball game. See "Coover's Grand Slam," 113–114, in* Aethlon *7:1 (Fall 1989): 113–120.*

excitement, the reader lets strange names slip past while telegraphic exclama-
tions flash across the surface of hypotactic prose. Henry, giddy with joy and
anxiety, is involved both as spectator and participant, a proprietor-as-fan fully
engaged with the game and what it means. He watches the gestures of the grandstand as well as the action on the field, sees fans cheer, clap, eat hot dogs, drink
beer. So intently is Henry focused on the sights and sounds of the ballpark that
the reader is hardly aware of him; like Henry, the reader is

> caught up in it, witnessing it … this great ball game, event of the first order, tremen-
> dous moment: *Rookie pitcher Damon Rutherford, son of the incomparable Brock
> Rutherford, was two innings — six outs — from a perfect game!* Henry, licking his
> lips, dry from excitement, squinted at the sun high over the Pioneer Park, then at
> his watch: nearly eleven, Diskin's closing hours. So he took the occasion of this
> seventh-inning hometown stretch to hurry downstairs to the delicatessen to get a
> couple sandwiches [3–4].

Its first paragraph is a splendid epitome of the novel. Its interpenetrating fictions,
its evocative yet unsentimental depiction of baseball, the texture of Henry's life
all crowd into this luminous moment. When Henry looks at the sun, then
checks his wristwatch and hurries downstairs for late-night delicatessen, the
reader understands that the UBA is as real to him as hunger. When one considers that Henry's excitement is a response not to real-life baseball but to a
game that is modeled after it, one appreciates the seriousness of his commitment. Like every passage in which Henry envisions his created world, this scene
implicates the reader in the proprietor's belief in that world's reality. Most
importantly, the first paragraph indicates that the baseball game Henry is watch-
ing/playing has become the crystalizing moment of the story that he has already
started, in his own mind, to write.

Henry not only finds himself motivated by an impulse to play, to be "*in
there, with them,*" but also conceives a will-to-interpretation that constructs
Damon Rutherford's perfect game-in-the-making as "*history!*" Pitching a perfect game is exceedingly difficult and seldom achieved; Henry recalls that only
two or three perfect games have occurred in the UBA and that a Rookie has
never pitched one. Knowing that the odds are against Damon, Henry prepares
himself "for the lucky hit that really wouldn't be lucky at all, but merely in the
course of things" (11) — a sign that he yearns for a truly extraordinary event. As
Damon faces the final batter, Henry rues the fact that his very nearness to perfection courts a last-minute "storybook spoiler," a bleeder or dunker, the see-
ing-eye base hit that ruins the perfect game without changing anything else.
Even worse, such a hit always seems to dribble off the bat of an ordinary player,
a nobody — as if the baseball gods amused themselves by blasting the "epochal
event" with something "less than commonplace, a mediocrity … a utility
ballplayer never worth much and out of the league a year later" (15). As if hedging his enthusiasm against the disappointment lurking in the dice, Henry contemplates an aesthetic of anticlimax. Contemptuous of this familiar scenario,

which denies the making of "*history!*" as if by accident, Henry raises his own stake in the completion of the pattern. If Damon succeeds, his perfect game will possess special meaning, Henry decides, not only because he is a Rookie, but because he is the son of "*the incomparable Brock Rutherford,*" the greatest pitcher in UBA history. Thus, Damon's perfect game already exists in Henry's mind as more than what it is: not simply "a new thing" but an opportunity for "immortality" (11, 4).

To interpret this game as "More than just another ball game" (3) is, ironically, also to diminish it, for the gesture that seeks to confer meaning on the outcome of a game filches value from play's sheer process. The search for meaning endeavors to define a telos that, by its nature, tends to represent the game in utilitarian terms and to elide the autotelic nature of all play, including contests with the purpose of distinguishing winner from loser. Recreative pleasure, which is psychological and physical, is inherent in playing the game for its own sake; it does not depend on outcomes. Indeed, for the true player or amateur, the game embodies neither use nor meaning; it is what it is, its process a sufficient end in itself.[9] In this respect, game differs from novel, which is written and read as a narrative oriented toward a significant, signifying end. On the other hand, the narrative process of every novel — and a reader's experience of any book — is a continuum of fulfillment and failure, its telos a formal, although not necessarily defining, endpoint. More simply: Just as one cannot determine the quality of a baseball game exclusively by its ninth inning, so does a novel's meaning depend on the story's unfolding as well as its ending — despite the reader's tendency to privilege the meaning-making capacity of the end. Henry recognizes the value of process but has grown unsatisfied with its autotelic pleasures. Consequently, he invests the playing of the game with a meaning of his own, thereby mitigating the thrill of unpredictable play with the premeditated designs of art. Despite recognizing the difference between game and novel, Henry concentrates on making the game signify as a narrative that he considers "*history!*" — or, as one may say, a kind of fiction.

As a narrative, Damon's perfect game provides a fitting sequel to the Brock Rutherford story, which Henry remembers fondly (8, 64–66). Reading Damon's perfect game in the context of UBA history, Henry discerns a pattern in the confluence of events, an implicit promise that the seemingly pointless succession of games, players, and seasons will reveal its comprehensive logic and yield a significance that transcends the incidental aspects of play. Henry's enthusiasm, the naked power of his desire to locate meaning in the UBA, impels him to regard the perfect game as an aesthetic rather than a ludic event, and Damon Rutherford as a metaphoric figure whose self-assured demeanor is a sign of "his

[9]*The notion that "process is essence" is familiar to devotees of both sport and literature. In* Take Time for Paradise: Americans and Their Games *(New York: Summit Books, 1989), A. Bartlett Giamatti defends "autotelic activity, whether called play or study or leisure or artistic activity" as something that is an end in itself and whose purpose is "to achieve a state of being ... that is like what religion often describes, but which is not the sole possession or province of religion" (Giamatti 38).*

total involvement, his oneness with the UBA" (9). Motivated in part by an overwhelming sense of story, Henry interprets the perfect game as restorative of the
Association's glorious past. Seeking something to alleviate the tedium of an
unremarkable season, Henry perceives the quality of *kairos,* or "significant
time,"[10] in Damon's moment of perfection. During the ordinary run of days and
games, time is just something to be lived through and baseball a more or less
pleasant way of helping it pass. Without something special at stake, a rare or
remarkable event to infuse play with meaning, "even a home run was nothing
more than an HR penned into the box score; sure, there was a fence and a ball
sailing over it, but Henry didn't see them.... But ... when someone like Damon
Rutherford came along to flip the switch ... even a pop-up to the pitcher took
on excitement, a certain dimension, color. *The magic of excellence*" (14). *Kairos*
infuses the actions occurring within its frame with special clarity and a repleteness of meaning, a sense of fulfillment inhering in the moment. This temporal
space is the eternal present of the novel, in which events transpire in the light
of their imminent end. Resonant yet finite, such events possess an urgency that
compels one's attention, while time and the rigors of its keeping seem to melt
away. Baseball, with its illusion of eternal presentness, is an apt figure for the
kairos of fiction, yet even the clockless game can seem hemmed in by the minutes, an exercise driven by *chronos,* the "tick-tock" of ordinary time. Damon's
performance restructures simple chronology as "the time of the heroes,"[11] an
interlude of temporal intensity in which every second does not merely "count"
but is fraught with significant action.

The perfect game inspires Henry to revise his reading of UBA history so
that Damon's "*excellence*" may be more perfectly commemorated. This revisioning subjects a history that has hitherto seemed complete and self-justifying to an emendation that reads it as a prefigurement of the present crisis.[12] In
keeping with the traditional content of the baseball trope, Henry constructs a
relationship between Damon's precocious "*excellence*" and his father's exemplary career. When Brock Rutherford and four of his peers who have entered
the UBA in year XIX merit Hall of Fame election, Henry thinks of XIX as "Year
of the Rookie," just as the XX's become the "Celebrated Era of the Pioneers" after
Brock has led the team to a succession of pennant-winning seasons (59, 8).

---

[10]*The conceptions of* kairos *and* chronos, *and of a fiction's imminent end, are derived from Frank Kermode's* The Sense of an Ending: Studies in the Theory of Fiction *(New York: Oxford University Press,
1967), especially 35–64.*

[11]*What Novak calls the "time of the heroes" describes the temporal context of Damon's perfect game:
"In the sacred time of sports, the time of the heroes occasionally breaks through. No one dictates the
moment. It comes when it comes. But by preparing oneself, by laboring steadily, by forcing one's attention and concentration to the highest pitch possible, one may not lose the opportunities which suddenly
and surprisingly appear" (Novak 130).*

[12]*"It is the New Testament that lays the foundation for both the modern sense of epoch ... and the modern distinction between times: the coming of God's time (kairos) ... as against the passing of time,
chronos. The notion of fulfillment is essential; the kairos transforms the past, validates Old Testament
types and prophecies, establishes concord with origins as well as ends" (Kermode 48).*

Damon's perfect game subsumes these markers under a new epochal title that valorizes the father's accomplishments while intensifying the aura of fulfillment gathering around the son. Remembering Brock's dominance, Henry strikes on an encapsulating phrase and wonders, "Was he calling it that now? The Brock Rutherford Era?" Henry realizes that Damon is not only shaping the future but is "doing something to the past, too" (22).

Henry's judgment is not mere hindsight. The phrasing of his thought recalls the eternal presentness of literary texts that, according to T. S. Eliot, shapes the history of literature. All works of literary art, Eliot explains, exist coterminously within an "ideal order" of "relations, proportions, values" (presumably within the mind of the reader or critic).[13] When a new poem, play, story, or novel enters this order, it changes the pre-existing relationships among the prior works so that their myriad aesthetic qualities remain vital and coherent, albeit differently perceived (by the reader or critic). Thus, the entire established order, which was complete without alteration before the new work appeared, becomes refreshed or renewed as a result of the "supervention of novelty." This phenomenon, Eliot maintains, is "conformity between the old and the new" (Eliot 50). If one considers Damon, and specifically his perfect game, a novelty, one recognizes that Henry's integration of the perfect game into UBA tradition suggests not only a sensitivity to context but an analogy of baseball to literary art. Recast in Eliot's terms, Damon's poem is "really new" because no Rookie has ever composed one of comparable quality, and no son of a great poet has improved so markedly on a precursor's work (Brock has pitched two no-hitters but never a perfect game [11]). Damon's achievement readjusts (as Eliot would have it) the "relations, proportions, values" of Brock's career, which seems more important now that the perfect game has reprised it in exalted form. At the same time, the reordering that Damon enacts on the past necessarily involves him in the glorification of his father's legacy: The next and last time Damon pitches, the occasion is Brock Rutherford Day at Pioneer Park.

Henry's readjustment of UBA history to highlight "The Brock Rutherford Era" seems appropriate, yet this impulse to historicize past and present as episodes of an ongoing story is a sign of the proprietor's insistence that causality, progress, and moral coherence shape the development of what are really non-contingent events. The celebratory "Day" that Henry contrives is an example of his impulse to burden the game with an aesthetic rationale. Brock Rutherford Day allows Henry to satisfy his impatience to see Damon pitch again (just two days after the perfect game), and authenticates the transfer of vital power from father to son. As the symbol and cause of "a new Rutherford era" (31), Damon is the poetically just pitcher to exalt the proceedings to the level of art: "It was *more* than history, it was, it was: *fulfillment!*" (66). In staging what should be an ordinary game as a theatrical piece (Brock and other old-time Pioneers

[13]T. S. Eliot, "Tradition and the Individual Talent," 50, as reprinted in The Sacred Wood (1920; reprinted, New York: Methuen, 1983), 47–59.

in the grandstand, "stuntflying and skywriting over the Park and fireworks and flowers for all the ladies" [65]) and forcing Damon to pitch out of turn, Henry violates UBA protocol. Affording Damon special treatment is not just an indication that he "meant more to [Henry] than any player should" (38), but evidence that Henry is willing to use his greater knowledge to influence Damon's fate. Concerned that the young pitcher might falter in outings after his perfect game, Henry realizes that it would be prudent to protect him. As proprietor, Henry can construct Damon's participation to the best advantage in order to ensure his elevation to Ace status, "without which no great career was possible" (39). Having determined that Damon should have, must have, a "great career" because of who he is and what he has done, Henry understands that scripting a storybook "*fulfillment!*" is his prerogative. Although it would deny the internal logic of the Association, as well as the spirit of its rules, Henry is tempted to meddle against the dispassionate outcomes of luck and chance if doing so will shelter his favorite from the uncertain fortune immanent in the conscienceless, ahistorical dice. This plan foreshadows Henry's overly determined authorship of the UBA in the latter half of the novel; similarly, the objections that Henry advances against such meddling foretell the confusion that besets the UBA as a result of his later interventions. Considering an egregiously manipulative proprietorship from the perspective of Barney Bancroft, Damon's manager, Henry concedes that it is a temptation he must resist because Barney "didn't know what Henry knew" (39). The "functional details" (56) of the UBA are invisible to its characters, Henry reminds himself, and this internal logic must be categorically respected if the Association is to remain a worthwhile enterprise. Thus, Damon Rutherford must negotiate his fate within the context of the game, on the terms dictated by play. If Damon fails, surrenders so many hits and runs that he is ranked as a Regular rather than an Ace, Henry can do nothing but watch and endure it. To do otherwise — that is, to direct the course of Damon's career — would be to compromise the game's integrity: "he'd set his own rules, his own limits, and though he could change them whenever he wished, nevertheless he and his players were committed to the turns of the mindless and unpredictable — one might even say, irresponsible — dice. That was how it was. He had to accept it, or quit the game altogether" (40). These ruminations arguably provide the best available gloss on chapter eight, in which Henry has seemingly "quit the game" and the players strut and fret a nervous hour on a prefabricated stage. The tension between his notion of what should happen and the multifarious possibilities offered by the dice epitomizes the dilemma Henry confronts every time the process of play undoes his sense of story. Driven by dice whose sums are defined on preformulated charts, the UBA unfolds without any awareness of precedent or what Henry has identified as its history. The Association's *modus operandi* is radically ahistorical — which is to say, ludic rather than aesthetic and, therefore, inherently conscienceless — despite the countervailing historical conscience that Henry possesses and with which he tries to endow it. The proprietor's careful record keeping and detailed recollection of players and games (45–46, 58–62) can only interpret or embellish the dice-decreed results. And the dice, "heedless of history yet makers of it" (16), exercise their power with a vengeance when Damon bats against Jock Casey on Brock Rutherford Day.

Like an author fighting a novel that will not develop into the story he wishes to tell, Henry resists the crux of Damon's death. Nothing will avail, however, to circumvent the moment; having rolled 1-1-1 twice consecutively, Henry is preternaturally certain of the fatal outcome yet powerless to affect the course of events. He cannot conceive of a reasonable excuse to pinch-hit for Damon, and removing him arbitrarily seems superstitious, even paranoid. Henry's quandary is basic to the writing of fiction. His narrative having arrived at a major crux, the author must decide between opposed alternatives: Allow the story to proceed along the lines it seems itself to dictate or enforce his will upon it. The choice Henry makes will determine the shape of the narrative he writes hereafter. Whether he lets Damon bat or sends up a pinch hitter, Henry foresees unpredictable repercussions: "what if he pulled him and then — as had always been the case — Casey threw an ordinary number? The second no-hitter … would be out the window … and all for nothing. … And what about Damon, getting jerked from the game like that, what would his attitude afterwards be? What would he make of it? There was more than one risk here" (71). Henry's involvement with his characters is complete; to him they are real men who are at risk in whatever plots he might devise. In contradistinction to the "irresponsible" dice, Henry himself is weighted with conscience, believing himself responsible for the lives he has set in motion. Generally, he declines to meddle in these lives because of the aftereffects he might unknowingly precipitate. And so, deciding that "There's nothing to be done about it…. Play it out" (71), Henry rolls. Against the odds, triple snake eyes come up for the third time in a row. The result on the Chart of Extraordinary Occurrences seals Damon's fate: "1-1-1: *Batter struck fatally by bean ball*" (70) is the verdict the "irresponsible" dice announce on Damon's career, effectively truncating with a bang and a whimper the story that Henry has been composing with such care. Damon's death-by-beanball freezes the action while Henry's mind races, searching for a way to remediate his sudden loss. He extends his hand to scramble the dice, "trying to stop, trying to back up" (73), then realizes he cannot undo what has become, contrary to his intentions, "*history!*" "*Les Jeux sont faits,*" Sartre would say; Henry thinks, "But do what? The dice were rolled" (73).

Having lost his protagonist and the promise of "*fulfillment!*" betokened by Damon's precocious glory, J. Henry Waugh, "utterly brought down, brought utterly to grief, buried his face in the heap of papers on his kitchen table and cried for a long bad time" (76). Evidently, Damon's fatal injury is also, metaphorically, Henry's traumatic wound, and his effort to recover from it the project of his exile. In chapter three, exile is figured as a period of mourning, in which Henry ransacks his interpretive repertoire for a morally coherent response. Incapable of maintaining even the meager relationships of his outside life, J. Henry Waugh temporarily vanishes from the text. His mind retreats to the Association and inhabits it with a kind of schizophrenic skittishness, living out the responses of various characters to Damon's death (93–123). Henry himself seems to stand by, a passive observer awaiting a resolution. The representation of this process displays Robert Coover's pyrotechnic creations, the febrile intensity of his imagined worlds, and resists excerption, for the virtuosity of this performance lies particularly in its seamless extension over narrative time.[14] Interpretation of Damon's death is polyphonic. Rag Rooney, the impious manager of the Haymakers, derides the apotheosis of the Rutherfords with characteristic vulgarity, asking a UBA veteran, "'Now, honestly, don't that Brock Rutherford crap twist your balls, Tim?'" Rooney proposes his own reading of the Era: "'Crock Rubberturd'" (111). Skepticism is a possible response to the aborted "*fulfillment!*" Another is offered by Sandy Shaw, an ex-player who commemorates the UBA in folksong. Drunk and distressed, Henry sings Sandy's ballads in Pete's, a local bar, oblivious to the spectacle he makes of himself. Within the microfiction, Pete's Bar is Jake's Bar, a fitting scene of commiseration for the UBA veterans who gather there (93–103). Interestingly, Henry remains distant from the attitudes of reconciliation available at Jake's. Even the privileged perspective of UBA chancellor Fennimore McCaffree, who watches the proceedings on a bank of closed-circuit televisions, cannot vouchsafe consolation to the inconsolable Henry.

McCaffree's overview of the Association represents Henry's proprietary omniscience, but its chief purpose is to identify a mimetic form that will allow the narrative, which is evolving beyond Henry's control, to assimilate Damon's death. The development of this form is crucial to the novel's long dénouement, for it describes the alternative structure that emerges from Henry's blatant intervention. While Sandy sings of Damon and the pitch that killed him, McCaffree ponders how such fictions help the players cope with unprecedented tragedy. Sandy's "dreams and legends" mediate truth, McCaffree decides, by casting cold fact in an assimilable form: "Men needed these rituals, after all, that was part of the truth, too, and certainly the Association benefited by them. Men's minds being what they generally were, it was the only way to get to most of them..." (103). The mimetic form that Fenn McCaffree discovers is ritual. Assuming that truth is ambiguous, that it is created in part by the fictions used to express it, McCaffree concludes that ritual is as legitimate a form as history for interpreting experience. To become sufficiently powerful, however, any ritual that Henry might construct from season LVI must include a counterplot to stand in opposition to Damon Rutherford's untimely death. Sensing that "The only conceivable forms of meaningful action at a time like this were all illegal," McCaffree sets the counterplot in motion by wondering whether Jock Casey, the pitcher who has thrown the lethal beanball, has acted with malicious intent (104). This possibility is tacitly affirmed (yet never proven), so that Casey's (alleged) intentionality justifies (if not excuses) the "illegal" measures that

---

[14]See Shelton 84–85; Caldwell 165–166.

Henry takes to exact retributive justice. Once enforced, Casey's punishment completes the framework of what will become Damonsday's ritualistic action.

Irony doubtlessly accounts for Coover's making Fenn McCaffree a Legalist and "the social construct ... his central concern" (101), for it is the UBA's prevailing ludic order, which defines its social construct, that Henry undermines by violating the rules of play. By monitoring the illegal actions through McCaffree, Henry can break the rules and deplore doing so, all within the context of the game. "Illegal" measures seem necessary to Henry when the dice stymie his efforts to sabotage Casey's performance. Despite figuratively loading the dice, Henry is unable to exert his will: Casey and his team continue to win. To Henry, this pattern seems a gross insult added to grievous injury. Casey and the Knickerbockers, however, are the antagonists of the narrative that Henry is composing; their success, which begins with Damon's death, is the heart of the counterplot. In the latter part of the Brock Rutherford Day game, which Henry resumes after the period of mourning, Casey and the Knickerbockers excel. Apparently indifferent to Damon's death, they play as if inspired, pitching and hitting and running the bases with heightened skill and unseemly arrogance. It is not merely that they win but that they win easily and, Henry feels, with a sense of gloating. In the narrative that Henry constructs, Casey and the Knicks are a perfect nemesis.

Emerging from grief's stupor, Henry peers at the UBA through an alcoholic haze and tries, in the grip of exhaustion, "to put all that scene back together again" (124). Like Humpty-Dumpty, his "Head cracked like an egg" (74), Damon cannot be mended; his wound is fatal, his exile from teammates and friends everlasting. Although the pinch runner who takes his place on the bases completes the circuit and scores the game's first run, the symbolic homecoming is hollow. Henry's enthusiasm has ebbed, his imagination disengaged from the action. This attitude reveals his original commitment as a peccadillo, pathetic and slightly mad. Trying to pep himself up, Henry "even said out loud: 'All right, fellas, a little pepper now, let's wake up!'— but he heard himself talking to a wooden kitchen table all too plainly, and he thought: what a drunken loony old goat you are, they oughta lock you up" (127). Henry's idiosyncratic demeanor, which has made him a likable personality, now seems desperately obsessive, even monomaniacal. He plays out the fatal game with the intention of discovering a recomposition of the shattered pattern, having decided that "either something happened — something in short *remedial* — or into the garbage bag with the whole works" (127–128). The dice, however, continue to dictate a contrary narrative. The Knickerbockers lash out a succession of hits and score eighteen runs in the final four innings, the *coup de grâce* administered by Casey himself in the form of a come-backer that breaks the new pitcher's finger. Disgusted and appalled, the proprietor concedes defeat: "That was too much. Henry threw the dice across the kitchen" (130). Henry's exasperation with the "irresponsible" dice signifies his desire to conduct the game free of the tyranny of chance and foreshadows the consummation of that wish.

Before abandoning the UBA-as-game, Henry resorts to alternative strategies in attempting to establish what he considers a legitimate compensatory pattern.

Resisting an impulse to "quit the game. Burn it" (141–142), Henry chooses to immerse himself in its process, what one might conceive (mindful of Stein's advice in Conrad's *Lord Jim*) as the "destructive element" of its play. Although this option courts disappointment, Henry pursues it in a spirit of optimism and even anticipates replacing Damon with a new player, who might be destined for greatness:

> The thought cheered him some, and then on the bus, he had other ideas. First of all, that the circuit wasn't closed, his or any other: there were patterns, but they were shifting and ambiguous and you had a lot of room inside them. Secondly, that the game on his table was not a message, but an event: the only signs he had were his own reactions; if these worsened, it might be best, after all, to close down the Association.... But first he should finish out this season [143].

Damon's death has altered UBA history, but only by resuming play will Henry discover how. Perhaps the season's aggregate results will describe a narrative of renewal, with another talented Rookie at its center. The imperative to play the season to its end is characteristic of Henry; he cannot renounce even the keeping of fielding statistics, "the dullest job," because of a sense of historical coherence: "there were all those fielding records already established, and what would they mean if they had no challengers?" (54). Similarly, the Knickerbocker's manager, Sycamore Flynn, cannot agree that the rest of season LVI might well be canceled, or "that they close down the Association" (117) as a sign of respect for Damon, for the UBA's continuity over time is the source of its meaning.[15] The UBA's past, Sycamore realizes, will mean nothing if the Association ceases to exist. The more disturbing question is whether this loss of meaning itself means anything. Sycamore has "No answer: only dread" and so resigns himself to taking part when the action resumes (117). In the present circumstances, meaning is recoverable only if the process continues.

In playing out the season, however, Henry compromises the stochastic terms that define the game. He attempts to effect certain results, to direct the action in order to create a meaningful pattern *ex cathedra,* by every means short of flagrantly manipulating the dice. When the Pioneers sink below .500 and the Knickerbockers, and especially Casey, continue to win, Henry is faced with an outcome that is not only "Disappointing" (151) but that seems to indicate the assertion of a separate intentionality that opposes his will and the stratagems he uses to exert it. Despite forcing Casey into dire game situations and sometimes even "[tossing] the dice in advance to make sure he was going to get hit," Henry finds Casey able to hold his own, even to prevail (152). To Henry, such outcomes are perverse, perhaps diabolical, as if the dice were expressing active "malevolence, rather than mere mindlessness" (152). Even Chancellor McCaffree, who watches the action on four simultaneously-playing televisions, cannot

---

[15]*Roy Caldwell likens the keeping of records to the writing of narrative: "By rolling the dice and recording the results, the player generates a narrative sequence ... an arrangement from which a story may be deduced. Each element in the sequence is an empty configuration waiting to be endowed with further meaning" (Caldwell 164).*

discern the logic of the "radical transformation" (145) that is reshaping the UBA. Playing 60 games in 24 hours, the proprietor has only selectively updated the statistics and written only brief accounts into the Book, introducing a strange uncertainty into league affairs: "For all Fenn McCaffree's pretense at efficiency, the truth was the books just were not being kept, and no one knew exactly anymore what was happening" (151). McCaffree's surveillance of all UBA activity causes a telling cognitive dissociation, for he (Henry as McCaffree) monitors the repercussions of his (the proprietor's) untoward conduct seemingly without knowing that (Henry) is causing it. This sense of uncertainty intensifies over the next 48 games, which Henry condenses to some 12 hours' playing time by forgoing all statistics and log entries. By recording only winners and losers, Henry assures himself that the Knickerbockers suffer continual defeat; he also knows that he is destroying the UBA. At this point, the Association's coherence and integrity count for less than Henry's obsessive desire to "bring Casey and the Knicks to their knees, see them drop behind the Pioneers in the standings, if only for a day. But, in mocking irony, the more he crushed the Knicks, the more the Pioneers fell away ... as though they were running from him, afraid of his plan" (176). Like an author driving himself to finish a novel, Henry sprints toward the end of the season without pausing to consider the fine points of his work. His labor deforms the UBA, which loses its continuity; the absence of records betokens chaos, incoherence, death. By focusing on his intended outcome, to vanquish Casey and his team, and ignoring the other aspects of the created world, Henry degrades the art of composition to a mere exercise, the tracing of a predetermined pattern. And before he even completes the figure, Henry understands that his intentions have come to nought.

Having failed to yield the "something ... *remedial*" (128) that its proprietor has demanded, the game exhausts his patience. Henry's efforts to salvage the UBA-as-game culminate in his inviting an uninitiated player into the diamond-inscribed world. It is a desperate measure, but Henry realizes that if he shares the UBA, he might be able to save it. The game he attempts to play with fellow accountant Lou Engel demonstrates, however, that Henry has conceived the Association in such elaborate particularity that no one else can fully participate. Although well-meaning and generous, Lou has no sense of the Association's virtual reality and no comprehension of the necessities that allow it to maintain its logic and coherence. Even before play begins, while he is explaining the interactions of the dice and charts, Henry feels disassociated, "miles away somehow" (183). When Lou notices that Jock Casey, his starting pitcher, is a Rookie, and that two Ace pitchers have been held in reserve, he gently admonishes his friend, as if Henry were trying to fix the game. Henry, realizing that his own pitcher is an Ace, admits to himself that Casey's selection might appear suspect. Still, he refers to the pitching rotation to defend himself: It is Casey's regular turn. Lou is not interested in fine points, however, and insists on a last-minute substitution:

> "Aw, come on now, can't I pitch one of these other boys? How about this fella Whitlowe Clay?"

"I suppose so, but he pitched two days ago—"

"Yeah, but he's tough," argued Lou, grinning. "I'll start with ole Whitlowe." He erased Casey's name and wrote in Clay. "Where'd you get these names from, the funny papers?" The whole thing was fast becoming pointless [183].

Lou continues in this fashion, making substitutions based on the rankings of various players, including some who Henry knows have been slumping. Having entered the UBA's ongoing process without any knowledge of its antecedent action, Lou must strategize on the basis of superficial evidence. His most glaring false move is to play Casey as a batter rather than a pitcher. This decision betrays a misunderstanding not only of the UBA but of real baseball, as Henry explains:

"The Rookie status for pitchers only helps them as pitchers, not hitters."

"Oh? why not?" Absent question, spurred by vexation more than curiosity.

"Just the rules, Lou. It's what I was saying, maybe you ought to let me explain more before we start, see, there's a lot of special things about errors and injuries and relief pitchers and pinch hitters and lead-off hitters and pinch runners and clean-up hitters and—" [184].

Lou's approach is relentlessly practical: to field the best team possible, insofar as he can determine quality by a player's paper reputation. Each of his substitutions distorts the Association's internal logic to serve the purposes of the present game. Lou's improvised lineup is based not on the pitching rotation, the manager's hunches, the minutiae of match-ups or abilities, but on expediency. To Lou such revisions are matters of no import; to Henry, who clings to verisimilitude even as he compromises it, Lou's jocular remarks and obtrusive managing are insults, for they implicitly say not merely that the game is not real but that it is not even serious play. As Henry apprehends with painful clarity, Lou regards the UBA as a game for boys. His questions reveal the ludic structure for what it is: arbitrary, conventional, ultimately meaningless. For Lou to play the game as Henry would wish, no amount of explanation would suffice. Still, he tries; amidst pizza and beer and Lou's chummy attempts to interest Henry in the cinema by retelling, in an unintentionally discontinuous, haphazardly backtracking fashion, the plot of a movie he has seen, they play. Lou's uncunning juxtaposition of his own preferred fictive reality to Henry's game distracts them both, and the resultant collision of imaginary worlds reduces the UBA to a beer-sodden shambles (177–199). In trying to accommodate this poor player, Henry perceives the truth of a long-standing assumption: Sharing the UBA on the level of commitment necessary to preserve its distinctive mimesis is impossible.

In the wake of repeated disappointments, Henry surrenders to the desire he now realizes has haunted him since Damon's death. First by manipulating the dice to alter the previous throw of 2-6-6, "a lot less than he'd hoped for" (198), Henry contrives a second consecutive 6-6-6. With Jock Casey on the mound, the stage is literally set for the final act of the morality play that Henry has scripted to redeem the prior accident. Even the fortuitous appearance of the poetically just batter does not escape his notice and seems like an invitation to force a completion of the refractory pattern: "Who was up next? The catcher Royce

Ingram. Damon's battery mate. Poetic. Indeed" (200). Understanding that the action he contemplates will commit him to participation in the UBA forever after, Henry inscribes his intention into the game with all of the premeditation of a writer revising his prose. He shakes the dice and then, with a whispered apology to Jock Casey, "[sets] them down carefully with his right [hand]. One by one. Six. Six. Six" (202). The third consecutive "roll" of 6-6-6 yields the intended result on the Chart of Extraordinary Occurrences: "*Pitcher struck fatally by linedrive through box*" (200). By executing/sacrificing/murdering/crucifying Jock Casey, Henry recuperates the significance of Damon Rutherford and invests his accidental death with new meaning; and "this is conformity between the old and the new" (Eliot 50).

The fearful symmetry of these two deaths satisfies Henry's aesthetic, which seeks a pattern to organize the disparate episodes of the game. In terms of narrative, Casey's death is the climax of the counterplot and an answer to the original story's demand for moral coherence and justice based on causality. Its upshot is the removal of chance from the game; after the manipulated outcome, play is conducted strictly according to the proprietor's sense of what should happen: "Players hit balls, moved around bases, caught flies, but as though at rest, static participants in an ancient yet transformed ritual. Journalists quit writing, just watched.... Good pitchers threw strikes, bad ones gave up hits to good hitters, while bad hitters went hitless. Boys watched grimly, older than old men, and old men hardly watched at all" (203). As a result of its proprietor's intervention, the UBA becomes less a game and more a prescripted ritual; indeed, the status of the UBA-as-game becomes permanently ambiguous at this point. The conformity of play to its probable results, the loss of vital interest, the cessation of writing, all indicate that Henry manipulates the dice to bring the season to an appointed conclusion. Curiously, as authorial intentionality increases, *kairos* gives way to *chronos*. Action that has retained the possibility of transcendence, that at times has unfolded in a luminous present, becomes a series of rote gestures performed to the accompaniment of a ticking clock. The moment is neither replete with play nor bright with "*The magic of excellence*" (14); only ordinary events enter this world, and all of these are predictable. Henry has banished play's ready pleasures, which a game offers moment to moment, to relieve the UBA (and himself) of the pain of chance disappointment. At this point, the novel that Henry is composing is a flat reflection of the game whose rough edges it is supposed to refine.

The work of composition, however, is incomplete. To integrate season LVI into the greater UBA scheme, Henry conceives of yet another fiction: a history of the Association's first 56 years. Henry projects Pioneer manager Barney Bancroft as this book's author and imagines that the work itself might be "a little controversial, the exposure of some pattern or other" (211). A written history is necessary, Henry believes, because the log entries and raw material of records and statistics require a thorough reckoning and an insightful analysis. Only in this way can the ragged threads of UBA activity be woven into an intelligible pattern. The theme of Bancroft's tome, as Henry anticipates it, is that "perfection wasn't a thing, a closed moment, a static fact, but *process,* yes, and the process

was transformation" (212). In Henry's mind, this transformation includes a closing of ranks, a reunification of the UBA after the deaths of Damon Rutherford
and Jock Casey. His scheme entails Bancroft's becoming chancellor, Sycamore
Flynn's replacing Bancroft as manager of the Pioneers, and Brock Rutherford's
taking Sycamore's place as manager of the Knickerbockers (216). As if to validate this reformation, Barney's "compact league history" will be entitled *The
UBA in the Balance* and reveal the political evolution of the Association (another
process) from Boggler to Legalist to Guildsman predominancy in a way that
constructs "the Rutherford-Casey event as the culminating moment" (216). Its
designation as "history" notwithstanding, the manifest fictionality of this project is obvious, particularly when one recalls Henry's conception of what constitutes history: "you can take history or leave it, but if you take it you have to
accept certain assumptions or ground rules about what's left in and what's left
out" (49). Clearly, Henry opts to "take" history into the realm of fiction, a move
that guarantees that someone will be "'writing it down'" (50) to commemorate
and interpret it. In its incarnation as history, the UBA becomes non-ludic and
exclusively textual: Nothing is meaningless and accident cannot displace the logic
of events, for everything is inscribed into an overarching narrative.

Rewriting the UBA as history prepares it for further transformation, which
ostensibly removes the proprietor from its proceedings while dispersing his
thoughts among a cast of confused and anxious players.[16] By chapter eight,

[16]*On Henry's status in chapter eight the critics vary. Roy Caldwell sees him as the invisible God of the
UBA: "a Flaubertian narrator, he has refined himself out of existence" (Caldwell 168). Frank W. Shelton concludes that "speculation about ... Henry ... would be useless" and that "the problem is insolu-
ble and does not matter, for the world Henry created remains alive" (Shelton 89); see "Humor and
Balance in Coover's The Universal Baseball Association, Inc." in Critique: Studies in Modern Fiction 17:1 (1975): 78–90. Judith Wood Angelius argues that "the problem at least matters" (Angelius 169)
and locates Henry in "the character of Paul Trench" because he "embodies the same negative charac-
teristics ... feels insecure, insignificant, paranoid, and lonely" (Angelius 171); see "The Man Behind the
Catcher's Mask: A Closer Look at Robert Coover's Universal Baseball Association" in University of Den-
ver Quarterly 12:1 (1977): 165–174. Ann Gonzalez reads Henry's absence as a sign of his "artistic decision to detach himself from his creation," not a sign of insanity or death (Gonzalez 109); see "Robert
Coover's The UBA: Baseball as Metafiction" in The International Fiction Review 11:2 (1984): 106–109.
Richard Alan Schwartz argues, "by the book's conclusion Henry has disappeared; he is either dead or
crazy" (Schwartz 145); see "Postmodernist Baseball" in Modern Fiction Studies 33:1 (Spring 1987):
135–149. Michael Oriard judges Henry "insane" because of "his inability to maintain contact with concrete reality, his need to create an illusory world governed by order and rationality" (Oriard 240). Brenda
Wineapple comments, somewhat apocalyptically, that Henry "has 'killed' himself, and yet the game proceeds without him" (Wineapple 72); see "Robert Coover's Playing Fields" in Iowa Review 10:3 (1979):
66–74. Richard Crepeau opines that "It almost seems logical when Henry finally disappears inside the
UBA, its rituals and history. It is also a bit frightening" (Crepeau 116). Neil Berman maintains that
"Henry's identification with the Association is so total that ... all play and no work have made no Henry"
and that "Henry Waugh is not merely central to his play-world, he is the play-world and all its players
simultaneously. He is schizophrenic, but he is god" (Berman 99, 102). Cordelia Candelaria believes that
Henry has suffered a nominal "self-destruction (that is, disappearance)," yet discerns his presence in
Hardy Ingram, whose "ruminative questioning ... parallels the attitude expressed earlier by Waugh"
(Candelaria 127). If one agrees that Henry is always the author of the UBA, one may conclude that in
chapter eight his consciousness is reflected by the thoughts of the UBA personalities, just as it is throughout. The attitude of every figure in chapter eight can be traced to ideas at least tentatively held by Henry,
so it seems that his mind is still at play even if the text does not mention him by name.*

which occurs 101 UBA years after the events of the first seven chapters, Henry has established a new mimesis to compensate for the lost story of Damon's *"fulfillment!"* The "annual rookie initiation ceremony, the Damonsday reenactment of the Parable of the Duel," subsumes the separate deaths of Damon Rutherford and Jock Casey in a single ritual that obsessively reenacts the fatal events of season LVI. Described but never shown to the reader, this ritual remains "an Association secret" (220), yet it, and not any game, is the focus of attention on Damonsday CLVII. The Caseyite and Damonite sects that monopolize the debate are committed not to playing baseball but to the analysis and interpretation of history (230–237). Similarly, the players spend their time discussing the import of the ceremony and wondering whether the rookies playing Damon and Casey will truly die.[17] The preliminaries of the rookie initiation ceremony do, indeed, resemble the preparations for a religious ritual that will commit "human" sacrifice (yet only figments of Henry's imagination will perish), all of it based on a postmodern myth constructed from now-legendary events.[18] The import of Damonsday, however, is not simply that the UBA has, by Henry's rigging of the dice, reversed the process that long ago transmuted religious rites into sport. Rather, the carefully staged scene, its incorporation of each least element of Damon's death-by-pitched-ball and Casey's retributive execution, is the expression of J. Henry Waugh's authorial imperative to create enduring significance from the random events of the game. Although nominally absent, Henry still acts as author and reader of the game/novel. Thus, if the Association does, contrary to logic, "knock off [its] best young talent every season" (220), Hardy Ingram will accept his fate as this season's Damon, for doing so will recuperate the compelling power of season LVI's primal scene. In this sense, the UBA, once an organization committed to contesting athletic pre-eminence, has itself come home to baseball's origin as an ancient ritual consecrated to the memorialization of mythic figures and their sacrificial deaths. Ironically, this homecoming, merely formal or figurative at best, occasions neither healing and reconciliation nor rebirth, but an antagonistic confrontation that ends, presumably, in another death.

---

[17]*In chapter eight, the UBA "has passed into ... the Age of Interpretation" (Caldwell 168). The players "vie with one another to explain the meaning of the world.... They write books, found and join religious sects, construct philosophical systems" (Caldwell 169).*

[18]*Critics generally agree about the thematic purpose of Damonsday, despite the ambiguous status of J. Henry Waugh in the proceedings. An interesting reading of Damonsday in the context of The UBA as a whole is propounded by Arlen J. Hansen in "The Dice of God," which sees Einstein's famous rejoinder to Heisenberg's uncertainty principle as being played out in Coover's fiction. "God does not play dice with the universe," Einstein asserted, losing in his metaphor the distinction between the objectivity of behavior of subatomic systems and "the knowability of a system's parts" (Hansen 51). The point is that quantum mechanics is so theoretically radical that the figures of speech a scientist might use to describe it can falsify the theory by engaging conceptions and assumptions that the theory inherently refutes (Hansen 51–52). Just as a new language is often required by science, so are new myths and new stories the special creative province of the novelist (according to Coover, says Hansen, 53, 57–58), for new forms will eventually be needed when the old forms cease to be useful or satisfying. Damonsday is the new myth, the product of "re-mythification," that J. Henry Waugh creates to redress the failure of the old-style UBA (Hansen 57–58). See also Candelaria 126–128.*

While disparate voices, caustic and skeptical, maintain a noisy dispute about the purposes of Damonsday (229–237), Hardy Ingram (descendant of Royce, Damon's catcher) self-consciously sustains the fictional role assigned to him. "Death" does not frighten Hardy Ingram because it no longer threatens Henry with chaos, the disruption of pattern. Certain deaths are integral to this narrative, for Henry interprets them to be so; even Barney Bancroft's assassination, coming only a year after *The UBA in the Balance*, can be — must be — assimilated. The alternative — that Bancroft's murder is not a "synthesis for the Duel" — is unacceptable, for then "maybe it just happened. Weirdly, independently, meaninglessly. Another accident in a chain of accidents: worse even than invention. Invention ... implies a need and need implies purpose; accident implies nothing, nothing at all" (224–225). Invention, the process by which reality becomes fiction, ultimately implies purpose: a telos that is immanent in a narrative as its author prospectively regards the narrative's ending. The novel, like the game, embodies its own significance without reference to any exterior reality because its narrative unfolds, refolds, expands and prolongs itself in an eternal present suffused with meaning. Yet the novel differs from the game to the extent that it refers to its end, its result or purpose, as a formal necessity of significant time.[19] The novel's formal promise of "*fulfillment!*" distinguishes it from the game, whose purpose is its self-justifying process and whose results are morally vague. Like life, a game is conducted not in pursuit of its ending, in the sense of ultimate meaning or "*fulfillment!*" but for its process, which is made provisionally meaningful by the player or spectator's knowledge that it is finite — that it will come to an end. To those obsessed with fiction's signifying form, reality's random flux must be unbearable. Chance, accident, the absence of pattern signify nothing yet often characterize events of the real world and, what is more worrisome to Henry, the world of the game. To interpret these events is to transform them into fiction or its related form, history, both of which blur the truth of the original moment in the very process of recording it.[20]

Thus, the Damonsday participants, whether they subscribe to the dogma of the opposed Caseyite or Damonite factions, or to one of the competing theories (also propounded in books) that depict other UBA personalities as "the real heart and point of the Parable of the Duel" (223), suspect that the truth is obscured by the proliferating interpretations, which cast doubt on the most basic facts: "Some writers even argue that Rutherford and Casey never existed — nothing more than another of the ancient myths of the sun, symbolized as a victim slaughtered by the monster or force of darkness" (223–224). Like Sandy Shaw's ballad of Damon's death, the Damonsday ritual is less concerned with

---

[19]"*All such plotting presupposes and requires that an end will bestow upon the whole duration and meaning. To put it another way, the interval [between* tick *and* tock] *must be purged of simple chronicity, of the emptiness of* tock-tick, *humanly uninteresting successiveness. It is required to be a significant season,* kairos *poised between beginning and end*" (Kermode 46; see also 44–49).

[20]See Heisenberg's uncertainty principle, as explained by Arlen Hansen in "The Dice of God," 50.

factual truth than with giving Henry a way to inscribe the verdict of the irresponsible dice indelibly into the UBA. Henry realizes that the Damonsday reenactment is willfully accepted as true or as an expression of the wish for meaning. An elaborate dumb show of sin and retribution, this ritual is no less arbitrary than a game or a novel in the codification of its rules and its delineation of form. This knowledge disturbs Henry, for it denies Damonsday, as well as the original events of season LVI, any ultimate meaning; truth, like fiction and history, is fabricated from reality rather than manifest in it. In this context, the criterion of value becomes experiential: the joy of the game, the book, the life, not for what it means in the light of its imminent ending but for what it is in itself. If the time-space of the game retains the quality of *kairos*, it inheres in the process of play.

The self-sufficiency of play causes Henry some anxiety, which he registers through Paul Trench, the Rookie catcher who plays Royce Ingram to Hardy's Damon. Paul worries about the futility of play and the game's refusal to reveal whatever meaning it might possess. His frame of reference is experiential, but he either does not recognize the irreducible value of experience or finds it unconvincing. His fear is free-floating, all-encompassing and, at the same time, too complicated to be put into words. Doubtful of his own beliefs and a reluctant participant in the Parable of the Duel, Paul Trench is caught in a limbo between diffidence and eschatological despair:

> Beyond each game, he sees another, and yet another, in endless and hopeless succession. He hits a ground ball to third, is thrown out. Or he beats the throw. What difference, in the terror of eternity, does it make? He stares at the sky, beyond which is more sky, overwhelming in its enormity. He, Paul Trench, is utterly absorbed in it, entirely disappears, is Paul Trench no longer, is nothing at all: so why does he even walk up there? Why does he swing? Why does he run? Why does he suffer when out and rejoice when safe? Why is it better to win than to lose? Each day: the dread. And when, after being distracted by the excitement of a game, he returns at night to the dread, it is worse than ever, compounded with shame and regret. He wants to quit — but what does he mean, "quit"? The game? Life? Could you separate them? [238].

The "excitement of the game," which comes from playing it, is the best antidote to "the terror of eternity." Baseball's atemporal scheme and counterclockwise movement are poignant expressions of every person's unreasonable hope for immortality, which alone could invest any individual life, always finite in accomplishment and duration, with ultimate meaning. Why, in the face of eventual death, do we expend the effort to sustain life? Because the process of living, the successive, gathering action of any life, defers our confrontation of mortality, and the deferral of death is our closest approach to eternal youth. J. Henry Waugh, childless and unmarried, bereft of friends, seeks youth or an illusion of it, which he momentarily recaptures in the self-confident serenity of Damon Rutherford. Recognizing that Damon "will someday have to hang up his cleats like all the rest," Henry feels melancholy (49); when Damon dies prematurely, the fictions that Henry has devised to offset the knowledge of his final end are exposed as self-conscious falsifications. And yet, willing oneself to believe in these fictions can make them, for practical purposes, real. Knowledge of the truth abides — "the dread" is not expungeable — but consciousness, relying on its sustaining fictions, represses or eludes it. When one's sustaining fictions fail, consciousness is obliged to contemplate two irreconcilable ideas simultaneously: the desire for eternal life and the inevitability of death. At this point, it is a triumph of the spirit, as well as a test, as F. Scott Fitzgerald would have it, "of a first-rate intelligence ... to hold two opposed ideas in the mind at the same time, and still retain the ability to function."[21] Paul Trench, introspective and doomed, plays the game, "suffer[s] when out and rejoice[s] when safe" and cannot quit because the game is the thing he has, the sustaining fiction that remains intelligible amidst a welter of interpretive creeds, none of which he espouses.

Similarly, the most redemptive feature of Damonsday is not the ritual sacrifice, if the sacrifice of young athletes is indeed what Henry requires to consecrate an accident, nor the myths and counter-myths that swirl around season LVI and its legacy, but the game itself, its essential gestures recapitulated in the once-and-future elaborations of play. Recalled by "Damon" (Hardy Ingram) to his love of the game, Paul Trench sets aside his gloom, the sense of being dwarfed by the expanse of all space and time, and draws solace from the luminosity of the present moment:

> "Hey, wait, buddy! you *love* this game, don't you?"
> "Sure, but..."
> Damon grins. Lights up the whole goddamn world. "Then don't be afraid, Royce," he says.
> And the black clouds break up, and dew springs again to the green grass, and the stands hang on, and his own oppressed heart leaps alive to give it one last try.
> And he doesn't know any more whether he's a Damonite or a Caseyite ... doesn't even know if he's Paul Trench or Royce Ingram ... it's all irrelevant, it doesn't even matter that he's going to die, all that counts is that he is *here* and here's The Man and here's the boys and there's the crowd, the sun, the noise.
> "It's not a trial," says Damon, ... hands working the new ball. ... "It's not even a lesson. It's just what it is." Damon holds the baseball up between them. It is hard and white and alive in the sun.
> He laughs. It's beautiful, that ball. He punches Damon lightly in the ribs with his mitt. "Hang loose," he says, and pulling down his mask, trots back behind home plate [242].

Registering the tangible presence of the rubbed-up ball, red stitches livid against the horsehide, Paul Trench returns to the game-in-itself, reminded that playing it is designed to sustain him. He regards the scene with a reawakened consciousness and recovers enough of his equanimity to participate in the fiction

---

[21]F. Scott Fitzgerald, "The Crack-Up" (1936), 69, as reprinted in The Crack-Up, edited by Edmund Wilson (1945; reprinted, New York: New Directions Books, 1956), 69–84.

of Damonsday.[22] Playing Damon's part, Hardy Ingram participates wholly, uses "Royce" instead of Paul's own name, and invokes the game for "what it is": not a myth nor the fulfillment of a pattern, not "a trial ... not even a lesson," but a brave hedge against doom, an expression of willful forgetfulness of final things in an extended season of play.

The final exchange between Hardy Ingram and Paul Trench reiterates the novel's major themes. The game's being "just what it is" and the ineluctable modality of the baseball "alive in the sun" recapture the pretextual past of *The Universal Baseball Association*, when J. Henry Waugh was satisfied by the game-in-itself, the performances of its players, the progress of its seasons. To the extent that its ending symbolically reprises its origin, the narrative gestures at closure and approaches — but never quite returns to — home. The final dialogue reasserts the game's raw beauty, portending that Damonsday will not transpire as it presumably has many times in the past. The tingling that Hardy Ingram feels "just behind his left ear" (222), like the avenging tingle that Paul Trench feels in his hands, "a power there he neither wants nor asked for" (240), are signs of a potential, premature doom that may yet be circumvented if the proprietor throws the dice without prejudice and desists from interfering in the outcome. Chance, which has decreed that Damon Rutherford would die, has incited J. Henry Waugh to displace the game with a sterile ritual, but restoring chance to the artifact will reverse this process and transform the unregenerative, unsustaining ceremony into a new Era of play. If Henry can recommit himself to play's rejuvenating process — if he can trust the game-within and not the ritual to sustain him — the UBA might again become "good for him," the thing that "[keeps] him young" (6).

At novel's end, however, ritual has not come full circle back to game. The pattern is incomplete in terms of the baseball trope, for the ninth chapter, which would constitute the final inning of Robert Coover's complex game, does not exist. Presumably, Coover declines to complete the pattern to avoid domesticating J. Henry Waugh's experience of the UBA with a comfortable passage home. With the suspended action of Damonsday CLVII and the unthrown baseball "hard and white and alive in the sun" (242), the future of the UBA and the destinies of its players are left in doubt. On the other hand, J. Henry Waugh has already come home and apparently plays, or ritualizes, the game in unbroken solitude. Having been fired by Zifferblatt over the telephone (Henry is already at home), the proprietor takes up residence within the UBA and vanishes from the world of accounting firm and delicatessen, as well as from the printed page. Although he has resisted this outcome, Henry has always thought of home and the UBA together: "He was headed for home, returning to his

---

[22]Brenda Wineapple notes Paul Trench's political disengagement and sense of philosophical relativism: "There are no sustaining or immutable and knowable truths. The self is diverse, not primal.... And, most importantly, time consists of endless beginnings, re-enactments, repetitions, and creative renewal, for time is lived and shared experience. With Paul Trench, we are restored to life by means of our fictions" (Wineapple 73).

league and all its players" (44). Ultimately, Henry forgoes the balance between his real world and the universe of his game, "that rhythmic shift from house to house" (141), and comes home permanently to the UBA in a way that exiles him from all human companionship. Such a homecoming is not so much incomplete as it is darkly ironic, for it does not afford the protagonist the expected reunion with self or family, but buries him in a deeper, seemingly irremediable isolation. In an apparent prelude to madness, J. Henry Waugh disappears into his own obsessive imagination. The fantasized ballplayers are Henry's nominal family and friends, and so this homecoming to the UBA, the playing field of his mind, is the truest one he can enjoy.

Having attempted to script his game as if it were a novel, J. Henry Waugh discovers that the process of composition often thwarts an author's intention. Like a game, fiction seems in its unfolding to possess a life of its own. There is a difference, but it is one only of degree. Loading the dice mitigates the game's susceptibility to chance but does not insure it. Played this way, the game becomes an expression of revisable authorial intention: a novel. Once the dice are manipulated and a particular outcome coerced, the artifact becomes predestined and static: a ritual. In the end, both the UBA and its proprietor are imprisoned in a ritual that does not evolve despite being repeatedly enacted. Conversely, no two games are quite the same, no matter how many games one plays. As a game, its outcomes affected by accident and chance, the UBA is, like real baseball, more nearly a metaphor for life's progress than it is an analogue of a novel's composition. Chance is the ungovernable, unpredictable factor in all games, aleatory or ludic, and the element that differentiates any game from the purposeful intentionality of art.[23] And yet, these dynamics resist simplification. The novel, written *in medias res* of its author's life, may imitate life's flux and round into being through a series of nominal mishaps. Only the author knows the whole process of his book's composition, just as J. Henry Waugh alone comprehends his Association's history and future dispensation. In this sense, novel and game are analogous forms, each a fictive artifact whose meaning is more a matter of belief than an objective quality. By aligning novel and game in so tenuous a comparison, Robert Coover suggests that the novel, in both the process of composition and its eventual reading, escapes one's control. The narrative's unanticipated developments liberate it time and again, denying its author perfect mastery of his fiction, frustrating the reader's wish for perfect comprehension. In this sense, an author can never write a perfect game, nor the reader observe one. Lack of total control means that literary intentionality is imperfect, which implies a diminishment of a novel's end, or purpose, as being the most accurate index of its meaning. Baseball, too, is a fiction whose process is

---

[23]In "Sport, Art, and Aesthetics: A Decade of Controversy (1978–1988)," Daniel J. Herman reviews the debate attending the proposition that sport, whether "purposive" or "aesthetic" (according to David Best's taxonomy in Philosophy and Human Movement), is never art and can never be successfully analogized to art. See The Achievement of American Sport Literature, edited by Wiley Lee Umphlett (Madison, NJ: Fairleigh Dickinson University Press, 1991), 158–164.

more compelling than its end, in both senses of that word. Meaning inheres in the story's being told, the game's being played, the "how" of narrative rather than its terminal "what," for chance — or inspiration — might intervene at the unlikeliest moment to trace a pattern that remains invisible to the author until it is complete.

◆ Conclusion ◆
Coming Home
Baseball in American Fiction

And so, finally, he'd found his way back to baseball. Nothing like it really. Not the actual game so much — to tell the truth, real baseball bored him — but rather the records, the statistics, the peculiar balances between individual and team, offense and defense, strategy and luck, accident and pattern, power and intelligence. And no other activity in the world had so precise and comprehensive a history, so specific an ethic, and at the same time, strange as it seemed, so much ultimate mystery.
— Robert Coover, *The Universal Baseball Association, Inc., J. Henry Waugh, Prop.*

Baseball fiction implicates the reader in the same kind of exchange that characterizes the reading of all fiction. Faced with a new text, one begins tentatively, looking for signs of orientation. The narrative voice is likely to seem strange, its turns of phrase unanticipated, its language unfamiliar, so that making sense is difficult. One continues reading as an act of faith, trusting the narrative to clarify itself. Sentence by sentence, the reader grows accustomed to the voice and its figures, and moves more easily from page to page. Readers who are peers, who are close in age, education, and experience (and have gender in common), will read a given book to similar effect, with similar affect. And yet, no two persons bring the same qualities to reading, and so never take away exactly the same impressions of any book; what one instantly forgets, the other remembers forever, and so forth. Then, too, the knowledge one brings to reading partly determines the meaning that a book will have for him. Reading is not merely personal or idiosyncratic, but unique. For much of the experience, the reader's comprehension of the text is inchoate; assuming a well-wrought book, uncertainty gradually subsides and narrative coheres. Responding to the author's cues, a reader makes his own sense — of characters and their actions, of scenes and their contexts, of sentences, of words — and effectively constructs an inimitable text.

Once read, a book changes. Its pages remain as printed, but the reader's response, fleetingly formed in the act of reading, evaporates in a moment, precipitates again, vanishes, regathers, and can never be duplicated. Modestly,

provisionally, intending his work for an audience of one (and for only one reading, because the reader, too, changes as a result of having read; it is impossible
to read the same book twice), the reader helps mentally to compose, if not physically to write, the book he reads. The lion's share of the work is the author's.
The author is responsible not only for what appears in the book but also for its
context: how it is presented and in what relation to what other things. Juxtaposition and deferral, repetition and pacing, the structure of sentences (simple
or complex? paratactically discrete or hypotactically enfolded?), the framing of
language and selection of words (plain diction? Latinate? slang? descriptive?
figurative? and where, when, in relation to what?), the relative lengths of paragraphs, of chapters, of the book itself condition the reader's reception of the
text and provide the raw material, authorially refined, upon which his imagination plays. Like marriage, reading and writing is a partnership of sorts, an
informal collaboration to which each party brings a peculiar matrix of expectations and desires, talents, ambitions, anxieties, flaws, preoccupations, secrets,
dreams. No writer ever wrote without a sense of audience, and no reader ever
finished a book without asking, at some point along the way if not at the end,
just what its author meant by it.

If the foregoing essays indicate a single conclusion, it might be that the
baseball content of American fiction is as significant as the reader is willing to
make it. Like the meaning of a novel or the importance of a game, the literary
currency of baseball is a fiction in which one chooses to believe — a sustaining
fiction, perhaps, that one constructs for oneself, that we construct together, to
restore the interest of a game loved in childhood and neglected thereafter, to
rediscover the thrill of first impressions: the scent of a new glove, and feeling
one's hand inside it; the buzz of a fastball, the unnerving arc of the curve; the
wooden bat connecting with the hard ball, the full, almost liquid feeling of pure
contact, and the loud crack, and the ball springing into the air; the moment of
picking a favorite player, yes, *him!* and feeding hope on each pitch, each hit,
every catch and throw, living one's life through how he plays the game and
dying a little death with him when he retires; of pushing through the turnstile,
finding the right ramp, striding up through shadows into a wash of reflected
light, the grandstand rising behind and blue seats streaming away, and the jewel-
green field, lit so brightly it stuns the eyes, shimmering in the night like a mirage
floating on the edge of a desert. A luminous sight, composed with the clarity
of a world that is closer to perfection, it is enough to strike one motionless. Dispersed in the expanse, the uniformed players possess visible grace, an eloquence
of power and motion that, to an ordinary man, truly does seem larger than life.
Absorbed in admiration, the spectator is returned to himself by 40,000 voices,
the sensation of that human roar reverberating inside his chest. These impressions and a hundred others, the configurations of ballparks, the colors of dirt
and grass, the designs of uniforms, the demeanors of players and their names,
persist in the mind without asking to be remembered. For baseball is not just
memorable; it is compelling. It delivers us from a dead season, returning with

life in the spring, keeps us reliable company through the bright summer, and reaches its shattering conclusions in autumn twilight. All the time spent watching, the days and nights, late games from the coast, listening to radio baseball in the car, in bed with closed eyes, fighting sleep: all of that paying of attention has its effect, and its meaning. It is not just so many hours lost, so many thousands of hours taken away from this brief life, but indicative of habits of mind and temperament. Proceeding pitch by pitch, unhurried by the clock, baseball demands patience. Over the course of a season it can develop in ways impossible to anticipate and then, with only one strike to throw or one play to make, change utterly, for better or worse. Faith is essential in approaching it; so is optimism, for baseball is haunted by failure. The most capable hitters succeed three times out of ten — perhaps, if they are especially adept, thirty-five times out of every hundred. The most victorious teams lose 40 percent of their games. No one who has played baseball has not been humbled by it, and no one who has succeeded at it, who has gotten the winning hit, thrown the clinching pitch, made the saving catch, forgets how it felt to match an ideal of performance to its enactment.

Some of that feeling is recoverable in baseball fiction. Depictions of players and games, even when these are fictitious, evoke impressions of baseball as one has known it. Allusions to actual players, to historical games, to notable events like the Black Sox Scandal, create a sense of continuity, not only between word and world, text and reality, but between author and reader. Writing baseball is essentially a friendly gesture. *Here,* the author tacitly says, *is something familiar, something you will recognize, and enjoy.* Baseball allusions take for granted the reader's familiarity with the game, presume his knowledge of its contexts, past and present. It is possible to ignore these figures, just as it is possible to ignore other allusions to persons, events, and phenomena. In many cases it might be that relatively little is lost. A reading of *The Sound and the Fury* does not come to grief if the reader cannot identify "that fellow Ruth," just as *A Portrait of the Artist as a Young Man* retains its drama for a reader unaware of the private indiscretion and public disgrace of "Poor Parnell!... My dead king!" — or does it? Without knowing what he is missing, the reader knows that he is missing something. Ignore enough allusions, synecdoches, and other tropes, and reading becomes impoverished, an exercise of following words across a page without perceiving their gathering force. Under such a handicap, why read at all? Is *The Old Man and the Sea* as satisfactory a story if one ignores "the great DiMaggio" and the other baseball names? Santiago is destitute, his life reduced below subsistence, his language pared down to essentials. To slight the baseball content is to steal a portion of the old man's humanity and empty the fiction of half its meaning, thefts by which one deprives oneself of the pleasures of the text.

In baseball novels these pleasures can be remarkable. One must, however, find the books that take the subject matter and its representation seriously enough to create a smart, original, entertaining narrative. Unfortunately, most baseball novels are trifling things. Readers cannot help but notice the uneven prose, the lapses of aesthetic judgment, the absence, finally, of literary merit. Badly written, absurdly plotted, these books give baseball fiction its ragamuffin reputation. Like bad fiction of other sorts, poor baseball novels indulge, in roughly equal measure, in sentimentality and falseness. The latter flaw is a result of a writer's not trusting the material to stand on its own. Having chosen baseball as the vehicle of fiction, some authors still doubt that it can embody literary meaning and so force the game into symbolic implausibilities: to be more than what it is. The invention of a metaphysical or supernatural *über*-text is usually unconvincing, despite the example of *The Natural;* like Lardner's comic realism, Malamud's deft transposition of mythic archetypes might be superficially imitated without being intrinsically equaled. The sentimental impulse, on the other hand, is potentially present in all baseball fiction; it is the author's job to resist it. Owing, perhaps, to a lingering sense that no novel "about" a game is to be taken seriously, sentimentality is also the unfortunate legacy that juvenile sports fiction has bequeathed to the adult genre. Having read and, *as boys,* loved boys' baseball books, some writers fall into their jejune idiom, simplistic distinctions, and overwrought excitement. Clichés, a chief feature of boys' baseball tales, are especially ill-suited to the creation of complex fictive worlds. Baseball is so familiar that translating it into a fiction free of clichés is difficult. Certain figures — of language, of character, of plot — are repeated as if in reflex and have come to be expected; if they do not appear, the reader is likely to feel not only that something is missing but that something strange is going on. It would much improve the genre's overall quality if one had this sensation of strangeness more often. Instead, most writers rehearse the clichés of baseball fiction as unthinkingly as they draw breath, fulfilling their readers' expectations and producing derivative (and superfluous) baseball novels.

The ultimate cause of these frailties might lie in baseball itself. Knowing the game, mindful of the attributes of a good novel, one comes to realize that baseball is not easily adapted to the dynamics of literary fiction. For all of its formal similarity to the novel, baseball resists the telos of narrative and the development of complex fictional characters. A baseball game is like a story, but if the story's telling is to amount to more than transcribed play-by-play, the writer must transform the game into a narrative of consequence and import. If the protagonist is a baseball player, he must have a life away from the diamond, conceive thoughts that are not diamond-shaped, perform actions that are not diamond-bound. In itself, baseball means nothing. It is beautiful to watch, exciting to play, but its meaning comes from without, from the imaginative responses of its players and fans. A novel can never be about baseball in the sense that it can be about love, greed, the soul's own pain. Baseball is not a theme, it is not a character, it is neither an ideological position nor a system of ethics. Baseball is a game. It is played by men who contest its outcomes with competitive passion and physical pride, and the conflicts inscribed in its play are momentarily resolved, pitch by pitch. For these conflicts to be meaningful, they must refer to a concern beyond strikes and outs, hits, runs, and errors. The resolution, which the reader prospectively contemplates as he reads, must convey the sense of something greater at stake than the final score.

As if its literary origins and their repercussions were not sufficiently vexing, baseball fiction's major trope — that of exile and homecoming — also invites sentimentality, for it has nostalgia built into it. Nostalgia, literally homesickness, is the genre's fatal flaw. Like the player, a character whose fictive career is shaped by the diamond's formal logic will always find himself drawn to revisit his past and the origin hidden within it. The hankering for home is powerful, and the protagonist, like the ballplayer, has every reason to complete the passage. Home is where the heart is, the place the heart knows best, the familiar space of safety and repose. But the action, as even Busher Keefe understands, is elsewhere. Like other American myths, the self-sufficiency of home is nice to believe in — another sustaining fiction that belief can make true. Experience, however, and the baseball novel itself suggest that the best adventures occur far afield of one's domestic contexts. One might say that the wayfarer comes home to tell the story of his odyssey because the audience is more likely to be sympathetic. In itself, homecoming means the end of adventure, the beginning of rest. The longing for such domestic returns will yield a weak narrative unless the author complicates, varies, or otherwise surprises the simple inevitability of the journey.

The most telling feature of the best baseball fiction is its resistance to simple closure. The genre's four seminal works describe homecomings that are either failed, incomplete, or complicated by dissatisfaction or anxiety. In *You Know Me Al*, Jack Keefe decides at the last minute not to return to his hometown and embarks instead on a circumnavigation of the globe. Having been preoccupied with coming home, Jack has his mind changed for him again and, with a company of fellow players, lights out for the territories and beyond. Despite a sensation of premature nostalgia at the prospect of leaving his wife and child, Busher Keefe commits himself to an extended season, a self-imposed exile of play. In *The Natural*, Roy Hobbs, desperate to recapture the lost time and inner peace of his boyhood, cannot distinguish the Imaginary from the Real and so cannot come home to himself. Blind to the ways of reconciliation, unwilling to surrender his vanity or adapt himself to the passing of time, Roy strikes out in his final inning, dying a death that is not just the little death of athletes but the inception of a greater exile. Despite the home runs he hits, Roy Hobbs never comes home at all. In *The Southpaw*, Henry Wiggen returns to Perkinsville to marry his hometown girl, yet finds his picture removed from the place of honor in Borelli's Barbershop and himself confronted with the task of having to write a book to correct the distortions of the sporting press. Left-handed in temperament as well as in physical inclination, Henry's refusal even to pretend to humble down to the ethos of an organization man alienates him from the spirit of his time. His homecoming is tasked by the rigors of authorship, and the southpaw himself is beset by a sense of having been mistreated by his team, the other players, the sportswriters, and the fans. In *The Universal Baseball Association*, coming home marks the onset of a more ominous separation. Having abandoned the balance between work and play, life and art, J. Henry Waugh removes himself from the ordinary world and commits his being to the world of his game, which he pursues with ritualistic complexity within the confines of his apartment. Trapped inside the spaces of his own omniscience, the dark diceman of the UBA inhabits home as a prisoner, a psychological and physical shut-in condemned to an exile of solitary confinement.

The game-playing career of J. Henry Waugh embodies the primary dilemma of all authors of fiction: how to assimilate life's disparate elements to an aesthetic vision while preserving their essential truth, then to deploy the transformed material in a purposive yet flexible pattern that discovers meaning in the course of its unfolding. The key to literary art, as Henry Waugh realizes but cannot attain, is trusting the creative process, the incremental construction of scene and story, its shaping, stripping down, and refashioning, the accretion of words that is the imagination working on (or playing with) the material of experience. Without undue second-guessing, self-censorship, or tyrannical assertions of authorial intent, the literary imagination will eventually find the critical balance between "strategy and luck, accident and pattern" that shapes the playing of baseball games and the playful composition of the baseball novel.

♦ *Appendix* ♦
Views from the Press Box
The Critical Literature

> *Criticism, analysis, reflection is a natural response to the existence in the world of works of art. It is an honorable and even an exalted endeavor. Without it, works of art would appear in a vacuum, as if they had no relation to the minds experiencing them. It would be a dismal, unthinkable world with these shooting stars arousing no comment, leaving no trace. But it is the mind of the critic, somehow, the establishment of his own thought and values, that counts; and that establishment is the authority of the voice, whether it comes from creative work in the arts or creative work in criticism. ... It is not a question of right or wrong specific opinions, but of the quality of the mind.*
> — Elizabeth Hardwick, interview in *The Paris Review*

As the reader will have noted, *Home Games* is hardly the first critical study of baseball fiction. A number of studies of sport literature published in the last two decades have influenced the present author's selection of primary texts and interpretive themes; indeed, *Home Games* has taken its present form in part as a response to the insights and omissions of prior scholarship. Previous critics have defined the field of inquiry quite well, and some have been scrupulous in providing comprehensive accounts of practically every American novel written around our major sports. These books have helped to legitimize sport literature criticism and deserve notice. Moreover, *Home Games* attempts, in addition to offering its own readings of baseball fiction, to synthesize certain principles and motifs that have been in play for many years. A summary of some of the major themes explored by other critics will help the reader discern how these ideas have been adapted to the purposes of the present study.

Two useful inquiries into sport literature appeared in the same year. Leverett T. Smith's *The American Dream and the National Game* (1975) and Wiley Lee Umphlett's *The Sporting Myth and the American Experience* (1975) both address the general topic of sport in literature in their respective attempts to articulate the broader cultural significance of sports in America. *The American*

Dream and the National Game endeavors to create a dialogue between the products of what its author calls, respectively, "high" and "popular" culture. This dialogue reveals that "works of 'high' culture" (literature) address "all the contradictions" of the general culture and provide, as a virtue of their special coherence, "models" by which to analyze the works of "popular" (sports) culture.[1] From this premise, Smith examines "the changing relation of sport and society" and identifies "what values are attributed to games, sports, or other kinds of leisure activity" (4). Like many studies of game, play, and sport, *The American Dream and the National Game* begins with the theories of Johan Huizinga, as propounded in *Homo Ludens* (1938) and, to a lesser extent, in *In the Shadow of Tomorrow* (1935). Smith draws variously from the conception of play presented in these books, but Huizinga's notion of play's essential separateness from "'ordinary' life or 'real' life" (quoted by Smith 12) is the key element underlying Smith's analysis of sport in cultural and literary contexts. According to Huizinga, "Play is a voluntary activity ... [that] always belongs to the sphere of festival and ritual — the sacred sphere." Thus, "Play is distinct from 'ordinary' life both as to locality and duration. It is 'played out' within certain limits of time and place. It contains its own course and meaning ... [and] creates order, *is* order." Play's primary quality is "that at a certain moment it is *over*" (quoted by Smith 12–13). This definition, at once complex and limiting, informs Smith's readings of selected American fictions.

For the purposes of *Home Games*, Smith's discussion of Ring Lardner's fictional busher, Jack Keefe, has proven most useful. The explications of certain moments and characters of Hemingway's fiction are also valuable, both for the light they shed on that author's rhetoric of play and because this analysis informs Smith's discussion of *The Southpaw*. The chief merit of *The American Dream and the National Game*, as far as students of sport literature are concerned, is its copious use of primary texts to establish the cultural and historical contexts of sport literature. In terms of baseball contexts, Smith is especially thorough when he turns his attention to Ring Lardner. A careful evaluation of Lardner's nonfictional baseball writings allows the critic to argue persuasively that Lardner lost his youthful enthusiasm for baseball not primarily as an aftereffect of the Black Sox Scandal but because the introduction of a livelier baseball and the vogue of home run hitting changed the essential quality of the game Lardner had known from boyhood.[2] This distinction might strike some

---

[1]*Leverett T. Smith*, The American Dream and the National Game *(Bowling Green, OH: Bowling Green University Popular Press, 1975), 5.*

[2]*Ring Lardner had grown up with the "inside" baseball of John McGraw and Ty Cobb, which gave "really intelligent managers a deserved advantage and smart ball players like Cobb and Jim Sheckard a chance to do things" (Smith 125; see 121–126). After Babe Ruth demonstrated the efficacy of the home run and quickly established its popularity among the paying customers, baseball became a game that also rewarded power and strength. Intelligence, the application of strategy in specific game situations, and the skills required by the hit-and-run, the bunt, and the stolen base were diminished by a relative lack of appreciation among fans. Because these plays were less frequently attempted, they were less successfully performed. It is easy to imagine the cycle of incremental degradation that practically erased the dynamics of "inside" baseball from the professional's repertoire by the late 1950s.*

readers as meaningless, yet the Black Sox Scandal,[3] usually figured as baseball's fall from a state of ludic grace, conventionally (and arbitrarily, for game-fixing had been a problem even before the start of baseball's professional era in 1869[4]) marks the end of baseball's "innocence" and the beginning of its corruption by money. The prominence of a fixed World Series, especially one in which the losing team is perceived to be much more talented than the winner, no doubt accounts for the notoriety of the Black Sox Scandal and the special persistence of the myths associated with it. And yet, the construction of baseball's pre–Black Sox "innocence" and Babe Ruth's "redemption" (in 1920[5]) of the "fall" of 1919 suggests that thoughtful observers often interpret the vulgar machinations of the sports world as a postfigurement of sacred events.

The inevitable conclusion is that the manner in which Americans watch, participate in, and respond to their favorite games reveals major assumptions of American (multi)culture. It is not too much to claim that the nation's sporting life can define the prevailing national character. Sport's revelatory quality supplies Wiley Lee Umphlett's premise in *The Sporting Myth and the American Experience*. Umphlett reads the representations of the athlete and other sporting characters as a means by which American fiction "[tells] us a great deal about ourselves — our shortcomings, obsessions, and failures as well as our finer moments."[6] This orientation to American sport fiction is guided by the critic's supposition that sport reflects the culture as well as influences it. Sport is a key to "understanding Americans as a people," for "We can perhaps learn more about a people through how they play a game or use their leisure time than we can through how they involve themselves with their day-to-day occupations" (9). From his investigation of sport in literature, the critic discovers that Americans are beset by "the feeling of eternal division" (11). Umphlett discerns such a division in "Rabbit" Angstrom, John Updike's ex-high school basketball star, and in the social conflicts of the late 1960s and early 1970s, when *The Sporting Myth and the American Experience* was conceived and written. The development of fictional characters like Updike's Rabbit describes part of "our moral evolution as a people" (11), for the "sporting hero" attempts to "reconcile the rift between the dream and the actuality" as a means to self-knowledge (21). The hero's trial is a "fictional pattern ... of the *encounter*," which obliges him to chose, in confronting the demands of nature and society, "between a self-effacing code of behavior or his own private self-interests" (21). By examining "the development of an American literary type from primal innocence to 'complex fate'"

---

[3]*See page 42* supra, *note 12.*

[4]*Harold Seymour, Baseball: The Early Years (1960; reprinted, New York: Oxford University Press, 1989), 52–56, 87–88. In the nineteenth century, the practice of "fixing" a baseball game was called "hippodroming." According to Seymour, the first fix to be revealed involved an amateur game between the New York Mutuals and the Brooklyn Eckfords on September 28, 1865 (Seymour 53).*

[5]*See Preface, page 6* supra, *note 8.*

[6]*Wiley Lee Umphlett, The Sporting Myth and the American Experience: Studies in Contemporary Fiction (Lewisburg, PA: Bucknell University Press, 1975), 10.*

(11) and judging the sporting hero according to his "performance ... the quality of his basic actions" (21), Umphlett endeavors to reveal "our moral destiny"
(11). Using this approach, the critic evaluates *You Know Me Al, The Natural,
Bang the Drum Slowly,* and *The Universal Baseball Association, Inc., J. Henry
Waugh, Prop.*

By contrast, Neil Berman comments at length on just one of these books
in *Playful Fictions and Fictional Players* (1981). Berman, interested in demonstrating the seriousness of play and the indivisibility of American games and
culture, chooses to address a greater variety of sport fiction. The "major and
representative novels" that Berman selects envision a "world that is actively hostile to any manifestation of freedom, any play" and that "manages to deaden"
the play "it pretends to allow."[7] The central assumption of this study is drawn
from Jacques Ehrmann's claim that "To define play is *at the same time* and *in
the same movement* to define reality and to define culture."[8] As Berman explains
Ehrmann's revision of Huizinga, play becomes not merely an alternative version of reality but an activity and attitude of mind that displaces the "workaday" or routinely "real" world. To the extent that sport fiction succeeds in
representing play's reality to its players, it "suggests that an unplayful world is
in fact unreal" (15). Following Erhmann's lead, Berman claims not that "play
and sport are like 'life'" but that "play and sport *are* life — or should be, if sport
were always play" (15). In a rhetoric of assertion that sometimes seems to echo
the claims of Michael Novak's *The Joy of Sports* (1976),[9] Berman states his position with utmost clarity: "The play-attitude is as serious and real as any other
existential phenomenon" (15). The "unplayful," and therefore "unreal," world
that Berman finds most compelling in baseball fiction is the accountant's life
of J. Henry Waugh in *The Universal Baseball Association.* Although Berman
finds other baseball novels interesting and mentions some of them in passing,
it is to Coover's ingenious fiction that he devotes an entire chapter — the final
chapter of his book. *The Universal Baseball Association* is, Berman writes, "a natural climax to this study," for it presents "a completely internalized play-world
with its own myths and rituals" (10). This "play-world" is not opposed to "seriousness, work, or reality," for Henry's baseball game thrives in his imagination — and on the page — as "the real world" and "makes the world of accounting
seem unreal by comparison" (10). Of sport fiction generally, Berman argues that
it focuses the reader's attention on "man's play nature" and "the significance of
games and game playing in contemporary culture" (4). The genre itself contradicts the "dualism" of thinking that "the world of the game" and "the real
world" are mutually opposed (7). Inevitably, sport fiction leads its critics,
Berman claims, to question the traditional "intellectual oppositions" that align

[7]*Neil Berman,* Playful Fictions and Fictional Players: Game, Sport, and Survival in Contemporary
American Fiction *(Port Washington, NY: Kennikat Press, 1981), 8.*

[8]*Jacques Ehrmann, "Homo Ludens Revisited" in* Yale French Studies *41 (1968); quoted by Berman, 6.*

[9]*See page 190 supra, note 4.*

play with gratuitousness, sterility, leisure, literature, and unreality, and associate work with usefulness, fecundity, seriousness, science, and reality (6). Interpreting sport fiction allows the critic to reveal both the seriousness of play and the importance of his culture's games (4).

In *Laurel & Thorn* (1981), Robert J. Higgs is less interested in defining and evaluating the sport fiction genre and more attuned to the incarnations of the athlete-as-character. To describe the literary athlete, Higgs formulates a model of opposed "conformist" and "rebel" types, then complicates the model by associating these types with notions of the "Apollonian" and "Dionysian" that allude both to Nietzsche and to classical conceptions.[10] The Apollonian is "artificial," and the athlete of this type is "attempting to conform to some stereotyped conception of completeness" that includes "the dispensation of knowledge, the banishment of evil, and the control of nature" (9). The Apollonian is "unrealistic, immature, though giving the illusion of maturity, and, if given enough prominence, tyrannical and oppressive" (9). Conversely, the Dionysian is "natural" and this athlete "is the neurotic who wants to be himself ... the true 'natural' who has accepted his body as himself and feels no need to conform to an Apollonian order" (10). The Dionysian is "narcissistic" and regressive rather than self-actualizing, yet "not self-deceived as the Apollonians are because he has no self to deceive" (10). A third figure, the athlete-as-Adonis, seems to stand in a medial position between the Apollonian and the Dionysian, remaining essentially in revolt against "both authority and nature" and all "stereotyped definitions of what it means to be a man" (11). Adonis is "almost the antithesis" of Dionysus, Higgs explains, yet also a "Dionysian figure" who is so like the original that "significant distinctions between some ancient versions of Dionysus and Adonis" are "virtually impossible" (10). Adonis will neither "kill himself" nor "uncritically conform" but does "seek knowledge ... for the sake of self" and "reminds us that body and self must be united on the side of nature and not on the side of conformity and control as Apollo would have us believe" (11). Living in "a world of tension, pain, struggle, and hope," Adonis demonstrates "the imperfectibility of man and ... the hubris of those who would assume to spell out the best manner of reconciling body and mind" (11). The Adonic figure seems to combine a revolt that is less extreme than the Dionysian with a form of self-control that is less categorical and self-stultifying than the Apollonian. The variations among these figures are clearest when Higgs applies the constructs to specific literary characters: Nebraska Crane, Thomas Wolfe's part-Cherokee baseball hero, is an Adonic figure, the natural or folk hero (125–127); Jim Randolph, Wolfe's "southern [football] knight," is an Apollonian type, the sporting gentleman (127). Generally, the Apollonian is found in "the busher, the sporting gentleman, the apotheosized WASP, the booster alumnus, the muscular Christian, and the brave new man" (9); the Dionysian is recognizable "as

[10]Robert J. Higgs, Laurel & Thorn: The Athlete in American Literature *(Lexington: University Press of Kentucky, 1981), 8–9.*

the familiar babe, bum, or beast" (10); and the Adonic subsumes "the folk hero, the fisher king, the scapegoat, the absurd athlete, and the 'secret' Christian" (11). Most importantly, Adonis possesses *aidos*, which Higgs defines as a special kind of humility that is not expressed in self-effacement but does include the courage and ability to fight or compete fairly. Higgs applies this taxonomy to baseball characters in *You Know Me Al*, *The Natural*, and *Bang the Drum Slowly*, as well as to sporting figures in a variety of American novels, including *The Great Gatsby*, *Elmer Gantry* (1927), and Walker Percy's *Lancelot* (1977).

The task of defining the sport fiction genre and the challenge of delineating its sporting characters are cojoined by Christian K. Messenger in a seminal contribution to the critical literature of game, play, and sport. *Sport and the Spirit of Play in American Fiction: Hawthorne to Faulkner* (1981) investigates the "play impulse" in works by Washington Irving, James Fenimore Cooper, Ring Lardner, F. Scott Fitzgerald, Ernest Hemingway, and others, in addition to the study's subtitular names. This book places sport at the center of American culture, where it mediates the inherent conflict between America's frontier heritage — the people's arduous task of exploring and settling "a vast continent, confronting nature in the raw and often calling on only their own 'raw' physical natures as tools or weapons in an unequal contest," and America's religious heritage, its Puritan circumspection that has "engendered a profound mistrust of play and sport."[11] Sport, Messenger argues, enables Americans "to bring their physical natures into conjunction with the tenets of the mind and the yearnings of the spirit" (1). Messenger's approach involves identifying the varieties of play, as the concept is explored in the respective works of Johan Huizinga (*Homo Ludens*) and Roger Caillois (*Man, Play, and Games* [1961]), and adapting their classifications to his own taxonomy.[12] Like Berman in *Playful Fictions and Fictional Players*, Messenger uses the contributions of Caillois and Ehrmann to expand Huizinga's conception of play. Again, the critic insists that play is not opposed to seriousness or reality and that sport has become, in late twentieth-century America, a powerful secular ritual in its approach to the sacred. In citing the "welter of meanings" associated with sport, Messenger indicates that the contemporary debate reaches beyond the classifications of Huizinga and Caillois (6). Still, in his readings of Hawthorne, Twain, Faulkner, Hemingway, Lardner, et al., Messenger applies these terms to the types of play that inform the fictional representations of characters and their actions.

The protagonists of sport fiction possess definitive qualities that are determined by the type of games they play and the historical contexts of their

---

[11]*Christian K. Messenger,* Sport and the Spirit of Play in American Fiction: Hawthorne to Faulkner *(New York: Columbia University Press, 1981), 1.*

[12]*Combining the definitions propounded by Huizinga and Caillois, Messenger offers the following terms to describe the varieties of play:* "agon— *a competition for something, a contest with rules;* paidia— *the most spontaneous of free play;* ludus— *the most rule-bound and organized form of play;* alea— *games of chance;* mimesis— *a representation of something;* mimicry— *acting by participants, simulation by the audience;* ilinx— *an irrational state induced by hypnosis, drugs, or emotional exaltation" (2–3).*

appearance. Messenger posits "Three specific heroic models" to delineate these figures: "the Ritual Sports Hero, the Popular Sports Hero, and the School Sports Hero" (8). The Ritual Sports Hero is an "Adamic figure who seeks self-knowledge" and competes "against self or natural adversaries." He has "both surpassing skill and great dignity" and often lives in the wilderness for long periods. The Ritual Sports Hero is an individualist who plays for self. This "personal, isolated frame of competition" often places him in conflict with society (8). His sport assumes the form of ritual and includes activities like hunting, trapping, fishing, and exploration; thus, "play is often work of the most creative and healing sort" and is related to "primitive sacrificial sports and the sports of antiquity where rites sustained culture" (10). This hero's "sporting motions and victories are serious and private"; "sport is a revelation" (9). The Popular Sports Hero is a product of the American frontier. He is "democratic, raw, humorous, and unlettered" and appears initially as a "hunter, physical wild man, gambler, or shrewd confidence man." His sport evolves from "his work with horse, rifle, and riverboat" in a natural environment and later becomes the "popular" sport of industrial society, which he plays in urban arenas before the gaze of thousands (8). He is, or becomes, the professional competitor who plays the game for "immediate extrinsic rewards: money, fame, records"; sport is "a contest" (9). The School Sports Hero originates in Eastern colleges, where his education includes a "militant sporting ethic" (9). For the School Sports Hero, the sporting experience is play undertaken "in preparation for life's work." Sport teaches him about himself and "about lessons in courage and discipline that he can apply to life and society outside the arena" (9–10). Educated, more genteel than the others, he is trained to play a prominent role in society, which generally admires him and regards him as a "potential leader." He plays his (college's) games for "externalized goals [and] personal gratification" (10) but finally to win "society's praise," to "establish his place as leader or spokesman"; sport is "a test" (9). By applying these categories to sporting characters, the critic demonstrates that the athletic figures of early twentieth-century American fiction are descendants of nineteenth century legendary and folkloric types.

The evolution from folkloric to athletic hero reflects the transition of the sport fiction genre from moralistic juvenile tales to a literature with a claim on the attention of adults. Michael Oriard surveys this genre and its changing typologies in *Dreaming of Heroes* (1982).[13] Oriard aligns baseball fiction with three other modes (football, boxing, and basketball) that emphasize the athletic performance, off-the-field exploits, and personal character of the athletic hero. Working with Joseph Campbell's model of the mythological hero, a figure divinely incarnated and situated at the heart of a culture-specific version of the monomyth, Oriard discerns an analogous, albeit "plebian" (36), manifestation

[13]*Michael Oriard,* Dreaming of Heroes: American Sports Fiction, 1868–1980 *(Chicago: Nelson-Hall, 1982).*

of the mythic hero in the athletes of American sport fiction.[14] Oriard makes
no grand claims for the athletic hero—he recognizes the limited self-awareness
and egocentric sense of responsibility that disqualify the professional ballplayer
from legitimately serving as a truly mythic, in a sense sacrificial, cultural
hero[15]—and argues instead that the athletic hero, like the mythic hero, is caught
up in a process of initiation and maturation unique to his cultural context.
This portrayal is especially appropriate to the early representations of athletic
heroes in juvenile fiction, such as the Frank Merriwell stories, but also to
the subsequent avatars of the athlete in literary novels. Oriard's study offers
informative material on the dime novel and pulp fiction of the late nineteenth
and early twentieth centuries and offers a detailed account of their formulaic
narratives (29–36).[16] As a cultural symbol, the baseball player is sufficiently
complex to evoke several distinctive American types: "the premier natural"
(77); a "descendent of American frontier heroes" (60); a "solitary figure ... the
self-sufficient but social man whose imaginative origin as the rugged individualist of the American frontier makes him in many ways the most distinctly
American of sports heroes" (59–60); and "the companion figure to the self-
made man in the pantheon of American mythic heroes ... deeply rooted
in American folklore" (76). These descriptions overtly place baseball fiction
within a cultural context; Oriard's avowed purpose is to establish the credibil-
ity of sport fiction as a subgenre that expresses the mainstream positions (what
Oriard calls "the norm") of American culture that are implicitly lost or opposed
in the "extreme positions [of] our more complex novels" (23). The "thematic"
(22) orientation of the study, which is also fortuitously chronological, allows
Oriard to use sport fiction and its treatment of its subject matter to illuminate
the changing preoccupations of American society and to reveal these changes
as part of the historical development of American culture. On this basis, Oriard
covers baseball fiction from the Frank Merriwell stories of Gilbert Patten
to adult novels like *You Know Me Al*, *The Natural*, *The Southpaw*, *Bang the Drum
Slowly*, *The Great American Novel* (1973) and *The Universal Baseball Association*.

Both Michael Oriard and Christian K. Messenger have subsequently published ambitious new studies of sport in American literature and culture. Messenger's *Sport and the Spirit of Play in Contemporary American Fiction* (1990)
extends the author's inquiry to contemporary novels concerned primarily with
sports and the representation of sporting characters. In this volume, Messenger shifts the focus from the Ritual, Popular, and School sports heroes, which

[14]See Joseph Campbell, The Hero with a Thousand Faces *(1949; 2d ed. 1968; reprinted, Princeton, NJ:
Princeton University Press, 1973), 17–20, 30–40, and* passim.

[15]See Cordelia Candelaria, Seeking the Perfect Game: Baseball in American Literature *(New York:
Greenwood Press, 1989), 72–74.*

[16]Christian K. Messenger also examines the boy's dime novel and pulp sports fiction in Sport and the
Spirit of Play in American Fiction, *131–179.*

he judges to be in "decline or transformation,"[17] and proposes a new theoretical model to articulate "a structural semantics for the study of sport and play in contemporary American fiction" (xiv). This construct is the Greimas semiotic square, which the critic adapts to his purpose by designating its quadrants as, respectively, "individual sports heroism," "collective sports heroism," "anti-heroism," and "play." In this scheme, "individual sports heroism" occupies the upper left quadrant and figures as the "logical contrary" of "collective sports heroism," which is placed in the upper right. "Play," the "negation" of individual sports heroism, fills the lower left, and its logical contrary, "anti-heroism" (the "negation" of collective sports heroism) takes the remaining lower right corner (12–14). If one were to draw the "four-term homology" (12), or to refer to the series of squares that chart the movement from general to specific theory (13–14), the position of each term would resolve itself without confusion. Such a diagram offers the additional benefit of revealing that anti-heroism is the "relation of contradiction" vis-à-vis individual sports heroism; likewise, "play" is the "direct contradictory" of collective sports heroism (13–14). The immediate purpose of employing this system is, according to Messenger, "organizational": to simplify "an inventory of characters, scenes, and plot to a constructed series of contraries and their generated negations" (14).

The critic's larger purpose is to apply his rendition of the semiotic square to "a significantly large number of texts from many areas of sports fiction" in an effort to "[identify] ... a continuing social drama of sport in society that actualizes the issues of freedom (play) and constraint (rules, competition)" (2). The justification for resorting to this particular model is its capacity to allow "play and sport ... [to] co-exist in a full field of relations where play may be seen as the basis for sport but also as its implied opposite and critic" (11). Furthermore, the semiotic square describes how individual "heroes and heroines of sports fiction" play "between content and form in the realm of aesthetics" (10, 11) by engaging in the "play toward origins" and "the play beyond categories" (8). Thus, the semiotic square is especially suitable to "mapping the arena" (12) of sport fiction: it reveals "the play of differences in sport ... a constant movement between oppositions" that configures the athlete's relationship to team and self (18). In the process of determining what is (or belongs to) self and what is the property or right of the team, the athlete discovers, Messenger explains, a desire to "'play back to' the origins of [his] physical delight" (18), both in terms of his adept, talented body and of his game in its pure or "innocent" form — before the game became a job or obligation. At the same time, the athlete realizes a desire to "'play beyond' limits, get beyond self and the body's limitations to do what has never before been achieved" (18). The typical outcome of these conflicts involves the "'play between' ... absolutes or terminal crises," in which the athlete negotiates the demands of the collective and

---

[17]Christian K. Messenger, Sport and the Spirit of Play in Contemporary American Fiction (New York: Columbia University Press, 1990), xiii.

the desires of the self, the team and the individual, "allegiances and ... rebellions" (18).[18]

In baseball fiction, Messenger notes that the "play toward origins ... is always a 'coming home'" and that "the quest for 'home' and origin [is] matched by a ceaseless wandering, a state of exile" (317). Baseball's unique "timelessness," the nominal freedom of its play from clock time, creates, Messenger believes, "in both players and spectators the expectancy of varied narrative" and provides in its many pauses (between actions, between innings) those useful lulls or "narrative interstices, for telling and re-creation" (316). Baseball's temporal and spatial freedoms are figures of what the critic identifies as "the play beyond [limits]" (318), whereas "the play between [individual and collective selves]" involves the process of traversing the semiotic square, "with *individual sports heroes* moving fluidly from *collective sports heroism* to *anti-heroism* and back to *play*, resisting capture by their imaginative response" (Messenger's italics, 317). This model aptly describes the phases of many a fictive ballplayer's career, but the critic's application of the semiotic square to baseball fictions is less indispensable than the allusive, insightful readings he offers of baseball novels. *The Natural, The Universal Baseball Association, The Great American Novel,* and *Bang the Drum Slowly* attract sustained attention and receive complete readings, and other novels, notably *Sam's Legacy* (1974), *The Seventh Babe* (1979), *Ironweed* (1983), *Almost Famous* (1982), and *The Southpaw,* inspire extensive commentary. Like other critics of sport fiction, Messenger tends to overrate the quality of some baseball novels, yet the reach of his coverage, which extends from John R. Tunis's *Young Razzle* (1949) to Don Snyder's *Veteran's Park* (1987) is impressive. Such comprehensiveness has many attributes and two drawbacks: the critic evaluates so many novels that his remarks on most of them tend toward capsule summary and snap judgment; and differences of literary quality are blurred in the rush to cite the next example. In fairness, it is clear that adjudicating matters of craft is less to the critic's purpose than is marshalling a catalogue of evidence to support his detailed readings and validate his theoretical premise. The general assumption seems implicitly to be that one must define the genre, locate its relevant texts and account for them in theoretical terms, before separating the wheat from the chaff. In baseball fiction there is, unfortunately, a lot of chaff— as even the simply descriptive sections of Messenger's commentaries illustrate.

A similar assumption may be adduced from the succinct commentaries of Michael Oriard's *Sporting with the Gods* (1991). Believing that "no claim for pattern can be convincing without quantity of evidence,"[19] Oriard surveys

[18]*The progress of the sports hero around the semiotic square, beginning in "free Play" and moving through "Individual Sports Heroism," "Collective Sports Heroism," "Anti-Heroism," then either back to Collective Sports Heroism or forward to Play, is sketched in general terms by Messenger on 15 and briefly applied to three textual examples on 19–22.*

[19]Michael Oriard, Sporting with the Gods: The Rhetoric of Play and Game in American Culture (New York: Cambridge University Press, 1991), xvi.

innumerable texts in order to "explore the cultural history of a metaphor ... that says life is a game" (ix). The method is one of comprehensive reading: to "trace the histories of a number of rhetorical figures—images, similes, metaphors, analogies—that express heroic codes, strategies of survival, states of being, life itself as 'sport,' 'game,' or 'play'" (xi–xii). The scope of Oriard's study is prodigious—it begins in the colonial period and ends in the 1980s—and the range of textual evidence encompasses prose texts, primarily fictions, by mostly major American writers from James Fenimore Cooper to John Updike. The critic's main endeavor is to delineate the "shifting definitions" of the "key terms" (*game, play, sport*) during the course of American cultural history, and on this basis to interpret "[American] society's inner life, its understanding of human possibility" and to present "a concrete record of cultural transformation" (xii–xiii). The general goal is to establish a critical discourse in which the "cultural dichotomy" of work and play can be analyzed, to the end of situating it among the standard "conflicts between nature and civilization, individual and society, self and other" (xiii). Given this thematic approach and some 350 years of literature to which to apply it, the critic has little time or space specifically to address baseball fiction. Oriard's interest in game, play, and sport is so generalized, his textual evidence drawn from sources so otherwise disparate, that *Sporting with the Gods* reads from its first chapter as a history of American prose fiction in terms of its ludic language, content, and concerns. The study is exhaustive of its subject, but students interested in baseball fiction will find its discussion generally relevant yet, in specific cases, collateral.

Indeed, each of the foregoing studies takes as its subject(s) sport literature and/or sport in literature. Whether perceived as interrelated topics or two parts of a single subject, sport (in) literature includes so great a number and variety of texts that one finally suspects that every American novel ever written contains an allusion to sport, the figure of a game, or some element of play. Studies that address the subject(s) of game, play, and sport are remarkable for the breadth of their respective discussions. Of necessity, however, they seldom provide thorough readings of baseball fiction. Happily, Cordelia Candelaria supplies in *Seeking the Perfect Game* (1989) much of what is lacking. Candelaria narrows the field of inquiry by investigating only baseball in American literature. *Seeking the Perfect Game* surveys "the baseball imagery and metaphor" of American fiction to demonstrate how the literary use of baseball creates "its own fictive universe."[20] Essentially, Candelaria's thesis is her perception of an evolution in the mimetic mode of baseball fiction, ranging from the "allegory and romanticism of its earliest forms to the realism and solipsism of its contemporary renderings" (2). Abetting this shift, prose style and narrative strategy move from "linear, mostly one-dimensional narratives to those presented multidimensionally in the fragmented chronology usually derived from ironic,

[20]*Cordelia Candelaria, Seeking the Perfect Game: Baseball in American Fiction (New York: Greenwood Press, 1989), 2. Citations are noted parenthetically.*

autotelic viewpoints" (2). The critic contends that these developments parallel baseball's evolution from an ancient fertility rite to a modern, stylized game of abstracted gesture and symbol. This study has a number of distinguishing features: It offers perceptive readings of *The Natural, The Río Loja Ringmaster,* Harris's "Author" Wiggen tetralogy, *The Great American Novel,* and *The Universal Baseball Association, Inc., J. Henry Waugh, Prop.;* it overrates *Sam's Legacy* and *Babe Ruth Caught in a Snowstorm* (1973); it tends to undervalue *The Celebrant* (1983). In assembling the theoretical scaffolding of its argument, *Seeking the Perfect Game* provides two valuable services: It summarizes the Egyptian origins of baseball, which Robert W. Henderson reveals in *Ball, Bat and Bishop* (1947),[21] and engages in parts of its interpretive commentary the categories of Apollonian, Dionysian, and Adonic, which Robert J. Higgs adduces in *Laurel & Thorn* to explicate the representation of the baseball player in American fiction (8–9, 20–21). Perhaps most important in terms of the present work, Candelaria locates many allusions to baseball in canonical American fiction. Although the critic describes these moments as "Literary Fungoes" (51) and often does little more than identify them, her scrupulous efforts to glean baseball allusions from novels not about baseball have tacitly encouraged the essays in Part I of *Home Games.*

The respective critical writings of Christian K. Messenger, Michael Oriard, and Cordelia Candelaria offer coherent approaches to reading baseball (and other sport) fiction, and useful interpretations of its seminal texts. The respective studies by Wiley Lee Umphlett, Neil Berman, Robert J. Higgs, and Leverett T. Smith also make significant contributions to the critical inquiry by offering literary terms in which to think about the interrelated subjects of sport (in) literature, the athletic or sporting hero, and the baseball novel. Undoubtedly, new studies will appear in the near future and aspire to comprehensiveness (either of baseball or all sport literature) and system-building.[22] Baseball fiction and

---

[21]*Robert W. Henderson,* Ball, Bat and Bishop: The Origin of Ball Games *(New York: Rockport Press, 1947; reprinted, Detroit: Gale Research, 1974).*

[22]*At least two studies have appeared since the present work was conceived and written. Both* Making the Team: The Cultural Work of Baseball Fiction *(Chicago: University of Illinois Press, 1997), by Timothy Morrison, and* Ground Rules: Baseball & Myth *(Chicago: University of Illinois Press, 1996), by Deeanne Westbrook, examine baseball fiction in considerable detail.* Making the Team *is mainly a cultural study; mooting distinctions of literary quality, Morris argues that "the cultural work and ideological constructions of adult baseball fiction are continuous with those of juvenile baseball fiction" despite "the rhetoric that denies and conceals this continuity" (3). The continuity and its denial can, Morris claims, "provide a model for insights into the cultural construction of ... both 'genre' and 'serious' [literature], and into the functions of literature as a cultural value" (3).* Ground Rules, *more properly a literary study of baseball fiction, engages structuralist (Levi-Strauss) and poststructuralist (Eric Gould,* Mythical Intentions in Modern Literature*) theories of myth and "Mythicity" (Gould's neologism), as well as Lacanian conceptions, to explicate selected texts of baseball fiction. Westbrook claims that "this body of texts — baseball literature — has the status of a functional modern mythology" (9), that it "[constitutes] a genuine American mythology" (1). Insofar as it discusses* The Natural *and* The Universal Baseball Association *at length,* Ground Rules *would probably have contributed much to my readings of those novels. Regrettably, I was unaware of the book's existence until relatively recently, long after I had written (and rewritten)* Home Games.

the criticism of it are still relatively new topics in literary studies, so a certain amount of effort must be devoted to identifying the texts that belong to the genre and classifying them according to one or more essentially descriptive taxonomies. The moment, however, has arrived for a criticism of baseball fiction that focuses on selected texts and, by its selection of texts, makes some distinction between the books that we will read, study, and discuss hereafter and those that will fade into the background. One may describe this project as a modest form of canon-building, the prospect of which should cause no one discomfort; literary scholars constantly build, dismantle, and reconstruct the respective canons of every literary tradition they can identify. Indeed, the ongoing formation of a malleable canon is always necessary, for it supplies the context that critics need to make sense of individual works. Such a project is necessary for baseball literature if this young tradition and its criticism are to be taken seriously within the academic discipline of literary studies and by the greater intellectual community. If we continue to write about *Shoeless Joe* and *The Universal Baseball Association* in the same chapter and fail to explain that the latter is something like a work of literary genius and the former a sentimental fantasy, phony and self-indulgent, our academic colleagues will not trust our discernment. The likely result is that both novels — and their critics — will be dismissed as trifling. *Home Games* aspires to contribute, in an admittedly limited way, to the project of canon-building. The book's implicit argument is that the baseball novel is properly a part of the American literary tradition — that *The Natural* is as legitimate an artistic expression of certain of our preoccupations as *The Scarlet Letter* and as worthy of critical attention. The same assumption underlies the investigation of baseball allusions in canonical texts. The point is not that baseball allusions are more important than other tropes but that baseball allusions carry meanings that are important even to readers who are uninterested in baseball — or would be, if these readers knew what they were missing. Ideally, Part I will assist these readers, not only in making sense of the specific allusions it explicates but also in unpacking the baseball tropes that readers will encounter if they continue to read American fiction. Then, too, reading baseball allusions with a critical eye encourages one to accept the baseball novel as a serious literary endeavor. Chapters six through nine attempt detailed readings of four exemplary baseball novels to demonstrate what sustained critical attention might yield if it were applied to the best work in the genre. If these attempts are successful, the reader will not merely accept the readings offered herein but will return to the primary texts, re-read and rethink them, and formulate his own interpretations to stand alongside the essays of *Home Games*.

Index

Note: Fictional characters are distinguished from historical personages by being indexed according to their first names. Thus, Roy Hobbs is indexed as "Roy Hobbs" and Jack Keefe as "Jack Keefe," whereas Babe Ruth is indexed as "Ruth, Babe" and Ty Cobb as "Cobb, Ty."

Adventures of Huckleberry Finn, 20, 31, 161 [headnote], 164, 165, 165*n7*, 171, 171*n14*, *n15*, 172*n16*

Aeneas, 103*n22*

aleatory (defined) 191*n5*; 212; see also 226*n12*

Alexander, Charles C., cited 31*n21*, 70*n10*, 78*n20*, 81*n22*, 87*n5*, 95, 105*n26*, *n27*, 106*n29*, 126*n15*, 140*n27*

Almost Famous (David Small), 8, 230; reunion in, 14

Angell, Roger: on Joe DiMaggio, 110*n41*; as originator of serious baseball journalism, 185, 185*n25*

antibaseball fictions, 15

anti–Semitism: in *The Great Gatsby,* 46; in American fiction, 46*n19*; in the sporting press, 46*n20*; in *The Sound and the Fury,* 55–56

Asinof, Eliot: on Black Sox Scandal, 42, 42*n12*, 43*n14*, 45; on Babe Ruth in 1920, 6*n8*

Auerbach, Eric, 9*n1*; 86

Babe Ruth Caught in a Snowstorm (John Alexander Graham), 7, 232

Bang the Drum Slowly, 7; epigraph of (quoted) 15; 162*n1*, 173*n17*, 224, 226, 228, 230, 232

baseball: early history of, 17, 23–25, 28–29; Egyptian roots of, 146*n9*, 232; seasonal rhythm of, 216–217; analogized to literary art, 9–14, 197; resistance to literary art, 218–219; quest for home, 10; freedom from clock time, 13, 101, 155, 196, 209, 217, 230; diamond, 13, 15, 26, 27, 64–65, 66, 68, 69, 177*n20*; in American fiction, 22; and writing, 24–25, 167–169; visibility and difficult beauty of, 26; healthy effects of, 27–28; purist mentality of, 28–29; cultural resonance of, 30, 146, 147, 147*n11*; U.S. postage stamps of, 4*n2*; around-the-world tours of, 34, 34*n26*, 140, 140*n27*; as a "worrying thing," 64–66, 76–77; quality of failure in, 217; American archetypes of, 66–68; wartime, 94*n13*; minor league, 125, 125*n13*; hazing of rookies, 3, 126, 126*n15*; and life, 187, 212, 216–217

baseball allusions: signature themes of, 9, 31, 61, 62; as rhetorical artifice, 16, 217; in selected texts (summarized), 17–18; reader of, 215–216; potency of, 36; fathers and sons, 40, 77, 99–105; realistic and impressionistic, 62; "pastoral" versions of, 64*n4*, 65; dream of glory, 66–67; rites of passage, 74–76; in *A Connecticut Yankee in King Arthur's Court,* 32–33; in *The Great Gatsby,* 17, 41–42 (quoted); in *The Sound and the Fury,* 17, 53; in *You Can't Go Home Again,* 63 (quoted), 64–65 (quoted), 66 (quoted); in *Of Time and the River,* 68–69 (quoted), 70 (quoted); in *A World I Never Made,* 72 (quoted), 73 (quoted); in *No Star Is Lost,* 74 (quoted), 74–75

(quoted), 75 (quoted), 76–77 (quoted);
in *Father and Son,* 78 (quoted), 79
(quoted), 80 (quoted), 81 (quoted), 82
(quoted); in *My Days of Anger,* 83
(quoted); "The Three-Day Blow," 17, 86–
87 (quoted), 90 (quoted); in *A Farewell
to Arms,* 17, 93 (quoted), 96 (quoted),
97 (quoted); in *The Old Man and the
Sea,* 18, 100 (quoted), 102 (quoted), 104
(quoted), 109 (quoted), 112 (quoted)
baseball novel: characterized, 2–3; qualities of successful examples, 115, 217;
inferior versions of, 8, 115–117, 217–218;
origins in boys' pulp fiction, 116, 116*n1,*
218; trope of exile and homecoming in,
10, 14–15, 18–19, 219–220, 230; tropes of
father and son in, 166–169; protagonist
of, 14–15; reader of, 215–216; resistance
to literary art, 218–219; susceptibility to
cliché and sentimentality, 218–219; and
literary art, 220
Berman, Neil, cited 188*n3,* 192*n6, n7,*
206*n16,* 226, 232; summarized 224–225
Bildungsroman (defined), 20*n16*
"bird dog" (defined) 82*n23*
Black Sox Scandal: 3, 6, 47, 217, 223; in
The Great Gatsby, 17, 41–45; summarized
42*n12;* 78*n20;* 83; Ring Lardner's reaction to, 45, 222; James T. Farrell's reaction to, 83*n24;* "prefigured" in "The
Three-Day Blow," 87*n6*
Bloom, Harold (quoted) 165*n9*
"bonehead" (defined) 91*n11;* and Heinie
Zimmerman, 86, 89, 89*n9,* 91*n11;* and
Fred Merkle, 91*n11*
boys' baseball books: 18*n14,* 116, 116*n1,* 161
[headnote], 161, 165, 165*n6,* 218, 228
Brown, "Three-Finger," 40*n9*
Browning, Robert, dramatic monologues,
121, 142
"busher" (defined), 121*n1*

Caillois, Roger, 226, 226*n12*
Campbell, Joseph, 13*n8,* 227, 228*n14*
Candelaria, Cordelia, cited 16*n10,* 16*n11,*
64*n4,* 71*n12,* 109*n39,* 116*n2,* 122, 122*n4,*
138*n24,* 146*n9,* 147*n10,* 163*n3,* 170*n12,*
171*n15,* 188*n3,* 192*n6,* 206*n16,* 207*n18,*
228*n15,* 232; summarized 231–232
Cartwright, Alexander Joy, 23–24
"caught off base" (defined) 96*n15*
The Celebrant (Eric Rolfe Greenberg), 232
Chase, Richard, on the Romance, 145*n5*
Chaucer, 14
Cincinnati Red Stockings, 29*n18*

Civil War, 27, 28*n15,* 29, 54, 55, 60
Cobb, Ty: baseball tactics of, 5*n6,* 222*n2;*
in *The Great American Novel,* 7; 31,
31*n21;* on Three-Finger Brown's curveball, 40*n9;* 78; reputation as great ball
player and shrewd businessman, 78*n20;*
as a baseball "writer," 81*n22;* 82; rookie
hazing of, 126*n15;* Lardner's praise of,
126*n16;* depicted in *You Know Me Al,*
129; autobiography of, 185*n26*
Collins, Eddie, 78, 78*n20,* 82, 89*n9,* 127*n19*
*A Conneticut Yankee in King Arthur's
Court:* baseball in, 32–35 (quoted 32–
33); publication date of, 34; figures and
tropes of exile and home in, 32–35
Coover, Robert, 2, 20, 22, 187–188, 193,
200, 207*n18;* quoted 215 [headnote], 224
Coveleski, Stanley, 65–66, quoted 66
Creamer, Robert: on Babe Ruth, 5; quoted
51 [headnote]; 56*n8, n9,* 58, 58*n16;* as
originator of serious baseball biography,
185

Danny O'Neill, 17, 61, 62, 71–83; linking of
baseball and Catholicism, 73, 78, 80;
"discovery" of, 80–81; as a writer of
baseball fiction, 81–82 (quoted 81)
Doubleday, Abner, 28*n15*
DiMaggio, Joe: 3, 18, 217; as allusion, 36;
as synecdochic name, 86, 99, 112–113;
career span, 107*n34;* baseball skills of,
110*n41;* salary of, 110–111, 110*n42;* legend
of, 113*n45;* as the professional's pro, 99,
107*n32,* 111–113, 112*n44;* as team player,
107, 107*n35;* as unique champion, 108,
108*n38;* as injured combatant, 108–111;
as inspirational figure, 100, 103, 106,
108–109, 109*n39;* 110*n41;* 110*n42;* allusions to, in *The Old Man and the Sea*
(quoted), 100, 102, 104, 109

Ehrmann, Jacques, 224, 226
Eight Men Out (Eliot Asinof), 6*n8,* 42*n12,*
43*n14,* 45
Einstein, Albert, 207*n18*
Eliot, T. S., 48, 62*n2,* 146, 197, 205
Emerson, Ralph Waldo, 151; quotation
from "The American Scholar," xi (epi-
graph)

A Farewell to Arms, 2, 17, 85; baseball allusions in, 93–99 (quoted 93, 96, 97);
Babe Ruth in, 93–94; bravery in, 97–98;
tropes and figures of exile and home in,
17, 93–96, 98–99

Farrell, James T., 17, 36, 61; as realistic baseball writer, 62, 71; baseball allusions of, inexactly characterized, 71*n12;* on difficulty of becoming a major league player (quoted), 82; omission of Black Sox Scandal from *Father and Son,* 83; baseball allusions of, summarized, 83–84; reaction to Black Sox Scandal, 83*n24*

Faulkner, William, 1, 16, 36, 51, 52, 117, 226

Father and Son (Farrell), 73, 77–83, 77*n18;* pederast in, 79–80 (quoted 79); figures and tropes of exile and home in, 78; baseball and writing, 80–82

Federal League, 76*n17,* 77*n19,* 133, 133*n21*

Fitzgerald, F. Scott, 1, 17, 36, 44, 46, 117, 226; on Ring Lardner, 37–38 (quoted), 123*n8;* on *You Know Me Al,* 38, 123; disdain for baseball, 38; use of baseball in *Gatsby,* 40, 41*n11;* aspirations for *Gatsby,* 41; quoted 210; see also *The Great Gatsby*

Forster, E. M., 142, 142*n31,* 160

Frank Merriwell pulp serial, 116, 116*n1,* 161, 228

Franklin, Benjamin, 49; 49*n21*

Frost, Robert, quoted 23 [headnote]

Frye, Northrop: quoted on the Romance, 143 [headnote]; cited 145*n6*

Gehrig, Lou, 4*n2,* 56, 66

Giamatti, A. Bartlett, quoted: on the conventional aspect of sports, 11*n4;* on the Romance, 14; on baseball and narrative, 115 [headnote]; 187 [headnote]; on autotelic activity, 195*n9*

Gould, Stephen J.: on Babe Ruth's home run hitting, 6*n8;* on the Cardiff Giant fraud, 28*n15*

The Great American Novel (Roth), 7, 228, 230, 232

The Great Gatsby, 2, 3, 9, 148*n13,* 154, 226; sports in, 39, 47; signature scene of (quoted) 41–42; baseball allusion deleted from, 41*n11;* Meyer Wolfshiem in, 17, 42–49; Nick Carraway in, 41–42, 43–44, 46, 48; Jay Gatsby in, 39–42, 43, 45, 47–49; Tom Buchanan in, 39; Jordan Baker in, 39, 47–48; Mr. Gatz in, 40, 48; Jimmy Gatz in, 39–40, 48–49; Dan Cody in, 45, 49; anti–Semitism in, 46; money and business in, 44, 45–46, 47, 49; religion in, 44–45, 46; folk heroes in, 45, 45*n18;* figures and tropes of home in, 17, 41*n11,* 46, 48, 49; romantic idealism in, 48–49

Hardwick, Elizabeth, quoted, on the nature and value of criticism, 221 [headnote]

Harris, Mark, 2, 7, 15, 16*n10,* 166*n10,* 171, 171*n15,* 172, 183, 232; as "editor" of *The Southpaw,* 20, 175; "Horatio at the Bat," cited, 16*n10,* 117*n6,* 165*n6;* remarks on *The Southpaw* (quoted), 118; remarks on *Bang the Drum Slowly* (quoted), 162*n1;* remarks on craft, 163*n3;* fictional treatment of baseball in *The Southpaw,* 161–163

Hawthorne, Nathaniel, 226; in *The Great American Novel,* 7; on "the human heart," 14; 20; fictional material of, 29; predicament of, 30; on the Romance, 144–145, 144*n3,* 154

Hemingway, Ernest, 1, 16, 17–18, 36, 117, 166*n10,* 222, 226; in *The Great American Novel,* 7; sports in the writings of, 85, 90*n10;* macho code of, 90; language of, 95–96; thematic use of baseball allusion in "The Three-Day Blow," 92–93; use of baseball allusions in *A Farewell to Arms,* 94–99, 96*n15;* on football, 98, 98*n16;* use of baseball allusions in *The Old Man and the Sea,* 99–100, 106–108, 106*n31,* 109*n39,* 112–113, 112*n44*

Henry Wiggen (in *The Southpaw):* exile and homecoming of, 20, 119, 162–163, 172–185, 219–220; as "Author," 20, 161–163, 167–172, 184–185; reading of, 164–166, 169; formative experiences of, 162–167; "innocent" baseball ethos of, 162, 165–167, 166*n10,* 172; "crises" of, 162, 172, 180–184; sense of identity of, 174; "inside" story of, 20, 161–162, 167, 170, 172–184; alienation of, 172, 174; wound of, 174–176, 178–180; left-handedness of, 161, 169–170, 176–177, 181–182

Higgs, Robert J.: cited 6*n7,* 64*n5,* 232; summarized 225–226

home: in baseball fiction, 9–10, 14, 17–21, 115, 219–220; in baseball (home plate), 13; as "nodal point," 13*n8;* as unifying theme, 17; in *You Know Me Al,* 19, 120, 121, 122, 125–126, 128–133, 135, 137–142, 219; in *The Natural,* 19–20, 119, 144, 148, 150–153, 155–156, 158–160, 219; in *The Southpaw,* 20, 119, 161–163, 174, 181, 184, 219; in *The Universal Baseball Association,* 20–21, 119–120, 187, 189–190, 201, 207, 211–212, 220

Home Games: origins of, 1–2; rationale for, 8, 18*n13,* 221, 232–233; structure of, 9;

critical premises of, 15–16, 16*n11*, 21–22, 221–233; overview of content, 16–21
The Huge Season (Wright Morris), quoted 15
Huizinga, Johan, 222, 224, 226, 226*n12*

It Looked Like For Ever (Mark Harris), 162*n1*, 171*n13*, 183*n23*, 232

J. Henry Waugh (in *The Universal Baseball Association*), 224; exile and homecoming of, 20–21, 119–120, 220; as writer/author, 190–194, 197–199, 203–205, 207; as game-player, 187–189, 194, 198, 220; as creator and sustaining force of the UBA, 188–189, 191–192, 192*n6*, 207; psychic wound of, 21, 199–201
Jack Keefe (in *You Know Me Al*), 3, 122*n2*, *n3*, 222; exile and homecoming of, 19, 120, 140–142, 219; taunted, 16*n12*, 135; as protagonist/narrator, 121, 127; self-portrait of, 121–122; narrative voice of, 122–125, 131, 142; language of, 122–124, 122*n4*, 128, 130–132, 137, 141; insecurities and anxieties of, 3, 124–128, 130–131, 133–135, 138–139; exiles of, 128, 131, 140–142; character development of, 136–142, 138*n24*
James, Henry, 29–30, 31*n21*; on Hawthorne, 30 (quoted), 30*n20* (quoted)
Joyce, James: quoted 39*n4*, 44*n17*, 217; Leopold Bloom, 14; stream-of-consciousness narrative, 123

Kahn, Roger, 125*n13*, 185
kairos (defined) 13; in *The Universal Baseball Association*, 196, 205, 208–209
Kazin, Alfred: quoted 61 [headnotes]; quoted 161 [headnote]
Kermode, Frank: cited 13, 196*n10*; quoted 196*n12*, 208*n19*
Knickerbocker Base Ball Club, 23–25; rules of, 24–25

Lardner, Ring,16*n12*, 18; 222, 226; preference for "inside" baseball, 5*n6*; 126*n16*, 222*n2*; as author of baseball fiction, 31; F. Scott Fitzgerald on, 37–38; devaluation of his own fiction, 38, 117*n3*, 123–124, 123*n11*; reaction to Black Sox Scandal, 45; Virginia Woolf's opinion, 61*n1*; as inimitable author of *You Know Me Al*, 116–117, 218; his characters characterized, 121 [headnote], 123*n7*; as recorder

of vernacular speech, 122–124; satiric treatment of, 123*n10*; Jack Keefe baseball stories of, 138, 138*n25*, 139*n26*, 142*n30*; Edmund Wilson's comment on, 185
Lieb, Fred: quoted on Babe Ruth, 57; books of, 57*n10*

Mack, Connie, 77*n19*, 142*n29*; in *Father and Son*, 81–82, 81*n21*
Malamud, Bernard, 7, 16*n10*, 19, 117 (quoted), 118 (quoted), 143, 144*n3*, 146, 146*n9*, 147, 154, 161, 218
Mantle, Mickey, 7, 66
Marquard, Richard "Rube," quoted 67
Mathewson, Christy, 40*n9*; 68, 69*n9*, 70, 70*n10*, 105*n27*, Lardner's praise of, 126*n16*
McGraw, John: preference for "inside" baseball, 5*n6*, 222*n2*; and 40*n9*; 87, 87*n6*, 89, 89*n9*, 91, 91*n11*, 140, 140*n27*, 141
Melville, Herman, 29; in *The Great American Novel*, 7
Mencken, H. L., on Ring Lardner's characters, 121 [headnote]
Messenger, Christian K.: cited 2*n1*, 10*n2*, 18*n14*, 26*n11*, 29*n17*, 38*n3*, 40*n9*, 43, 90n10, 98*n16*, 107*n32*, 116*n1*, *n2*, 117*n3*, *n4*, *n5*, 118, 123, 123*n7*, 143*n1*, 147*n10*, 160, 165*n5*, *n6*, *n8*, 170*n12*, 171*n15*, 228*n16*, 232; summarized 226–227, 226*n12*, 228–230, 230*n18*
mimesis (defined) 9*n1*, 226*n12*; see also 145, 153–154, 187, 231
mimicry (defined) 226*n12*; in *No Star Is Lost*, 74–75
Most Valuable Player Award, 56, 56*n7*
My Baseball Diary (Farrell): on Ed Walsh's 1911 no-hit game, 71–72 (quoted 72); on difficulty of becoming a major league player, 82 (quoted)
My Days of Anger, 73, 83 (quoted)

The Natural: 2, 7, 8, 68, 161, 167*n11*, 218, 224, 226, 228, 230, 232, 233; as precursor, 9; as antibaseball fiction, 15, 160; as a seminal work, 18, 118–119; magical realism of, 118, 145–147, 153–155; as a first novel, 117; Malamud's remarks about, 117–118; language and mimesis of, 19–20, 144–146, 153–154; fertility god in, 104*n23*; critical history of, 143, 146–148; plot summarized in mythic terms, 147–148; and the prose Romance, 143, 144–146, 154–156, 160; as a composite of

Romance and Novel, 145–146; and myth, 146–148, 146*n8, n9,* 160, 185, 187; preter–Natural events in, 154–155; tropes and figures of time in, 143–144, 147–153, 155–160; **Roy Hobbs** in, 143–144, 146*n9,* 147–160; **Memo Paris** in, 148, 149, 153–154, 156–159; **Iris Lemon** in, 143, 148, 154–160; primal scene of, 150–151; tropes and figures of exile and home in, 144, 148, 150–153, 155–156, 158–160, 219

Nebraska Crane, 17, 62, 63–66, 64*n4,* 64*n5,* 83, 225; humor of, 64–65

Nick Adams, 17; in "The Three-Day Blow," 86, 88–93

No Star Is Lost, 73; baseball and sibling rivalry in, 74–75; rites of passage in, 74–77; figures and tropes of exile and home in, 74–75

Novak, Michael, quoted 37 [headnote] 190*n4,* 196*n11;* cited 44*n16;* see also 224

Odyssey (Homer), 14

Of Time and the River, 2; baseball in, 68–71; home in, 70

The Old Man and the Sea, 2, 3, 9, 15–16, 18, 85, 93, 217; **Santiago** as father figure in, 99–101, 103; as teacher in, 100–103; as figure of Christ in, 107; as prideful code hero in, 108; as committed craftsman in, 111–112; importance of baseball in keeping Santiago alive, 101–103, 217; conversations of Santiago and Manolin in, 99–103 (quoted 100, 102); **Joe DiMaggio** in, 99–100, 103–104, 106–113, 217; DiMaggio as inspirational figure in, 100, 103, 106, 108–109; as the professional's pro in, 99, 107*n32,* 111–113, 112*n44;* as team player in, 107, 107*n35;* as a unique champion in, 108, 108*n38,* ; as an injured combatant in, 108–111; as synecdochic name in, 86, 99, 113; **Dick** and **George Sisler** in, 102, 104–105, 104*n24,* 105*n25;* **John McGraw** in, 102, 105, 105*n26, n27,* 106*n29;* **Leo Durocher** in, 102, 105, 106*n28;* synecdochic naming in, 85, 99, 112–113; fathers and sons in, 99–105, 112; ineffectiveness of baseball allusions in, 99*n19,* 106, 106*n31;* tropes and figures of exile and home in, 18, 100–103, 106, 109–110, 112

Oriard, Michael, cited 18*n14,* 38*n2,* 45*n18,* 116, 116*n1,* 117*n5,* 123*n10,* 138*n24,* 147*n10,* 165*n6,* 170*n12,* 171*n15,* 192*n6,* 206*n16,* 232; summarized 227–228, 230–231

Pilgrim's Progress, 14

"Ring" (F. Scott Fitzgerald), quoted 37–39

The Río Loja Ringmaster (Lamar Herrin), 8, 232; quoted 9 [headnote]; as anti-baseball fiction, 15

Romance (defined), 144–145, 145*n5;* 14, 143, 145*n6,* 154

Roth, Philip, 7, 16*n10*

Rothstein, Arnold, 42, 42*n12,* 43, 43*n14;* 47

Roy Hobbs (in *The Natural*): as a Ruthian figure, 7; as a Shakespearean "natural," 19*n15;* belatedness of, 19, 148–150, 157, 159; exile and homecoming of, 19–20, 119, 144, 151–152, 155–156, 159–160, 219; character of, 143–144, 147–160, 147*n12,* 148*n13,* 150*n14,* 152*n15, n16,* 157*n17,* 162, 167; final insight of, 159–160; antagonistic relationship to time, 144, 148–151, 155–158; failed quest of, 143, 144, 146–148, 149–150, 152, 156–160; conception of home, 144, 150–153, 156, 158

rules: conventional aspect of, 11–12, 74, 204, 209; redefining, 12, 24, 28; inequitable or disregarded, 96, 98*n16,* 99; constraining aspect of, 198, 206; breaking of, 175–176, 201–203

Ruth, Babe, 1–7, 36, 78; cultural context of, 3–6; early life, 5; nicknames of, 5, 58*n16;* legends of, 6, 6*n8,* 51 [headnote], 223; semiotics of, 3–7; in *The Great American Novel,* 7; reinvention of baseball, 6*n8,* 31, 139, 222*n2;* as allusion, 36; early baseball career of, 56*n8,* 94*n14;* hitting prowess, 56*n9;* contemporary accounts of, 57; annual salary of, 57*n13;* mixed ethnicity of, 58–59; in *The Sound and the Fury,* 1, 17, 53–54, 56–60, 217; in *Sam's Legacy,* 7, 59*n18;* in *A Farewell to Arms,* 93–94

Sam's Legacy (Jay Neugeboren), 7, 59*n18,* 230, 232

Sanctuary (Faulkner), baseball allusion in, 51–52 (quoted 51)

Santiago (in *The Old Man and the Sea*): as committed craftsman 111–112; as father figure 99–101; as figure of Christ 107; as prideful code hero 108; as teacher 100–103

The Seventh Babe (Jerome Charyn), 7, 230

Seymour, Harold, cited 23*n2,* 24, 24*n5,* 25, 28*n15,* 29*n16,* 29*n18,* 34, 34*n25,* 35, 56*n7,* 76*n17,* 94*n13,* 105, 111*n43,* 133*n21,* 223*n4*

Smith, Leverett T.: cited 5*n6,* 18*n14,* 46*n20,* 56*n9,* 90n10, 107*n32,* 112*n44,* 122*n3,*

126n16, 138n24, 147n10, 166n10, 232; summarized 221–223

Smith, Red, quoted on Babe Ruth, 57

The Sound and the Fury: 1, 3, 9, 217; **Jason Compson** in, 1, 3, 17, 52–55, 57–58, 59–60; money and business in, 52–55, 58–60; baseball allusion in, 53 (quoted); Babe Ruth in, 1, 17, 53–54, 56–60; anti-Semitism in, 55–56; figures and tropes of home in, 17, 54–55, 59–60

"southpaw" (defined), 177n20

The Southpaw, 2, 162n2, 222, 228, 230, 232; as precursor, 9, 185; precursors of, 165n9, 171; reunion in, 14, 20; as a seminal work, 18, 118–119; as a first novel, 117; contrasted to prior baseball fiction, 161; formal realism of, 20, 118, 161, 185, 187; language and mimesis of, 20, 161, 171–172, 172n16; as an American *Bildungsroman,* 20, 161; problems of authorship, 169–172, 219; **Holly Webster** in, 20, 162–164, 169–171, 174–179, 175n19, 183–185; **Pop** in, 20, 162–172, 176, 181, 181n21, 184; **Aaron Webster** in, 20, 162–164, 171–172, 181n21, 184; **Sam Yale** in, 162, 165–166, 166n10, 172–173, 176, 179; **Dutch Schnell** in, 162–163, 172, 174, 176–179, 184; **Krazy Kress** in, 162, 165, 172, 177–178, 180–182, 182n22, 184; **Patricia Moors** in, 162–163,172, 176–178, 182–183; **Red Traphagen** in, 172n16, 173, 173n17, 178; Korean War in, 181–182, 181n21, 182n22, ; **Henry as "Author"** in, 20, 161–163, 167–172, 184–185; Henry's "inside" story in, 20, 161–162, 167–168, 170–184; left-handedness in, 161, 169–170, 176–177, 181–182, 219; Henry's "crisises" in, 162, 172, 180–184; cynicism in, 173, 173n17, 178, 181–182; Henry's "innocent" baseball ethos in, 162, 165–167, 166n10, 172; baseball and writing in, 167–169; money in, 176, 179–180, 183, 185; scenes of confrontation, 177–180, 182–184; figures and tropes of exile and home in, 20, 161–163; 173–185, 219–220

Spalding, Albert Goodwill, 28n15, 34, 34n26

Speaker, Tris, 22, 68, 69n9, 70, 70n10, 72

The Sun Also Rises, 15, 98

synecdoche (defined), 16n12

synecdochic naming (defined), 85; "Heinie Zim" as an example of, 89; "the great DiMaggio" as an example of, 99, 107–113

"The Three Day Blow," 16, 17–18, 85; baseball allusion in, 86–93; temporal ambi-guity in, 86–88, 87n4, 87n5, 87n6; Heinie Zimmerman in, 86–87, 89, 91, 93; figures and tropes of exile and home in, 17–18, 88–89, 91–92

A Ticket for a Seamstitch, 162n1, 232

trope (defined), 10n3

Twain, Mark, 226; in *The Great American Novel,* 7; as commentator on 19th century baseball, 17, (quoted) 31, (quoted) 32–33, 34–36; as recorder of vernacular speech, 122, 171n15; narrators of, 123, 123n7; as precursor, 171

Umphlett, Wiley Lee, cited 18n14, 90n10, 107n32, 117n5, 122n2, 125n14, 147n10, 148n13, 150n14, 152n15, 212n23, 232; summarized 223–224

The Universal Baseball Association, 2, 20, 215 (quoted), 224, 228, 232, 233; as precursor, 9; precursor in, 197; as antibaseball fiction, 15, 211–212; as a seminal work, 18, 118–119; as baseball metafiction, 118–119; as a fiction-within-a-fiction, 187–188; microfiction of, 188–89, 200; macrofiction of, 188–189, 206n16; language and mimesis, 21, 187–189, 200, 204, 207; **virtual reality** of, 193, 193n8, 199, 203–204; **time** in, 196, 202; **game** in, 21, 187, 191, 193–195, 198, 201, 203, 205, 208–212, 220; **work** in, 190n4, 202–203, 220; **play** in, 190n4, 191–192, 195, 198, 202, 204–205, 209–211, 220; and **ritual,** 21, 187, 200–201, 205, 207–212, 220; and **history,** 187, 191, 194–200, 202, 205–209; and the **novel,** 187, 190–191, 193–197, 199, 203, 205, 208–209, 212; and **process,** 187, 190–192, 195, 202, 204–209, 211–212; and **pattern,** 193, 195, 197, 201, 203–205, 208, 211, 213; and **fulfillment,** 192, 196–200, 207–208; *kairos* and *chronos,* 196, 196n12, 205, 208, 208n19, 209; **J. Henry Waugh** as writer/author, 190–194, 197–199, 203–205, 207; as player in, 187–189, 194, 198; as creator and sustaining force of the UBA, 188–189, 191–192, 192n6, 207; the Book of, 191–193, 203; wound(s) of J. Henry Waugh and Damon Rutherford, 199–201; counterplot of, 200–202, 205; reunion in, 206; Damonsday in, 189, 201, 207–211, 207n18; sustaining fictions in, 188, 209–211, 211n22; tropes of paternity in, 190, 193, 196–198; tropes and figures of exile and home, 187, 189–190, 199, 201, 207, 211–212, 220

Updike, John, 223, 231

Walsh, Ed, 71–73, 72*n15*, 80, 83, 126, 126*n18*
Washington, George, 4, 6
Wilson, Edmund: quoted 85 [headnote]; on Ring Lardner, 185
Whitman, Walt: as commentator on 19th century baseball, 17; as amateur baseball player, 23; as baseball writer (quoted), 25–26, 35–36; poetic voices and images of, 26–27; "Song of Myself" (quoted), 26, 27; on relevance of baseball to American culture (quoted), 27; on the curveball (quoted), 28–29; 31; baseball images of, compared to Thomas Wolfe's, 71; figures and tropes of exile and home in, 26–27
Wolfe, Thomas, 17, 36, 61–62, 225; description of Tris Speaker, 22, 68; as realistic chronicler of baseball work, 64–65 (quoted); baseball allusions of, inexactly characterized, 64*n4;* as visionary of baseball dreams, 66 (quoted); as impressionist writer of baseball, 68–71 (quoted 68–69, 70); baseball allusions of, summarized, 83–84
A World I Never Made, 2, 9, 61, 71–73; figures and tropes of exile and home in, 72–73
World Series: [1903], 31, 223; as allusion, 36, 87*n6*, 88, 88*n7;* [1912], 68–71, 69*n9*, 70*n10*, 71*n11;* 84; [1917], 82–83, 87*n5*, 89;

[1918], 94*n13*, [1919], 41–42, 43, 48, 83, 83*n24;* as a rite of a secular religion, 44

You Can't Go Home Again, 9, 61; baseball in, 62–68 (quoted 63, 64–65, 66); **Nebraska Crane** in, 63–66; figures and tropes of exile and home in, 17, 63–64, 64*n5*, 66–68; humor in, 65
You Know Me Al, 3, 224, 226, 228; as precursor, 9; as antibaseball fiction, 15, 185*n24;* zeugma in 16*n12*, 135; as first literary baseball novel, 18; as a seminal work, 18, 118–119; comic realism of, 117, 118, 187; language and mimesis of, 19; 31, 122–124, 128, 130–132, 137, 141; Fitzgerald's opinion of, 38, 123; **Jack Keefe** in, 121–142; **Florrie** in, 131–133, 135–136, 139–141; **Kid Gleason** in, 127, 134–135, 135*n22*, 137–139, 139*n26;* **Al** in, 125–126, 125*n14;* first-person narration in, 127; humor in, 121–124, 129, 131, 133–135, 140–141; theme of exile in, 128–133, 135, 137, 139*n26*, 140–142; linking of baseball and romance in, 128–129; homecoming forestalled, 130–133; paradox in, 130, 140–141; paternity in, 136–137, 136*n23;* tropes and figures of exile and home in, 120, 121, 122, 125–126, 128–133, 135, 137–142, 219

zeugma (defined) 16*n12;* in *You Know Me Al*, 135